Nazi Empire

Drawing on recent studies of the links between empire, colonialism, and genocide, *Nazi Empire: German Colonialism and Imperialism from Bismarck to Hitler* examines German history from 1871 to 1945 as an expression of the aspiration to imperialist expansion and the simultaneous fear of destruction by rivals. Acknowledging the important differences among the Second Empire, the Weimar Republic, and the Third Reich, Shelley Baranowski nonetheless reveals a common thread: the drama of German imperialist ambitions that embraced ethnic homogeneity over diversity, imperial enlargement over stasis, and "living space" as the route to the biological survival of the German *Volk*.

Shelley Baranowski is Distinguished Professor of History at the University of Akron. She is the author of *Strength through Joy: Consumerism and Mass Tourism in the Third Reich* (2004); *The Sanctity of Rural Life: Nobility, Protestantism, and Nazism in Weimar Prussia* (1995); and *The Confessing Church, Conservative Elites and the Nazi State* (1986) and the co-editor, with Ellen Furlough, of *Being Elsewhere: Tourism, Consumer Culture, and Identity in Modern Europe and North America* (2001).

Praise for *Nazi Empire*

"For more than a decade now, historians have been rediscovering that the best key to the question of the continuities of German history is to be found in the histories of German expansionism since the mid-nineteenth century. Admirably attuned both to the longer-term patterns and to the Nazi empire's terrible specificities, with an assured grasp of detail and a clear analytical vision, Shelley Baranowski has given us the best critical synthesis yet of that steadily mounting scholarship."

– Geoff Eley, University of Michigan

"This fine new political history of Germany between 1871 and 1945 does a wonderful job of synthesizing all of the most recent literature in English and German. In particular, Baranowski offers an insightful and judicious discussion of continuities and discontinuities across this period of German history, and a careful analysis of what 'empire' meant to successive generations of Germans."

– Suzanne L. Marchand, Louisiana State University

"Linking the Nazi regime, the Holocaust, and colonialism has become a controversial hypothesis in recent years, raising fears in some quarters that the Holocaust's uniqueness might be questioned. Shelley Baranowksi's achievement in *Nazi Empire* is to transcend the problem by embedding the genocide of European Jewry into a broad historical narrative while preserving its distinctive features. Reasonable yet provocative, at once sober and humane, this book is a chilling portrait, as she puts it, of 'the Third Reich's own horrific contribution to the history of European imperialism.'"

– A. Dirk Moses, University of Sydney and
the European University Institute, Florence

"In this ambitious book, Shelley Baranowski, an expert on the history of Nazi Germany, defines for readers what was distinctive about the Nazi version of racial empire. At the same time, she offers a valuable guide to the growing literature on German colonialism and its links to Nazism."

– Lora Wildenthal, Rice University

Nazi Empire

German Colonialism and Imperialism
from Bismarck to Hitler

SHELLEY BARANOWSKI

University of Akron

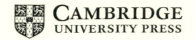

CAMBRIDGE
UNIVERSITY PRESS

CAMBRIDGE UNIVERSITY PRESS
Cambridge, New York, Melbourne, Madrid, Cape Town, Singapore,
São Paulo, Delhi, Dubai, Tokyo, Mexico City

Cambridge University Press
32 Avenue of the Americas, New York, NY 10013-2473, USA

www.cambridge.org
Information on this title: www.cambridge.org/9780521674089

First published 2011

Printed in the United States of America

A catalog record for this publication is available from the British Library.

Library of Congress Cataloging in Publication data
Baranowski, Shelley.
Nazi empire : German colonialism and imperialism from Bismarck
to Hitler / Shelley Baranowski.
p. cm.
ISBN 978-0-521-85739-0 – ISBN 978-0-521-67408-9 (pbk.)
1. Germany–Colonies–History. 2. Germany–Territorial
expansion–History. I. Title.
JV2017.B37 2010
325'.343–dc22 2010026353

ISBN 978-0-521-85739-0 Hardback
ISBN 978-0-521-67408-9 Paperback

For my students

Contents

Figures

Maps

Preface

This book originated several years ago at the suggestion of Frank Smith of Cambridge University Press, who asked me to write an accessible text on the Third Reich for undergraduates. Having devoted my career up to this point to writing on more specialized topics, I jumped at the chance to survey a field that has produced a huge and scarcely manageable literature. In fact, *Nazi Empire: German Imperialism and Colonialism from Bismarck to Hitler* has become much broader in its chronological scope than Frank intended. I am thus very grateful to him for allowing me to go beyond what he originally envisioned to explore German history from the Second to the Third Reich as a problem of empire. Although I hope that this book will appeal to its intended audience, I have found its organizing principle sufficiently fascinating, and challenging, to want to pursue it further in the future. Suffice to say, I am indebted to Frank for encouraging me to develop a project with long-term as well as short-term possibilities.

As this project has taken shape, I have been privileged to work with Eric Crahan, my editor at Cambridge, who has professionally guided the manuscript to completion, patiently answering my questions and concerns along the way. Jason Przybylski ably handled the details that accompanied the transition from submission to production, as did Bindu Vinod, who capably supervised the production process. Cambridge's anonymous readers of my original prospectus and the first draft offered thoughtful criticisms and suggestions, which I hope the final product reflects. My thanks go as well to Volker Langbehn and Mohammad Salama for giving me the opportunity to present an earlier version of my work at the stimulating interdisciplinary conference, entitled "Germany's Colonialism in International Perspective," that they organized at San Francisco State University in September 2007. Catherine Epstein generously shared parts of her forthcoming book on Arthur Greiser, the Nazi leader of the Warthegau. I deeply appreciate the help of the staff of the German Federal Archives, Digital Picture Archive, in Koblenz which supplied many of the illustrations in this book. The same applies to Jim Retallack of the University of Toronto and the German Historical Institute in Washington, D.C., who gave me permission to reproduce a map from the GHI's "German History in Documents and Images." Last but certainly not least, the staff of the Photo Archive of the United States Holocaust Memorial Museum was very forthcoming in providing me with additional images from their superb collection. The views or opinions expressed in this book and the context in which the images are used do not necessarily reflect the views or policy of, nor imply endorsement by, the Holocaust Museum.

I conclude with my thanks to sources of support closest to home. A faculty development leave from the University of Akron gave me the time to compose a workable first draft. For more than twenty years I have been fortunate to work with a wonderful group of colleagues in the history department, who have provided a collegial and intellectually stimulating environment. I am especially grateful to Stephen Harp, who read and commented on a portion of an earlier version of this work. My students, both past and present to whom this book is dedicated, have personified the indivisible bonds between one's teaching and one's scholarship. And, as always, my love to my husband Ed and to my family.

Introduction

In her controversial report from Jerusalem on the 1961 trial of the
Nazi war criminal Adolf Eichmann, the German-Jewish political phi-
losopher Hannah Arendt struggled to define the significance of the Nazi
regime's attempt to exterminate the Jews. She was certain of the defen-
dant's guilt and the appropriateness of the death sentence imposed on
him. Against widespread international criticism of Israel's kidnapping
of Eichmann in Argentina to bring him to justice, she defended the
right of the Israeli court to try him. Nevertheless, Arendt resisted the
court's claim that the "final solution" amounted to the culmination of
centuries of antisemitism. Instead she believed that the Judeocide was
a "new crime, the crime against humanity – in the sense of a crime
'against the human status,' or against the very nature of mankind."
Genocide, she continued, "is an attack upon human diversity as such,
that is, upon a characteristic of the 'human status' without which the
very words 'mankind' or 'humanity' would be devoid of meaning." As
"a crime against humanity," the Nazi effort to make the Jews "disappear from the face of the earth" was indeed "perpetrated upon the
body of the Jewish people." Yet, "Only the choice of victims," she said,
and "not the nature of the crime, could be derived from the long history of Jew-hatred and anti-Semitism."[1]

This insight from the Eichmann trial has drawn less attention over
the years than Arendt's depiction of Eichmann as a bland careerist and
her biting criticism of Jewish leaders in occupied Europe, who in her

---

[1] Hannah Arendt, *Eichmann in Jerusalem: A Report on the Banality of Evil*, revised and
enlarged ed. (Harmondsworth, Middlesex: Penguin, 1984), 268–9.

view, contributed to their own destruction.[2] Historians of Germany have rediscovered Arendt of late, but they have focused on her sprawling and problematic work, *The Origins of Totalitarianism*, to apply her insights regarding the contributions of European imperialism to the emergence of totalitarian regimes in Europe after World War I and the Nazi genocide against the Jews during World War II.[3] The determination to apply imperialism and empire as categories of analysis to generate fresh insights into the historical development of Germany, which Arendt's work has spawned, has produced a lively debate between two competing perspectives. The first focuses on the long-term impact of Imperial Germany's maritime colonialism before the Great War, and explores the possible continuities between Imperial German colonial practices and the Third Reich.[4] A second and more recently articulated position that challenges the first recognizes that "Germany," be it the Holy Roman Empire until its dissolution in 1806, or the Second Empire after 1871, was a continental empire well before it ever ventured overseas. That legacy and the longstanding German fascination with and dread of the "east," Russia especially, carried important consequences, notwithstanding the nationalist imaginings of German colonies overseas that extended at least as far back as the Revolution of 1848.[5]

---

[2] *Eichmann in Jerusalem*, 116–26, esp. 125. For the latter point, Arendt built upon the documentation in Raul Hilberg's pioneering *The Destruction of the European Jews* (Chicago: Quadrangle Books, 1961).

[3] *The Origins of Totalitarianism* (New York: Meridian, 1972). *Origins* was first published in 1951.

[4] Exemplary in this regard is Jürgen Zimmerer, "Colonialism and the Holocaust: Towards an Archeology of Genocide": in *Genocide and Settler Society: Frontier Violence and Stolen Indigenous Children in Australian History*, ed. A. Dirk Moses (New York and Oxford: Berg): 49–76; "Holocaust und Kolonialismus: Beitrag zu einer Archäologie des genozidalen Gedenkens," *Zeitschrift für Geschichtswissenschaft* 51, no. 12 (2003): 1098–119; "Die Geburt des 'Ostlandes' aus dem Geiste des Kolonialismus: Die nationalsozialistische Eroberungs-und Beherrschungspolitik in (post-)kolonialer Perspektive," *Sozial.Geschichte: Zeitschrift für historische Analyse des 20. und 21. Jahrhunderts*, 19, no. 1 (2004): 10–43; and his recent book, *Von Windhuk nach Auschwitz: Beiträge zum Verhältnis von Kolonialismus und Holocaust* (Münster: LTI, 2007). See also Benjamin Madley, "From Africa to Auschwitz: How German South West Africa Incubated Ideas and Methods Adopted and Developed by the Nazis in Eastern Europe," *European History Quarterly* 35, no. 3 (2005): 429–64.

[5] See Edward Ross Dickinson, "The German Empire: an Empire?" *History Workshop Journal* 66 (2008): 129–62; Russell Berman, "Colonialism, and no end: The other continuity theses," in *Colonial (Dis)-Continuities: Race, Holocaust, and Postwar German*, eds Volker Langbehn and Mohammad Salama (New York: Columbia University Press, forthcoming); and Robert Gerwarth and Stephan Malinowski, "Der Holocaust als 'kolonialer

Yet such starkly posed alternatives limit the ways in which "empire" as a category of analysis applies to Germany, and not only because Germany's two-dimensional imperial ambitions, continental and maritime, warrant further assessment as to how each stood in relation to the other. Rather, comparative studies that explore the links between empire, colonialism, and genocide are offering new ways to historicize the Nazi regime's obsession with the biological endangerment of the German *Volk* and its mutually reinforcing remedies, the acquisition of "living space" (*Lebensraum*) at the expense of the Slavs and the extermination of the Jews. Using the fifteenth-century "reconquests" (*reconquistas*) of Christian Spain against the Moors and the Muskovite princes against the Mongols as examples, A. Dirk Moses argues that, "the founding of empires can be linked to the experience of a society's having been colonized and subjected to imperial conquest and rule," often leading to the expulsion or destruction of the one-time colonizer. Moses suggests that this insight could prove especially relevant to National Socialism, a German "national liberation movement," for which the acquisition of a vast empire would exterminate millions, and especially the Jews, who were perceived as the pernicious agents of foreign colonization and contamination.[6] Yet Moses' argument also applies to the combination of brashness and pessimism that characterized the imperialism of the Second German Empire. If far less extreme than the Third Reich, pre–World War I aspirations to an even larger empire than the post-1871 entity joined two goals, creating internal cohesion and marginalizing domestic "enemies," and the achievement of global power. Major ruptures and discontinuities indeed punctuated the history of the "first" German unification from

---

Genozid'? Europäische Kolonialgewalt und nationalsozialistischer Vernichtungskrieg" *Geschichte und Gesellschaft* 22 (2007): 439–66; and "Hannah Arendt's Ghosts: Reflections on the Disputable Path from Windhoek to Auschwitz," *Central European History* 42, no. 3 (2009): 279–300. On the "east" in the German imagination, see Gerd Koenen, *Der Russland-Komplex: Die Deutschen und der Osten 1900–1945* (Munich: C.H. Beck, 2005); *Traumland Osten: Deutsche Bilder vom östlichen Europa im 20. Jahrhundert*, ed. Gregor Thum (Göttingen: Vandenhoeck and Ruprecht, 2006); Wolfgang Wippermann, *Die Deutschen und der Osten: Feindbild und Traumland* (Darmstadt: Primus Verlag, 2007); and Vejas Gabriel Liulevicius, *The German Myth of the East: 1800 to the Present* (Oxford and New York: Oxford University Press, 2009).

[6] A. Dirk Moses, "Empire, Colony, Genocide: Keywords and the Philosophy of History," in *Empire, Colony, Genocide: Conquest, Occupation and Subaltern Resistance in World History*, ed. A Dirk Moses (New York and Oxford: Berghahn, 2008): 30–40. See also the telling comparisons in Mahmood Mamdani's *When Victims Become Killers: Colonialism, Nativism, and the Genocide in Rwanda* (Princeton and Oxford: Princeton University Press, 2001), 12–3.

1871 to 1945. Nevertheless, the insecurities of Imperial Germany, which were interwoven in the triumphs that followed unification, established a pattern that would intensify through war, defeat, and economic crisis.

This book, a synthesis that draws primarily upon the findings of recent scholarship, argues that Germany offers an example of a less-appreciated "tension of empire," the aspiration to imperialist expansion and the simultaneous fear of dissolution at the hands of its imperialist rivals. That tension arose from the memory of the late medieval decline of German settlements in the Slavic lands of Eastern Europe, the religious conflict of the Reformation and the Thirty Years War, the decentralization and eventual break-up of the Holy Roman Empire under Napoleon, the triumphant but "incomplete" unification of 1871, which left large communities of ethnic Germans beyond the boundaries of the Second Empire, and finally, Imperial Germany's defeat and "subjugation" at the end of World War I. If the boundaries between European colonizers and the indigenous peoples they colonized were fluid and subject to contestation, as Frederick Cooper and Ann Laura Stoler famously observed over ten years ago,[7] the boundaries between becoming or being an empire and being bested by imperialist rivals could be equally impermanent and unstable. Through German eyes, beginning with the educated middle classes that propelled the drive to German unification in the nineteenth century, the prospect of sudden and devastating reversal lay barely hidden beneath the promise of a globally powerful Germany. The volatile combination of ambition and dread, which was embedded in a religious and millenarian vision of national death and resurrection,[8] informed the determination to challenge European imperialist rivals and ultimately the United States. At the same time, the perceived "failure" to eliminate social, religious, and ethnic divisions at home led increasingly to the demonization of domestic "enemies," who appeared to be the agents of foreign foes. That tendency, already evident during the Second Empire, grew more pronounced under the Weimar Republic, which many Germans saw as the noxious offspring of the Entente's depredations. In their view an unholy alliance of liberals, "Marxists" and especially Jews

---

[7] Frederick Cooper and Ann Laura Stoler, *Tensions of Empire: Colonial Cultures in a Bourgeois World* (Berkeley/Los Angeles/London: University of California Press, 1997), 7.

[8] Kevin Cramer, *The Thirty Years' War and German Memory in the Nineteenth Century* (Lincoln and London: University of Nebraska Press, 2007), and Norbert Elias, *The Germans: Power Struggles and the Development of Habitus in the Nineteenth and Twentieth Centuries*, ed. Michael Schröter and trans., Eric Dunning and Stephen Mennell (New York: Columbia University Press, 1996), 5–8.

presided over the post–World War I Weimar "system," doing the bidding
of Germany's foreign "colonizers."

Although the desire to recover and extend Germany's prewar maritime
empire persisted among former colonial administrators and public intellectuals after the Great War, Germany's defeat, the collapse of the Hohenzollern
monarchy, and what was perceived as a punitive postwar peace settlement
meant that the acquisition of a continental "living space" became central to a German resurgence. Catapulted into power as the expression of
populist and elite discontent unleashed by the Depression, the National
Socialists would combine the projects of empire and genocide. Although
markedly different from the vision of a restored and modernized Holy
Roman Empire that infused the nationalism of Catholics before World
War I, the Nazi "Greater German Reich" would, unlike the Bismarckian
and predominantly Protestant "lesser Germany," be invulnerable to foreign conquest and dismemberment. As a corrective to the failure of the
Second Empire to realize its imperialist ambitions before and during the
Great War, an expanded German *Lebensraum* would provide the resources
to compete with, and triumph over, the Nazi regime's imperialist rivals. It
would forge a harmonious and racially purified empire that by subordinating, expelling, or killing its enemies would ensure the domination of the
German master race, a final triumphant resurrection over a past of unfulfilled aspirations. Because Jews mythically personified Germany's foreign
and domestic enemies, they embodied the fragile boundaries between the
dream of expanding and maintaining an empire and losing it through military defeat and racial pollution. As Isabel Hull has argued recently, German
military doctrine had long presupposed that victory in war required the
complete destruction of the enemy.[9] The Third Reich would distinguish
itself by eliminating the enemy *behind* the enemy.

Despite the long imperial history of Germany, *Nazi Empire* limits its
chronological focus to the "first" German unification (the second being
in 1990), the period between the founding of the Second Empire to
the demise of the Third Reich. During the 1960s and 1970s, choosing
this particular chronological frame would have been unexceptional in
light of the controversy that the historian Fritz Fischer unleashed with
his *Germany's War Aims in the First World War*, published in 1961.[10]

[9] Isabel Hull, *Absolute Destruction: Military Culture and the Practices of War in Imperial
Germany* (Ithaca and London: Cornell University Press, 2005).

[10] *Griff nach der Weltmacht: Die Kriegszielpolitik des kaiserlichen Deutschland, 1914–1918*
(Düsseldorf: Droste, 1961). Fischer went further in his *War of Illusions: German Policies*

By identifying continuities in the imperialistic war plans of the Second
Empire and Third Reich, Fischer influenced a generation of scholars to
investigate Germany's "deviation" (*Sonderweg*, or "special path") from
the liberal democratic west as the source of its descent into fascism.
Dominated by an agrarian and industrial elite, the Second Empire pursued imperialism and ultimately war to shore up its power against the
rise of the German labor movement. Although weakened by revolution
and military defeat in 1918, the elite recovered enough to put the Nazis in
power in 1933, again to secure its social and political domination.[11] This
book does not restore the "special path" argument, which historians since
the 1980s have progressively dismantled.[12] Yet with due allowance for the
discontinuities between the founding of the Second Empire and the end
of the Third Reich, a common thread emerges. Imperial Germany and its
two successors staged the drama of German imperialist aspiration, the
eschatology of ethnic homogeneity over diversity, imperial enlargement
over stasis, and *Lebensraum* as the route to biological survival.

As the European order changed during the nineteenth century from a
conglomeration of dynastic empires to a composition of hybrids, that is,
empires that strove to become internally cohesive nation states, Imperial
Germany was potentially the most destabilizing because it anticipated
further enlargement even as it partially fulfilled German nationalist
aspirations of long standing. Although the "Iron Chancellor" Otto von
Bismarck temporarily contained expansionist ambitions in favor of internal consolidation and stabilizing the concert of great powers, Imperial
Germany's military might and rapid economic growth increased the pressure to compete for preeminence with other "world empires." That pressure grew all the more intense because of Bismarck's seeming inability to
contain domestic "enemies," especially ethnic minorities and the emerging
German left. Yet Germany's acquisition of protectorates overseas and its
efforts to establish informal empire on the continent, resulted in its near
total diplomatic isolation. That predicament, coupled by the anxieties
generated by the transnational migration of Slavs and Jews, gave rise to
a radical nationalist fear of annihilation that encouraged the disastrous

---

from 1911 to 1914, trans. Marian Jackson (London: Chatto and Windus, 1969) by argu-
ing that Germany bore the sole responsibility for the outbreak of war in 1914.

[11] Exemplary in this regard was Hans-Ulrich Wehler's *Das Deutsche Kaiserreich 1871–1918*
(Göttingen: Vandenhoeck and Ruprecht, 1973).

[12] The onslaught began with David Blackbourn and Geoff Eley. See their *The Peculiarities
of German History:Bourgeois Society and Politics in Nineteeth-Century Germany* (New
York and Oxford: Oxford University Press, 1984).

brinkmanship at the commanding heights of the Reich government in the summer of 1914. "Preventive war" was to be the antidote to international "encirclement," and as an important by-product, internal division.

If the Second Empire represented the potential of German nation and empire building, its defeat, the loss of its overseas empire, and its partial dismemberment after World War I reawakened earlier experiences of division and victimization by the European great powers, made more intense by economic crisis and deep domestic political divisions. To be sure, the Weimar republic was by no means destined to fail or was the viscerally antirepublican, anti-Marxist, and antisemitic radical right, from which the Nazi movement would emerge, destined to succeed. During the tumultuous first four years of the republic's life, the threat of foreign intervention and the Entente's desire to stabilize the German economy undermined radical nationalist and imperialist putschism. Furthermore, during Weimar's "middle years" between 1924 and 1929, a rough economic stabilization and a tenuously restored European state system that was partially willing to entertain German revisionist claims against the postwar peace settlement, allowed the republic to establish a degree of legitimacy. Yet, in addition to destroying the global economic and political order, the Great Depression propelled a new movement to power, the National Socialists, who defined their imperialism not only against the "bourgeois" revisionism of the republic, but also against what they deemed as the absurdity of Wilhelmine imperialism, its prioritizing of commercial over racial ends. Although economic objectives, the acquisition of raw materials and labor, were deeply embedded in the Nazi *Lebensraum* project, they were the means to more important goals, settlement, ethnic cleansing, and the racial revitalization of the *Volk* as to key to its German invulnerability.

Genocide, often the outcome of colonial conquest, has been a disturbingly common historical and contemporary problem.[13] The Nazi variant, the regime's solution to the "incomplete" unification of 1871, the defeat and collapse of 1918, and the crisis of the European state system between the wars, was the most extreme manifestation of a longstanding European problem, the tension between the maintenance of empire with all of its diversity and the struggle for ethnic and ideological

[13] For extensive comparative studies, see Ben Kiernan, *Blood and Soil: A World History of Genocide and Extermination from Sparta to Darfur* (New Haven and London: Yale University Press, 2007); and Mark Levene's *Genocide in the Age of the Nation State.* Vol. I, *The Meaning of Genocide,* and vol. II, *The Rise of the West and the Coming of Genocide* (London and New York: I. B. Tauris, 2005). A third volume is forthcoming.

homogeneity. Without the Nazis' obsession with the mythical power of the Jewish "enemy" and the long history of antisemitism, of course, the Holocaust would not have happened. Yet the distinctive characteristic of the Holocaust that total war reinforced, its remarkable consistency, in which Hitler's charismatic authority unleashed the ideologically murderous zeal and personal ambition of thousands of the Reich's epigones in the field, transformed the homogenizing capacities of the European nation states into what Arendt termed the "attack on human diversity as such." By ensuring the triumph of an empire that was to last a millennium, the Nazi "living space," cleansed of "undesirables" and "subhumans," would end the tension between dominion and annihilation.

I

From Imperial Consolidation to Global Ambitions

Imperial Germany, 1871–1914

The unification of Germany, which followed Prussia's victories over Denmark in 1864, the Austrian Empire in 1866, and France in 1871, produced a new territorial state with formidable military power, economic potential, and expansionist ambitions. Having triumphed three times in succession over enemy armies, the German "Second Empire" promised to become, for many of its citizens, the more effective successor to the first, the Holy Roman Empire, and thus the heir to Rome itself. Following the dreams of the revolutionaries of 1848, many imagined that the new Germany was but the first stage in the achievement of a dominion that would extend beyond its present borders to include ethnic Germans scattered throughout Europe, a realm that would reach as far as Constantinople and the Black Sea.[1] Imperial Germany came nowhere close to achieving that goal during its forty-seven-year lifespan. Yet by the beginning of the twentieth century, its export industries, which included electrical engineering, pharmaceuticals, chemicals, metals, finished goods, and machine-tool production, had transformed it into Europe's most dynamic economy.[2] Germany's rapid economic growth over a short period, second only to that of the United States after the

---

[1] Richard J. Evans, *The Coming of the Third Reich* (New York: Penguin Press, 2003), 6–7; Wolfgang Mommsen, *Der Erste Weltkrieg: Anfang vom Ende des bürgerlichen Zeitalters* (Frankfurt am Main: Fischer Taschenbuch Verlag, 2004), 96–7; and MacGregor Knox, *To the Threshold of Power, 1922/33: Origins and Dynamics of the Fascist and National Socialist Dictatorships*, vol. 1 (Cambridge: Cambridge University Press, 2007), 54–7.

[2] Niels P. Peterson, "Das Kaiserreich in Prozessen ökonomischer Globalisierung," in *Das Kaiserreich transnational: Deutschland in der Welt 1871–1914*, eds. Sebastian Conrad und Jürgen Osterhammel (Göttingen: Vandenhoeck and Ruprecht, 2004), 55–6.

Civil War, testified to its emergence as one of three new global players, along with America and Japan, that would rival the dominant European empires, Great Britain and France. The multiplication of industrialized and industrializing empires hastened global commercialization and the frenetic scramble for colonies in previously inaccessible parts of the globe that characterized the last third of the nineteenth century. At a time when global imperialist competition weakened the concert of European great powers that stabilized the continent after the defeat of Napoleon more than a half century earlier, the ambitions that Germany's military prowess and economic power spawned, reflected in its determination to "catch up" with and surpass Europe's leaders, meant that Germany would play a pivotal role in that competition.

In the 1860s, the prime minister of Prussia, Otto von Bismarck, opportunistically promoted unification to expand Prussian power, dissolve the German Confederation (the loose association of German states constructed after the defeat of Napoleon led jointly by Prussia and the Austrian Empire), and co-opt liberal nationalists, who sought a united Germany with constitutional limitations on monarchical power. Despite bitter battles between Prussian liberals and Bismarck over the accountability of the government and its military to parliament, the expectation of the commercial, legal, and cultural benefits of unification, for which Prussian economic power was indispensable, divided the liberal movement and worked to Bismarck's advantage. The Prussian army's impressive performance contributed to unification on Bismarck's terms, as did the fear of many liberals in Prussia and in other German states that a "ring" of enemies, especially France and Russia, would continue to profit from a politically fragmented Central Europe. Only unification under Prussian leadership would allow Germany to compete with other empires.[3] The ethnic tensions arising from Prussia's past as a colonizer, precipitated by the large number of Poles in its eastern territories of Silesia, West Prussia, and Posen, which Frederick the Great annexed during the eighteenth century, proved equally relevant to liberal sentiment. The demands of liberal revolutionaries in 1848 for a German national state provoked Polish rebellions in Prussia's eastern provinces, which had remained outside of the German Confederation. The Polish uprising in 1863 against the Russian Empire caused Prussian liberals especially to believe that too much democracy would bolster the political influence of

---

[3] Harald Biermann, *Ideologie statt Realpolitik"; Kleindeutsche Liberale und auswärtige Politik vor der Reichsgründung* (Düsseldorf: Droste Verlag, 2006), 239–53.

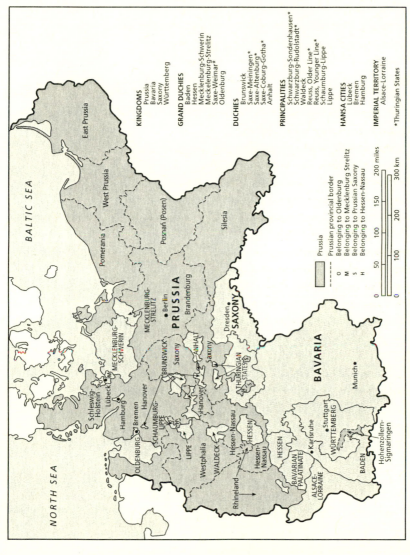

MAP 1.1. Germany, 1871–1918. Although the unification of Germany created a modern territorial state, its composition of numerous smaller entities bore the stamp of Germany's past divisions.

Source: © German Historical Institute, Washington, DC/James Retallack, 2007, German History in Documents and Images. Cartography by Mapping Solutions, Alaska.

Polish elites, who espoused democratic and nationalist ambitions of their own. Liberal suspicions of Polish disloyalty, which fed from perceptions of Polish cultural inferiority, made the protection of German nationhood more urgent to liberals than democratization.[4]

In addition to dreaming of an expanded continental Reich, German liberals had long integrated overseas colonies in their hopes of spreading German culture and completing the German nation. Like those of a German continental imperium, liberal dreams of an overseas empire originated well before the Revolution of 1848.[5] As well as imagining German settlements along the Danube basin and southern Russia, scientific periodicals, novels, travelogues, and the liberal press advocated the pursuit of colonies in the Middle East, East Asia, and the South Seas. They also envisioned settlements of patriarchal German families in the Americas that would solidify the familial relationship between Germans at home and the diaspora abroad. Moreover, a precedent existed from Prussia's earliest history to support a future overseas empire: the construction of a fortress on the Gold Coast in 1683 by the Elector of Brandenburg, Friedrich Wilhelm. Although surviving as a Prussian outpost for only seventy years, after which Frederick the Great shifted his attention to the integration and settlement of Upper and Lower Silesia, the fortress represented Brandenburg's engagement in networks of international trade, which included the transport and sale of slaves.[6]

---

[4] See Philipp Ther, "Beyond the Nation: The Relational Basis of a Comparative History of Germany and Europe," *Central European History*, 36, no. 1: 53–6; Todd Kontje, *German Orientalism* (Ann Arbor: University of Michigan Press, 2004), 106–209. On the pre-unification history of the hostility of Bismarck and Prussian liberals toward Prussian Poles, see Richard Blanke, *Prussian Poland in the German Empire (1871–1900)* (New York: Columbia University Press, 1981), 1–16.

[5] Susanne Zantop, *Colonial Fantasies: Conquest, Family, and Nation in Precolonial Germany, 1770–1870* (Durham and London: Duke University Press, 1997); Hans Fenske, "Imperialistische Tendenzen in Deutschland vor 1866. Auswanderung, überseeische Bestrebungen, Weltmachtträume," *Historische Jahrbuch* 97/98 (1978), 337–83; F.L. Müller, "Der Traum von der Weltmacht:" Imperialistische Ziele in der deutschen Nationalbewegung von der Rheinkreise bis zum Ende der Paulskirche," *Jahrbuch der Hambach Gesellschaft* 6 (1996/7): 99–183; Bradley Naranch, "Inventing the *Auslandsdeutsche*: Emigration, Colonial Fantasy, and German National Identity, 1848–71," in *Germany's Colonial Pasts*, eds. Eric Ames, Marcia Klotz, and Lora Wildenthal (Lincoln and London: University of Nebraska Press), 21–40; and Matthew P. Fitzpatrick, *Liberal Imperialism in Germany: Expansionism and Nationalism, 1848–1884* (New York and Oxford; Berghahn Books, 2008), 27–72.

[6] On this episode, see Ulrich van der Heyden, *Rote Adler an Afrikas Küste: Die brandenburgisch-preussiche Kolonie Grossfriedrichsburg in Westafrika*, 2nd ed. (Berlin: Selignow, 2001).

Because of the aspirations to an expanded Reich, the constitution of 1871 assigned to the Imperial state the task of promoting colonization. By the 1880s, a largely middle-class public promoted the acquisition of colonies and the projection of global power as the most effective means of achieving national cohesion and spreading German culture.[7] Social Darwinian ideas, which grew popular in the decades following unification, presupposed a global struggle for survival among world empires, in which only Germany's triumph as a global hegemon could guarantee its long-term survival and prosperity. To be sure, nation and empire building had become mutually reinforcing tasks for all European great powers. Managing or acquiring diverse territories was essential to the status of a world power, yet so was ensuring cultural and civic uniformity, which were crucial to social and economic modernization. Yet this dilemma was more intense in Germany, where a long history of intervention and containment by more centralized and more powerful states, and the emigration of millions of Germans, especially to the Americas, encouraged a nationalism that fused pride and aggression with insecurity and pessimism.[8] The Second Empire's multiethnic composition and the presumption of colonialism in the Imperial constitution laid the foundation for its distinction among the great powers: the aspiration to an overseas and enlarged continental empire. Although the United States and Italy entertained similar ambitions, America remained peripheral to continental European rivalries until World War I because its primary sphere of influence lay in the Western hemisphere. Italy could equal neither Germany's economic performance nor its military prowess despite its own rapid industrialization.[9]

---

[7] Arne Perras, *Carl Peters and German Imperialism 1856–1981: A Political Biography* (Oxford: Clarendon Press, 2004), 7.

[8] On the tension between nation and empire, see Sara Friedrichsmeyer, Sara Lennox, and Susanne Zantop, *The Imperialist Imagination: German Colonialism and Its Legacy* (Ann Arbor: University of Michigan Press, 1998), 19; Frederick Cooper and Ann Laura Stoler, *Tensions of Empire: Colonial Cultures in a Bourgeois World* (Berkeley, Los Angeles, and London: University of California Press, 1997), 22; and Edward Ross Dickinson, "The German Empire: an Empire?" *History Workshop Journal* 66 (2008): 129–62. On German insecurities, see Norbert Elias, *The Germans: Power Struggles and the Development of Habitus in the Nineteenth and Twentieth Centuries*, trans. Eric Dunning and Stephen Mennell (New York, 1996), 3–8.

[9] See Pascal Grosse, "What Does German Colonialism Have to Do with National Socialism? A Conceptual Framework," in Ames et al., *Germany's Colonial Pasts*, 120; and especially the extensive comparison between Italy and Germany in MacGregor Knox, *To the Threshold of Power, 1922/33: Origins and Dynamics of the Fascist and National Socialist Dictatorships*, vol. 1 (Cambridge: Cambridge University Press, 2007), 58–139.

THE ELUSIVE CONSOLIDATION: THE LIMITS OF
BISMARCKIAN NATION BUILDING

Mindful of Imperial Germany's precarious position, Bismarck disconnected the projects of national consolidation and expansion. He opted instead for internal consolidation under Prussian leadership while forcefully rejecting territorial enlargement.[10] To that end, he alternated between negotiation and coercion to contain what he and his allies viewed as oppositional and divisive forces at home that would weaken the Reich internally and externally. Although often effective in the short term, Bismarck's attempts to marginalize those whom he and his political allies labeled "enemies of the Reich" deepened internal divisions and convinced many that domestic conflict heightened the Reich's vulnerability. Imperialism came to the fore as the means of resolving that problem.

Bismarck's challenges began with the opposition to unification from his own eastern Prussian landowning caste, the Junker nobility, whose compromises with the Hohenzollern monarchy had aided the consolidation of Prussia in the seventeenth and eighteenth centuries. By guaranteeing an imperial state that preserved Prussian hegemony and limited democratization, Bismarck tempered the fear of most Junkers that absorption in an enlarged Germany would weaken their political and social influence. Because Prussia comprised nearly 60 percent of the Empire's territory, its monarch Wilhelm I became the German emperor or kaiser, and the Prussian general staff assumed command of the Imperial army, which was in turn accountable solely to the emperor. Similarly, federal ministers, the majority of them Prussian by virtue of holding comparable offices in that state, owed their appointments to the kaiser rather than being chosen from the dominant parties in the Imperial Reichstag. As a consequence, ministerial responsibility meant obedience to the crown and not to parliament. The Reichstag could neither introduce legislation nor dictate the timing, amount, or duration of military appropriations. Furthermore, Prussia dominated the upper house, the Reichsrat. Rather than being elected democratically, the Reichsrat consisted of the appointed representatives of the twenty-five German states. Because Prussia controlled more than one-quarter of the votes in the upper house and Bismarck served simultaneously as the Prussian prime minister and imperial chancellor, Prussian power was, not surprisingly, sufficient to block amendments to the Imperial constitution.

---

[10] Lothar Gall, *Bismarck: The White Revolutionary*, vol. 2, *1871–1898*, trans. J.A. Underwood (London, Boston, Sydney: Allen and Unwin, 1986), 40–1.

FIGURE 1.1. Prince Otto von Bismarck, ca. 1875. In keeping with the prestige of the Prussian military, the victories of which enabled the unification of Germany, Bismarck regularly wore an army uniform as Imperial chancellor and prime minister of Prussia.
Source: Bundesarchiv Koblenz, Bild 183-R29818.

Yet Prussian power was far from absolute. Although testifying to the achievement of unification, the Imperial constitution bore the traces of Germany's past as a conglomeration of smaller entities, amounting to a treaty laboriously negotiated among the sovereign states of the German Confederation.[11] The federal states retained significant

---

[11] Christopher Clark, *Iron Kingdom: The Rise and Downfall of Prussia, 1600–1947* (Cambridge, MA and London: Belknap Press of Harvard University Press, 2006), 557; Katherine Anne Lerman, *Bismarck: Profiles in Power* (London: Longman, 2004), 138–56.

autonomy despite the extension of Imperial authority in the realms of currency, law, transportation, justice, public health, and social welfare. The states retained their own legislatures, ruling dynasties, and, in the cases of Saxony, Bavaria, and Württemberg, even armies, although they were placed under Prussian command. Likewise, the arts, religion, and education remained state prerogatives. The implications of Imperial Germany's federal structure resided most clearly in its system of revenue generation, in which the states alone retained the power of direct taxation. The Reich's revenue intake was limited to the contributions of the states, the imposition of tariffs, fees on services, and indirect taxes on consumption, the inadequacy of which in the years immediately before World War I would provoke bitter debates as to who would foot the bill for the construction of battleships. Despite the growing identification with the German Reich after 1871, much of which was expressed in commemorations that celebrated the nation as the extension of the local and regional values,[12] regional and local particularism coexisted with nationalism. Seemingly entrenched regional loyalties caused nationalists to fear that the creation of a united Germany had done little to overcome the divisions that had made Germans the pawns of European power politics since before the Thirty Years War. Moreover, the "lesser German" (*kleindeutsch*) variant of unification that triumphed in 1871, having excluded Austria and other German ethno-linguistic enclaves in Europe, did not include all Germans. Having arisen from Prussia's destruction of the German Confederation, Imperial Germany was essentially the product of partition and secession.[13] The "incompleteness" of unification and the fear of internal fragmentation would be a recurring theme that, over the long term, would strengthen the case for expansion, especially after Bismarck departed from the scene.

Because of its potential for expressing the popular will, the Reichstag exposed the fault lines of Imperial society. Despite the constitutional limits on its power, it became the primary forum for nationwide political mobilization because it was chosen by universal male suffrage in elections that were generally free of irregularities. Although it could not introduce legislation, which was the government's prerogative, it could debate its merits under the scrutiny of an expanding mass media. Religious and

---

[12] Alon Confino, *The Nation as a Local Metaphor: Württemberg, Imperial Germany, and National Memory, 1871–1918* (Chapel Hill and London: University of North Carolina Press, 1997), esp. 97–209.

[13] See David Blackbourn's perceptive remarks in his *The Long Nineteenth Century: A History of Germany, 1780–1918* (New York and Oxford: Blackwell, 2003), 184–5.

ethnic minorities, and eventually the German labor movement, used the Reichstag as a forum for advancing their interests in ways that challenged the nationalizing and homogenizing efforts of the Imperial state.[14] With the triumph of the predominantly Protestant National Liberal Party in the 1873 national elections, one of two liberal parties that arose from the split of the liberal movement in the 1860s, the first source of conflict – religious difference – moved to center stage. The National Liberals and the older liberal party, the Progressives, rejoined to support Bismarck in their "Battle for Culture" (*Kulturkampf*) against the Catholic Church, a campaign that fused anticlericalism, a contempt for "superstition," and a Protestant nationalism that deemed Catholicism synonymous with disloyalty, not least because the Catholic population included ethnic minorities.

Protestants held a sizable majority over Catholics, comprising nearly two-thirds of the Empire's citizenry and dispersed unevenly between a Lutheran majority and a Reformed or Calvinist minority. Despite that majority, which might otherwise have instilled confidence in their position, Protestant nationalists equated the fight against Catholicism with resistance to foreign domination. Thus, Martin Luther emerged as a national hero for having rebelled against the tyranny of the Roman Catholic Church. The Swedish King Gustavus Adolphus, who battled the armies of the Holy Roman Empire during the Thirty Years War, represented the promise of 1517, a Protestant Reich liberated from Rome and France, which the restorationist Peace of Westphalia of 1648 ultimately betrayed.[15] The annexation of Alsace and Lorraine from France, combined with the large Polish population in the eastern Prussian provinces and Catholic majorities in Baden, Bavaria, and the Rhineland, exacerbated confessional antagonisms and the ethnic tensions arising from Prussia's colonial heritage. Convinced that Catholic sympathies lay with Austria and France, Germany's defeated enemies, and with the ultramontanist and antimodernist Pope Pius IX, the government expelled Catholic religious orders, removed refractory bishops, imposed state control over the appointment and education of clergy, and decreed civil marriages as

[14] Blackbourn, *Long Nineteenth Century*, 201. On the limits of the government's ability to influence the Reichstag and manipulate the electorate, see Margaret Lavinia Anderson, *Practicing Democracy: Elections and Political Culture in Imperial Germany* (Princeton: Princeton University Press, 2000).

[15] Kevin Cramer, "The Cult of Gustavus Adolphus," in *Protestants, Catholics and Jews in Germany, 1800–1914*, ed. Helmut Walser Smith (Oxford and New York: Berg, 2001), 97–120; and Kevin Cramer, *The Thirty Years' War and German Memory in the Nineteenth Century* (Lincoln and London: University of Nebraska Press, 2007), especially 51–93.

compulsory. The intent was to punish Catholic "backwardness," irrationality, and internationalism as inherently opposed to the "progressive,"
"modern," and Protestant German nation. Liberals especially objected
to the Jesuits, whom they suspected of encouraging an irrational and
emotional feminine piety through regular confession and other forms of
devotion. The relationship between Catholic women and Jesuit priests
challenged the authority of fathers, whose patriarchal leadership of the
family imperial law had enshrined, and underwritten, the pernicious
influence of the Jesuits in the public sphere.[16]

To be sure, tensions eased between Protestants and Catholics in the
decades after unification. Regular church attendance among Catholics
declined over time, and Catholics who were in business and the professions, although underrepresented in the population compared to
Protestants, pushed for the social and political integration of their coreligionists. Nevertheless, the minority status of Catholics and the defensiveness of the Catholic Church remained a feature of German politics
until after World War II. Hostile to liberalism because of its secularism
and to Imperial bureaucratic homogenization, which refused to allow
space for Catholic distinctiveness and local traditions, the nationalism
of Catholics diverged sharply from the Protestant variant. Instead of
the Protestant Reich standing tall against the tyranny of Rome and the
Habsburgs, the Catholic view of the nation recalled the "greatness" of the
Holy Roman Empire. The same Gustavus Adolphus, whom Protestants
venerated, emerged in the Catholic perspective as the seventeenth-century
version of Napoleon Bonaparte, who unleashed the ills of secularism and
revolution against the Imperial constitution, the embodiment of German
civilization. Similar to Protestants, Catholics believed that the Peace of
Westphalia was disastrous, for it ushered in another two centuries of
German weakness and foreign intervention. Yet for the latter, the tragedy
lay in the defeat of reforms that would have modernized and strengthened the Holy Roman Empire.[17]

After the death of Pope Pius in 1878, the worst effects of the Battle
for Culture abated in most of Germany. Yet anti-Catholic measures

[16] Roisin Healy, *The Jesuit Specter in Imperial Germany* (Boston: Brill Academic Publishers,
    2003), 21–83, 117–72; Michael Gross, *The War against Catholicism: Liberalism and the
    Anti-Catholic Imagination in Nineteenth-Century Germany* (Ann Arbor: University of
    Michigan Press, 2004), 185–239.
[17] Helmut Walser Smith, *German Nationalism and Religious Conflict: Culture, Ideology,
    Politics 1870–1914* (Princeton: Princeton University Press, 1995), 61–78: Cramer, *Thirty
    Years War*, 204–16.

continued to be imposed on Alsatians and Lorrainers and the two and a half million Prussian Poles, most of them concentrated in the eastern Prussian frontier where, from the government's perspective, the combination of confession and ethnicity posed special "dangers" to German security. In Alsace and Lorraine, pitched battles took place between Protestant bureaucrats and the local church over diocesan boundaries, the instruction of priests, and the clerical role in education that continued until 1918. In Prussian Poland, decrees that mandated German as the language of instruction in the schools and for the conduct of business in the courts and bureaucracy accompanied the decrees of the Battle for Culture, an assault against Poles that would only deepen in the 1880s and afterward. With the growing number of Polish agricultural workers on large landed estates and Polish wage earners in the coal mines and factories of the Ruhr, the Battle for Culture took on a double meaning with the defense of German culture against the Polish migration from the Russian and Austro-Hungarian Empires.[18] Even in the rest of Germany, religious conflict solidified a powerful Catholic subculture, the political potency of which formed during the religious revivals following Prussia's annexation of the Rhineland and Westphalia after the Napoleonic wars, as well as the brief liberal victories during the Revolutions of 1848.[19] The Center Party, founded in 1870 to represent the religious interests of both confessions, became transformed as a result of the conflict with Bismarck into the political voice of Catholics, claiming 80 percent of the Catholic vote in the 1874 Reichstag elections. A luxuriant popular piety that centered on apparitions of the Virgin Mary linked politics and religion through the trope of suffering at the hands of the Imperial state, which Catholics viewed as simultaneously (and ironically) Protestant and secular.[20]

[18] On the Battle for Culture and the ethnic struggle, see Lech Trzeciakowski, *The Kulturkampf in Prussian Poland*, trans, Kataryna Kretkowska (Boulder, 1990); Dan P. Silverman, *Reluctant Union: Alsace-Lorraine and Imperial Germany 1871–1918* (University Park, PA: Pennsylvania State University Press, 1972), 71–110; Blanke, *Prussian Poland*, 17–37; and William W. Hagen, *Germans, Poles and Jews: The Nationality Conflict in the Prussian East, 1772–1914* (Chicago and London: University of Chicago Press, 1980), 128–31. On the impact of Polish labor, see especially Sebastian Conrad, *Globalisierung und Nation im Deutschen Kaiserreich* (Munich: C.H. Beck, 2006), 150–3.

[19] Gross, *War against Catholicism*, 29–73; Jonathan Sperber, *Popular Catholicism in Nineteenth-Century Germany* (Princeton: Princeton University Press, 1984), 39–98.

[20] Matthew Jeffries, *Imperial Culture in Germany, 1871–1918* (Houndsmills, Basingtroke, Hampshire: Palgrave Macmillan, 2003), 17; David Blackbourn, *Marpingen: Apparitions of the Virgin Mary in Bismarckian Germany* (New York: Vintage Books, 1994), esp. 76–99 and 202–49.

Religion joined with ethnicity was but one source of division. Class
became another. The emerging German labor movement constituted
a "threat" to domestic order and cohesion, temporarily mitigating
Bismarck's assault against Catholicism in the interests of containing the
left. Founded in 1875 as the Socialist Workers' Party of Germany (subsequently renamed the Social Democratic Party, or SPD, in 1890), the
Socialists spoke for an increasingly urbanized proletariat and a growing number of industrial wage earners. Combining political and social
goals, the party advocated the redistribution of wealth and property, the
expansion of the powers of the Reichstag, and the elimination of unequal
franchises in state legislatures, particularly in Prussia where the division
of the electorate among three classes disproportionately benefited large
landed estate owners. In 1878, responding to two assassination attempts
against the emperor by perpetrators with no known connection to the
Socialists, Bismarck launched what he hyperbolically described as a "war
of annihilation" against the "rats in the country."[21] Passed by a conservative majority in the Reichstag, the Anti-Socialist Law that Bismarck
introduced outlawed the party and banned Socialist meetings and publications. Although the law permitted the Socialists to run as candidates
for parliamentary elections, the experience of repression forged a durable Social Democratic subculture that survived the Law's expiration in
1890. Amplified by numerous party-sponsored cultural organizations,
and drawing its support primarily from working-class neighborhoods
where lifestyles and cultural practices differed from those of the middle
classes,[22] the SPD became both reformist and revolutionary. Its Marxian-
inspired Erfurt Program of 1891 predicted the intensification of the class
struggle between the bourgeoisie and the working class, a conflict that
would inevitably culminate in the overthrow of capitalism. The second
part of the program, however, emphasized short-term needs, better wages,
improved working conditions, and the reform of the political system
beginning with the elimination of the three-class franchise in Prussia.

Despite an emerging gradualist sensibility in the SPD, middle- and
upper-class Germans commonly perceived the Socialists as traitors, or
"fellows without a fatherland." The SPD's Marxian-inspired solidarity with the international proletariat and its vision of a democratized

---

[21] Lerman,*Bismarck*, 181.
[22] This despite the evidence that SPD increasingly won the votes of craftsmen, rentiers, and
retail clerks. See Jonathan Sperber, *The Kaiser's Voters: Electors and Elections in Imperial
Germany* (Cambridge: Cambridge University Press, 1997), 66–9.

nation threatened Imperial Germany's mix of bourgeois nationalism and dynasticism. Bismarck's introduction of social insurance in the 1880s to cover illness and accidents, and later pensions and disability coverage – all of which were supposed to give workers a stake in the imperial system – did little to mitigate social tensions. The propertied classes' fear of socialism made certain that no Protestant middle-class party captured a significant working-class constituency. Although over time, younger Catholic workers increasingly gravitated to the SPD, only the Center and, to a lesser extent, the parties representing national minorities won the allegiance of workers. Confessional loyalty remained important even among Catholic workers in the Ruhr who, despite their resentment of unsympathetic priests and bourgeois coreligionists, formed their own unions to oppose oppressive Prussian officials and anticlerical Social Democratic labor organizers.[23]

Antisocialism became an essential lubricant to the political functioning of the Second Empire during the Bismarckian era as the chancellor struggled to forge parliamentary majorities loyal to the government. The bourgeois hostility to the left and the increasing demand for tariff protection from industrial and agrarian interests in the wake of the long recession that took hold two years after unification led to the formation of the "iron and rye" cartel, composed of the National Liberals and two parties, the Free Conservatives and the Conservatives, which articulated the views of industry, large-scale commercial interests, and estate agriculture, respectively. The combination of antisocialism and protectionism mitigated the religious divide as the Center, which spoke for the interests of Catholic peasants, joined the cartel to vote for the imposition of protective tariffs on foreign commodities. While such an alliance hardly destroyed the Center's potential as an opposition, common economic interests and a hatred of the left fostered expedient cooperation.

The Center's pragmatism, however, did little to relieve the pressure on ethnic minorities, nor did it entirely assuage Protestant suspicions of Catholic disloyalty. In fact, Bismarck intensified his assault in the 1880s against ethnic "enemies," beginning with the Poles. Once again, he counted on the support of liberals, whose anticlericalism derived not only from the trope of conniving priests preying on the vulnerability of women, but also from visions of priests forcing the conversion of German spouses in

---

[23] Michaela Bachem-Rehm, *Die katholischen Arbeitervereine im Ruhrgebiet 1870–1914: Katholisches Arbeitermilieu zwischen Tradition und Emanzipation* (Stuttgart, Berlin, and Cologne: Kohlhammer, 2004), 93–190.

mixed marriages. Yet the special harshness of the Battle for Culture in regions where ethnicity and religion formed a combustible mix not only failed to tame the nationalism of Polish elites, it also politicized the Polish rural masses into resistance. That, in turn, moved the chancellor and his parliamentary allies to impose new measures to punish a troublesome minority. Between 1883 and 1885, the Prussian government at Bismarck's behest forcibly expelled thousands of recent nonnaturalized Russian and Galician Polish immigrants, a then-unprecedented act in peacetime.[24] The crackdown at the Reich and Prussian levels, which began with the Battle for Culture, represented a departure from the Prussian government's pragmatism in dealing with its Polish subjects before unification. Whereas previously the Prussian crown respected the integrity of Polish culture and the Polish language as long as Poles remained loyal, believing that market forces would encourage German settlements to alter the ethnic balance, the postunification Prussian government intervened directly to suppress resistance by forcing assimilation.[25]

Poles were by no means the only ethnic minority to be subjected to colonial subjugation, which wavered between "civilizing" and marginalizing the colonized. In addition to the Alsatians and Lorrainers annexed after the Franco-Prussian War, Danish nationalists in Northern Schleswig, which Prussia claimed from Denmark in 1864, were deemed at least potential "enemies of the Reich." In the new western borderlands, the efforts of German educators to nationalize primary school pupils did not differ noticeably from those of the French, and in fact the Germans often proved more accommodating to local sensibilities than their predecessors.[26] Yet in a more successful migration than occurred in Prussian Poland, German settlers, many of whom financed, owned, and managed industrial development, flocked to Alsace and Lorraine between 1871 and 1914. Germans dominated the student bodies of provincial universities, while German administrators imposed exceptional laws to keep the native populations under control.[27] Arguably, however, the hostility to the Poles ran deeper. Although assimilating Poles remained the goal

---

[24] Hagen, *Germans, Poles, and Jews*, 132–5; Smith, *German Nationalism and Religious Conflict*, 185–205.

[25] Clark, *Iron Kingdom*, 579.

[26] Stephen L. Harp, *Learning to Be Loyal: Primary Schooling as Nation Building in Alsace and Lorraine* (Dekalb, IL: Northern Illinois University Press, 1998), esp. 19–105.

[27] Silverman, *Reluctant Union*, 60. Dieter Gosewinkel, *Einbürgern und Ausschliessen: Die Nationalisierung der Staatsangehörigkeit vom Deutschen Bund bis zur Bundesrepublik Deutschland* (Göttingen: Vandenhoeck and Ruprecht, 2001), 191–211.

of government policy, and intermarriage between Poles and Germans was never outlawed, Poles were commonly stereotyped as primitive and anarchic, wallowing in filth and unable (or unwilling) to lift themselves out of poverty.[28] Such arrogance belied the insecurities associated with the history and memory of the successful German colonization of the Baltic regions in the Middle Ages, and its subsequent decline with the devastation of the Black Death, the rise of the Polish-Lithuanian Commonwealth, and its defeat of the Teutonic Knights. Frederick the Great's conquests in the eighteenth century and the creation of the new German Empire after 1871 only partially compensated for the loss of a much larger expanse of territory.[29]

In 1886, the Prussian government formed its new Settlement Commission to institute a colonization program that would combat the flight of Germans from the east to the industrial regions of the west. A nettlesome problem with major long-term consequences, the departure of Germans for better-paying employment elsewhere and the reliance of estate agriculture on Polish immigrant labor, the government sought unsuccessfully to counter the "polonization" of the eastern frontier. Although its program gave priority to the purchase of Polish estates and the creation of villages exclusively composed of transplanted German peasants, the necessity of creating economically viable plots limited its impact. Despite having settled some 130,000 Germans over thirty years, which easily exceeded the number of settlers in Germany's overseas colonies,[30] they did not come close to equaling the number of Germans who moved west, some 940,000 between 1886 and 1905.[31] The support for settlement came from the ruling coalition in the Prussian parliament, particularly the National Liberals who were as fervent as Bismarck in their determination to reverse the "decline" of German culture in the east. Other measures to promote Germanization, including the tightening of state control over education and the imposition of the German language in primary and secondary schools, directly targeted

[28] Philipp Ther, "Deutsche Geschichte als imperiale Geschichte: Polen, slawophone Minderheiten und das Kaiserreich als kontinentales Empire," in *Kaiserreich transnational*, 137–41.

[29] On the history and memory of the colonization, see Debórah Dwork and Robert Jan van Pelt, *Auschwitz: 1270 to the Present* (New York and London: W.W. Norton, 1996), 17–65.

[30] Conrad, *Globalisierung*, 149.

[31] See Uwe Mai, *"Rasse und Raum": Agrarpolitik, Sozial-und Raumplanung im NS-Staat* (Paderborn: Ferdinand Schöningh, 2002), 16–22; Blanke, *Prussian Poland*, 55–91.

Polish cultural nationalism in ethnically Polish regions. Although the impact of the settlement program was minimal, not least because few Polish estates were economically hard-pressed enough for the Prussian government to buy them out, the Bismarckian initiatives yielded two significant outcomes. By promoting ethnic contestation, they magnified tensions between Catholic Germans and Poles. In order to prove their loyalty to the Empire, Catholic bishops became agents of Germanization among their Polish parishioners. Moreover, although limited to replacing Germans who had emigrated and to imposing linguistic and cultural uniformity on the Poles, the failure of Imperial German initiatives would weaken confidence in the state's ability to force assimilation. It would encourage more aggressive colonization proposals in the future to erect a dam against the "Slavic flood." If Germanization would not take root, so those proposals opined, then harsher measures would.[32]

The suspicion of minorities was not confined to the institutions of state. Antisemitism generated a populist response, as massive structural changes in the economy and the long recession overlapped with the state's assaults against the Poles. In the 1880s, at the same time that the Prussian government expelled Russian and Galician Poles and established its eastern settlement program, lower middle-class demagogues, Hermann Ahlwardt, Otto Böckel, and the Protestant court chaplain Adolf Stöcker among them, vented their frustrations at Germany's legally emancipated, increasingly urbanized, prosperous, and assimilated Jewish minority, as well as the influx of unassimilated Jews from the Austro-Hungarian and Russian Empires. Despite winning seats in the Reichstag into the 1890s, single-issue antisemitic parties did not survive because of conflicts among them.[33] Yet the political utility of antisemitism became irresistible to the major political parties as they sought to broaden their mass support. If the "rowdy," demagogic antisemitism of populists such as Böckel and

---

[32] William W. Hagen, *Germans, Poles, and Jews: The Nationality Conflict in the Prussian East, 1772–1914* (Chicago and London: University of Chicago Press, 1980), 132–5: Smith, *German Nationalism and Religious Conflict*, 185–205; Dwork and van Pelt, *Auschwitz*, 48–50.

[33] The most recent work to examine the fortunes of the antisemitic parties is Massimo Ferrari Zumbini's *Die Wurzeln des Bösen: Gründerjahre des Antisemitismus; Von der Beismarckzeit zu Hitler* (Frankfurt am Main; Vittorio Klostermann, 2003). Yet still valuable are Richard H. Levy, *The Downfall of the Anti-Semitic Political Parties in Imperial Germany* (New Haven: Yale University Press, 1975); Paul W. Massing, *Rehearsals for Destruction: a Study of Political Anti-Semitism in Imperial Germany* (New York: Harper, 1949); and Peter G.J. Pulzer, *The Rise of Political Anti-Semitism in Germany and Austria* (Cambridge, MA: Harvard University Press, 1988), originally published in 1964.

Ahlwardt lost organizational cohesion, the Center, National Liberals, and especially the Conservatives, whose platform of 1892 called for rolling back the civil rights of Jews, appealed to the populist anti-Jewish feeling of peasants, artisans, and small shopkeepers, for whom the Jew personified a increasingly concentrated industrial economy that disadvantaged them.[34]

The adoption of antisemitism by political leaderships and the huge rural pressure group affiliated with the Conservative Party, the Agrarian League, contributed to a broader trend that characterized Imperial Germany after the 1880s, that is, its acceptability to the social and intellectual elite. By the 1870s and early 1880s, Germany's most popular historian Heinrich von Treitschke, fearing the cultural consequences of Jewish immigration from the east, demanded the elimination of Jewish distinctiveness through assimilation even as he implied its impossibility. By contrast, Treitschke grudgingly acknowledged that the Poles were capable of Germanization.[35] Yet if Treitschke only hinted at the ineradicable difference of Jews, the inventor of the term "antisemitism," the writer Wilhelm Marr in 1873, explicitly cast Jews as a different race altogether than Christian Germans. Their pernicious characteristics were immutably and irrevocably defined by blood. Jews were less important as flesh-and-blood individuals, however, than as the personification of the signs of economic and cultural degeneration: free-market and free-trade liberalism, international mobile capital, socialism, and especially racial mixing, the result of increasing intermarriage, which antisemites believed threatened German "purity."[36] Although Eastern European Jews (*Ostjuden*) garnered most of the attention for their "oriental" appearance, despite the fact that the majority consisted of transients seeking emigration to America from

[34] James Retallack, *The German Right 1860–1920: Political Limits of the Authoritarian Imagination* (Toronto, Buffalo, and London: University of Toronto Press, 2006), 334–9.

[35] On Treitschke, see Helmut Walser Smith, *The Continuities of Germany History: Nation, Religion, and Race across the Long Nineteenth Century* (Cambridge: Cambridge University Press, 2008), 171–4; and John Weiss, *Ideology of Death: Why the Holocaust Happened in Germany* (Chicago: Ivan Dee, 1996), 128–42. The still indispensable analysis of elite adoption of antisemitism in order to rally a populist base is Hans-Jürgen Puhle's *Agrarische Interessenpolitik und preussischer Konservatismus im wilhelminichen Reich (1893–1914): Ein Beitrag zur Analyse des Nationalismus in Deutschland am Beispiel des Bundes der Landwirte und der Deutsch-Konservativen Partei* (Hannover, Verlag für Literatur u. Zeitgeschehen. 1966).

[36] Although the rate of intermarriage was below 10 percent in 1900, an indication of continued Jewish endogamy, the increase in that percentage was sufficient to attract the attention of antisemites. See Shulamit Volkov, *Germans, Jews, and Antisemites: Trials in Emancipation* (Cambridge: Cambridge University Press, 2006), 259.

Germany's seaports, Jewish immigration from the east became the excuse
for including assimilated Jews in a larger, right-wing crusade to disenfranchise and disempower. The Prussian government expelled Russian
and Galician Jews along with the Poles.[37] Unlike anti-Polish feeling,
which the Imperial and Prussian states orchestrated directly to suit their
political ends, populism initially propelled the growth of antisemitism.
Nevertheless, the acceptability of antisemitism among elites, and especially the growing belief that to be Jewish meant the opposite of being
German, testified to a fearful and exclusionary nationalism intensified by
the colonial roots of Imperial Germany's Prussian core and the stubborn
resistance to a homogenizing Germanization by Imperial Germany's ethnically diverse population.

German antisemitism was neither entirely home grown, nor was it
uniquely vitriolic. The enormous influence in bourgeois circles of the
works of the French racist Joseph Gobineau and the Briton Houston
Stewart Chamberlain underscored the transnational cross-fertilization
of antisemitism, which the popularization of Darwinism increasingly
redefined. Pogroms arising from fears of blood libel, such as in Xanten
in the Rhineland and in the West Prussian town of Konitz in 1900,
drew sustenance from the waves of antisemitic violence that erupted
throughout Central and Eastern Europe from the 1880s to World War
I.[38] Comparatively speaking, German Jews faced fewer legal and social
disabilities than Jews in the Austro-Hungarian and Russian Empires, and
they confronted fewer episodes of antisemitic violence. Moreover, when
violent outbreaks did occur, Jews received more police protection from
antisemitic mobs. Despite discrimination, which kept them out of the
officer corps, the senior civil service, and prestigious academic positions,
Jews in general enjoyed a high degree of social and political integration,
especially in the cities. The burgeoning market for mass entertainment
and spectacle after 1890 opened doors for Jewish entrepreneurs and
entertainers, underscoring the relative openness of prewar German society compared to what would follow after 1918 and certainly after 1933.[39]

---

[37] Jack Wertheimer, *Unwelcome Strangers: East European Jews in Imperial Germany* (New
York: Oxford University Press, 1987), 9–41 and 43–74; Steven E. Aschheim, *Brothers
and Strangers: The East European Jew in German and German Jewish Consciousness*
(Madison: University of Wisconsin Press, 1982), 59–79.

[38] See Helmut Walser Smith, *The Butcher's Tale: Murder and Anti-Semitism in a German
Town* (New York: W.W. Norton, 2002).

[39] See Till van Rahden, *Jews and Other Germans: Civil Society, Religious Diversity, and
Urban Politics in Breslau, 1860–1925*, trans. Marcus Brainard (Madison: University of

Nor was there any cause celèbre in Imperial Germany comparable to the Dreyfus Affair in France, where the vitriolic antisemitism surrounding the sensational trial and conviction of an Alsatian Jewish officer exposed bitter political divisions over the legitimacy of the Third Republic and the "crisis" of French masculinity arising from France's defeat at the hands of Prussia.[40]

Nevertheless, if hostility toward Jews amounted to a global and ancient prejudice, and its intensity reached nowhere near the levels of World War I and its aftermath, its appearance as the expression of the insecurities of German national identity made it potentially dangerous. Despite their divergent conceptions of the nation, Protestants and Catholics united in memorializing, indeed celebrating, the Christian communal violence against Jews that between 1350 and 1550 destroyed scores of Jewish settlements. Those memories merged with more recent, and more painful, recollections of the Napoleonic invasion and its consequences: the confiscation of church property, the elimination of communal autonomy, and the legal emancipation of German Jews whose subordination and exclusion communities previously regulated.[41] Antisemitism not only became a "cultural code," that is, a discourse that for the antisocialist and antiliberal right could conceptualize Germany's deep social and political divisions in simplified terms, it would also become linked to Germany's imperialist mission abroad and to its imperialist rivals as Germany strove to achieve its global "place in the sun" – rivals that would become enemies as war approached. As early as 1893, the imperialist and antisemitic publicist, Friedrich Lange, who profoundly influenced the thinking of leading figures of the radical nationalist and imperialist Pan German League, integrated antisemitism in his broader campaign for the moral rebirth of the nation through "pure Germanism." He combined demands for cultural homogenization and the expulsion of Jews from German society with the call for autarky, imperialist expansion, and finally war as an historical necessity to enhance Germany's global standing.[42]

Wisconsin Press); Marline Otte, *Jewish Identities in German Popular Entertainment, 1890–1933* (Cambridge: Cambridge University Press, 2006).

[40] See Christopher Forth, *The Dreyfus Affair and the Crisis of French Manhood* (Baltimore and London: Johns Hopkins University Press, 2004).

[41] Smith, *Continuities of German History*, 74–114.

[42] Volkov, *Germans, Jews, and Antisemites*, 115; Geoff Eley, *Reshaping the German Right: Radical Nationalism and Political Change after Bismarck* (New Haven and London: Yale University Press, 1980), 53, 246–7. See also Christian Davis, "Colonialism, Antisemitism, and Germans of Jewish Dissent in Imperial Germany" (PhD diss: Rutgers University, 2005), 41–6.

PRAGMATIC COLONIALISM OR EXPORTING "GERMANNESS": OVERSEAS IMPERIALISM, AND BISMARCK'S FORCED RETIREMENT

Consistent with his emphasis on internal consolidation, Bismarck pursued a foreign policy that, although it promoted German hegemony in Central and Western Europe with a credible military force to back it up,[43] stressed the preservation of the existing Reich and the intra-European dynastic order. The conservative and dynastic solidarity expressed in the Three Emperors League, which in 1873 joined Germany with Austria-Hungary and Russia, was the culmination of Bismarck's efforts to reassure both that Imperial Germany would not extend its borders to include Germans beyond the Reich.[44] Nevertheless, in 1884 and 1885, the state's forays into overseas imperialism accompanied the ratcheting up of anti-Polish and anti-Jewish feeling at home, an indication that Bismarck's ability to separate national consolidation from expansion was waning. The anti-Polish measures and the acquisition of colonies owed much to Bismarck's need to maintain workable parliamentary coalitions of "national" parties in Prussia and the Reich as the utility of antisocialism temporarily subsided and difficult economic issues, especially tariff protection for agriculture, divided the National Liberals.[45] In order to counteract the losses that the National Liberals suffered in the national parliamentary elections of 1881, Bismarck sought to capitalize once more on powerful bourgeois nationalist sentiments that implicitly fused repression of the Poles with the acquisition of colonies abroad.[46] Having appreciated the popularity of overseas colonization in the Free Conservative Party that represented powerful commercial, industrial, and landed interests, and the National Liberals, who saw the acquisition of colonies as a means of reversing their electoral fortunes, Bismarck used the opportunity to rebuild a coalition of "state-supporting" parties.[47] Moreover, Bismarck sympathized with commercial, banking, and manufacturing interests, which hoped a presence overseas would provide raw materials, markets, trading posts, and opportunities for investment. Bismarck's apparently

---

[43] See Konrad Canis, *Bismarcks Aussenpolitik 1870 bis 1890: Aufstieg und Gefährdung* (Paderborn: Ferdinand Schöningh, 2004), 85–108.

[44] Gall, *White Revolutionary* vol. II, 40–60; Lerman, *Bismarck*, 208.

[45] Sperber, *Kaiser's Voters*, 180–9.

[46] Cf. Conrad, *Globalisierung*, 143–4.

[47] Hartmut Pogge von Strandemann, "Domestic Origins of Germany's Colonial Expansion under Bismarck," *Past and Present*, no. 42 (1969): 140–59; and Fitzpatrick, *Liberal Imperialism*, 116–31.

sudden interest in colonies did not attest to a far-reaching scheme to acquire colonies to compensate for economic crises at home, diffuse domestic tensions, weaken the appeal of Social Democracy, and stabilize the imperial system, as was once argued.[48] Yet the chancellor did understand the appeal of imperialism to precisely those parties and interests, which he considered essential to a reliable government. Such a coalition would continue the Empire's consolidation while marginalizing the left and ethnic minorities, the "enemies of the Reich." The failing health of Kaiser Wilhelm handed Bismarck another issue that the acquisition of colonies could potentially resolve. Fearing the impending ascension to the throne of Crown Prince Friedrich and his English wife Victoria, whose suspected liberalism held the potential for bolstering the electoral fortunes of the left-liberal Progressives, Bismarck calculated that overseas colonialism would heighten nationalism at home, keep the liberal parties divided, and tie the new kaiser's hands with a reliably "national" majority in the Reichstag.[49]

Bismarck's decision was a godsend to the private adventurers, entrepreneurs, and prominent Free Conservative aristocrats, who composed the membership of the two-year-old German Colonial Society, and pro-colonial elements in the Foreign Office. Following the widely publicized activities of the missionary and publicist Friedrich Fabri in Angola, and adventurer-entrepreneurs such as Adolf Lüderitz in Southwest Africa and Carl Peters in Zanzibar, Bismarck placed under imperial "protection" the West African harbor of Angra Pequeña, Southwest Africa, the Cameroons, Togoland, the northeastern portion of New Guinea, several Micronesian and Melanesian islands, and a portion of East Africa – all between April, 1884 and February, 1885. In addition to the startling suddenness of the German initiatives, which clearly unsettled London, Bismarck's apparent support of the dubious tactics of Carl Peters in Zanzibar and East Africa seemed a de facto endorsement of Peters' very public desire to challenge British claims in the same region, a desire that temporarily served Bismarck's own domestic purposes. Bismarck's convening of the Berlin West Africa Conference in November of 1884 arose from a mixture of motivations. In addition to preventing colonial rivalries from

---

[48] Hans-Ulrich Wehler, *Bismarck und der Imperialismus* (Cologne; Berlin, Kiepenheuer u. Witsch, 1969). Wehler's position has remained unchanged with some modifications. See his *Deutsche Gesellschaftsgeschichte*, vol. 3, *Von der "Deutschen Doppelrevolution" bis zum Beginn des Ersten Weltkrieges 1849–1914* (Munich: Vandenhoeck and Ruprecht, 1995), 980–90.

[49] Canis, *Bismarcks Aussenpolitik*, 212–4.

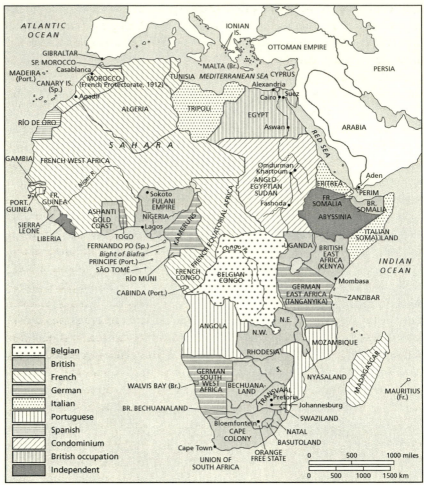

MAP 1.2. The Partition of Africa, ca. 1876–1894. This map, indicative of the mounting competition among European empires during the last quarter of the nineteenth century, also illustrates Germany's own desire to acquire its "place in the sun." In addition to its African possessions (Southwest and East Africa, Togo, and the Cameroons), Germany acquired a ninety-nine-year leasehold in Qingdao (Kiaochow) in China's Shandong Province, as well as part of Samoa and several other South Pacific islands.
Source: Robin W. Winks and Joan Neuberger, *Europe and the Making of Modernity, 1815–1914* (Oxford and New York: Oxford University Press, 2005), 271.

destabilizing intra-European relations by establishing spheres of influence that would allow open markets and ease of trade among the European powers, he also sought to define "civilized" standards for dealing with African peoples, whose absence from the bargaining table signified their legal demotion to the status of children. Yet Bismarck's desire to direct French attention to sub-Saharan Africa, thus defusing French claims to the return of Alsace Lorraine and using France as a counterweight to British power, was equally important.[50]

In fact, Bismarck's comparatively modest colonial agenda was becoming outmoded. At a time when the restiveness of colonized peoples and the insatiable need of a global economy for raw materials, markets, and labor pushed other European states to impose more direct control over their possessions, Bismarck envisioned an inexpensive, informal colonialism with as little state management as possible. The commercial concessions on the ground that he supported would operate effectively enough. Moreover, the electoral losses of the Progressives, the old kaiser's surprising recuperation, the installation of a conservative government in London that was friendlier to German interests, and above all the need to keep the Russian and Austro-Hungarian Empires from coming to blows in the Balkans, reduced the impulse to further expansionism.[51] Nevertheless, the lure of colonies to the commercial and professional middle classes testified to the reawakened fusion of national consolidation and imperialism that would grow impatient with Bismarck's limited objectives, his seemingly unaggressive caution, and his putative inability to contain "enemies of the Reich." In addition to promoting its commercial benefits, bourgeois imperialists deemed colonialism as essential to developing a strong German nationalism as the antidote to internal fragmentation and the dissolution of national identity through emigration to the Americas. Thus, as Friedrich Fabri, Carl Peters, and other activists claimed, acquiring its own colonies for settlement would allow Germany to divert the overflow of the German population overseas while exporting the German language and nationality as the way to compete with its imperialist rivals, particularly Great Britain. Colonies would enable economic prosperity, deepen national pride, and replace what Peters believed was the longstanding cosmopolitanism of Germans with a virile ethnic consciousness, honed if necessary by force of arms. Unlike German migrants to the Americas, these new settlers would retain their identity rather than assimilate to their host nations. In maintaining their ethnic integrity, the

[50] Dirk van Laak, *Über alles in der Welt: Deutscher Imperialismus im 19. Und 20. Jahrhundert* Munich: C.H. Beck, 2005), 66–7; Gerrit W. Gong, *The Standard of 'Civilization' in International Society* (Oxford: Clarendon Press, 1984), 6; David Simo, "Colonization and Modernization: The Legal Foundation of the Colonial Enterprise; A Case Study of German Colonization in Cameroon," in *Germany's Colonial Pasts*, 99 Canis, *Bismarcks Aussenpolitik*, 209–29; Gall, *Bismarck, White Revolutionary*, vol. II, 140–6.
[51] Canis, *Bismarcks Aussenpolitik*, 229.

German language and culture would prevail. Consistent with the Social Darwinian zeitgeist and bourgeois imperial imaginings of long standing, Peters maintained that expansion furthered the struggle among nations for global superiority. As had been true for the British Empire, the extension of German cultural and economic power worldwide would enable Germany to prosper and strengthen national pride. Yet Germany would not merely become one imperialist power among others, according to Peters. It would become globally dominant. Consistent with the combination of pride and dread that characterized the imaginings of German nationalists, Peters maintained that the failure to pursue imperialism would be disastrous, for it would result in the extinction of the Germans as a people.[52]

Although willing to assert Germany's interests overseas, Bismarck opted to negotiate competing European claims to Africa, which the Berlin West Africa Conference made clear. His deference to Hamburg commercial interests, which sought a modus vivendi with the British, subsequently translated into a growing impatience with Peters, whose reckless adventures encroached upon British interests. Most notable was Peters' foray into the Equatorial Province between 1888 and 1890 to rescue the German-born agent of the Egyptian khedive, Emin Pasha, whom the Mahdist uprising had displaced. Yet this was no mere rescue. Rather, Pasha became the instrument for Peters to establish the province as the core of a future German Central Africa (*Mittelafrika*), the wide territorial expanse of which would compare to the British Cape-to-Cairo axis. Inspired by the Prussian victories at Königgratz and Sedan, Peters' murderous attacks on indigenous populations, especially the Masai, unsettled the chancellor. Peters refused to subordinate his mission to government oversight and deliberately undermined an Anglo-German agreement against annexations in the rear of the other power's sphere of interest. By the mid-1890s, Peters' adventures would cease to attract support at home as his behavior aroused fears that he had alarmingly "gone native," having murdered his African concubine and her lover in a jealous rage. Claiming that he had married the woman according to "Muslim" and "African" customs, Peters created a furor in the Foreign Office and the Reichstag, especially the Center, which condemned his sham union as

---

[52] Perras, *Carl Peters*, 31–99; Hartmut Pogge von Strandmann, "Consequences of the Foundation of the German Empire: Colonial Expansion and the Process of Political-Economic Rationalization," in *Bismarck, Europe, and Africa: The Berlin Africa Conference 1884–1885 and the Onset of Partition*, eds. Stig Förster, Wolfgang J. Mommsen, and Ronald Robinson (Oxford: Oxford University Press, 1988), 105–20.

FIGURE 1.2. Carl Peters and his African servant Ramassan, 1894. In addition to demonstrating the continuing prestige of the military by wearing a uniform, Peters' bearing suggests the virility that was integral to German imperialist imaginings and crucial to national consolidation.
Source: Bundesarchiv Koblenz, Bild 183-S40874.

having undermined the sanctity of marriage. For the time being, however, Bismarck's refusal to support the Emin Pasha expedition cost him the support of the National Liberals and Free Conservatives, the key parties in his governing coalition.[53] The chancellor was thus left with few means of preserving his position once his inability to contain the "enemies of the Reich" was exposed.

[53] Perras, *Carl Peters*, 167.

The stunning results of the March 1890 Reichstag elections, which produced major increases for the Social Democrats, Center, and Progressives at the expense of the government's coalition irretrievably damaged Bismarck's position. The chancellor's defeat aggravated the already existing alienation between Bismarck and the new Kaiser Wilhelm II. Having ascended the throne in 1888 after the death of Wilhelm I and brief reign of Friedrich III, Wilhelm had little patience with the power that Bismarck had accumulated during his predecessor's reign. Envisioning himself as a modern ruler with a gift for exploiting the mass media, unlike his grandfather who rarely ventured beyond his Prussian domain and Bismarck for whom Prussian authority was central, the new kaiser neither shied from asserting his royal prerogatives nor from ruling as a national monarch. Where Bismarck had failed to achieve a genuine national integration, Wilhelm would reconcile all factions and parties, and enable Germany to realize its providential destiny as a world power.[54] Faced with massive strikes by workers in the Ruhr and the Rhineland, the kaiser opposed Bismarck's demand for the renewal of the Anti-Socialist Law, as well as Bismarck's introduction of an even tougher law packaged with a threat of a coup against the Reichstag if the legislation did not pass.[55] Unlike Bismarck's laissez-faire approach to management–labor conflicts and his outright repression of the Social Democrats, the kaiser opted for using the state not only as a mediator but also as the instrument of factory inspections and protective legislation. Such measures, he hoped, would weaken the attraction of workers to socialism, which as the elections made clear, neither the Anti-Socialist Law nor Bismarck's innovative social insurance program had dampened.[56] Yet Bismarck's departure testified to more than just divisions over social policy. It signified the rise of a more aggressive imperialism overseas and to the east of the Reich's borders. Given expression at the commanding heights of government, especially the kaiser who rejoined the projects of expansion and national integration, and mobilizing the industrial, commercial, and educated middle classes, imperialism also worked its way into the practices of the German military, informed the scientific underpinnings of human classification, and influenced the semiology of an emerging mass culture.

---

[54] See Clark, *Iron Kingdom*, 587–92.
[55] For the details surrounding Bismarck's fall, see John C. G. Röhl, *Wilhelm II: The Kaiser's Personal Monarchy, 1888–1900* (Cambridge: Cambridge University Press, 2001), 200–305.
[56] Kathleen Canning, *Languages of Labor and Gender: Female Factory Work in Germany, 1850–1914* (Ithaca and London: Cornell University Press, 1996), 134–7.

CHALLENGING THE "WORLD EMPIRES": GERMAN
IMPERIALISM IN THE WILHELMINE ERA

Within weeks of Bismarck's resignation, the Imperial government over-turned a key element of Bismarckian foreign policy by allowing the Reinsurance Treaty with Russia to lapse. Having committed Germany to aid Russia if it were attacked by Austria-Hungary, and Russia to back Germany if it were attacked by France, the treaty protected Germany against the threat of a two-front war. Although the incompatible interests of Russia and Austria-Hungary placed enormous stress on the Three Emperor's League even before Bismarck's resignation, organized interests from within the Imperial government, led by a powerful anti-Russian faction in the foreign ministry, Wilhelm's closest confident Philipp Eulenberg, the chief of the general staff, Count Alfred von Waldersee, and the kaiser's new chancellor, Leo von Caprivi, collectively hastened the treaty's demise.[57] Economic clashes and immigration conflicts between Germany and Russia undoubtedly contributed to the government's decision to dispose of the treaty. Protective tariffs to protect German agriculture, which continued to reflect the political influence of large estates, provoked retaliatory tariffs by Russia against German manufactured goods. The unceremonious return of Polish agricultural labor to Russia after the harvest, the result of a compromise to limit their presence to the growing season, only aggravated Russian resentment.[58]

But other calculations intervened as well. The prominent Baltic German historian of Russia, Theodor Schiemann, whom tsarist Russification had driven from his homeland, influenced the German general staff to intensify its war planning against the tsarist empire. Anxiety at Russia's growing financial and military power constituted a significant motivation, inasmuch as Waldersee especially was convinced that Jewish bankers, including Bismarck's own financial advisor, Gerson Bleichröder, had engineered significant increases in German capital flows to the Russia Empire.[59] Thus, Bismarck's strategy for ensuring that Germany, Austria-Hungary, and Russia would not come to blows over the Balkans, a volatile region which

[57] Lamar Cecil, *Wilhelm II: Prince and Emperor, 1859–1900* (Chapel Hill and London: University of North Carolina Press, 1989), 188–90. On the impact of Russian-Austro-Hungarian tensions, see Clark, *Iron Kingdom*, 552–3.
[58] Volker Berghahn, *Imperial Germany, 1871–1918: Economy, Society, Culture and Politics*, rev. ed. (New York and Oxford: Berghahn Books, 2005), 256–7.
[59] Troy Paddock, "Creating an Oriental *Feinbild*," *Central European History* 39, no. 2 (2006): 232–4: Röhl, Wilhelm II 210. On the significance of the cross border mobility of ethnic Germans from beyond the Reich's borders, see Dickinson, "German Empire," 150–4.

the post-Napoleonic Concert of Europe had not taken into account, went by the boards. Germany committed itself wholeheartedly to the Triple Alliance with the Austro-Hungarian Empire and Italy.[60] The consequence was not long in coming: anti-German voices in St. Petersburg encouraged Russia to transform its economic ties with France into a political and military alliance, which Bismarck had long striven to prevent.

To compensate for the deteriorating relations between Russia and Germany, Bismarck's successor and Wilhelm's new chancellor, the career military officer and chief of the admiralty Leo von Caprivi, worked to secure Anglo-German amity. Caprivi agreed to cede a portion of Zanzibar to Britain in return for the North Sea island of Heligoland as part of his larger, and ultimately futile, goal of cementing an Anglo-German alliance. Yet, in addition to the fury with which imperialist circles responded to the news of the agreement, frustrated by what they saw as Germany's stagnation as a colonial power, the underlying goal of the pact did little to counter balance the new emperor's undisguised determination to overtake the British Empire and to construct a large navy to sustain it.[61] Great Britain's desire to reposition itself in the face of increased global competition and German assertiveness, personified in Wilhelm's plebiscitary appeals to the public at large and the staging of popular ritual demonstrations of German naval prowess, contributed to Germany's subsequent diplomatic isolation.[62] It unsettled the continental balance of power that proved increasingly unable to absorb the vested interests of Europe's great powers and the blatantly expressed ambitions of their challengers.

Enthusiasm among the professional and commercial middle classes reinforced the emperor's predilection to enlarge the Imperial navy and to challenge Great Britain's rule of the high seas. In 1895, following the failure of the British adventurer Leander Starr Jameson to overthrow the Boer-led government of the Transvaal Republic and to expand British economic influence in Southern Africa, Wilhelm congratulated the Transvaal's president and expressed sympathy for the Boers, which inflamed British public opinion against Germany. If indicative of the kaiser's spectacularly incompetent diplomacy, in which this case would not

---

[60] John C. G. Röhl, *Wilhelm II: The Kaiser's Personal Monarchy, 1888–1900* (Cambridge: Cambridge University Press, 2001), 342.

[61] Canis, *Bismarcks Aussenpolitik*, 385–6.

[62] Jan Rüger, *The Great Naval Game: Britain and Germany in the Age of Empire* (Cambridge: Cambridge University Press, 2007), 198–250.

be the only episode, Wilhelm's support for the Boers proved popular at home, especially among officials, academics, clergymen, professionals, and entrepreneurs. Even Social Democratic workers who were known to oppose colonialism shared in the anti-English sentiment that the Boer War generated.[63] By the end of the decade, middle-class imperialists had formed the Navy League, the first of several important imperialist pressure groups, membership of which reached 300,000 with an even larger number of affiliates.[64]

Unlike the army, which was perceived as more Prussian than German, a navy in Wilhelm's view would fuse the tasks of national consolidation and the global extension of German influence known as "world policy" (*Weltpolitik*). By becoming a genuinely national institution linked to the broader goal of a maritime empire, a powerful navy would both strengthen the "national" parties and isolate or co-opt those parties most likely to resist it – the SPD, the left-liberal Progressives, and the Center. The government's unwillingness to support Carl Peters after the scandal of his "marriage" directly resulted from the fury that it created in the Center, the votes of which it needed to secure a future naval program.[65] More important, unlike the army, which retained its Prussian character, the navy would unify a fragmented society divided by competing ideas of the nation, a goal that the kaiser pursued through popular spectacles such as ship launches and fleet reviews that blended regional symbols and imagined histories into a coherent fiction of German unity.[66] A navy would solve the problem that had arisen during Germany's confrontation with Great Britain over the independence of the Transvaal, that is, the inability to back its sympathy with Britain's enemies with ships large and numerous enough to challenge the British. Finally, a navy would become a key instrument in Germany's response to rapidly changing international realities. With the expansion of the American economy, the rise of Japan, and the increasing tendency of the European great powers to ward off competition by sealing off their empires with high tariffs, Germany needed new instruments to compete in a transformed environment.[67]

[63] Richard J. Evans, *Proletarians and Politics: Socialism, Protest and the Working Class in German before the First World War* (New York: St. Martin's Press, 1990), 174–6.

[64] Eley, *Reshaping the German Right*, 70.

[65] Perras, *Carl Peters*, 230

[66] Rüger, *Great Naval Game*, 140–64; Canis, *Von Bismarck zur Weltpolitik: deutsche Aussenpolitik 1890 bis 1902* (Berlin: Akademie Verlag, 1999), 223–56.

[67] Christopher Clark, *Kaiser Wilhelm II: Profiles in Power* (Harlow: Longman, 2000), 130–8.

FIGURE 1.3. Visit of Kaiser Wilhelm II on board the *S.M.S. Hansa II*, ca. 1899. To the Kaiser, the navy conjoined the imperial projects of world policy and national cohesion.
Source: Bundesarchiv Koblenz, DVM 10 Bild-23-61-18.

   In 1897, the kaiser appointed Alfred Tirpitz as naval minister, who, as a devotee of the American naval strategist Alfred Thayer Mahan, believed that without a strong navy as leverage against its maritime rivals and as an instrument of colonial expansion, Germany could not become a global power. Similar to Carl Peters in his replaying the fear of annihilation lurking within the promise of greatness, Tirpitz connected empire with national survival. Germany's failure to compete with its imperialist rivals would return it to an agrarian country that would once again be divided and dominated by its neighbors.[68] In addition to checking the French and Russians, Tirpitz's "risk" theory intended a fleet large enough to threaten Britain close to its own shores, thus serving as an effective means of extracting colonial concessions. The navy's range was to be impressive. It would anchor Germany's new presence in the Far East, begun in the same year with the seizure of China's Jiaozhou Bay and the acquisition of a fifty-kilometer leasehold surrounding it on the southern coast of the Shandong Peninsula, ostensibly in retaliation for the murder of two German Catholic priests.

---

[68] Raffael Scheck, *Alfred von Tirpitz and German Right-Wing Politics, 1914–1930* (Atlantic Highlands, NJ: Humanities Press, 1998), 13–14.

Following a skillful propaganda campaign, Tirpitz shepherded a naval bill through the Reichstag with a budget large enough to build nineteen battleships and thirty-two cruisers, using the murder of the priests to win over the Center, which had been previously cool to a naval build-up. A second and even larger naval appropriations bill sailed through the Reichstag in the wake of rising anti-British sentiment accompanying the British victory in the Boer War.[69] Imperialism would continue to meet opposition, if not to the principle necessarily but at least to some of its consequences, especially from the Center and Social Democratic parties, and from some Progressives. Nonetheless, an alternative pattern was emerging: The opposition was never strong enough to undermine the widespread conviction, entrenched especially among influential sectors of the middle classes, that Germany deserved to be a global power.

Imperial Germany's quest for its "place in the sun," as the state secretary for foreign affairs Bernhard von Bülow termed it, brought important consequences because of the scale of its ambitions and the provocative manner in which those claims were advanced – provocations that were by no means limited to the kaiser's infelicitous handling of the art of diplomacy. Tirpitz's high-risk program of heavy battleships was not the only program that weakened the prospects for improving Anglo-German relations, or even the kaiser's loud support for the Boers. Because the German naval construction program prompted the British to accelerate their own naval enlargement, which included its Dreadnaughts, the government was forced into a seemingly endless naval race in which no amount of expenditure could ensure German superiority on the high seas. In addition, German commercial competition in Asia, the Middle East, Africa, and Latin America, with its self-conscious assertion that Germany was overtaking Britain economically, increasingly challenged Britain's confidence in its ability to maintain its global hegemony. Even infrastructural projects such as the Berlin-to-Baghdad railroad, ostensibly undertaken to promote "progress" as a member of an international consortium, alienated the British, who perceived a German threat to the Suez Canal and the Persian Gulf.[70] Germany's heavy-handed attempts in 1905 and 1911 to weaken French control of Morocco and extend its commercial interests in North Africa, unsettling in the process the Anglo-French Entente Cordiale, confirmed the British and French in their desire to resolve their colonial differences to meet a common threat. Taken together, the Imperial government's assertiveness destroyed the cornerstone of Bismarck's foreign policy, the diplomatic isolation of Prussia's

[69] Cecil, *Wilhelm II*, 316–7, 335.
[70] van Laak, *Über alles in der Welt*, 93–4.

adversary in the final war of unification; yet implicitly or otherwise, that was the point. Bismarck's seemingly modest strategic ambitions were no longer consonant with the perspective of Wilhelmine imperialists, for whom the alternative to world policy was weakness and decline.

German initiatives in Europe became equally contentious. In addition to encouraging British fears that Germany aspired to continental hegemony in the manner of Napoleon, they multiplied the points of tension with the Russian Empire. On top of the ongoing conflicts over protectionism, immigration, and financial policy, negative images of Russia in the German mass media as "Asiatic," "despotic," and menacing increased the nervousness of the tsarist government over German intervention in southeastern Europe, prompting Russia to deepen its economic and military ties to France. In 1904 and 1905 the kaiser did attempt to conclude a new alliance with Russia in order to neutralize the Franco-Russian alliance that the parties had concluded ten years earlier. Yet negotiations came to naught because Germany would not abandon its desire to achieve continental supremacy.[71] The German economic and commercial penetration in Europe was substantial, amounting to three-quarters of all exports by 1914.[72] It included joint ventures in France, Belgium, and Luxembourg, and burgeoning trade with Scandinavia, Romania, and especially the Lower Danube and Turkey. Following Bismarck's dismissal, German commercial, railroad, banking, and military overtures to the Ottoman Empire, which the Iron Chancellor had begun, resulted in an increased German presence. By the early twentieth century, German dealings with the Ottomans emphasized educational, economic, and cultural initiatives rather than occupation or annexation, for there were strategic advantages in appearing more consensual and less intrusive than Germany's western rivals. Many in the foreign office and prominent public intellectuals such as Paul Rohrbach sympathized with the Ottomans' efforts to reassert sovereignty, recalling Germany's own history as the pawn of foreigners. Yet however "benign," German market concessions and German military influence on the Ottomans further strained relations with Britain, France, and Russia.[73]

[71] Robert R. McLean, "Dreams of a German Empire: Wilhelm II and the Treaty of Björkö of 1905," in *The Kaiser: New Research on Wilhelm II's Role in Imperial Germany*, eds. Annika Mombauer and Wilhelm Deist (Cambridge: Cambridge University Press, 2003), 119–42; Paddock, "Creating an Oriental *Feinbild*," 214–43.

[72] Blackbourn, *History of Germany*, 253–4.

[73] On German activities in the Ottoman Empire, see Ulrich Trumpener, *Germany and the Ottoman Empire 1914–1918* (Princeton: Princeton University Press, 1968), 3–20; and most recently Malte Fuhrmann, *Der Traum vom deutschen Orient: Zwei deutsche Kolonien im Osmanischen Reich 1851–1918* (Frankfurt: Campus, 2006), 142–382;

Although Russia spent its borrowed French money on the purchase of German goods, German activity in a region that the tsars had long considered vital to Russian security became increasingly explosive, particularly when economic and military power converged. Thus, the mission in 1913 of General Otto Liman von Sanders, who was sent to Constantinople to rebuild and "Germanize" the Ottoman army as a potential ally in a war against Russia after its disastrous failures in the first and second Balkan wars, hardened Russia's determination to control the Dardanelles.[74] Finally "encircled" by an alliance composed of former adversaries once bitterly at odds with each other over competing colonial claims, Germany was left with but one reliable ally, the Austro-Hungarian Empire. Beset by deep interethnic conflicts at home, which Serbia's pan-Slavism exacerbated, Austria-Hungary was arguably the most trigger happy of the major European powers in the years leading up to World War I. Seeking to capitalize on the Turkish defeat by Italy in North Africa, Austria-Hungary precipitated an international crisis in 1908 by annexing the former Ottoman provinces of Bosnia and Herzegovina. Well before July, 1914, its general staff had already been contemplating a preventive war against the Serbs. The irony of Germany's predicament was inescapable: Having achieved unification by divorcing the Habsburgs, Germany's claim to world power had the effect of linking its fortunes to the very same dynasty.

In light of its economic significance, which vastly exceeded the value of Germany's overseas possessions, the spread of its industrial and commercial influence in Europe reinforced Germany's claim to continental preeminence, a desire that the kaiser himself explicitly enunciated early in his reign and exactly what Germany's rivals feared. Yet that wish was by no means confined to the commanding heights of the state. Wilhelm's penchant for bolstering his popular standing by exploiting the plebiscitary potential of the mass media further legitimated and intensified the bourgeois imperialism, which contributed to Bismarck's fall. Matching the impulse to world policy exemplified by the Colonial Association, the Navy League, the Colonial Society, and the Imperial League against Social Democracy, and antisemitic groups that saw colonies as an antidote to their failure to disenfranchise Jews at home, other pressure

and Fuhrmann again, "Germany's Adventures in the Orient: A History of Ambivalent Semi-Colonial Entanglements," in *Colonial (Dis)-Continuities: Race, Holocaust and Postwar Germany*, eds. Volker Langbehn and Mohammad Salama (New York: Columbia University Press, forthcoming).

[74] Alan Kramer, *Dynamic of Destruction: Culture and Mass Killing in the First World War* (Oxford: Oxford University Press, 2007), 102–3,

groups yearned for an expanded German continental dominion. The Pan German League and Eastern Marches League, the latter more commonly known by the acronym "*Hakatisten*," which combined the names of its founders, pulled no punches in criticizing the government if it seemed too timid or too willing to compromise in asserting German imperial interests.

Founded as the General German League in 1891 and headed initially by a close associate of Carl Peters, the Pan German League was reorganized in 1894 under the more effective leadership of Ernst Haase. Antagonism toward Caprivi's Heligoland-Zanzibar treaty prompted the League's founding. The Pan Germans vehemently criticized the government's alleged timidity in expanding Germany's overseas colonial holdings. Caprivi's willingness to allow estate owners to hire more Polish seasonal workers as long as those workers returned to their native land after the harvest became the raison d'être of the *Hakatisten*, founded during the same year as the reconstitution of the Pan Germans. Although mythologizing Bismarck as the antithesis of the Imperial government's post-Bismarckian weakness,[75] ironic in light of the circumstances surrounding the Iron Chancellor's removal, both pressure groups implicitly rejected Bismarck's claim that Germany was a "satiated" power. Instead, Germany was to emerge as a major player among world empires. Confidence in Germany's military and economic power motivated such claims. Yet the chronic insecurity embedded in German nationalism was at least as important. Obsessed by Germany's strategic vulnerability in comparison to other empires – Britain, the United States, and especially Russia – the Pan Germans and *Hakatisten* came to rethink the foundations of German foreign policy. As the ostensible patron of Slavs, the Russian Empire figured prominently because of the "flooding" of the German east by Polish immigration from Austrian Galicia and Russia, the dependence of large landed estates in eastern Prussia on Polish agricultural labor, and the higher Polish birthrate. According to the Pan Germans, who by the first decade of the twentieth century moved beyond an ethno-cultural definition of Germanness to a racial and biological one, immigration undermined the Prussian colonialization of the east. Together the Pan

---

[75] Richard E. Frankel, *Bismarck's Shadow: The Cult of Leadership and the Transformation of the German Right, 1898–1945* (Oxford and New York: Berg, 2005), 29–42. On the impact of Bismarck's fall on the media's personalization of politics and its increasingly negative portrayal of the kaiser, see Martin Kohlrausch, *Der Monarch im Skandal: Die Logik der Massenmedien und die Transformation der wilhelminishcen Monarchie* (Berlin: Akademie Verlag, 2005), 102–18.

Germans and *Hakatisten* sought to promote German settlements, ban the influx of cheap Polish labor outright, and expel Prussian Poles to the United States.[76]

As the antidote to the Polish "flood" and as the protectors of German communities outside the Reich's borders threatened by "Russification" or "Magyarization" (the nationalizing obsessions of neighboring states),[77] the Pan Germans stood at the forefront in pushing for the continental consolidation of ethnic Germans in one polity. In their view, the Second Empire, for all of Bismarck's skill in bringing it into existence, amounted only to the first stage in the completion of a genuine "national state." An expansion that merged political and ethnic boundaries was now required. The new Reich would include not only the existing German Empire, but also Polish and Baltic territory, the Habsburg lands, Romania, Switzerland, Luxembourg, the Flemish-speaking parts of Belgium, and Holland. By the eve of World War I, the Pan German leader Heinrich Class, who had been elected to his position in 1904, was calling for the expulsion of foreign Jews and second-class citizenship for the rest, as well as the ethnic cleansing of Germany's troubled eastern border regions, a nasty innovation that World War I and its aftermath would only intensify.[78] To address a common obsession as to the consequences of emigration, the League pushed for the support of German communities abroad, including preserving their citizenship, so that they would not lose their identity.[79]

The Pan Germans personified an imperialism that, following the inchoate imaginings of preunification nationalists, became increasingly two dimensional. In addition to promoting continental expansion, they also

---

[76] Conrad, *Globalisierung*, 134–7; Peter Walkenhorst, *Nation-Volk-Rasse: Radikaler Nationalismus im Deutschen Kaiserreich 1890–1914* (Göttingen: Vandenhoeck & Ruprecht, 2007), 80–165.

[77] Naranch, "Inventing the *Auslandsdeutsche*," 34.

[78] Daniel Frymann (pseudonym for Heinrich Class), *Wenn ich Kaiser wär: Politische Wahrheiten und Notwendigkeiten* (Leipzig: Dieterich, 1912), 75–6; Walkenhorst, *Nation-Volk-Rasse*, 252–80.

[79] In addition to Walkenhorst, see Roger Chickering, *We Men Who Feel Most German: A Cultural Study of the Pan German League 1886–1914* (Boston, London, Sydney: George Allen and Unwyn, 1984), 74–101; Woodruff D. Smith, *The Ideological Origins of Nazi Imperialism* (New York and Oxford: Oxford University Press, 1986), 83–112; Dennis Sweeney, "The Racial Economy of *Weltpolitik*: Imperialist Expansion, Domestic Reform, and War in Pan German Ideology, 1894–1918," www.sitemaker.umich.edu/german-modernities.files/sweeney.doc. Accessed 16, June 2010; Smith, *Continuities of German History*, 208–10; and Rainer Hering, *Konstruierte Nation: Der Alldeutsche Verband 1890 bis 1939* (Hamburg: Christiens Verlag, 2003), 110–219.

supported world policy, advocating coaling and cable stations, commercial and industrial concessions in Asia Minor, more subsidized steamship lines, and the German presence on the Jiaozhou Bay. Despite its impressive economic growth to date, Germany would not survive and prosper, according to the Pan Germans, unless it acquired an empire commensurate with its economic weight. Yet by articulating a theme that would emerge with greater force after World War I when a weakened France and multiple weak successor states in Eastern Europe made it more plausible, the Pan Germans, and especially Heinrich Class, gave priority to one dimension over the other.[80] They claimed that the extension of German living space in Europe was the precondition for the expansion of Germany's overseas empire. In addition to enhancing Germany's economic resources, which would be essential to contending with its imperialist rivals, the acquisition of living space would mean the expulsion of the Poles and the revitalization of German ethnicity through settlement. It would repeat the achievements that had laid the foundations for the emergence of Prussia and Austria as great powers in the first place, the medieval German settlements in Slavic lands and along the Baltic coast. In pondering the loss of millions of German settlers to the United States, who contributed to America's rise as a world power but sacrificed their language and culture in the process, Class posed a counterfactual question: "What would have happened if those millions had remained attached to their homeland and then [were] used in a wonderful, well-planned settlement of the ancient German soil in Eastern Europe? Without question the dominant position of Germandom (*Deutschtum*)would have been assured for all time."[81] Class' idea would prove extraordinarily durable.

Although its size was seemingly insignificant – its membership never exceeded more than 22,000– the Pan German League enjoyed an influence disproportionate to its numbers.[82] Its base of support in the politically active and well-connected middle classes, its ties to the media, its intersections with other nationalist organizations, including the 300,000-member Agrarian League, magnified its influence. Public officials and

[80] See Woodruff Smith, *Ideological Origins*, 110; and Walkenhorst, *Nation-Volk-Rasse*, 182–225.
[81] Heinrich Class, *Deutsche Geschichte in Einheit mit 24 Vollbildern und unter bunten Karte des deutschen Siedlungsgebiet in Mitteleuropa* (Leipzig: Dieterich'sche Verlagsbuchhandlung, 1914), 440. On Pan German expansionist plans, see also Geoffrey Stoakes, *Hitler and the Quest for World Dominion* (Leamington Spa and New York: Berg, 1986), 39–41.
[82] Berghahn, *Imperial Germany*, 215.

secondary-school teachers, who envisioned themselves as the bearers of German culture and the personification of the authority of the state, played an especially prominent role. Similarly, the 50,000-member Eastern Marches League, which was composed of Protestant pastors, school teachers, and government officials who resided in the Prussian east, belied its relatively small membership with a substantial influence within the Prussian government.[83] Although emerging in response to a setback in overseas imperialism and drawing much of its early leadership, including Carl Peters, from the Colonial Society, the principal contribution to German imperialism of the Pan Germans and *Hakatisten* was the articulation of a German-dominated east that reimagined an enlarged nation in starkly racial and biological terms, a polity purified of foreign elements. Not only would Germany hold sway economically, it would also institute population policies grounded in racial hierarchies constructed according to putatively immutable differences, the aim of which was no longer the Germanization of Poles but rather their physical removal.[84]

In common with antisemites who defined "Germanness" (*Deutschtum*) against its negation, the "Jew," radical nationalists soon found "the Jew" useful to explain what they perceived as a global competition among empires for survival.[85] Indeed, the emergence of a racially and biologically grounded antisemitism, coupled with the colonial attitudes and ruling strategies imposed on other ethnic minorities, polished the lens through which Germans viewed their subject peoples overseas.[86] Moreover, what had first emerged as a "cultural code" among the right for describing domestic social ills, urbanization, the rise of Social Democracy, and democratization, antisemitism discursively expanded to personify Germany's imperialist rivals. To the Pan Germans, continental expansion was the antidote to the insidious workings of "international Jewry" that prevented Germany from assuming its rightful place among the world powers. The Pan German demand for living space at the expense of Slavs to the east so that the German population would have room to grow and prosper would be the key to combating the Jews as well as the Poles. The ethnic cleansing of Slavs would give Germany the resources to counterbalance

[83] Hagen, *Germans, Poles and Jews*, 175; Chickering, '*We Men*,' 114–5.
[84] Sweeney, "Racial Economy."
[85] Russell A. Berman, *Enlightenment or Empire: Colonial Discourse in German Culture* (Lincoln and London: University of Nebraska Press), 133.
[86] Sebastian Conrad, "Eingeborenenpolitik in Kolonie und Metropole," in Conrad and Osterhammel, *Kaiserreich transnational*, 126–7; Smith, *Continuities of German History*, 167–210; Dickinson, "German Empire," 134–5.

British power and its accompaniment, the "global Jewish spirit," as the prelude to further overseas colonization. The notion of preventive war against Russia was not simply the brainchild of the general staff or even the governing elite. The Pan Germans promoted the idea in the decade before World War I, fearful of Slav population growth, the rapidity of Russian industrialization thanks to French loans, and the Russian penetration of the Balkans. The founding of the Army League in 1913 by the Pan German August Keim, which had a significant presence in garrison towns, represented the shift in emphasis to building German ground forces against the threat in the east.[87] Even if the German press, including conservative publications, did not advocate a preventive war, it increasingly cast the Russian Empire as alien – as "Asiatic" and thus having nothing in common with Europe.[88]

Like the image of Bismarck, which nationalists enshrined as a model of toughness and daring during the wars of unification, German military tactics mirrored the combination of aggression and dread of postunification imperial fantasies. Drawing from Prussia's experience with *francs tireurs*, French guerrilla snipers, who bedeviled supply and transportation lines after Prussia's supposedly "decisive" victory at Sedan, the army settled on what it considered an appropriate military doctrine: In the event of war, the enemy was to be totally destroyed. Its practices of rooting out French guerrillas so as to defeat the adversary before foreign mediation could rob Prussia of its victory, prompted radically punitive measures – shooting suspected guerrillas, mutilating prisoners, and razing towns in a "kill or be killed" scenario – that found no justification in international law.[89] Prussia's military victories, although more contingent and less impressive than they appeared to contemporary observers,[90] inspired Carl Peters' murderous and racially motivated campaigns against Masai villages in equatorial Africa in the 1880s. To him, colonization necessitated the construction of the "natural" hierarchy of German colonizers over black Africans, whose resistance would be overcome by military force,

---

[87] Weiss, *Ideology of Death*, 120; Marilyn Shevin Coetzee, *The German Army League: Popular Nationalism in Wilhelmine Germany* (New York and Oxford: Oxford University Press, 1990), 3–43.

[88] Paddock, "Creating and Oriental *Feinbild*," 214–43.

[89] Isabel V. Hull, *Absolute Destruction: Military Culture and the Practices of War in Imperial Germany* (Ithaca and London: Cornell University Press, 2005), 110–30.

[90] See Geoffrey Wawro, *The Franco-Prussian War: The German Conquest of France, 1870–1871* (Cambridge: Cambridge University Press, 2003), who suggests that Prussia's victory owed more to the poor performance of the French than to its own military superiority.

already sanctified by having established Germany's continental power. Antisemites, who found Peters a frequent visitor to their circles, championed violence against Africans, who in addition to possessing similar characteristics as Jews, provided a compensatory target for their failure of their campaign at home to disenfranchise and expel Jews.[91]

The military's doctrine of annihilating the enemy carried over to the management of Germany's colonies overseas during the Wilhelmine era, beginning in German East Africa where warfare between the German Protection Force and the Hehe people was nearly constant between 1890 and 1898. Evolving from selective punishment to outright annihilation through the use of hunger as a weapon, some 150,000 Hehe were killed.[92] The case of German Southwest Africa became even more notorious. In 1894, the combination of missionary work, the potential for extracting raw materials, climatic conditions suitable for farming, and competition for land from Britons and Afrikaners had convinced the Imperial government to extend direct control over the colony to build German settlements at the expense of the indigenous Herero and Nama peoples. Settlers, according to the plan of the Imperial German Colonial Office, were to become the outpost of "Germanness," organizing rural communities grounded in the values of hard work, thrift, the patriarchal family, and ethnic unity. In turn, the settler homesteads would become the alternative to a metropole divided by social conflict. The idealization of independent German "farmers," who combined bourgeois and aristocratic "virtues," envisioned the paternalistic rule of colonists over "natives." In turn, colonial German communities would serve as the antidote to Social Democratic democratization at home. Inasmuch as those values expressed a utopian vision of a new type of social order, a racially privileged society, they depended on the brutal expropriation of native lands made easier by a cattle plague epidemic that decimated Herero herds, the destruction of the natives' cattle-based economy and tribal culture, and the erection of a system of apartheid aimed at creating a pool of cheap, docile African labor.[93]

---

[91] Davis, "Colonialism," 111–28.

[92] Thomas Morlang, "'Die Wahehe haben ihre Vernichtung gewollt.' Der Krieg der 'Kaiserlichen Schutztruppe' gegen die Hehe in Deutsch-Ostafrika (1890–1898)," in *Kolonialkriege: Militärische Gewalt im Zeichen des Imperialismus*, eds. Thoralf Klein und Frank Schumacher (Hamburg: Hamburger Edition, 2006), 80–108.

[93] For German Southwest Africa, see the still indispensible works of Helmut Bley, *Namibia under German Rule* (Hamburg: LIT Verlag, 1996), first published in 1968 and Horst Dreschler, *Südwest Afrika unter deutscher Kolonialherrschaft* (Stuttgart: Franz Steiner

When, in 1904, the Herero fought back by attacking German farmers who had encroached on their land and killing mostly male settlers,
the kaiser immediately assigned the task of suppressing the revolt to the
general staff. The military leadership, having engineered the sacking of
the colonial governor, Theodor Leutwein, for his alleged laxity toward
the natives, appointed the virulently racist General Lothar von Trotta, a
veteran of the Franco-Prussian War whose track record of ruthlessness
included the brutal crushing of a revolt in East Africa in 1896 and his
participation in quelling the Boxer Rebellion in China in 1900. Under
orders from Trotta, who scorned Leutwein's preference for mobilizing
Africans as labor, the German Protection Forces conducted a vicious
three-year campaign against the Herero and Nama peoples. German military tactics included quarantining their captives in the Omaheke Desert,
poisoning their water holes and wells, deporting them to other German
colonies, and imprisoning survivors in concentration camps with little to
no provisioning. The concentration camp at Shark Island off the coastal
city of Lüderitz became, for all practical purposes, a death camp, the
victims of which succumbed to starvation and disease. In Trotta's view,
the "natives" had to give way much as the Indians had to disappear in
favor of Euro-Americans, and to a large degree he succeeded. Neither
women nor children were spared. At minimum, an estimated 60 percent
of the Herero and Nama perished.[94] For those who survived, their way
of life was destroyed. With few exceptions, "natives" were not permitted
to own land, breed cattle, or raise horses. Confined to designated locations with no more than ten families each, they became forced laborers
for the colonizers. Although less publicized than the Herero War because
it was conducted locally rather than initiated from Berlin and because
it used native mercenaries rather than Germans, the suppression of the
millenarian-inspired and trans-tribal Maji Maji revolt in southern and
western Tanganyika, the result of German attempts to force African

Verlag, 1996), first published in 1966; and more recently Jürgen Zimmerer, *Deutsche
Herrschaft über Afrikaner: Staatlicher Machtanspruch und Wirklichkeit im kolonialen
Namibia* (Münster: LIT Verlag, 2004); and Daniel Joseph Walther, *Creating Germans
Abroad: Cultural Politics and National Identity in Namibia* (Athens, OH: Ohio University
Press, 2002). Others such as Birthe Kundrus, *Moderne Imperialisten: Das Kaiserreich im
Spiegel seiner Kolonien* (Vienna: Böhlau Verlag. 2003); George Steinmetz, *The Devil's
Handwriting: Precoloniality and the German Colonial State in Qingdao, Samoa, and
Southwest Africa* (Chicago and London: University of Chicago Press, 2007), esp. 75–239,
focus on the colonial imaginaries of the occupiers, as well as the social dynamics among
them.
[94] Hull, *Absolute Destruction*, 30.

peasants to work on German cotton plantations and cede their hunting rights, cost even more African lives. Using the despoliation of crops and seizure of livestock to induce famine in the rebellion's geographical center, 300,000 died, most by starvation.[95]

Because Nazi crimes loom large in the history of Germany, finding similarities between Imperial colonial warfare and Nazi ethnic cleansing and genocide later seems irresistible. Although the slaughter of the Herero and Nama was less centralized and bureaucratized than the Nazi regime's "final solution," the obsession with "military security" and hatred of the enemy ensured a genocidal outcome. The loathing of the Herero in particular, which the Germans shared with other Europeans and which crowded out the possibilities for a less-violent confrontation,[96] seemingly paralleled the Nazi regime's hatred of the Jews, which increased the probability of deadly results. In a manner that revealed the free, if inchoate and superficial, associations that connected disliked peoples at home and abroad, Germans on the ground in Namibia often equated the putative cunning and craftiness of the Herero to that of "furiously bartering Jews."[97] Thereafter, the systematic exploitation of native labor and the construction of a system of apartheid, the gravitation of prominent veterans of African campaigns to the Nazi Party after World War I, and the persistent, nagging fears of racial mixing might have constituted a bed of experiences that would shape the Third Reich. Moreover, warfare in Africa captured the popular imagination at home in insidious ways, deepening the legitimacy of imperialism, and along with it notions of German cultural and racial supremacy, which the National Socialists also tapped. The military's murderousness, so it has been argued, breached a taboo against genocide that would come back to haunt.[98]

---

[95] On the rebellion and its consequences for German rule, see Thaddeus Sunseri, "The *Baumwolle Frage*: Cotton Colonialism in German East Africa," *Central European History* 34, no. 1 (2001): 31–51; John Iliffe, *Tanganyika under German Rule, 1905–1912* (Cambridge: Cambridge University Press, 1979), 82–165; and Susanne Kuss, "Kriegsführung ohne hemmende Kulturschranke: Die deutschen Kolonialkriege in Südwestafrika (1904–1907) und Ostafrika (1905–1908)," in Klein and Schumacher, *Kolonialkriege*: 209–47.

[96] See Steinmetz, *Devil's Handwriting*, 124–33.

[97] Ibid., 183.

[98] See especially Jürgen Zimmerer, "Colonialism and the Holocaust: Towards an Archeology of Genocide," in *Genocide and Settler Society: Frontier Violence and Stolen Indigenous Children in Australian History*, ed. Dirk A. Moses (New York and Oxford: Berghahn Books, 2004), 49–76; "Holocaust und Kolonialismus: Beitrag zu einer Archäologie des genozidalen Gedankens." *Zeitschrift für Geschichtswissenschaft* 51, no. 12 (2003): 1098–1119; and "Die Geburt des 'Ostlandes' aus dem Geiste dem

Yet Imperial Germany was not Nazi Germany. Despite the horror of the German wars in Africa, the Imperial German suppression of colonial revolts did not differ significantly from the violent campaigns of other colonizing powers during the nineteenth century, which aimed either to destroy the economic independence of indigenous peoples or, if necessary, remove them altogether in order to ensure the competitiveness of metropoles in a modern global economy.[99] Indeed, the military practices that the Union Army deployed during the American Civil War, which derived from its leadership's experiences in fighting Indian wars, informed an ironic critique of the Prussian army's performance during the Franco-Prussian War. Invited to meet the Prussian General Staff, including Helmut von Moltke, the American General Philip Henry Sheridan, an observer of the Franco-Prussian conflict, expressed amazement at what he perceived was the Prussian army's traditionalism. Drawing on his own colonizing past, which he and his compatriot William Tecumsah Sherman subsequently visited on the Confederacy, Sheridan recommended that the Prussians engage in "total" war, and make French civilians suffer until their government capitulated.[100] The German military's conduct in Africa, which was obviously more radical than what Sheridan observed over two decades earlier, adhered to a common pattern.

In addition, the small number of German soldiers involved in Namibia paled in comparison to the millions mobilized on the eastern front during World War II. The competition for space and resources among industrialized nations, to which Germany contributed, embraced a "civilizing

---

Kolonialismus. Die nationalsozialistische Eroberungs-und Beherrschungspolitik in (post-)kolonialer Perspektive," *Sozial.Geschichte: Zeitschrift für historische Analyse des 20. und 21. Jahrhunderts* 19, no. 1 (2004): 10–43. See Benjamin Madley as well, "From Africa to Auschwitz: How German South West Africa Incubated Ideas and Methods Adopted and Developed by the Nazis in Eastern Europe," *European History Quarterly* 35, no. 3 (2005): 429–64.

[99] The Klein and Schumacher volume cited above, which includes German colonial wars with others during the era of high imperialism, is suggestive in this regard. See also Robert Gerwarth and Stephan Malinowski, "Der Holocaust als "kolonialer Genozid?" Europäische Kolonialgewalt und nationalsozialistischer Vernichtungskrieg," *Geschichte und Gesellschaft* 33 (2007), 444–50; Steinmetz, *Devil's Handwriting*, 69–70; and Dominick J. Schaller, "From Conquest to Genocide: Colonial Rule in German Southwest Africa," in *Empire, Colony, Genocide: Conquest, Occupation, and Subaltern Resistance in World History*, ed. A. Dirk Moses (New York and Oxford: Berghahn, 2008), 311.

[100] Michael Howard, *The Franco-Prussian War* (London and New York: Routledge, 2001), 380; Wolfgang Schivelbusch, *The Culture of Defeat: On National Trauma, Mourning, and Recovery*, trans. Jefferson Chase (New York: Metropolitan Books, Henry Holt and Co., 2001), 38–9.

mission" along with exploitation, one that claimed to bring "progress" to the colonized through educational uplift, advanced medical care, and infrastructural development.[101] And while the need to mobilize indigenous labor was common to the colonial administrations of both Southwest Africa and the Nazi east, ethnic cleansing assumed priority in areas that the Nazi regime designated for settlement until the strains of global war made the exploitation of labor imperative for all except the Jews. Finally, Imperial Germany's fractious party politics and social divisions left room for opposition to colonial policy and for the well-mobilized reaction to it, which saw imperialism as both the fulfillment of Germany's promise and as the means of subduing "enemies of the Reich." By contrast, the centralized and infinitely more repressive dictatorship of the Third Reich legitimated radical nationalism while permitting no such space for those most inclined to oppose it. The Nazi regime was the product of a broad consensus forged by military defeat, Germany's forced decolonization, and economic crisis after World War I that yearned for ethnic solidarity and the destruction of "enemies," who on political or racial grounds did not belong.

During the Wilhelmine period certainly, the political appeal of imperialism to the "state-supporting" parties presented formidable challenges to its opponents. Unlike Bismarck whose exploitation of imperialism to forge reliable coalitions raised expectations that exceeded the Iron Chancellor's ability to satisfy them, the more aggressive Wilhelmine imperialism at first paid dividends. The Imperial government's determination to build a larger navy derived partly from the need to identify national issues that would consolidate the Empire against its putatively less-trustworthy citizens, Social Democrats, Catholics, and minorities. Even many left-liberal Progressives abandoned their one-time anti-imperialism. In 1893 in fact, the Progressives divided into two parties, one that continued to oppose imperialism, whereas the other championed world policy as crucial to elevating Germany's global standing and building ethnic unity at home.[102] As a consequence, the government was able to push the first navy bill through the Reichstag in 1898 over the opposition of the Center and the SPD, tarring and feathering both as traitors to the Reich.

---

[101] Dirk van Laak, *Imperiale Infrastruktur: Deutsche Planungen für eine Erschliessung Afrikas 1880 bis 1960* (Paderborn: Ferdinand Schöningh, 2004), 142–6.

[102] Mark Hewitson, *Germany and the Causes of the First World War* (Oxford and New York: Berg, 2004), 150–1; Woodruff D. Smith, *The German Colonial Empire* (Chapel Hill: University of North Carolina Press, 1978), 146–7; Eric Kurlander, *the Price of Exclusion: Ethnicity, National Identity, and the Decline of German Liberalism, 1898–1933* (New York and Oxford: Berg, 2006), 38–46.

The blatant exploitation of imperialism mounted when in 1900 the kaiser appointed as chancellor the ardent world policy advocate, Bernhard Bülow, and even more so after the Social Democrats' impressive performance in the 1903 national and regional elections. For Bülow, world policy was crucial to forging unity at home, binding the kaiser to the nation, and undermining the parties that in his view promoted division.[103] Indeed the value of imperialism as a weapon against "enemies of the Reich," especially during and after the war in Southwest Africa, began to prove itself. Forced to call new parliamentary elections in 1907 in light of Center and Social Democratic opposition to the government's appropriations bill to cover the suppression of the African uprisings and compensate settlers for their losses,[104] Bülow unleashed a frontal assault against both parties, accusing them of treason for standing in the way of Germany's imperial mission. The result was the "Bülow Bloc," composed of the two conservative parties, the National Liberals, and left liberals sympathetic to imperialism. Bülow conceded the need to create an independent and more professional Colonial Office under Bernhard Dernberg, which emphasized infrastructure modernization and the comparatively gentler treatment of indigenous peoples.[105] Regardless, the new majority inflicted a major defeat on the opposition, especially the Social Democrats, who endured calumny similar to that voiced ten years earlier when the navy bill was passed. Because the election reawakened the anti-Catholic and anti-clerical invective of the Battle for Culture, the Center reined in its criticism of the German colonial administration and moderated its position toward colonial policy in order to burnish its credentials as a state-supporting party. The SPD's losses strengthened the hand of its minority of colonial advocates, who believed imperialism protected workers' jobs and ensured Germany's competitiveness against its rivals, and contributed to the party's decision to vote for war credits in 1914.[106]

---

[103] On Bülow's ideas of national integration, see Katherine Anne Lerman, *The Chancellor as Courtier: Bernhard von Bülow and the Governance of Germany, 1900–1909* (Cambridge: Cambridge University Press, 1990), 20–9; and Wehler, *Deutsche Gesellschaftsgeschichte*, vol. 3, 1139–41.

[104] John S. Lowry, "African Resistance and Center Party Recalcitrance in the Reichstag Colonial Debates of 1905/06," *Central European History* 39, no. 2 (2006): 244–69.

[105] Van Laak, *Über alles in der Welt*, 85.

[106] On the 1907 election, see Ulrich van der Heyden, "Die 'Hottentottenwahl' von 1907," in *Völkermord in Deutsch-Südwestafrica: Der Kolonialkrieg (1904–1908) in Namibia und seine Folgen*," eds, Jürgen Zimmerer and Joachim Zeller (Berlin: Ch. Links Verlag, 2003), 97–102, and Sperber, *Kaiser's Voters*, 240–54. On the Catholics and Socialism regarding imperialism, see Hewitson, *Germany and the Causes of the First World War*, 151–4.

The success of the Bülow Bloc owed much to the acceptability of imperialism to sizeable segments of the German population. To be sure, the lure of colonial possessions likely did not command the degree of attention that it did for the British and French. An important component of the academic elite revealed a deep appreciation of non-European histories and cultures that demonstrated the presence of alternative perspectives.[107] Nevertheless, imperialism hardly left the German public unaffected. Because nationalist myths were integrated into the promotion of literacy even before unification, tales of the medieval German colonization during the Middle Ages legitimated imperialism.[108] Broad swaths of Germany's middle class and even many workers accepted the justifications for the pursuit of empire. The subtle permeation of colonial knowledge generally and Social Darwinism specifically anchored the legitimacy of imperialism in ways that expressed the constancy of bourgeois visions of Germany's expanded global power beneath the turmoil of political debate. Racism and territorial expansion became normative to a degree that neither the paltry economic value of Germany's overseas colonies nor Germany's increasing diplomatic isolation, no matter how worrisome to a literate public, could disconfirm them. From the lofty perch of the academy, to popular fiction, to even the advertising that enticed German consumers, the ideas and symbols of imperialism were distributed and received. In addition to underwriting Germany's difficult relationships with other European powers, it also increased the pressure for a more restricted and exclusionary basis for citizenship.

Anthropologists, accustomed to popularizing their findings drawn from body parts, casts of bodies, and skulls from Germany's colonies, especially after the war in Southwest Africa, encouraged Germans to see themselves as racially distinct from Jews and other races. These complemented ethnographic studies of German school children, begun in the 1870s, which claimed to identify the different physical characteristics of Germans and Jews.[109] Having theorized colonized peoples as "natural," divorced from history, and as bodily objects of study deprived of subjecthood,

---

[107] See David Blackbourn, "Das Kaiserreich transnational. Eine Skizze," in Conrad and Osterhammel, *Kaiserreich transnational*, 321–2; and Suzanne L. Marchand's brilliant analysis of orientalist scholars, *German Orientalism in the Age of Empire: Religion, Race, and Scholarship* (Cambridge: Cambridge University Press, 2009), esp. 333–86.

[108] Knox, *To the Threshold of Power*, 54–5.

[109] Andrew Zimmerman, "Ethnologie im Kaiserreich: Natur, Kultur und 'Rasse' in Deutschland und seinen Kolonien," in Conrad and Osterhammel, *Kaiserreich transnational*, 204–12.

anthropologists and ethnographers by the 1890s had disseminated racial hierarchies that denied humanity to those defined as racially distinct. One of the principal goals of imperialism, the establishment of settler colonies, which would both preserve and project "Germanness," encouraged a closer affiliation between anthropology and eugenics, in which the reproduction of the community became essential to preserving ethnic purity, a new social order that increasingly assumed the absolute dissimilarity between Germans and racial "others."[110]

Far from being the ideology of antisemitic and racist intellectuals, Social Darwinism influenced Germany's political elite to such a degree that it was willing to accept war not only as as the consequence of the struggle among world empires, but also the means of overcoming the "decadence" of urbanism, materialism, socialism, and racial mixing. If Social Darwinism was common throughout Europe, it assumed a special intensity in Germany because it so clearly expressed the dilemma of German nationalism, the conflict between hubris and pessimism, the pride in German potential coupled with the fear that the struggle could be lost. Moreover, Germany's technological, scientific, and medical advances, which together contributed to Europe's most advanced economy, provided a distinctively modern foundation for racism by medicalizing all manner of social problems: alcoholism, crime, delinquency, chronic unemployment, and mental illness. Beginning in the first decade of the twentieth century, German academic scientists, the medical establishment, and welfare bureaucrats, fearful of the structural dislocations of industrialization, the teeming urban working-class slums and the transnational migration of foreign labor, talked openly of instituting racial "purification," or "racial hygiene," by "positive" and "negative" means to prevent the transmission of defective genes, including euthanizing the "unfit." Although the eugenics movement was not powerful enough to win the adoption of legislation to implement its goals, the effort to sustain racial hierarchies in Germany's colonial empire deepened the anxiety over the biological fitness of the population enough to assign "protective"

---

[110] Zimmerman, *Anthropology and Antihumanism in Imperial Germany* (Chicago and London: University of Chicago Press, 2001), 241–2; Pascal Grosse, "Turning Native? Anthropology, German Colonialism, and the Paradoxes of the 'Acclimatization Question.' 1885–1914," in eds. H. Glenn Penny and Matti Bunzl, *Worldly Provincialism: German Anthropology in the Age of Empire* (Ann Arbor: University of Michigan Press, 2003), 179–97; Pascal Grosse, *Kolonialismus, Eugenik und bürgerliche Gesellschaft in Deutschland, 1850–1914* (Frankfurt am Main, 2000), 18–192; and Fitzpatrick, *Liberal Imperialism*, 160–76.

measures to working-class women to ensure their maternal health. Yet imperialists also worried about the exposure to deadly diseases closer to home, especially from eastern Europe, heightening the desire to promote "German" hygiene to ward off the ill effects of contact with racially dangerous peoples.[111] The Nazi regime would go much further in positing the necessity of racial purification *before* the regime could embark on war. Nevertheless, the growing obsession with biological regeneration and the acquisition of living space as crucial to it put down roots under the Second Empire.

Social Darwinian ideas were not confined to the natural or social sciences. In addition to being disseminated in the press, popular literature became yet another means for legitimating imperialism and its underlying notions of race war. Popular fiction in the Wilhelmine era described Poles as racially different from the Germans. The so-called Eastern Marches novels (*Ostmarkromanen*) depicted seductive and suspiciously dark-skinned Polish women, whose sexual conquests inevitably polonized (i.e., defiled) blond, strong, and young, but naïve, German heroes. The settings for such novels, the uncivilized "wild east" where filth, degeneracy, and an untamed nature prevailed entrapped their protagonists in a swamp of decay.[112] Popular fiction after the Herero War explicitly justified the army's concentration camps and extermination programs in Social Darwinian terms. Allegedly unable to build permanent settlements, cultivate the land, or establish roots, the natives deserved to yield to the colonizers. Similar to the Jew who became the unyielding opposite of the German, Africans became the "other." In Gustav Frenssen's popular novel, *Peter Moor's Journey to Southwest Africa*, the elimination of the black threat served as the background to the hero's recognition that his personal fulfillment lay in his identification with the German ethnic community (*Volksgemeinschaft*). The hero's visits to German settlements with their immaculate and well-kept homesteads and model German housewives contrasted with the filth, nudity, and squalor of Africans.[113] Monuments

[111] Paul Julian Weindling, *Epidemics and Genocide in Eastern Europe 1890–1945* (Oxford: Oxford University Press, 2000), 3–42.. On the continuities between eugenics, racial science, and hereditary science in Imperial Germany and the Third Reich, see Eric Ehrenreich, *The Nazi Ancestral Proof: Geneology, Racial Science and the Final Solution* (Bloomington: Indiana University Press, 2007), 14–32.

[112] Ther, "Deutsche Geschichte als imperial Geschichte," in Conrad and Osterhammel, *Kaiserreich transnational*, 140; Kristin Kopp, "Constructing Racial Difference in Colonial Poland," in Ames et al., *Germany's Colonial Pasts*, 76–96.

[113] Nancy R. Reagin, *Sweeping the German Nation: Domesticity and National Identity in Germany, 1870–1945* (Cambridge: Cambridge University Press, 2007), 67–8.

to fallen German troops both in the colonies and the metropole embodied similar assumptions regarding the necessary sacrifices of German soldiers to advance the triumph of civilization over blackness.[114]

Moreover, the rise of a mass culture, fueled by the production of consumer goods and the increasing sophistication of advertising, contributed to normalizing colonial knowledge and encouraging the acceptance of imperialism. In addition to being demonstrations of power, ship launches and naval reviews in the North Sea became public spectacles and tourist destinations, even if attendees at times interpreted such rituals differently than intended by Tirpitz's Naval Office.[115] Beginning in the 1880s, popular spectacles (*Völkerschauen*), which displayed exotic peoples who performed "authentic" rituals and manufactured "native" crafts for sale, became an integral part of popular and middle-class leisure visits to zoos and industrial exhibitions. Building on older models of wonder and freak shows, these popular displays composed a virtual and sensationalized tourism that encouraged the imagination of "natives" as radically different. The advertising of consumer goods, partially adapted from the images of black minstrel shows from the American South, composed increasingly stereotypical racialized images of primitive Africans, complete with bones in noses, grass skirts, and thick lips, in turn subordinated to their white colonial overseers.

The widespread sympathy for the Boers in their conflict with the British – "Teutonic cousins," as Heinrich von Treitschke described them – became a mass market affair cultivated by the illustrated press. Yet because it directly involved the "defense" of German settlers against "savages," the Southwest Africa war especially brought the proliferation of commercial advertising that depicted African inferiority, along with its implicit justification for the violent suppression and exploitation of "native" labor. Because commercialized mass culture transcended party politics, and even the divisions of class, region, and religion to impose a new national identity, that of "consumer," its commodity racism might well have popularized imperialism even more effectively than the middle-class pressure groups, including the Colonial Society whose peddling of colonial wares failed to adapt to visual exoticism and sensationalism. The

---

[114] Medardus Brehl, "'Das Drama spielte sich auf der dunklen Bühne des Sandfields ab': Die Vernichtung der Herero und Nama in der deutschen (Populär-)Literatur," and Joachim Zeller, "Symbolischer Politik: Anmerkungen zur kolonialdeutschen Erinnerungskultur," in Zimmerer and Heller, *Völkermord in Deutsch-Südwest Afrika*, 86–96 and 192–208, respectively.

[115] Rüger, *Great Naval Game*, 93–139.

significant impact of commercialized images belied the relatively meager economic benefit of Germany's colonies.[116] By visually distinguishing
Germans from the "lower races" and masking the colonizers' violence
with suggestions of Germany's benevolent "civilizing" mission, mass
advertising did its part to fuse desires for empire and the construction of
German national identity. The spread of mass culture reinforced the trend
among ethnographers and anthropologists to abandon an earlier, more
cosmopolitan and Humboldtian understanding of a common humanity
and to embrace instead visions of "otherness" that, in addition to rendering racial hierarchies as biologically justifiable, postulated racial difference as less recognizably human.[117]

Nevertheless, despite its spreading acceptability, imperialism remained
a source of division. Leaving aside the Social Democrats, whose majority continued to oppose it, imperialism created contention among the
"state-supporting" parties. Although backing for world policy could
be found in the Conservative Party, the Prussian agrarians and Junkers
especially, fought tooth and nail against naval appropriations because of
their potentially negative implications for their privileges. The mounting
deficits associated with the Tirpitz plan increased the urgency of finance
reform that would have allowed the Reich, instead of just the states, to
tax directly. The proposed reform package presented to the Reichstag
in 1909 jeopardized the low tax assessments of Prussian agrarians, and
the Conservative Party's counterattack brought Bülow's resignation. In
addition, imperialism divided radical nationalists from the government.
Pressure groups operating outside of parliament attacked the Imperial
government unceasingly for its insufficient muscularity and leadership,
be it against Socialists, Catholics, Jews, and Poles, or especially against
Germany's foreign rivals.[118] Thus, in 1905, Bülow raised the hopes of
imperialists when he persuaded the kaiser to make a dramatic appearance
in Tangiers to disrupt one of the outcomes of the Entente Cordiale between
Britain and France, a French protectorate over Morocco. Yet a public furor
followed when at the Algeciras conference, convened in 1906 to defuse
the danger of war between Germany and France, Germany's diplomatic
isolation produced little to show for Wilhelm's grandstanding. In 1911

---

[116] David M. Ciarlo, "Consuming Race, Envisioning Empire: Colonialism and German
Mass Culture, 1887–1914" (Diss.: University of Wisconsin-Madison, 2003), 186–223.
[117] H. Glenn Penny, *Objects of Culture: Ethnology and Ethnographic Museums in Imperial Germany* (Chapel Hill and London: University of North Carolina Press, 2001),
131–219.
[118] See especially Hewitson, *Germany and the Causes of World War One*, 61–84.

the Foreign Secretary Alfred von Kiderlin-Wächter, with the backing of Bülow's successor as chancellor Theobald von Bethmann-Hollweg, tried a second time to fracture the Anglo-French Entente by sending German gunboats to the Moroccan port of Agadir. Engaging the Pan Germans as agitators, the Imperial government aimed to muscle the French into concessions. Again forced to back down once the risk of war presented itself, the government discredited itself with the very groups whom it had counted upon for support.

The kaiser's own penchant for discrediting himself added to the contentious relationship between radical nationalists and the Imperial government. In the wake of the failure at Algeciras, one of Wilhelm's closest advisors, Philipp Eulenberg, who was rumored to have been lukewarm toward the expansion of the navy, found himself battered by charges of homosexuality that sufficed to force his resignation.[119] In 1908, the kaiser's interviews with the American journalist William Bayard Hale and later with Sir Edward Stuart Wortley in the British paper, the *Daily Telegraph*, in which Wilhelm vacillated between jingoistic attacks on the British and professions of friendship to win over the British public, unleashed a storm of criticism across the political spectrum. The uproar forced Bülow to withdraw his support from the kaiser despite having vetted the articles before they went to press. Having infuriated the Conservative and National Liberal press, which condemned Wilhelm's inept attempts to assuage the British, the kaiser's most offensive remarks had the additional consequence of deepening Germany's international isolation.[120] And having assiduously courted the media from the beginning of his reign, Wilhelm inadvertently called his fitness as emperor into question as the nationalist and imperialist press became emboldened to bite the hand that stroked it.[121] The kaiser's attempted fusion of world policy and national integration blew up in his face.

The impact of imperialism came to a head between 1904 and 1914 as colonial wars overseas and conflicts with minorities at home threatened to alter the meaning and application of German citizenship. Overseas, the lordship of German settlers and soldiers over Africans and Pacific islanders was to be secured through apartheid, exercised especially through

---

[119] Isabel V. Hull, *The Entourage of Kaiser Wilhelm II 1888–1918* (Cambridge: Cambridge University Press, 1982), 109–45.

[120] Peter Winzen, *Das Kaiserreich am Abgrund: Die Daily-Telegraph Affäre und das Hale-Interview von 1908: Darstellung und Dokumentation* (Stuttgart: Franz Steiner Verlag, 2002), 19–91.

[121] Kohlrausch, *Monarch im Skandal*, 229–63.

bans on mixed marriages in German Southwest Africa in 1905, German East Africa in 1906, and German Samoa in 1912. Although discomfort regarding intermarriage between German settlers and African women had grown more pronounced over the previous decade, the Herero, Nama, and Maji Maji wars, defined as "race wars" by Germany, undermined the once-common assumption among colonists that relationships between German men and native women did not compromise racial hierarchy. The outlawing of mixed marriages deprived the mixed-race children of their rights to inheritance, as well as the right to German citizenship. In turn, German settlers were pressed to redefine themselves as a new racial elite untainted by miscegenation, imbibing the mythology of the thrifty, self reliant, hygienic, and racially pure German home. German settlers who married Africans were denied the right to vote in colonial assemblies. German feminists, eager to advance their own claims to citizenship, spearheaded the drive to find German wives for male colonists, who would become partners in the construction of racially elite farming families that would mitigate class divisions in the colonies.[122] Although, by the beginning of the twentieth century, interracial relationships had become a problem for all European colonial empires,[123] the system of racial privilege and segregation that the German colonial administration honed after the Herero War, which like the American South, would deny citizenship to anyone with so much as a drop of African blood, was distinctive in its severity.

For radical nationalists and imperialists in the Conservative and National Liberal parties in the Reichstag, as well as in the Pan German and Eastern Marches Leagues and Colonial Society without, the specter of miscegenation led to the demand that Reich citizenship be limited to whites.[124] The obsession with the migration of Poles to the mines and factories of the Ruhr, the influx of Polish agricultural workers from Russia and Galicia to work on East Elbian estates, and Jewish refugees from pogroms converged with the dread of "race war" overseas. By 1908,

---

[122] Lora Wildenthal, *German Women for Empire 1884–1945* (Durham, NC: Duke University Press, 2001), 79–171.

[123] See Ann Laura Stoler, *Carnal Knowledge and Imperial Power: Race and the Intimate in Colonial Rule* (Berkeley and Los Angeles: University of California Press, 2002).

[124] See Dieter Gosswinkel, *Einbürgern und Ausschliessen*, 214–18; and his comparative article, "Citizenship in Germany and France at the Turn of the Twentieth Century: Some New Observations on an Old Comparison," in *Citizenship and National Identity in Twentieth-Century Germany*, eds. Geoff Eley and Jan Palmowski (Stanford: Stanford University Press, 2007), 27–39.

the desire of the governing Bülow Bloc to punish the Center for its criticism of German colonial policy, and Polish resistance to the imposition of German as the language of instruction in the schools and the state-sponsored subvention of German settlers in the east, spawned decrees that justified the outright expropriation of Polish land and the imposition of other discriminatory measures that undermined the principle of equality before the law.[125] The cumulative impact of such measures resulted in the new Reich citizenship law of 1913. Although contrary to the fervent wishes of the radical right, the law fell well short of defining citizenship biologically and it preserved the possibility of naturalization for exceptional cases in which military service especially could enable a noncitizen to become one, citizenship was no longer defined by residence but by "community of descent."[126] That biological criteria did not prevail was due to the Socialist, Center, and Progressives, who in successive debates in the Reichstag opposed the antimiscegenation laws. Although revealing their own ambivalence toward interracial relationships, Catholics upheld the sanctity of marriage while the Socialists argued for humane treatment on the grounds of universally applicable human rights. Ironically, despite the parliamentary elections of 1912, which produced a shift to the left, the new citizenship law now deemed as legitimate state intervention in a previously sacrosanct institution, even as it confirmed the existence of an opposition that was strong enough to resist the imposition of colonial rules at home.[127]

FROM "A PLACE IN THE SUN" TO SEEDING THE STORM CLOUDS: GERMANY AND THE APPROACH OF WORLD WAR I

If the debate over the citizenship law testified to the modest success of the Center and Social Democratic opposition, the elections of 1912 provoked the furious reaction of radical nationalists. The SPD's electoral achievement threatened the army's privileged position in the Imperial

---

[125] The Bülow Bloc assumed that the Center was politically dominant in Polish-speaking regions, but it was not. The effect of the Bloc's anti-Catholic rhetoric and practice was to unite Polish nationalists and the Church. For this result in Upper Silesia, see James E. Bjork, *Neither German nor Poles: Catholicism and National Indifference in a Central European Borderland* (Ann Arbor: University of Michigan Press, 2008), 128–73.

[126] Wildenthal, *German Women for Empire*, 1–171; Blackbourn, *History of Germany*, 334; Gosewinkel, *Einbürgern und Ausschliessen*, 310–27.

[127] Helmut Walser Smith, "The Talk of Genocide, the Rhetoric of Miscegenation: Notes on Debates in the German Reichstag Concerning Southwest Africa, 1904–14," in Friedrichsmeyer, et al., *Imperialist Imagination*, 107–23.

constitution inasmuch as the party called for an end to military spending and reconciliation with Great Britain and France. It also pushed for democratization, the elimination of the three-class franchise in Prussia, and tolerance for minority languages and cultures. Despite clear signs that many Social Democratic leaders sought to achieve the party's gains by legal and parliamentary means, the marginalizing of "enemies of the Reich" had failed once again. Backed up by powerful trade unions that won substantial benefits for their wage-earning members, the Social Democrats had become the radical nationalists' worst nightmare. The following year, the SPD's parliamentary gains allowed the formation of majority in the Reichstag sufficient to pass a bill to tax landed estates. That encouraged an assortment of pressure groups ranging from the Pan German League to employers associated with heavy industry, and key leaders from the National Liberal and Conservative parties to form the "Cartel of Productive Estates." Advocating an aggressive foreign policy and even war as means to achieving imperialist goals, and a change in the constitution to eliminate the Reichstag, the Cartel voiced disenchantment with the Imperial government's weakness and the kaiser's inadequacies as a leader, which had grown evident since the Eulenberg scandal and the *Daily Telegraph* Affair. To the Cartel, only the use of force to preserve the survival of the fittest would ensure Germany's place as a world power and extend Bismarck's legacy. If right-wing militance was not the primary impetus for risky policies at the top, it did little to discourage the army and the civilian leadership from walking the precipice. As the international climate worsened in July of 1914 following the assassination of Archduke Franz-Ferdinand, the heir of the Austro-Hungarian throne in the Bosnian city of Sarajevo, the Imperial government could find few justifications for restraint as its febrile, trigger-happy ally sought revenge for the murder against a state whose very independence threatened the Dual Monarchy's survival.

Indeed, on August 1, 1914, the German general staff led by its chief Helmut von Moltke, launched a preventive war against France and Russia to remedy the consequences of Germany's often incoherent and unprioritized pursuit of overseas and continental empire.[128] Surrounded by enemies whose numerical strength, military reforms, railroad construction, and rapid rearmament programs would soon become more than a match for Germany and its ally, the German military opted for brinkmanship,

---

[128] Annika Mombauer, *Helmuth von Moltke and the Origins of the First World War* (Cambridge: Cambridge University Press, 2001), 182–226.

believing that victory would be more likely the sooner an attack was launched. The general staff calculated that defeating France first, then turning its attention to Russia before Russia was completely mobilized would allow the Reich to escape its "encirclement" and forestall a long, debilitating war that would ultimately mean Germany's ruin.[129] Although benefiting from the budgetary bills of 1912 and 1913, which expanded the army's size, the long-term diversion of tax revenues to the navy and the officer corps' own desire to preserve its political reliability and social exclusivity, had hampered the army sufficiently to place it at a strategic disadvantage compared to its enemies. Thus, the haste with which Moltke acted turned what was a poisonous but still local issue, Austria-Hungary's ultimatum to Serbia following the assassination of its archduke, into a world war.[130]

Europe's great powers, which struggled to secure national cohesion while maintaining multiethnic empires, each deserve at least a measure of blame for the outbreak of war, beginning with the Russian government, which initiated partial mobilization for fear that not risking war would fatally undermine Russia's prestige and invite revolution.[131] The Austro-Hungarian multinational empire, the survival of which its leadership saw as so threatened by Serbian nationalism that it drafted its plans to destroy Belgrade and partition Serbia two weeks before the archduke was murdered, bears even more responsibility.[132] Even Great Britain, the seemingly reluctant belligerent, which often escapes blame for resisting challengers to its global hegemony, stationed an expeditionary force in France and Belgium as early as 1908. At the same time, it commenced planning for an anti-German blockade.[133] Having imbibed Social Darwinian notions of global conflict among nations and races

---

[129] See Hull, *Absolute Destruction*, 159–81. Of special concern to the German general staff was the Duma's approval in June of major increases in the size of the Russian army, which would have been realized by 1917. See Mombauer, *Helmuth von Moltke*, 172.

[130] Annika Mombauer, "The First World War: Inevitable, Avoidable, Improbable or Desirable? Recent Interpretations on War Guilt and the War's Origins," *German History* 25, no. 1 (2007): 78–95.

[131] See Samuel R. Williamson Jr. and Ernest R. May, "An Identity of Opinion: Historians and July 1914," *Journal of Modern History* 79, no. 2 (2007): 335–87, for a summary statement of the scholarship.

[132] David Fromkin, *Europe's Last Summer: Who Started the Great War in 1914?* (New York: Alfred A. Knopf, 2004), 260. See also Kramer's assessment of each belligerent's responsibility in, *Dynamics of Destruction*, 69–113.

[133] John H. Morrow, Jr., *The Great War: An Imperial History* (London and New York: Routledge, 2004), 25.

for decades, most political and military leaders of the major European powers accepted the inevitability of war. The question was when and how great a war it would become. Yet Germany's refusal to restrain Austria-Hungary, indeed its gamble during the July crisis that Austria-Hungary could impose a fait accompli before its enemies reacted, proved decisive. Austria-Hungary's collapse would have left Berlin totally isolated.[134] The offensive-mindedness of the Schlieffen Plan, albeit with the younger Moltke's modifications of the original, put Germany in the Belgian channel ports that directly threatened London and the Thames estuary. If the chancellor and the general staff were under no illusion that backing Austria-Hungary would lead to a European war, Wilhelm adhered to the desperate hope that despite the "blank check" his government issued in support of its ally, a general war could be avoided.

Because of the centrality of the German-Austro-Hungarian axis to the outbreak of war, historians once emphasized Germany's "deviation" from the liberal democracies of the west. In doing so, they turned on its head the powerful sense of Germany's distinctiveness held by early twentieth-century German intellectuals, who in praising Germany's "special path" (*Sonderweg*) condemned "perfidious Albion" as the "materialistic" nation of shopkeepers embraced by the "Jewish spirit." Nevertheless, it is illuminating to compare Germany and another emerging empire, the United States. In the timing of their wars for national unification (the American Civil War having prevented the nation's disintegration), the rapidity of industrialization in both nations, and the magnitude of their imperial ambitions, in which continental dominion would provide the foundations for overseas imperialism, Germany and the United States resembled each other. The high priest of global naval power, Alfred Thayer Mahan, found a no more-devoted readership than in Germany, among them the kaiser and Alfred Tirpitz. Like Germany, the United States used its navy to challenge British interests, although the western hemisphere was its primary focus.[135] American commercial expansionism in Central and Latin America, proved to be a chronic source of irritation to the British during the nineteenth and early twentieth century, especially with the American construction and fortification of the Panama Canal.

[134] On the German government's and the army's willingness to gamble, see Hewitson, *Germany and the Causes of the First World War*, and Cramer, *Dynamics of Destruction*, 90–4.

[135] See Nancy Mitchell, *The Danger of Dreams: German and American Imperialism in Latin America* (Chapel Hill and London: University of North Carolina Press, 1999).

There were also broad similarities in the tensions between empire and nation building. If the American colonization of the continent at the expense of indigenous peoples assuaged the land hunger of an ethnically diverse white population, in contrast to German radical nationalists who sought to protect their own ethnicity, the conquest of the "wild west" was as essential to American vitality as transforming the "wild east." Indeed, the distinguished Leipzig geographer and Pan German, Friedrich Ratzel, who first coined the term "*Lebensraum*" (living space) acknowledged the similarity to his own work of Frederick Jackson Turner's frontier thesis that attributed American distinctiveness to its conquest of much of North America.[136] Moreover, the obsession with "miscegenation" underwrote Jim Crow–segregation in the post–Civil War South, as well as the German deployment of African labor after the colonial wars. It partially defined citizenship in both cases – regionally in the case of the South and colonially in the case of Germany – making the United States and Germany pioneers among the imperialist powers. Visions of total war against "savage" Indians influenced both the German colonial army in Southwest Africa and America's ruthless suppression of the Philippines insurrection in 1899, which took the lives of an estimated 200,000 Filipinos, again a reminder that the Imperial German conduct of its colonial wars did not distinguish the Second Empire from other empires.[137]

By 1914, however, the American overseas empire was "limited" to Latin America, the Philippines, and its commercial inroads in Asia, and notwithstanding the tensions between Britain and the United States, Bernhard von Bülow's efforts to forge an anti-British alliance between Germany and the United States failed to disrupt the American strategic reliance on the British navy.[138] The shared notion of Anglo-Saxon racial superiority increasingly united American and British elites, which encouraged the former to support the British Raj in India and the British side in the Boer War. The British endorsed the American war against Spain.[139] Germany's

---

[136] David Blackbourn, *The Conquest of Nature: Water, Landscape, and the Making of Modern Germany* (New York and London: W.W. Norton & Co., 2006), 294.

[137] In addition to Gerwarth and Malinowski, "Der Holocaust als "kolonialer Genozid"?, 444–5, see Franz Schumacher, "Niederbrennen, plunder und töten sollt ihr": Der Kolonialkrieg der USA auf den Philippinen (1899–1913), in Klein and Schumacher, *Kolonialkriege*, 109–44.

[138] On Bülow's assessments of the United States, see Rainer Pommerin, *Der Kaiser und Amerika: der USA in der Politik der Reichsleitung 1890–1917* (Cologne: Böhlau, 1986), 71–303.

[139] Walter L. Hixson, *The Myth of American Diplomacy: National Identity and U.S. Foreign Policy* (New Haven and London: Yale University Press, 2008), 92–3.

relationship with Britain, on the other hand, would have a different outcome. The prospect of the fall of France and Belgium to Germany, which would have put the Germans on the English Channel, amounted to the more immediate threat to the British Empire, while opposition to foreign entanglements ensured that the United States remained formally neutral until Germany's unrestricted submarine warfare and promises to Mexico to restore its lost territories after the 1846 war undermined it.[140] It was Imperial Germany's misfortune that its major competitors lay close to home.

In the end, the general staff had no stomach for negotiation or for the articulation of more limited aims, fearing that anything less than the annihilation of the enemy before the enemy destroyed it would result in Germany's complete destruction. And, the government, which had made a practice of fanning the enthusiasm of "loyal" Germans, found its options circumscribed, not least by the belief of Bülow's successor Bethmann-Hollweg that the Germans and the Slavs were somehow destined to engage in a "racial struggle" for survival.[141] Yet if the dogma of annihilating the enemy was rooted in German military culture and practice, much of its power lay in the qualities of bourgeois nationalism more generally, penetrating both the Protestant or Catholic variant despite their manifest differences. Drawing on deeply religious narratives of promise and tragedy derived from the imagination of Germany's covenant as God's chosen people and its historical experience of defeat and division, German nationalism amounted to an explosive cocktail of will to power and the fear of dissolution.[142] Public displays of military power, as its spiraling naval budgets and maritime spectacles demonstrated, devoted more attention to mitigating domestic divisions than explicating coherent and attainable objectives.[143]

As in 1871, when military victory in an international crisis alleviated domestic divisions, the Imperial government and its general staff now applied the same logic. If not the proximate motivation for plunging into war, which was to strike before Germany's enemies became insurmountable, the Imperial government's gamble would carry an important by-product. The victory that it fervently hoped would come about would rally Germans around the throne and weaken the pressure to reform the

[140] Niall Ferguson, *The Pity of War* (New York: Basic Books, 1999), 54–5, 163–4.
[141] Mombauer, *Helmuth von Moltke*, 152–3.
[142] Kramer, *Thirty Years' War*, 215–6.
[143] Rüger, *Great Naval Game*, 162–3.

imperial system to benefit the "enemies of the Reich."[144] Instead, the war
that the general staff anticipated and the political leadership condoned
would bring about the very thing that nationalists most feared, the German
Empire's defeat and the loss of its adjacent and overseas colonies. War
and defeat radicalized patterns that emerged during the Second Empire,
the ambition to world power and the pursuit of a cohesive nation defined
by ethnic homogeneity. Although the National Socialists would regret the
incompleteness of the Bismarckian unification and underscore the faults
of Imperial German domestic and foreign policy, they would build on the
Second Empire's legacies even as they catalogued its failures.

[144] Roger Chickering, *Imperial Germany and the Great War, 1914–1918* (Cambridge:
Cambridge University Press, 2004), 8.

2

From Dominion to Catastrophe

Imperial Germany during World War I

By the summer of 1914, the German overseas colonial empire ranked
third in territorial size and fifth in population compared to the seven other
European empires and the United States.[1] Its influence had grown in southeastern Europe and in the Middle East, a testimony to its eagerness to
flex its formidable economic and military power. Internally, however, the
nagging concern persisted that Germany remained incomplete territorially,
fragmented and disunited internally, and threatened continuously by its
European rivals. Class and religious divisions, which expressed different
conceptions of the nation, the state's inability to subdue and assimilate ethnic minorities, and the encirclement of enemies who challenged Germany's
position overseas and on the continent, stood in the way of Germany's hegemonic ambitions. For many, therefore, the war promised a solution. It ener-
gized nationalists, who saw the call to arms as an opportunity to unify the
nation permanently and demonstrate Germany's superiority in what was
quickly perceived as a battle for survival between civilizations: Germany
against the Slavic east and the Latin west. The transcendent German "community" (*Volksgemeinschaft*) would ultimately triumph over internal fractiousness and its decadent and materialist foes.[2] Although implicit in the
emergence of mass politics that redefined the Second Empire beginning
in the 1880s, the wartime expectation of a cohesive and homogeneous

---

[1] Lora Wildenthal, *German Women for Empire, 1884–1945* (Durham and London: Duke
University Press, 2001), 2.
[2] Steffen Breundel, *Volksgemeinschaft oder Volksstaat: Die "Ideen von 1914" und die
Neuordnung Deutschlands im Ersten Weltkrieg* (Berlin: Akademie Verlag, 2003), 29–92;
Kevin Cramer, "A World of Enemies: New Perspectives on German Military Culture and
the Origins of the First World War," *Central European History* 39, no. 2 (2006): 272–3.

"community" of Germans able to fulfill their providential role of completing the nation would be the conflict's most durable contribution to the German imperial imagination in the years to come.

To be sure, a less belligerent and apocalyptic vision would later compete with that of radical nationalists and imperialists. Given institutional expression in the Social Democratic Party, the Center, and the reunified Progressive Party, this vision imagined a moderate peace without forced annexations and the imposition of a fully constitutional state. A democratized nation would replace the semi-authoritarian Wilhelmine system. Nevertheless, the advocates of radical nationalism, militantly imperialist, authoritarian, anti-semitic, and populist – would come to dominate German policy during the conflict until the war's privations and the war weariness that accompanied them opened more space for the opposition to press its claims. Yet even then, radical nationalism suffered only a temporary defeat. The turbulent beginnings of the Weimar Republic would encourage the resurgence of a more-exclusive imagined "community," purged of its political and racial enemies. Only a homogeneous "community" could expand Germany's borders, realize German aspirations to world power, and overcome the multiple weaknesses of Germany's postwar constitutional democracy, chronic economic crisis, internal division, and subjugation to the Entente.

EARLY VICTORIES AND IMPERIALIST DREAMS: GERMANY'S WAR AIMS

As the news of the July crisis intensified, the Imperial government's skillful, self-justifying narration of the events leading up to the war brought patriotic crowds into the streets, some among them singing the Imperial anthem, *Deutschland über Alles* (Germany above all). The reports of the Russian Empire's mobilization on July 31, followed in the coming days by Germany's declaration of emergency and its subsequent declarations of war against Russia, France, and Britain, brought volunteers eager to enlist in the military, swept up by the patriotic fervor and convinced that the war would be short. Their enthusiastic numbers included a young Austrian Pan German, who had recently immigrated to Germany from Vienna. Adolf Hitler cheered the news on Munich's Odeonplatz with the conviction that the war would give his life the purpose that the Dual Monarchy could not, serving the cause of the ethnic German nation.[3]

[3] Ian Kershaw, *Hitler 1889–1936: Hubris* (New York and London: W. W. Norton, 1998), 87–90; Brigitte Hamann, *Hitlers Wien: Lehrjahre eines Diktators* (Munich and Zurich: Piper, 1996), 573–4.

Having rejected the land of his birth, Hitler anticipated a trend that would grow more pronounced in the post–World War I Central and Eastern European "shatter zone" of imperial collapse and ethnic conflict, that is, the alienation of ethnic Germans beyond the Reich's borders from the nations where they resided.[4] Such excitement was by no means confined to aspiring, down-at-the-mouth artists. In addition to painting Manichaean and apocalyptic canvases that depicted the war as a battle between German "heroism" and the Entente's "materialism," or in the case of Russia "despotism," intellectuals viewed the unity of August of 1914 through the lens of Germany's previous resurrections, the aftermath of the Thirty Years War, the Battle of Leipzig in 1913 against Napoleon's armies, and the Franco-Prussian War in 1870.[5] Although fearful of the impact of the war's hardships, the prominent Freiburg historian Friedrich Meinecke could not resist blessing the conflict as an opportunity for national regeneration through renewed idealism, a heightened sense of community solidarity, and individual sacrifice for the greater good.[6]

In reality, the rapturous proclamations of "community" belied the potential for marginalizing and persecuting "enemies" that such nationalism contained, as newspapers published rumors of foreign spies plotting to poison the drinking water.[7] Moreover, the crowds drew disproportionately from a narrow constituency composed of the urban upper and middle classes, and especially intellectuals and university student fraternities. The numerous peace demonstrations organized by women and Social Democrats received little press coverage. So did other palpable expressions of anxiety, which included the hasty withdrawal of savings from banks, the hoarding of food, and nervous attempts to seek exemption from military service. War enthusiasm resonated poorly in rural areas because peasants knew that the outbreak of hostilities would deprive them of labor and animals just as their crops ripened for harvest. Faced with the prospect of losing sons, husbands, and brothers to the front, rural women expressed a pessimism and uncertainty that neither nationalistic propaganda nor menacing images of the enemy

4 Ulf Engel and Matthias Middell. "Bruchzonen der Globalisierung: Globale Krisen und Territorialitätsregime – Kategorien einer Globalgeschichtsschreibung," *Comparativ* 15 (2005): 5–38.
5 See Kevin Cramer, *The Thirty Years' War and German Memory in the Nineteenth Century* (Lincoln and London: University of Nebraska Press, 2007), 225.
6 Roger Chickering, *The Great War and Urban Life in Germany: Freiburg, 1914–1918* (Cambridge: Cambridge University Press, 2007), 72–3.
7 Michael Wildt, *Volksgemeinschaft als Selbstermächtigung: Gewalt gegen Juden in der deutschen Provinz 1919 bis 1939* (Hamburger: Hamburger Edition, 2007), 30.

could assuage.[8] Nevertheless, the government's claim that Germany mobilized in self-defense against its enemies, particularly Russia, and that it sought no territorial gains, gave rise to a two-dimensional myth that for a time contained opposition to the war. Germany was the victim of the Entente's aggressive "encirclement." In response, Germans would collectively sacrifice to defend their homeland, putting aside the deep class, regional, religious, and ethnic divisions that had long bedeviled them. On August 4, shortly after the announcement of Germany's declaration of war against France, Kaiser Wilhelm, seizing the opportunity to rebuild his rickety popular standing, proclaimed that the "peace of the fortress" or "civic peace" (*Burgfrieden*) now prevailed, creating a new wartime ethnic community that made internal division a thing of the past. The kaiser no longer recognized parties; rather, he knew only Germans.

Internal dissent crumbled as the seeming inclusiveness of the myth, with its imagined shared victimhood and sacrifice, encouraged "outsiders" to support the war in order to overcome their political marginalization. The conflict provided Jews and Catholics with an opportunity to demonstrate their patriotism. More than ten thousand Jewish men enlisted immediately after the war began, a fraction of the ninety-six thousand who would ultimately serve. Catholic elites compared the present call to arms to the medieval crusading sermons of Pope Urban II.[9] Like socialists elsewhere except in Russia and Italy, the German Social Democrats tempered their long-professed proletarian internationalism to join with the other parties in the Reichstag to authorize war credits. Trade unions affiliated with the Social Democratic Party suspended strikes, although the proclamation of the state of emergency that imposed martial law made it clear that coercion, and not simply consent, contributed to the declining resistance of the left. Although Social Democrats heatedly debated the party's response internally, the Reichstag fraction's support of the war effort came down to its belief that Germany *was* fighting a defensive

---

[8] For recent works that have questioned the extent of war enthusiasm in the German population, see Jeffrey Verhey, *The Spirit of 1914: Militarism, Myth, and Mobilization in Germany* (Cambridge: Cambridge University Press, 2000), 12–114; Christian Geinitz, *Kriegsfurcht und Kampfbereitschaft: Das Augusterlebnis in Freiburg: Eine Studie Zum Kriegsbeginn 1914* (Essen, 1998); and Benjamin Ziemann, *War Experiences in Rural Germany 1914–1923*, trans. Alex Skinner (Oxford and New York: Berg, 2007), 15–27.
[9] See Wildt, *Volksgemeinschaft*, 31–2; and Sven Oliver Müller, "Nationalismus in der deutschen Kriegsgesellschaft 1939 bis 1945, in *Die Deutsche Kriegsgesellschaft 1939 bis 1945*, Zweiter Halbband, *Ausbeutung,Deutungen, Ausgrenzung*, Jörg Echterkamp ed. (Munich: Deutsche Verlags-Anstalt, 2005), 18.

war against the Russian Empire, the most autocratic regime in Europe, thereby sharing in cultural assumptions about "Asiatic" Russia long in place. Social Democrats, except for their radical wing that expected revolution to arise from the ashes of imperialistic capitalism, hoped that constitutional reform, including the elimination of the three-class franchise in Prussia, would follow as the reward for their patriotism and loyalty to the crown. In addition, German victories would "liberate" the proletariat in enemy lands as the eschatology of war promised the ultimate victory of workers in and outside Germany.[10]

Contrary to the Imperial government's propaganda, the general staff's war was "defensive" only according to the logic of a preventive war unleashed against enemies, especially Russia, which Moltke believed would outstrip Germany in industrial capacity, manpower, railway networks, and weaponry within a few years. Moreover, if initially reticent about Germany's goals at the very beginning of the conflict, the government and the military soon formulated aims that extended well beyond the "defensive" containment of dangerous foes. Instead, Germany's war evolved into a campaign to achieve dominion over the European continent, an expanded network of overseas colonies, and global economic supremacy, diverse ambitions that had long been popular among the middle classes. For some, continental dominion would amount to an informal empire, a German-dominated customs union rather than territorial annexations. Yet the Pan German League's vision of a formal empire, the eastern regions of which were to be used for racial breeding and the resettlement of ethnic Germans, would ultimately move to the center of wartime imperialist discourse, benefiting from the extensive ties between leading Pan Germans, spearheaded by their leader Heinrich Class, and heavy industry. For the Pan Germans, the world war was a "racial war."[11]

Although Moltke's and Bethmann-Hollweg's assessment of Germany's present strategic position and coming prospects provided the primary motivation for backing Austria-Hungary's ultimatum to Serbia, the German armies' early progress on the battlefield encouraged the advancement of specific objectives. The intensity with which aims were articulated varied according to German fortunes at the front. Victories encouraged visions of an empire, while setbacks caused Chancellor Bethmann-Hollweg to seek

[10] Chickering, *Great War*, 76.
[11] Dennis Sweeney, "Race, Capitalism and Empire" The Alldeutscher Verband and German Imperialism," paper given at the Annual Meeting of the German Studies Association, Pittsburgh, PA, September 29, 2006; Müller, "Nationalismus": 19.

a separate peace to split the Entente, while publicly denying hegemonic or annexationist objectives that would disturb the "peace of the fortress" at home. For three reasons, however, expansionism defined the debates among the civilian and military leaderships for the duration of the conflict. First and most obvious, east central, eastern, and southeastern Europe, composed of the diverse nationalities of the German, Russian, Ottoman, and Austro-Hungarian Empires, became a major theater. Not only had the shrinkage of the Ottoman Empire, the designs of the Russian Empire on the Balkans, the ethnic divisions of Austria-Hungary that Serbian expansionism threatened, and the economic and geopolitical ambitions of Germany spawned the war in the first place, the war's subsequent deleterious impact inflamed German territorial ambitions until Germany had little choice but to sign the armistice agreement. Second, the longer the conflict lasted and the greater the hardship suffered by civilians, the more "necessary" territorial gains became, especially to the military and radical nationalists, to whom the pursuit of empire was key to maintaining morale on the home front, staving off domestic reform and ensuring that German troops would keep fighting. Third, apart from the intrinsic merits of securing an expanded empire beyond Europe, weakening the Entente from Germany's perspective meant an opportunity to exploit the vulnerability of Britain's overseas possessions and financial markets.[12] Besides, the decision of the British Committee of Imperial Defence to attack Germany's maritime possessions immediately with the aid of the troops of its allies and colonies meant that Germany's overseas empire would most certainly become a theater.[13]

At first, the German attack in the west caught the Entente off guard, despite the numerical inferiority of the German army. Modifying the famous 1906 memorandum of the then–chief of staff, Alfred von Schlieffen, who to compensate for German vulnerability in a two-front war proposed an annihilationist right-flanking movement into France by violating Belgian and Dutch vulnerability, Moltke bypassed Holland partially to shorten his supply lines. Yet the need for a neutral Netherlands adjacent to Germany, which could serve as a conduit for overseas trade in the event of a British blockade, proved even more important to Moltke, as did his belief in concentrating his forces at the fortress at Liège before

---

[12] Hew Strachan, *The First World War* (New York and London: Viking, 2003), 70.
[13] Stig Förster, "Vom europäischen Krieg zum Weltkrieg," in *Enzyklopädie Erster Weltkrieg*, eds. Gerhard Hirschfeld, Gerd Krumreich, and Irina Renz (Paderborn: Ferdinand Schöningh, 2003), 244.

Belgian forces could delay the German advance.[14] Although slowed by the Belgian and French sabotage of railroads, pressed to meet the invasion's exacting timetables, and deprived of forces that had been diverted to the southwest to prevent a French invasion of Germany through Alsace, the attack succeeded well enough. By the end of the first week of August, the German armies took Liège after fierce Belgian resistance and heavy German casualties, while the British and French armies scrambled to solidify their positions. After occupying Brussels by August 20th, putting the French and British Expeditionary Force in full retreat, the German armies entered France soon afterward.

Nevertheless, the unexpectedly rapid Russian mobilization brought initial setbacks for the Germans in the east, such that Moltke, then confident of victory in France, diverted two army corps from the western front to reinforce the German Eighth Army in East Prussia.[15] Under the command of the sixty-eight-year-old general Paul von Hindenburg, who had been called out of retirement, and Hindenburg's chief of staff Erich Ludendorff, who had boldly claimed credit for the victory at Liège, the Germans capitalized on the uncoded radio messages and poor communication among the Russian forces to win a major victory near the Masurian Lakes at the end of August. Ludendorff and Hindenburg, the latter having won promotion to field marshal, assumed the status of mythical national heroes for their victory in the eastern campaign, which had already been defined as a "racial struggle." Although content to leave the management of his army to Ludendorff, Hindenburg skillfully exploited the popular yearning for the truly national leader that Wilhelm failed to become, a leader who could transcend Imperial Germany's internal divisions and local identities.[16] "His" defeat of the Slavic enemy, the "Asiatic flood," underwrote his emerging status. For the sake of domestic consumption,

---

[14] Strachan, *The First World War*, vol. 1, *To Arms* (New York and Oxford: Oxford University Press, 2001), 179. For the debate on the Schlieffen Plan, see Terence Zuber, *Inventing the Schlieffen Plan: German War Planning, 1871–1914* (Oxford: Oxford University Press, 2002); and Isabel Hull's rejoinder in *Absolute Destruction: Military Culture and the Practices of War in Imperial Germany* (Ithaca and London: Cornell University Press, 2005), 160–5. Whereas Zuber sees Schlieffen's memorandum as advocating a defensive war in light of Germany's strategic deficiencies, Hull sees an "annihilative" strategy, which despite the subsequent modifications of Moltke and others, was consistent with German military practice since the Franco-Prussian War.

[15] Annika Mombauer, *Helmuth von Moltke and the Origins of the First World War* (Cambridge: Cambridge University Press, 2001), 243–9.

[16] Wolfram Pyta, *Hindenburg: Herrschaft zwischen Hohenzollern und Hitler* (Munich: Siedler, 2007), 93.

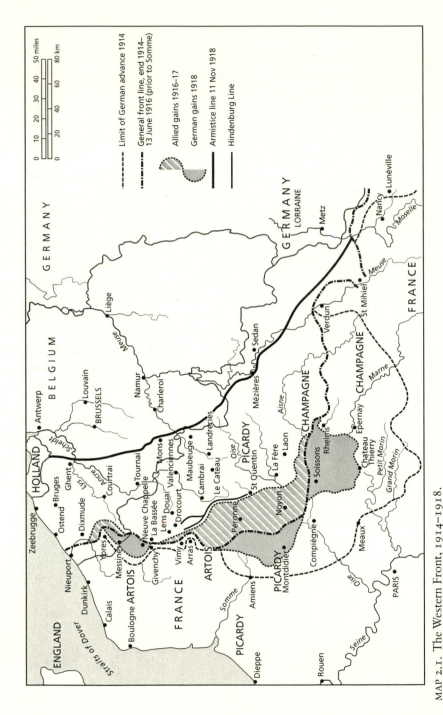

MAP 2.1. The Western Front, 1914–1918.
Source: Ian F.W. Beckett, *The Great War 1914–1918,* 2nd. ed. (Harlow: Pearson Longman, 2007), xxxii.

74

Hindenberg named the victory after the village of Tannenberg as the much-belated revenge for the Polish-Lithuanian defeat of the Teutonic Knights five hundred years earlier. If the Polish and Lithuanian victory in 1410 had signified the tragic late-medieval decline of the German crusading monastic order, the victory over Russia in 1914 announced the triumphant resurgence of German power.[17] Because Hindenburg's and Ludendorff's iconic victory on the eastern front contrasted sharply with what became a stalemate in the west, their stature would reinforce radical nationalist demands for territorial annexations.

Germany's rapid victories in the west during the first month of the hostilities, which sustained the hope that the war would soon be concluded, encouraged the articulation of expansive postwar goals. Under pressure from militant imperialists in the National Liberal and Conservative parities, heavy industry, and the senior bureaucracy, many of them with ties to the Pan German League, Bethmann-Hollweg composed his "September Program" during the second week of September of 1914 when German forces seemed well within reach of Paris. Political expediency deemed that the program be kept secret, for Bethmann-Hollweg, aware of its explosive potential, did not want to jeopardize the "peace of the fortress" by infuriating the Social Democratic Party, the left wing of the Center, and the Progressives, who advocated a negotiated peace and constitutional reform. Their willingness to approve war credits depended on the Imperial Government's claim that it was fighting a defensive war and would likely decline in proportion to German military advances beyond what was appropriate for a limited campaign. Bethmann was particularly worried about the Social Democrats, inasmuch as the party's initial support of the war temporarily overrode the opposition of workers in war-related industries, in which labor was obviously critical to armaments production.[18]

Although more conditional and less ambitious than the alternative proposals of the Pan German League and leading industrialists, the September Program proposed an empire of sufficient scope to permanently end Germany's historical vulnerability.[19] In Europe, it envisioned

[17] Strachan, *First World War*, vol. 1, 334.

[18] Roger Chickering, *Imperial Germany and the Great War, 1914–1918*, 2nd ed. (Cambridge: Cambridge University Press, 2004), 61–2.

[19] For Class's memorandum, see Rainer Hering, *Konstruierte Nation: der Alldeutsche Verband, 1880 bis 1939* (Hamburg: Christians, 2003), 134–5; and Woodruff D. Smith, *The Ideological Origins of Nazi Imperialism* (New York and Oxford: Oxford University Press, 1986), 168–85.

FIGURE 2.1. Photo of Field Marshal Paul von Hindenburg (left) and his chief of staff General Erich Ludendorff taken in 1916. By seemingly reversing the German retreat from the east in the late Middle Ages, the Battle of Tannenberg in 1914 elevated Hindenburg to the status of national hero. In addition to expanding their political power, Hindenburg and Ludendorff spearheaded radical nationalist demands for significant territorial annexations.
Source: Bundesarchiv Koblenz, Bild 146–1970–073–47.

"security for the German Reich in west and east for all imaginable time." France and Russia would be destroyed as great powers, in Russia's case by pushing it back as far as possible from Germany's eastern frontier and "her domination over the non-Russian vassal peoples broken." Because Bethmann-Hollweg wanted to keep outright annexations to a minimum to retain the possibility of a separate peace with Britain and avoid the incorporation of more subject peoples than he could manage, the program still imagined a cornucopia of gains. It expected the economic and military domination of France and Belgium, German control of the

Belgian coast and the mineral-rich Longwy-Briey basin, the annexation of Luxembourg, and a Central European customs union that would secure Germany's future as the industrial, technological, and financial hub. For good measure, the program envisioned the subordination of the Netherlands, Scandinavia, Austria-Hungary, Italy, and Romania. To supplement the continent as a market for industrial exports, Germany would construct a Central African empire extending from the east to west coasts by incorporating the French and Portuguese colonies, French Equatorial Africa, Angola, Mozambique, Togo, Dahomey, Senegal, and Gambia. Although the September Program was less precise about what would become of former Russian territories – whether Poland, Courland on the Gulf of Riga, Lithuania, Ukraine, and Finland would become satellite states or annexed outright – it nonetheless incorporated the demand of the Pan Germans for peasant settlements in eastern Europe and the exploitation of the region's raw materials. Finally, the program presupposed the continued German influence over Turkey, while the Berlin to Baghdad railroad would allow Germany to extend its ambitions to the Middle East and Asia.[20]

By the end of 1914, Bethmann-Hollweg was forced to shelve the September Program because the predictions of a quick victory had proven premature, and the left wing of the Social Democrats refused to support additional war credits. As a result, the chancellor sought to capitalize on the Hindenburg-Ludendorff victory in East Prussia to conclude a separate peace with Russia, which would at least relieve the pressure on the western front. Yet, although it contained liberal imperialist elements, such as a central European customs union, the September Program was neither a defensive "European Union" in response to Britain's involvement in the war, as one recent account implies,[21] nor did it merely express the temporary euphoria of victory. Apart from its unacceptability to the Entente, which would do whatever was necessary to defend its own empires, the Program's existence testified to imperialist aspirations that significantly exceeded those of other belligerents, aspirations that Bethmann's sleight-of-hand could not conceal. The September Program went well beyond the war aims of the British, which included the seizure of Germany's African colonies and substantial claims at the expense of the Ottoman Empire,

[20] Fritz Fischer, *Germany's Aims in the First World War* (New York: W.W. Norton & Co., Inc., 1967), 103–10.
[21] Niall Ferguson, *The Pity of War: Explaining World War I* (New York: Basic Books, 1999), 168–73.

and, as well, the goals of the French, which sought the recovery of Alsace and Lorraine, the annexation of the Saar, and the creation of satellite states on the left bank of the Rhine.[22] War plans were, to be sure, not the same as real gains enabled by military victories far from Germany's grasp, which was especially evident early on when Germany lost its holdings in Africa and the Far East. And Anglo-French imperialist ambitions, particularly at the expense of the Ottoman Empire, would have their own difficult consequences. Nevertheless, far from reining in German dreams of empire, the transformation of a short war into a long one made empire more compelling to those who hungered for it. An expanded Reich would be the suitable reward for outlasting foreign enemies in the battle of civilizations.

EVANESCENT VICTORIES AND LONG-TERM LIABILITIES, 1914–1915

However satisfying in the short run, Germany's triumph at Battle of Tannenberg and the initial victories in the west belied serious logistical problems, which crippled its ability to deal a knock-out blow against the Entente. The rapidity of the German advance though Belgium and France, which was calculated according to rigid, exhausting, and unrealistic timetables, undermined effective communication among the five invading armies, complicated the provisioning of the troops, and rendered the transport of artillery difficult at best. Moreover, Moltke's attempt to remedy those problems, that is, to move one army to the southeast to attack the retreating British and French forces, postponed the planned encirclement of Paris. As a result, the Entente forces regrouped at the Marne River east of Paris, stalling the Germans' advance during the first two weeks of September. Moltke's subsequent flanking movements, a desperate attempt to recover the initiative, failed, such that the western front became a 450-mile trail of trenches from Belgium to the Swiss border, in which opposing armies dug in for a conflict that evolved into the German general staff's worst nightmare, a two-front war of attrition that Germany had not been prepared to wage. Periodic attempts over the next four years by each side to break through the opposing army's line succeeded temporarily at most, creating bloody stalemates and nearly

---

[22] David Blackbourn, *A History of Germany, 1780–1918: The Long Nineteenth Century*, 2nd ed. (Oxford: Blackwell, 2003), 360–4; David Stevenson, *Cataclysm: The First World War as Political Tragedy* (New York: Basic Books, 2004), 112.

unfathomable casualties on both sides. Germany did overrun Belgium and it wrested control of the crucial industrialized regions of northeastern France. Nevertheless, the Battle of the Marne had proven sufficiently decisive to force Moltke to abandon his modified version of the Schlieffen Plan. Exposed to increasing attacks by rivals, who were captivated by their own expectations of a quick victory and blamed him for the failure to reach Paris, Moltke was replaced as chief of the general staff by Erich von Falkenhayn, the Prussian Minister of War.[23] Even worse from the German perspective, the outcome of the battle encouraged Italy, the Triple Alliance's weak link, to abandon the Central Powers for the Entente. Italy was promised major territorial concessions: Austro-Hungarian provinces with large Italian populations including the South Tyrol and Trentino, the Dalmatian coastline, and even western Anatolia. Thus, the Imperial government's fervent hope during the summer of 1914, that its modern-day repetition of the Roman feat at Cannae would subdue France before Russia mobilized, and that Britain would not honor its commitment to the Entente, collapsed like a house of cards.

Complicating matters further for the Germans, the Austro-Hungarian army, weakened by the direction of most of its troops to attack Serbia, fared poorly against the Russians armies in the Habsburg province of Galicia. By the end of 1914, the German High Command feared that the dual monarchy would collapse altogether. Even the Central Powers' victory over Serbia the following year would not have occurred without the reluctant contribution of German forces. That development illustrated the Central Power's most obvious liability aside from having resources inferior to those of the Entente; that is, the inclination to pursue separate agendas rather than to coordinate them jointly. Even the most basic requirement of an alliance in wartime, the sharing of information, could not be taken for granted. Only on the very day that Germany declared war against Russia did the German army's deputy chief of staff suggest to the German military attaché in Vienna that Austria-Hungary and Germany coordinate their mobilizations.[24] The Austro-Hungarian Chief of Staff Franz Graf Conrad von Hötzendorf did not learn of the seriousness of the German defeat at the Marne until late October of 1914.[25]

---

[23] Mombauer, *Helmuth von Moltke*, 250–71.
[24] Wilhelm Deist, "Die Kriegführung der Mittelmächte," in Hirschfeld et al., *Enzyklopädie Erster Weltkrieg*, 249.
[25] Mombauer, *Helmuth von Moltke*, 251.

The Ottoman Empire's decision in November of 1914 to ally with the Central Powers might well have given Germany two strategic benefits, additional troops that could be deployed against the British Empire in the Middle East where the Germans could not spare them, and overland routes to Central Asia and Africa through Anatolia. However, the revolutionary Turkish nationalist Committee for Union and Progress that now governed the empire pursued its own agenda, to liberate Turks in the Caucasus and further east as far as Persia and Afghanistan. To be sure, the German and Austro-Hungarian armies did rally in 1915 to win their greatest victories of the war under Falkenhayn. They seized most of Galicia and the Polish capital of Warsaw by August of 1915 and had taken the Lithuanian capital of Vilna by the second week of September. Until the end of the war, German troops occupied Russian Poland, Lithuania, and parts of the Ukraine. In addition to Bulgaria's decision to side with the Central Powers to recover Macedonia, which it had lost in the Second Balkan War, the improved defenses of the Ottoman Empire, thanks to German help, enabled the Turks in April of 1915 to inflict a disastrous defeat on the British and Dominion forces on the Gallipoli Peninsula on the Dardanelles straits. Finally, the combined forces of Austria-Hungary, Bulgaria, and Germany defeated Serbia by the end of 1915, thus opening a direct link between Berlin and Constantinople. Despite those triumphs, the Central Powers' advance into Russian territory ran out of gas as the Russian armies were able to establish new fronts. In the west, the German armies remained mired in the trenches, leaving the problem of Germany's strategic vulnerability unresolved.

The Entente's command of the seas, which comprised 59 percent of the world's steamer tonnage, exacerbated the Central Powers' dilemma. Its navies denied Germany access to ocean trading routes and cut it off from its overseas commercial markets and colonies. By the end of 1914, Germany had lost its hold on Jiaozhou Bay and its Chinese leasehold. It relinquished its Pacific islands north of the equator to the Japanese, who, when war broke out, sided with the Entente to gain control over Manchuria and Inner Mongolia, and to extend its influence in the Pacific. In Africa, the British occupied Togo in short order. Despite their lack of reinforcements from the metropole, German protection forces in Africa did force the Entente to commit considerable military resources, exactly what German strategists had hoped for. Thus, it took a lengthy campaign in 1915 by South African troops to subdue German Southwest Africa, and an equally difficult effort to wrest the Cameroons that same year. Although his enemies exaggerated the prowess of the German commander in East Africa, Paul von Lettow-Vorbeck, Lettow-Vorbeck's deployment of five thousand Askari fighters to wage guerrilla warfare allowed the territory to remain in German hands until the end of the war.[26]

Yet neither Lettow-Vorbeck's doggedness nor the ineptitude of the British at Gallipoli compensated for the Entente's maritime advantages. Although the negative effect of the British blockade of Germany's North Sea coast was limited during the first two years of the war, its initial phases resulted in a 25 percent drop in agricultural production. Mounting shortages of staples such as wheat and potatoes spawned restiveness among urban lower-middle- and working-class women, whose protests the government could not ignore.[27] The blockade and the Entente's naval superiority, which prevented Germany from obtaining food from alternative sources overseas, raised the prospect of further economic strangulation and extreme hardship for civilians the longer the war lasted. Germany depended on imports for its eggs, dairy products, fish, meat, and animal fodder, and much of its grain came from Russia, now Germany's enemy. Germany's strategic weakness and inferior resources to fight a multifront war deepened Falkenhayn's pessimism, which was intensified by the catastrophic loss of eighty thousand men in November of 1914 in what would become the first of three battles for control of the Flemish city of Ypres and its environs. Yet unlike Falkenhayn, who proposed a separate peace with Russia to divide the Entente, the hardliners within the German command, notably the "heroes" of Tannenberg, Hindenburg and Ludendorff, and the world policy champion, Alfred Tirpitz, gained the upper hand. That development was strengthened by the Entente's persistent refusals to accept Bethmann's offers of a negotiated settlement favorable to Germany. Following the advances against Russia in 1915, Hindenburg and Ludendorff emerged as the most committed annexationists in the military, along with Tirpitz who urged an all-out submarine offensive against Allied commerce to break the stalemate in the west.

[26] Stevenson, *Cataclysm*, 200–1; John H. Morrow, Jr., *The Great War: An Imperial History* (London and New York: Routledge, 2004), 58–60, and Woodruff D. Smith, *The German Colonial Empire* (Chapel Hill: University of North Carolina Press, 1978), 221–4.

[27] Chickering, *Imperial Germany*, 41. Although questioning the impact of the blockade by itself, Alan Kramer otherwise underscores Germany's food problem: *Dynamic of Destruction: Culture and Mass Killing in the First World War I* (Oxford: Oxford University Press, 2007), 154–5.

They were not alone. For many industrialists, state officials, and the educated middle class, the prospect of permanent territorial acquisitions found wide acceptance in the belief that Germany simply could not compete with other world empires without expansion. As a follow-up to the impassioned justification of German intellectuals in October of 1914 for the brutal conduct of the German military in Belgium, their answer to the indictment of the French intellectual Romain Rolland, university professors, artists, and writers launched another petition in early 1915, which demanded annexations in eastern and western Europe.[28] At minimum, they called for the dissolution of the Habsburg Empire and the merger of Germany and Austria, maintaining that the Bismarckian, "smaller German" unification, although a historical necessity in 1871, now required enlargement. The enthusiasm of the academic elite joined war aims and domestic reform in a way that called the legitimacy of the federalized Bismarckian constitution into question. If disagreeing on the nature of the system that would replace the Prusso-German monarchy, intellectuals agreed that the war provided an opportunity to create a revitalized and tautly unified nation instead of an empire beset by regional, ethnic, religious, and class conflicts. Even moderate intellectuals such as the Progressives' national leader, Friedrich Naumann, who after the initial blast of nationalist fervor at the war's beginning limited his demands for annexations and advocated a full constitutional political system at home, envisioned an expanded African empire, a voluntary customs union constructed on the British model of informal empire, and German settlements at the expense of Russia, particularly in the Baltic region with its Hanseatic past.[29] After Hindenburg and Ludendorff assumed supreme command of the army in August of 1916, annexationist and expansionist proposals for the east grew still more vehement, now including permanent claims to Lithuania and the Courland, and a global system of naval bases. Contrary to Bethmann-Hollweg, who believed that German continental domination with a minimum of annexations in Europe and additional colonies in Africa could be negotiated with Britain, hard-line annexationists around Hindenburg and Ludendorff sought Britain's total defeat.

[28] Peter Jelavich, "German Culture in the Great War," in *European Culture in the Great War*, eds., Aviel Roshwald and Richard Stites (Cambridge: Cambridge University Press, 1999), 44–5

[29] Robert Gerwarth, *The Bismarck Myth: Weimar Germany and the Legacy of the Iron Chancellor* (Oxford: Clarendon Press, 2005), 24–7; Breundel, *Volksgemeinschaft oder Volksstaat*, 98–102, 221–39. Kramer, *Dynamics of Destruction*, 29.

THE GERMAN OCCUPATION AND THE MAKING OF A CONTINENTAL EMPIRE

The economic and military weaknesses of the Central Powers, as reflected in the war's costs in lives and materiel, provided a strong incentive to deploy colonial practices in the regions that Germany occupied, most obviously the extraction of raw materials and the ruthless appropriation of labor. Unlike the British and French, Germany could not count on resources from its colonies overseas, which were meager enough even without the battles raging in Africa and the Entente's domination at sea.[30] Furthermore, the German military's failure to subdue France, the consequences of which had already become clear by the end of 1914, provided greater impetus to pursue draconian occupation policies, which undermined the few prospects that existed for a negotiated peace despite numerous peace feelers throughout 1915 and 1916 from the American President Woodrow Wilson and Pope Benedict XV. On the western front, the German armies had suffered 500,000 casualties and one-third as many in the east. The Battle of the Marne alone consumed more munitions per day than the German armies had used during the entire Franco-Prussian War.[31] The escalating monetary, material, and human costs of the war put a premium on economic organization at home, in which the military took the initiative. Every aspect of the domestic economy would be redirected to serve the war effort, to efficiently allocate crucial resources including food, draft additional troops, and to find new sources of labor to replace men who had been sent to the front. Those same costs also put a premium on the military's successful exploitation of resources in German-occupied Europe.[32]

Inside Germany, the military increased its power by virtue of the Prussian Siege Law of 1851, which had been incorporated in the Imperial constitution of 1871. In addition to military recruitment and the provisioning of troops, deputy district commanders from the army assumed responsibility for transportation, censorship, and the maintenance of public order. Even without that specific constitutional provision, as well as the military's nearly complete autonomy from civilian control, the war's inflation of the value of military expertise rendered the civilian

---

[30] Dirk van Laak, *Imperiale Infrastruktur: Deutsche Planungen für eine Erschliessung Afrikas 1880 bis 1960* (Paderborn: Ferdinand Schöningh, 2004), 172.

[31] Chickering, *Imperial Germany* 30, 35.

[32] Deist, "Die Kriegführung der Mittelmächte," in Hirschfeld et al., *Enzyklopädie Erster Weltkrieg*, 252.

leadership even less inclined than usual to challenge the general staff.[33] Yet, because military jurisdictions overlapped with those of civilian authorities, conflicts and confusion led to obvious inefficiencies. Despite the haste with which it was cobbled together, the management of war industries proved more effective because highly concentrated German industries entailed less of a need to organize from scratch. Under the direction of the chairman of the German General Electric Company, Walter Rathenau, the War Materials Section of the Prussian Ministry of War established twenty-five war materials corporations, each for a specific raw material, the boards of which drew from the firms that consumed each. Soaring corporate profits and centralized acquisition and allocations ensured that the production of munitions remained adequate.[34]

Maintaining sufficient and affordable food supplies was another story altogether. Shortages began with the blockade's interruption of imported butter, meat, and eggs, and the significant reduction in supplies of wheat. The need to provision soldiers at the front and workers in the cities, whose energy levels had to be satisfied to meet production targets, led to the introduction of price controls on agricultural commodities. Because those controls proved more effective in lowering agricultural output than in maintaining a steady supply of staples, the government imposed rationing. That and the good harvests of 1914 and 1915 mitigated the hardships somewhat, but the government's imposition of price ceilings on the primary sector thereafter, which was embodied in its Controlled Economy (*Zwangswirtschaft*), yielded few positive outcomes. Crop failures that increased malnutrition and the bitter resistance of peasants and large landed estate owners against government controls led to pitched battles between government inspectors and agricultural producers, while civilian dissatisfaction with the government's inconsistent and reactive rationing policies mounted.[35] In short, conditions at home did little to discourage the military from exploiting Germany's occupied territories, which military manuals had, in any case, already authorized. If the army's

---

[33] Hull, *Absolute Destruction*, 202.

[34] See Wilhelm Deist's extensive introduction and the supporting collection of documents in his *Militär und Innenpolitik im Weltkrieg 1914–1918*, 2 vols. (Düsseldorf: Droste Verlag, 1970). For an excellent summary of the beginnings of mobilization at home, see Chickering, *Imperial Germany*, 35–46.

[35] Belinda Davis, *Home Fires Burning: Food, Politics, and Everyday Life in World War I Berlin* (Chapel Hill and London: University of North Carolina Press, 2000), 24–113.

brutality against and exploitation of civilians in Europe did not equal Lothar von Trotta's genocidal assault against the Herero and Nama, the similarity between its wartime practices and colonialism was no coincidence in light of the all-or-nothing logic that propelled German war plans in the first place.

The occupation of Belgium and France enabled the application of methods drawn from the wars of unification and colonial campaigns afterward. The elements of German nationalism, the combination of hubris and desperation that launched Germany's preventive war, led not surprisingly to the exaggeration of dangers presented by civilians once the army moved into foreign territory. Because the success of Moltke's modified Schlieffen Plan depended on rapidity of movement in order to meet precise deadlines, the exhaustion of the troops, the lethal power of frightening new weapons, sabotage, and even modest resistance from the Belgian army encouraged brutal countermeasures from German soldiers against civilians. These included the destruction of property, the use of human shields, the taking of hostages, the imposition of exemplary punishments, and the mass executions of men, women, and children. Comparable to the draconian measures that the Austro-Hungarian army deployed against Serb civilians, German soldiers, with the full support of their superiors, killed six thousand Belgian civilians alone in August and September of 1914.

In part, the institutional memories of *franc tireurs* and the French republican *levée en masse* to resist the German invaders during the Franco-Prussian War motivated German conduct in 1914. Yet the fusion of colonial, Belgian, and domestic "enemies" in the minds of the German military leadership added to the mix. The equation of putatively unseen Belgian snipers with the vileness of the Herero, as well as the insurrections of Socialists and ethnic minorities at home, grounded the belief of even ordinary foot soldiers that they faced a war of annihilation. In light of that conviction, the military saw observing the canons of international law as an unaffordable luxury. Furthermore, because of the confessional affiliation of the dominant, French-speaking Walloons, anti-Catholicism contributed significantly to the carnage. The mainly Protestant units that invaded Belgium expressed a morbid fear of "ultramontane" Belgian priests who fomented rebellion, testifying to the profound and lingering impact of the Battle for Culture. Alternatively, the Imperial government, mediated through the Army League leader, August Keim, who was named governor of the province of Limburg, backed the Protestant Flemish national movement to weaken French influence and secure German domination in the future.[36]

Economic exploitation followed as a matter of course from Pan German and Social Darwinian imaginings, which influenced the officer corps in garrison towns before the war. Belgium's economic infrastructure was either destroyed outright or dismantled to benefit the occupation. By the beginning of 1915, the German command began to deport Belgian workers to Germany at the behest of industrialists to make up for the shortfall of labor at home. When the Belgians resisted, German occupational authorities cut public works assistance in order to cause unemployment, in the belief that doing so would pressure Belgian men to comply with the labor draft. Failing that, the occupation constructed a 300-kilometer electrified fence along the Belgian-Dutch border to prevent escape. The official policy of the German military called for the forced requisition of resources with its predictable results of malnutrition and disease among Belgian civilians. Were it not for the Committee for the Relief of Belgium (CRB), led by Herbert Hoover, and the occasional reluctance of the German governor general Moritz von Bissing to violate international law, widespread starvation would likely have occurred. The Germans applied similar tactics to occupied northern France, as well as Alsace and Lorraine, the populations of which had long been suspected of pro-French sympathies. The masses of forced laborers dragooned by the German military and the destruction and removal of industrial capital prompted Hoover, using a colonial metaphor, to describe German-occupied France as one big concentration camp. Industries and agricultural lands in northern France were totally destroyed.[37]

The conditions in the German-occupied east, once the front had been settled after the autumn of 1915, became arguably worse. The lack of attention and palliative relief from foreign sources, intensified by the withdrawal of Russian civil authority and the brutal population transfers and scorched earth practices of the Russian military, no doubt contributed. The occupiers, however, ensured that lives already made miserable would become even more so. Initially, the Germans conveyed

---

[36] John Horne and Alan Kramer, *German Atrocities, 1914: A History of Denial* (New Haven and London: Yale University Press, 2001), 89–174; Marilyn Shevin Coetze, *The German Army League: Popular Nationalism in Wilhelmine Germany* (New York and Oxford: Oxford University Press, 1990), 110. See also Jeff Lipkes, *Rehearsals: The German Army in Belgium, August 1914* (Louvain: Leuven University Press, 2007), especially 563–74, who highlights the central role of arrogant nationalism and militarism.

[37] Kramer, *Dynamics of Destruction*, 41–7.

a patronizing sympathy toward Poles whom they viewed as the victims of tsarism. Nevertheless, building on previous prejudices against ethnic minorities, German attitudes hardened into fears of a prehistoric and frighteningly vast expanse of territory with its disheveled and unregulated forests and its confusing hodgepodge of ethnic groups, whose multiple identities reminded the invaders of the particularisms that bedeviled their own nation. To manage the occupiers' fear, Ludendorff went beyond the extraction of labor and resources to introduce the massive transformation of the land and its people according to German cultural standard that took little account of local realities or sensibilities. German rule was harsh enough in Poland, which was placed under a separate civil administration. Poles had long inspired stereotypical and arrogant conceptions of disorderly, unclean, uncultured, and "primitive" Slavs, while their territory had encouraged radical nationalists to envision it as usable space for German settlers once the appropriate ethnic cleansing was instituted. But in the Courland, Lithuania, and parts of White Russia – the Ober Ost (Supreme Command of the East), which Ludendorff placed under the direct control of the military and out of reach of civilian oversight – the occupation pursued a program of regulation, manipulation, and intervention from above with minimal consideration for "natives." Building on the symbolic significance of the Battle of Tannenberg, the Ober Ost was conceived as the renovation and implementation of an historical precedent, the late-medieval German migration to the east and the Teutonic Knights' conquest of the Baltic coast.[38]

To be sure, Imperial German occupation policies in the east often assumed an instrumentalist complexity not achieved by the Nazi "drive to the east" (*Drang nach Osten*) less than thirty years later, the violence of which exceeded anything delivered by the belligerents of World War I. Although unsettled by the population mélange that they confronted, the Germans allowed a degree of ethnic distinctiveness by constructing schools and staging cultural productions with local actors, composers, and playwrights. Opening space for the cultural expression of locally spoken languages would make the "natives" appreciate their "liberation" from the Russian Empire and its imposition of Russification policies. Such practices, the occupation expected, would also facilitate the transmission

[38] Vejas Gabriel Liulevicius, *War Land on the Eastern Front: National Identity and German Occupation in World War I* (Cambridge: Cambridge University Press, 2000), 12–112, 151–75.

MAP 2.2. The German Ober Ost, 1915–1918.
Source: Vejas Gabriel Liulevicius, *War Land on the Eastern Front: National Identity and German Occupation in World War I* (Cambridge: Cambridge University Press, 2000), 60.

of German cultural values, such as cleanliness, obedience to authority, discipline, and hard work. Ironically, that policy extended to Jews, who in addition to experiencing less repression than under the tsars, also presided over the revitalization of Yiddish culture. As the German armies advanced eastward during the summer of 1915, German Jewish soldiers proved essential as interpreters and procurers of transport and supplies, while the German administration of the Ober Ost disproportionately represented Jews and Protestants.[39] The German attempt to deepen ethnic self-identification served its broader strategy of preventing Russia from ever regaining control while facilitating a permanent German foothold.[40] Compared to the Third Reich, Imperial Germany's operations in the east were positively benign.

Nevertheless, the contradictory mix of manipulation and repression undermined what pro-German sympathies might have been cultivated. The Ober Ost command instituted an inefficient but intrusive system of identification, issued bans on travel in an obsessive effort to limit the spread of "contagion," dragooned labor for Ludendorff's modernizing projects, such as road building and the erection of telegraph poles, and expropriated property to a degree that even mere subsistence was difficult. Ludendorff achieved one of his goals, a self-sufficient colony that would in turn provide the Reich with resources, particularly grain, but he did so at horrible cost. For Lithuania alone, the requisition statistics were staggering: 90,000 horses, 140,000 cattle, and 767,000 pigs. The occupation transferred to Germany resources valued at over 338 million marks while importing less than 78 million.[41] As in Belgium and France, men were pressed into labor service, many of the victims often collapsing and dying from malnutrition and disease. Punitive deportations, unburdened by the need for even a modicum of due process, were a regular occurrence.

Mounting resistance to the colonial practices of the German occupation in the Ober Ost, which would feed the ethnic nationalism that bedeviled Allied peacemakers later, demanded from the Germans' perspective even harsher countermeasures. Although unsuccessful in securing a docile population and an adequate stream of workers – the military's measures provoked anti-German uprisings – the occupation established perceptions and behaviors that would return with even more devastating vigor during the Third Reich. The Germans' experience with popular resistance confirmed German racial stereotypes

[39] Ibid., 113–50; Victor Klemperer, *Curriculum vitae: II: Erinnerungen 1881–1918*, ed. Walter Nowojski (Berlin: Aufbau Verlag, 1996), 466; Strachan, *First World War*, 148.

[40] Aviel Roshwald, *Ethnic Nationalism and the Fall of Empires: Central Europe, Russia and the Middle East, 1914–1923* (London and New York: Routledge, 2001), 116–25: Strachan, *First World War*, 148–50.

[41] Liulevicius, *War Land*, 73.

of Slavs as lazy, unclean, backward, incapable of creating a functioning state or advanced civilization, and a pernicious source of disease. The attempts of German authorities to contain the spread of typhus so that it would not contaminate the occupiers encouraged the introduction of the bacteriological techniques from the tropics, establishing a pattern that the Nazis would take to a greater extreme.[42] Rather than looking upon the district as composed of peoples with complex histories and cultures, albeit underdeveloped ones, who could be manipulated into submitting to German benevolence, the east evolved in German eyes into a project with the potential for realizing the Pan German vision of a vast space ripe for the civilizing effects of Germandom. It was to be a site for the implementation of a utopian vision of modern farms, roads, and efficient administration made possible by the investment of a superior people. By 1917, however, Ludendorff's transformative mission to uplift his subjects so that they would earn the blessings of German culture was receding in favor of plans for outright expulsions to make way for German soldier-farmers, who, following the pattern of medieval German colonizers, would make the land productive and defend it with their arms.[43]

More ominous still, German prisoner-of-war camps became laboratories for physical anthropologists to adapt more sophisticated techniques of racial differentiation and hierarchical ranking among Europeans themselves, techniques that they once again comfortably applied to exotic peoples overseas. Influenced by the radicalization of war aims, which even more sharply defined Germany's enemies as minacious "others," the captors held absolute power over their captives. Because the diversity of the prisoners, whose numbers included Asian and African colonial troops along with Europeans from enemy armies, reduced the significance of skin color, German anthropologists departed significantly from prewar disciplinary norms. When previously anthropologists were less inclined to attribute different racial characteristics to other Europeans, despite the growing prewar tendency to characterize Russia as "Asian," the war peeled away whatever reservations remained. While the Ober Ost administration extended the colonization of Slavs beyond the borders of Prussian Poland, German anthropologists documented the physical

[42] Paul Julian Weindling, *Epidemics and Genocide in Eastern Europe 1890–1945* (Oxford: Oxford University Press, 2000), 298–304.
[43] Liulevicius, *War Land*, 158–9.

characteristics of enemy prisoners, marking especially those captured on the eastern front as racially inferior.44

If its management of its territories was harsh, the Imperial German occupation fell well short of the genocide inflicted on its own subjects by its desperate ally, the Ottoman Empire. In claiming at minimum 800,000 victims and possibly double that number, the slaughter of the Armenians presaged the Nazi regime's own "solution" to the problems of imperial disintegration, ethnic competition and conflict, and conflicting political visions of post–World War I Europe, a parallel that Hitler himself allegedly recognized when he launched the German attack on Poland.45 Germany's long-term imperial ambitions and its short-term need for an ally in its Middle Eastern theater proved decisive in linking its fortunes to the new leaders of the Ottoman Empire, the Turkish Committee for Union and Progress (CUP). Well before it joined the war on the German side, voices within the CUP aspired to the creation of an ethnically and religiously homogeneous polity. A different sort of empire would compensate for the Ottoman defeats in the Libyan war of 1911 or the Balkan Wars of 1912 and 1913, not to mention the great powers' support for the independence of the Empire's Christian subjects. Unlike the Ottoman Empire of old, the most extreme elements within the CUP would no longer accommodate non-Turks. Unable to expel its Greek population through negotiation before the war broke out, the CUP deported thousands of Greeks into the interior of Anatolia to be used as forced labor until such a time when ethnic cleansing could be realized.46 Indeed the Ottomans' military capabilities were open to question. In early 1915, the Russians soundly defeated the Ottoman army at Sarikamish in the Causasus near the Russo-Turkish border, and even the Empire's victory at Gallipoli derived heavily from German support. Yet Ottomans' strategic virtue as a client state through which the Germans could cut off the

---

44 Andrew D. Evans, "Anthropology at War: Racial Studies of POWs during World War I," in *Worldly Provincialism: German Anthropology in the Age of Empire*, eds. H. Glenn Penny and Matti Bunzl (Ann Arbor: University of Michigan Press, 2003), 198–229.

45 See the work of Taner Akçam, *Armenien und der Völkermord: Die Istanbuler Prozesse und die türkische Nationalbewegung* (Hamburg: Hamburger Edition, 2004), and *A Shameful Act: The Armenian Genocide and the Question of Turkish Responsibility*, trans. Paul Bessemer (New York: Metropolitan Books, 2006).

46 Kramer, *Dynamics of Destruction*, 147–8. The degree of ethnonationalism in the CUP remains contested. For the argument that the Young Turks remained "Ottomanists" in conception, see Ronald Grigor Suny, "Truth in Telling: Reconciling Realities in the Genocide of the Ottoman Armenians," *American Historical Review* 114, no. 4 (2009): 934.

British from India was appealing. It promised a future German foothold in the Middle East at Britain's expense.

The closing of the Dardanelles to the Entente after Gallipoli emboldened the CUP to "solve" its Armenian "problem." Its suspicion of the pro-Russian sentiments of Armenians, its long-standing *revanchisme* in the wake of Ottoman defeats in the Balkans, years of resentment at British and French interventions, and above all, Russia's decisive defeat of Turkish forces in eastern Anatolia, where the Ottomans lost nearly eighty thousand soldiers, sparked genocide. In the spring of 1915, in the wake of a rebellion by Armenians at the Ottoman army's execution of five of their leaders, the shootings and pillaging began, followed by deportation of Armenians to its Arab provinces of Syria and Mosul. Confined to transit camps without food or water, forced into the desert or harsh mountain passages, shot and beaten along the way by Turks and Kurds both, the scale of the expulsion, which ultimately extended to the entire Anatolian Peninsula, was sufficient to demonstrate the government's intention, the outright extermination of a troublesome minority.

The genocide horrified the Germans in Turkey, who inadvertently became eyewitnesses. They included civilians such the pro-Armenian pastor Johannes Lepsius, and military and consular officers, such as Max von Scheubner-Richter, who later joined the Nazi Party as one of its earliest members, and even involved the deeply racist public intellectual Paul Rohrbach, who deemed Armenians capable of culture, unlike the Herero whose elimination he condoned while in service in Southwest Africa.[47] Nevertheless, possessing neither the linguistic skills nor the local knowledge that might have cautioned them against accepting the CUP's claim that the Armenians represented a dangerous fifth column, the German ambassador and German military officers attached to the Turkish army swallowed the official explanation of the Turkish authorities that "military necessity" made the deportations necessary. Despite Lepsius' efforts to document the crime, German public opinion extended little sympathy toward the Armenians.[48] If Imperial Germany's representatives in the Ottoman Empire did not aid the CUP in planning the genocide as was

---

[47] On Rohrbach, see Helmut Smith, *The Continuities of German History: Nation, Religion, and Race across the Long Nineteenth Century* (Cambridge: Cambridge University Press, 2008), 193–8, 204.

[48] The literature on the Armenian genocide is huge. In addition to Akçam, see Hull, *Absolute Destruction*, 263–90; Benjamin Lieberman, *The Terrible Fate: Ethnic Cleansing in the Making of Modern Europe* (Chicago: Ivan R. Dee, 2006), 98–114; Margaret Lavinia Anderson, "'Down in Turkey, far away': Human Rights, the Armenian Massacres,

once commonly asserted, German military habits of mind, which had long since recognized the abuse of civilians as integral to waging war, ensured an inconsistent and incoherent response. More to the point, if the CUP's campaign against the Armenians compromised the Ottomans' value as an ally by depriving its economy of the commercial skills and literacy of an important minority and diverted resources from its contribution to the war, the very objective of Germany's war, the enhancement of its global stature and imperial reach, invariably ruled out its intervention on behalf of the CUP's victims. In fact, the liberal imperialism that informed German activity in the Ottoman Empire since the first decade of the twentieth century derived from the German belief that the common experience of foreign intervention bound the Reich to the Ottomans. Just as in the past, the French had stood in the way of German aspirations to nationhood, so had the French and British blocked the Ottoman path to modernity and national consolidation.[49]

TOTAL WAR, DESPERATE MEASURES, AND THE END OF THE SECOND EMPIRE

Despite the resources that its occupation generated, Germany's liabilities exposed the long-term futility of enlarging its empire as the spoils of war. By 1916, the third year of the conflict, cumulative hardships experienced by civilians, the Supreme Command's increasingly intrusive and draconian management of civilian life, and the bitter and interrelated debate over war aims and political reform began to undermine the "peace of the fortress." The parties in which criticism of imperialist practices could be found, the Center, the Social Democrats, and the Progressives, became more vocal in the Reichstag as privations at home and the bloodletting abroad wore on their constituencies, who cared

and Orientalism in Wilhelmine Germany," *Journal of Modern History* 79, no. 1 (2007): 80–111. The view of Vahakn N. Dadrian, *German Responsibility in the Armenian Genocide: A Review of the Historical Evidence of German Complicity* (Watertown, MA: Blue Crane Books, 1996), that the German government was in on the planning of the genocide has been convincingly refuted by Donald Bloxham, *The Great Game of Genocide: Imperialism, Nationalism, and the Destruction of the Ottoman Armenians* (Oxford and New York: Oxford University Press, 2005), 115–33.

49 Malte Fuhrmann, "Germany's Adventures in the Orient: A History of Ambivalent Semi-Colonial Entanglements," in *Colonial (Dis)-Continuities: Race, Holocaust, and Postwar German*, eds. Volker Langbehn and Mohammad Salama (New York: Columbia University Press, 2010), and his *Der Traum vom deutschen Orient: Zwei deutsche Kolonien im Osmanischen Reich 1851–1918* (Frankfurt am Main: Campus, 2006), 109–382.

more for peace and the satisfaction of their hunger than annexations. Possessing fewer food supplies, natural resources, and manpower than the Entente, and fighting alongside allies who possessed smaller industrial bases, suffered massive internal tensions, and pursued war aims at odds with Germany's, the Second Empire's war moved closer to collapse, contrary to the wishful thinking of radical nationalists. Although the Imperial government and radical nationalist pressure groups succeeded in stifling the voices that favored a moderate peace and domestic reform for the first two years of the war, the opponents of annexations now became more competitive.

The year 1916 exemplified the meaning of "total war," a term that captures the enormous sacrifices in human life that the German government and military were prepared to make to stave off defeat. Expecting that the Austro-Hungarian armies would hold Russian forces in the east, Falkenhayn planned an offensive against France, which he believed was the Entente's weak link. Attacking the fortress in the French garrison town of Verdun in February, Falkenhayn hoped to decimate the French troops and force France to sue for peace and isolate the British. Yet despite German heavy artillery bombardment that enabled the military to take temporary possession of Fort Douaumont, the result was furious French resistance and a nine-month slaughter that, at the cost of 750,000 casualties on both sides, produced a net gain of three miles. In addition to having to commit forces to the bloody battle of the Somme that commenced in July, Falkenhayn had to divert troops to parry the Russian offensive in the east when Austria-Hungary diverted its troops to the Italian front. The naval standoff between Germany and Britain, which underscored the inadequacies of Tirpitz's expensive maritime project, proved inconclusive. Unable to patrol beyond the North Sea either to intercept commercial shipping or to break through the British blockade, the Germans had opted for unrestricted submarine warfare during the first fall of the war. Yet sinking ships without warning produced furious international protests in response. The torpedoing of the *Lusitania* in 1915, which entailed the loss of American civilians on board, threatened to bring the United States into the war. The Imperial government's and especially the kaiser's decision subsequently to suspend the attacks infuriated Tirpitz, whose insubordination caused Wilhelm to remove him from his position as state secretary in the naval ministry. Although British losses exceeded Germany's, the huge naval battle off the Jutland peninsula in May of 1916, failed to break the blockade.

In August, Romania's entry on the side of the Entente, occasioned by the Russian offensive and the Entente's agreement to Romania's annexation of Transylvania from Hungary, opened another front with which Germany would have to contend. Mounting criticism of Falkenhayn from senior army commanders pushed the kaiser to remove his chief of staff. Bethmann-Hollweg's reservations against unrestricted submarine warfare, which would only add to Germany's list of enemies, became increasingly neutralized. Wilhelm's chosen replacements for Falkenhayn, Field Marshal Hindenburg and General Ludendorff, proved momentous. Although the kaiser with good reason distrusted both as potential rivals who could displace him as the "people's tribune" – in fact, Hindenburg had come to personify the "spirit of 1914" better than the kaiser – their power base in the east, Falkenhayn's failed offensive, and mounting popular discontents left him with little choice. The emergence of the "heroes" of Tannenberg as virtual military dictators eclipsed Wilhelm's authority, brought more onerous demands on civilians to produce and sacrifice more, deepened domestic conflicts over war aims, and called the survival of the Bismarckian system into question.[50]

Confronted by battlefield stalemates that collectively boded ill for Germany's future, the new Supreme Command sought the total mobilization of the economy to boost production beyond what the militarily supervised war resource boards had to date accomplished. The Hindenburg Program and its subsidiary Auxiliary Service Law, modeled on Ludendorff's utopian initiatives in the Ober Ost,[51] envisioned huge increases in munitions, artillery, and machine guns by the spring of 1917 to be accomplished through the draft of an additional three million workers of both sexes between the ages of seventeen and sixty. Under the leadership of General Wilhelm Groener, who saw himself as the neutral mediator among industry, the state, and the military, the War Office of the Prussian Ministry of War centralized the acquisition and distribution of labor. Broadly comparable to the labor drafts in German-occupied Europe, the Auxiliary Service Law especially amounted to more than just

---

[50] For the documentary record of Wilhelm's insufficiencies as commander and his weakening influence after the first two years of the war, see Holger Afflerbach, *Kaiser Wilhelm II als oberster Kriegsherr in Ersten Weltkrieg: Quellen aus dem militärischen Umgebung des Kaisers 1914–1918* (Munich: R. Oldenbourg Verlag, 2005), and Afflerbach's summary, "Wilhelm II as supreme warlord in the First World War," in *The Kaiser: New Research on Wilhelm II's Role in Imperial Germany*, eds. Annika Mombauer and Wilhelm Deist (Cambridge: Cambridge University Press, 2003), 209–10. Pyta, *Hindenburg*, 91–113.

[51] Liulevicius, *War Land*, 55.

sheer fantasy. The attempt to efface the reality of insufficient manpower with a militarized vision of a self-sacrificing German "community" and the Supreme Command's belief in a compensatory act of will, introduced a distinctly fascist element into its programs. Yet, unlike the conditions in the occupied zones, Hindenburg and Ludendorff faced repeated challenges to their authority in the allocation of workers, food, and raw materials from civilian authorities in the Reich and state bureaucracies. Moreover, they had to make concessions to an increasingly vocal opposition in the Reichstag, even as they demonized as "internal enemies" the striking workers and women who resented being drafted to work in war industries.[52] Rather than win the Reichstag's unanimous and enthusiastic consent to the Hindenburg Program as the Supreme Command anticipated, the Social Democratic, Center, and Progressive parties instead wrested significant modifications to the Auxiliary Service Law. In return for approving the labor draft, workers won the right to representation on the military district and factory committees that allocated workers – committees that also arbitrated management-labor disputes. In addition, because neither industrialists nor the government could afford to alienate them, workers in munitions industries won the right to collective bargaining and the legal recognition of contracts arising from it. Rather than producing the militarized and hierarchical economy that Hindenburg and Ludendorff had hoped for, the result was a double dilemma. The Hindenburg Program not only failed to draft enough workers and significantly boost war-related production, it also emboldened the Reichstag's center-left coalition, gave a voice to the trade union leaderships, and spawned popular protests against worsening material conditions and a Supreme Command that promised continued authoritarianism and war without end.

Although the leftward swing of the 1912 elections spawned a radical nationalist counterattack in the Cartel of Productive Estates, the new center-left majority would hold the potential for increasing the influence of the Reichstag when circumstances warranted it. Despite the heavy battlefield casualties and the unpopularity of censorship, however, the victories of 1915 muted the opposition until food shortages, inflation, and exhausting workdays grew acute. The war unleashed a nationwide grassroots war

[52] MacGregor Knox, *To the Threshold of Power, 1922/33: Origins and Dynamics of the Fascist and National Socialist* Dictatorships, vol. 1 (Cambridge: Cambridge University Press, 2007), 227; Sven Oliver Müller, *Die Nation als Waffe und Vorstellung: Nationalismus in Deutschland und Grossbritannien im Ersten Weltkrieg* (Göttingen: Vandehoeck and Ruprecht, 2002), 223–37.

relief effort, particularly by women's organizations, which recast the political culture of the Kaiserreich in a less elitist and more populist direction.[53] Yet such demonstrations of popular commitment faded as the imperial and state governments proved increasingly unable to ensure an adequate food supply. Well-organized strikes on bread-and-butter issues, organized by the Social Democratic Party, began in the spring of 1916 and comprised the immediate context for the revisions to the Auxiliary Service Law, but they also pointed to chronic hardships that mocked the "peace of the fortress." Inflation, arising from the government's issuance of paper money not backed by gold, its inability to regulate wages and profits, and its decision to finance the war's spiraling costs by selling war bonds rather than raising taxes, hit salaried employees and white-collar workers particularly hard.[54] Skilled workers in war-related industries fared better because of their bargaining power. Regardless, higher prices for basic necessities, housing, fuel, soap, and clothing, and the disappearance of meat, fats, and butter, inequities in the rationing system, and the seemingly endless ersatz foods increased popular dissatisfaction, especially among workers in small shops who did not earn the high wages of munitions workers. In the words of one historian, "[s]carcity ruled the kitchen. So the dining table became the site of a daily ordeal. Foods appeared in ever more distasteful monotony and decreasing portions, which turned the term 'peacetime' (*friedensmässig*)) into a measure of opulence."[55] Morale suffered even in agricultural regions, such as southern Bavaria, where food supplies remained adequate despite the military's appropriation of draft animals and the decline of fodder and artificial fertilizers. Peasant women, forced to cope with the absence of male relatives, suffered from exhaustion and declining health as they struggled to farm with minimal help. Their inclination earlier in the war to interpret the loss of male relatives as "God's will," subsided with the growing conviction that the conflict was creating selfish and sinister war profiteers who benefited at the expense of the poor.[56]

By the winter of 1916 and 1917, a crisis confronted the Imperial government when the unseasonably cold weather that wiped out the potato crop compounded ongoing failures to ensure food deliveries. As

---

[53] Peter Fritzsche, *Germans into Nazis* (Cambridge, MA and London: Harvard University Press, 1998), 34–66.

[54] Gerald D. Feldman, *The Great Disorder: Politics, Economics, and Society in the German Inflation 1914–1924* (Oxford and New York: Oxford University Press, 1997), 25–51.

[55] Chickering, *Great War*, 266.

[56] Ziemann, *War Experiences*, 155–66.

a result, Germans were forced to eat the more weather-resistant turnip, which was normally used as animal fodder. In addition to provoking conflict in cities over the allocation of rations, the shortages and the measures taken to remedy them produced bitter division between town and countryside. In 1914, the government instituted its Controlled Economy, which imposed price ceilings on agricultural commodities in order to protect urban consumers from skyrocketing food prices. Although largely a failure, the new policy undermined the privileged position of farmers large and small, who had benefited from the artificially high prices induced by prewar tariff protection. In addition to price freezes, agricultural producers resented the military officers and local constables who seized livestock and grain, and the judges who imposed hefty fines on farmers who failed to comply. Urban consumers became accustomed to blaming peasants for hoarding and for exorbitant black market prices, while peasants in return complained that their food rations fell short of those of workers in war-related industries.[57] The urban-rural divide would persist after 1918 because the Weimar Republic's political divisions reproduced the clashing economic interests of urban consumers and rural producers.

Food demonstrations led by urban women became regular occurrences, indicative of the eroding confidence in the government and the growing self-assertion from below.[58] The declining availability of food disproportionately affected those who were least engaged in the war effort. Mortality rates for the very young and very old increased alarmingly. So did those of asylum and sanatorium patients, who in addition to ranking at the bottom of the pecking order in the assignment of rations, could neither hoard food when the supply permitted nor travel to the countryside on foraging expeditions. As a result, according to one estimate, over seventy thousand patients died of hunger, disease, and neglect.[59] Their disposability would serve as an ominous precedent for the future, as scarcity would encourage the hierarchical ranking of citizens according to

[57] On the impact of the Controlled Economy, see Robert G. Moeller, *German Peasants and Agrarian Politics, 1914–1924* (Chapel Hill and London: University of North Carolina Press, 1986), 43–67; Martin Schumacher, *Land und Politik:eine Untersuchung über politische Parteien und agrarische Interessen 1914–1923* (Düsseldorf: Droste Verlag, 1978), 33–84; Jens Flemming, *Landwirtschaftliche Interessen und Demokratie: Ländliche Gesellschaft, Agrarverbände und Staat 1890–1925* (Bonn: Verlag Neue Gesellschaft, 1978); and most recently, Ziemann, *War Experiences*, 166–81.

[58] Davis, *Home Fires Burning*, 137–218.

[59] Michael Burleigh, *Death and Deliverance:"Euthanasia" in Germany, 1900–1945* (Cambridge: Cambridge University Press, 1994), 11.

their ability to produce for the *Volk* "community." Comparative data for London, Paris, and Berlin underscored the "demographic crisis" that beset Germany between 1917 and 1919. While Berlin compared favorably with London and Paris in the life expectancy of its citizens before August 1914 and for the first two years of the war, the city's "excess deaths" afterward, particularly among infants, children, and women of all ages, illustrated the extent to which the Imperial government's inability to sustain public health had a deleterious impact. The scourges of measles, influenza, and tuberculosis took their toll.[60]

Battlefield reverses and the crisis in provisioning at home strengthened the case for the resumption of unrestricted submarine warfare against allied and neutral shipping. In February of 1917, Ludendorff, backed by a reluctant kaiser, committed himself to that course knowing that the United States, having previously endorsed Belgium's independence and having rejected a German-dominated Central Europe as inimical to its economic interests, would likely enter the war in support of the Entente.[61] In a clumsy attempt to tie the hands of the United States if it declared war on Germany, Germany encouraged Mexico to attack the United States in return for regaining Texas and New Mexico. Although gambling that U-boats would sink enough Allied ships to undermine the blockade, Ludendorff's decision brought an American declaration of war in April, exacerbating Germany's strategic bottleneck and further inflaming domestic political divisions at home. The huge American productive capacity and the prospect of fresh American troops in Europe to support the Entente made a German defeat ever more likely.[62]

Despite the Reichstag's modifications to the Auxiliary Service Law, the strikes continued into 1917 and 1918. The grievances expressed in them grew increasingly political, moving beyond bread-and-butter issues to demands for an immediate negotiated peace without annexations and constitutional reform at home. In April of 1917, in the wake of the February revolution in Russia and the overthrow of Tsar Nicholas II, the radicalization of industrial workers deepened divisions within the Social Democratic Party that had festered over the question as

---

[60] Jay Winter, "Surviving the War: life expectation, illness, and morality rates in Paris, London, and Berlin, 1914–1919," in *Capital Cities at War: Paris, London, Berlin 1914–1919* (Cambridge: Cambridge University Press, 1997), 487–523.

[61] Rainer Pommerin, *Der Kaiser und Amerika: Die USA in der Politik der Reichsleitung 1890–1917* (Cologne and Vienna: Böhlau Verlag, 1986), 344–76.

[62] Christopher Clark, *Kaiser Wilhelm II: Profiles in Power* (London: Longman, 2000), 235–6.

to whether to continue to finance the war. The party formally divided into the Majority Socialist Democratic Party (MSPD), which advocated support for the government as a means of winning political reforms, and the Independent Social Democratic Party (USPD), which refused to endorse war credits and opposed the Auxiliary Service Law. Even the USPD was beset by division between those who sought constitutional reform and the Spartacists, who called for anticapitalist revolution. Wilson's preference for a democratic Germany as a negotiating partner and the threat of a spillover of the revolution in Russia prompted the reformist coalition in the Reichstag to push its own agenda. Consisting of Majority Socialists, the Center, including its one-time imperialist leader, Matthias Erzberger, and the Progressives, who abandoned their imperialism in the wake of popular disaffection, the coalition passed a resolution in July 1917 that called for peace without annexations or reparations. In so doing, it withdrew its backing from the beleaguered Bethmann-Hollweg, whose tacking between reform and reaction, nego- tiated peace and annexations, failed to convince either the left or the right of his sincerity.

In fact, Bethmann-Hollweg's tentative overtures to the Reichstag, as well as the kaiser's own desperate attempts in his April 1917 Easter Message to pacify restive workers with the promise to eliminate the unequal and discriminatory three-class franchise in Prussia, gener- ated a new counteroffensive from the right. Bethmann-Hollweg's dis- missal and replacement by the stolid but effective Prussian bureaucrat Georg Michelis, instigated by the Supreme Command shortly after the Reichstag peace resolution, demonstrated the right's hostility to the chan- cellor's accommodations to the Reichstag and his less bellicose stand on submarine warfare. Moreover, the Supreme Command's determination to annex the Ober Ost and Ludendorff's attempt to guarantee sufficient manpower, resources, and land for German settlements, led in August of 1917 to the formation of the German Fatherland Party. As an umbrella organization founded by Alfred Tirpitz and Wolfgang Kapp, the new association brought together the radical nationalist and imperialist pres- sure groups, peasant and lower-middle-class interest groups, academics, industrialists, especially in heavy industry, estate owners, senior civil ser- vants, and militant annexationists in the military, and leading voices of the conservative and liberal parties. Like the prewar Cartel of Productive Estates, the Fatherland Party challenged the legitimacy of the Reichstag. Yet its sophisticated deployment of modern propaganda represented an important if unstable milestone in the development of a populist, racially

obsessed right.[63] Although dominated by prewar radical nationalist leaders, the new party's platforms incorporated vociferously populist appeals
in an attempt to harness the mass politicization that the war generated. In
addition to including anti-emancipationist women, who claimed a public
forum to articulate their vision of the nation's core values, the populist
surge combined a distrust of the monarchy for being too faint-hearted
in the pursuit of victory abroad and the containment of reformism at
home. It also endorsed a boundless expansionism untempered by the
harsh realities of Germany's military position.[64] As well as radicalizing
themes popular on the right since 1890, updated by its perceptions of
the sources of Germany's wartime predicaments, the Fatherland Party's
unambiguous biological racism attracted eugenicists who advocated sterilization and other means of eradicating undesirable traits from the Volk
"body." Rejecting constitutional reform, it proposed, in the words of one
historian, a "Bonapartist synthesis of military victory and popular military dictatorship."[65]

The Fatherland Party vented an abiding hostility toward Jews, who
personified socialism, democratic reformism, peace without annexations,
materialism, and speculation. The party's targets included corporate
"profiteers" such as the industrialist Walter Rathenau and the shipping
magnate Albert Ballin, "shirkers" who avoided military service, Eastern
European Jews whose immigration German Jews were supposed to have
aided, and the press that spread democratic or socialist "poison." It was
the most obvious expression of an increasingly vocal antisemitism that
by late 1916, provoked the military to take a census of Jews in its ranks,
in essence legitimating the myth of Jewish "shirkers." The party's multiple
hatreds testified to the collapse of the communal myth of 1914 and the
adoption of a vision of exclusionary racial "community" purged of undesirables and "enemies" that had put down roots before 1914 among radical

---

[63] Breundel, *Volksgemeinschaft oder Volksstaat*, 149–50. In rejecting earlier scholarly characterizations of the party as "pre-fascist," Heinz Hagenlücke's, *Deutsche
Vaterlandspartei: Die nationale rechte am Ende des Kaiserreiches* (Düsseldorf: Droste
Verlag, 1997), 248–71 and 388–411, suggests that its temporary success in mobilizing
broad constituencies could not conceal the long-term fecklessness of the prewar right's
populism.

[64] Elizabeth Harvey, "Visions of the Volk: German Women on the Far Right from the
Kaiserreich to the Third Reich, *Journal of Women's History* 16, no. 3 (2004): 155; van
Laak, *Imperiale Infrastruktur*, 178–80.

[65] Raffael Scheck, *Alfred von Tirpitz and German Right-Wing Politics, 1914–1930* (New
Jersey: Humanities Press, 1998), 67.

nationalists.[66] Acting on behalf of Germany's foreign foes, Jews conspired to destroy from within politically and biologically. Artur Dinter's spectacularly successful trilogy *Sins against the Blood*, the first volume of which appeared in 1917, powerfully reinforced widespread fears of contamination. The story woven by the war veteran, who would become one of the first members of the Nazi Party, melodramatically spun the tragic tale of an innocent German hero who married a half-Jewish woman. Although the hero's wife was a Christian, conversion provided no immunity against disaster as the couple's first child reproduced the hideously Jewish and apelike features of its mother. The legacy of the hero's sexual contact with a Jew follow him despite taking an Aryan woman as his second wife, for even that union produced a monster. *Sins against the Blood* went into fifteen editions and reached 1.5 million readers.[67]

The Fatherland Party failed to intimidate the Reichstag, which passed another resolution in October to abolish the discriminatory franchise in Prussia. Yet Russia's military weakness and the overthrow of tsarism in February of 1917 provided the Supreme Command with a golden opportunity to anchor German control of Eastern Europe permanently. Having already declared a future Polish kingdom in November of 1916, an entity with no discernible territorial integrity or independence, Bethmann-Hollweg proclaimed the creation of satellite states in Courland and Lithuania in April of 1917 at the command's urging. Although amounting to less than the outright annexation that Ludendorff had demanded and promising to forego attempts to Germanize local peoples, Ludendorff neither sacrificed his ambitions nor his expansive vision of an eastern empire, the resources of which would ensure German power in the future. In addition to offering land for German settlements, Courland and Lithuania would provide food and labor for a future war against Britain and the United States. The detailed plans of the head of the Ober Ost's interior ministry, Wilhelm Freiherr von Gayl, whose previous experience included directing the East Prussian Settlement Society, mapped out German fortifications, garrisons, settlements, and a customs union to

---

[66] Christhard Hoffmann, "Between integration and rejection: the Jewish community in Germany, 1914–1918," in *State, society and mobilization in Europe during the First World War*, ed. John Horne (Cambridge: Cambridge University Press, 1997): 89–104, Breundel, *Volksstaat oder Volksgemeinschaft*, 283–4. On the radicalization of antisemitism during the war and afterwards, see Werner Jochmann, *Gesellschaftskrise und Judenfeindschaft in Deutschland 1870–1945* (Hamburg: Hans Christians Verlag, 1988), 99–170.

[67] Cornelia Essner, *Die "Nürnberger Gesetze" oder die Verwaltung des Rassenwahns 1933–1945* (Paderborn: Ferdinand Schöningh, 2002), 32–4.

unite the economies of the new border states with Germany's.[68] Uniting the governor and Supreme Commander of the military in the same office, the new entities would answer only to the emperor.

The Bolshevik overthrow of the Russian provisional government in November of 1917, which the Supreme Command had indirectly aided by returning the Bolshevik leader, Vladimir Lenin, to St. Petersburg in a sealed train car earlier that year, promised to turn German dreams into reality. The Bolshevik armies could not withstand the German advance, which by February of 1918 had moved beyond Riga to Dorpat and Reval, putting St. Petersburg at risk. The Treaty of Brest-Litovsk between Germany and the Soviet Union, which was signed on March 3, 1918, and which the Germans imposed on the new Bolshevik government, was, to put it charitably, punitive. In addition to encouraging Finland, the Baltic States, and the Ukraine to withdraw from Russia and become client states of Germany, the Soviets were forced to cede portions of Poland and Belorussia, and three Armenian districts in the Caucasus to Turkey. The treaty essentially restored Turkey's pre-1879 frontiers, leaving the affected Armenians to a miserable fate at the hands of their nemesis. Altogether, Russia lost one million square miles of territory, fifty million of its population, nearly all of its coal and oil, three-quarters of its iron ore, half of its industry, and one-third of its railroads and agricultural lands. If the treaty necessitated the commitment of close to one million German troops to police the territories, thus reducing the number that could be sent to the western front, it nonetheless revealed the manner in which the war translated Pan German pipedreams into reality. The independence movements that mushroomed in the wake of the Russian Empire's fragmentation, especially Lithuania's, were ruthlessly suppressed. The military placed Baltic Germans at the head of local administrations, introduced censorship, and launched Germanization in the schools. Between Brest-Litovsk and the armistice, Germany installed a puppet government in Ukraine, subverting a Ukrainian independence movement that the Austro-Hungarian occupation had supported. Although the German military was ill-positioned to manage the huge expanse of territory under its control, its ambitions testified to the manner in which annexationism thrived during the latter phases of the war.[69] The Treaty of Bucharest with Romania, signed in

---

[68] Liulevicius, *War Land*, 202.
[69] Mark von Hagen, *War in a European Borderland: Occupations and Occupation Plans in Galicia and Ukraine, 1914–1918* (Seattle: University of Washington Press, 2007), 87–106.

May of 1918, demonstrated as well the temporary triumph of German imperialism. The defeat of Romania, after which the German occupation extracted huge amounts of Romanian grain and bankrupted Romania's economy, laid the groundwork for a pact that allowed Germany access to Romanian oil feeds for ninety years, securing an additional fuel supply for the empire of the future.[70]

Emboldened by the Brest-Litovsk agreement, Ludendorff launched a breakthrough attack in the west in the spring of 1918, believing that a final massive and victorious assault – one undertaken with no fewer than 192 divisions – would preserve the dream of German continental hegemony and undermine reformism at home. The Entente's counterattack and the subsequent failure of the spring offensive, which by the end of June cost Germany over nine hundred thousand casualties, exposed the hollowness of Ludendorff's gamble. By the end of the first week in August, the revival of the Entente's forces, replenished by an influx of 250,000 Americans every month, demoralized German enlisted men and officers enough to encourage their surrender, pulled the rug out from under Ludendorff, and set the stage for an Allied thrust through German lines.[71] The Turkish pursuit of Pan Turkish ambitions in the Caucasus, which left Mesopotamia open to Entente forces, the collapse of the Austro-Hungarian army, and Bulgaria's withdrawal from the war left the Germans badly exposed in the east. Nevertheless, if the Second Empire would not outlive military and domestic collapse, the annexationists' influence in high level circles and the military's control of information would persist.

In late September of 1918, the disintegrating state of affairs on the battlefield prompted Ludendorff to propose the formation of a government composed of the reformist parties of the Reichstag, the Progressives, Social Democrats, and the Center. It would ask for an armistice that would allow the army a respite to regroup for the "final struggle" (*Endkampf*), an apocalyptic, military-led popular uprising in the west, an evocation of the resistance against Napoleon. In staging a national rebirth to follow the impending military catastrophe, Ludendorff sought to protect the army from annihilation so that it could be used to prevent a Russian-style revolution at home that would destroy the military's power. He also

[70] David Hamlin, "'*Dummes Geld*': Money, Grain, and the Occupation of Romania in WWI." *Central European History* 42, no. 3 (2009): 451–71.
[71] Kramer, *Dynamics of Destruction*, 269–71. On the collapse of morale in the German army in the west, see Alexander Watson, *Enduring the Great War: Combat, Morale and Collapse in the German and British Armies, 1914–1918* (Cambridge: Cambridge University Press, 2008), 184–231.

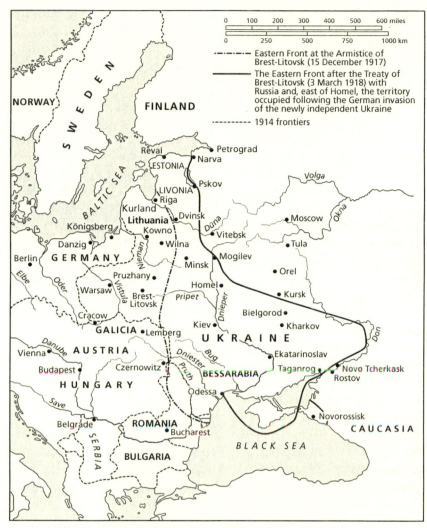

MAP 2.3. The German east after the Treaty of Brest-Litovsk, March 1918. Imperial Germany's sizeable gains at the expense of the Soviet Union would make it difficult even after its defeat to discredit the expansionist ambitions that had been central to the German war effort.

Source: Vejas Gabriel Liulevicius, *War Land on the Eastern Front: National Identity and German Occupation in World War I* (Cambridge: Cambridge University Press, 2000), 207.

hoped to extract favorable terms from the Entente, which did not want a repetition of the events in Russia. Germany would retain its gains of Brest-Litovsk, adjust the Franco-German border in Germany's favor, and impose German suzereignty over Belgium.[72] If he could not win those concessions, Ludendorff reasoned, Social Democrats, Catholics, and Progressives would assume the unpleasant responsibility of accepting the defeat. On October 4th, the kaiser appointed a new chancellor, Prince Max von Baden, whose opposition to unrestricted submarine warfare, the Supreme Command believed, would allow it to negotiate favorable armistice terms with President Wilson. He assumed power with the support of a reformist coalition which, in return for its participation, demanded that cabinet ministers be drawn from the leading parties in the Reichstag.

Events overtook Ludendorff's scheming, however. Prince Max and the Reichstag majority entertained their own popular *levée en masse* to defend the integrity of German territory, hoping that peace factions in the Entente nations would push their governments to conclude a fair and nonannexationist peace. Yet, by the end of October, Prince Max was forced to propose an armistice on the basis of the American president's Fourteen Points, and not just because of the continued Allied advances in the west. Indicative of widespread popular war weariness, disgruntled sailors in the North Sea port city of Kiel rebelled against their officers' orders to attack the British at sea in a last desperate battle. Their uprising launched a nationwide revolution, in which workers' and soldiers' councils, inspired by the Soviet model, compromised the government's control of events. After an extended debate over a plan initiated by the Supreme Command, which would have staged the kaiser's heroic death at the front to salvage the army's honor, Wilhelm abdicated and fled ignominiously to the Netherlands. For his part, Prince Max handed over the Reich chancellorship to Friedrich Ebert, the Majority Socialist leader. Ironically, the provisional government planned a popular uprising of national self-defense *against* Ludendorff's call for an immediate armistice. Although aborted by the pressure of events, the ruling coalition subsequently faced a barrage of radical nationalist invective, which accused "Marxists, pacifists, and Jews" of stabbing Germany in the back.[73] The Allied armistice terms

---

[72] Isabel Hull, "Military culture, Wilhelm II, and the end of the monarchy in the First World War," in *The Kaiser: New Research on Wilhelm II's Role in Imperial* Germany, eds. Annika Mombauer and Wilehlm Deist (Cambridge: Cambridge University Press, 2003), 251, and *Absolute Destruction*, 310–1.

[73] On this episode and the final discrediting of the Kaiser, see Michael Geyer, "Insurrectionary Warfare: The German Debate about a *Levée en masse* in October 1918, *The Journal*

seemed only to justify such a view: Germany was required to withdraw its armies east of the Rhine, repudiate the Brest-Litovsk Treaty, and surrender its fleet. To ensure Germany's cooperation, the Allied blockade remained in force.

The military's ability to shape the interpretation through which the German public would view military defeat owed not a little to the inability of the center-left coalition to push for major structural reforms after the kaiser abdicated. The opposition of the Progressives and Center to socializing the means of production reinforced the Majority Socialists' own reluctance to transform the economy or to challenge the existing economic, military, and bureaucratic leaderships. Had not the kaiser abdicated, the Majority Socialists would have accepted a constitutional monarchy. Their leaders, Ebert and Philipp Scheidemann, expected that fundamental social change and the socialization of the economy would evolve after the establishment of a liberal democracy, in which the Socialists would pull in enough votes to command a parliamentary majority. In the interim, Ebert concluded an agreement on November 10th with Ludendorff's successor as chief of staff of the Supreme Command, Wilhelm Groener, which promised that the army would support the new government and keep order in return for the government's protection of the army from reforms that would degrade the status of the officer corps. Several days later, an agreement between the Social Democratic trade union leader Karl Legien and the industrialist Hugo Stinnes ensured the recognition of trade unions by employers, collective bargaining, and the eight-hour day in return for the abandonment of socialization. The MSPD's concessions, however, divided the labor movement, and left in place institutions and leaders with little motivation to support the government beyond their fear of a more radical revolution. In fact, the Majority Socialists' willingness to secure the army against structural reform enabled its use as a force against popular revolution, and especially the uprising of the Spartacists, who in early 1919 were summarily crushed. The Russian Revolution had become a cautionary tale for the new coalition, which feared that it could succumb to a Bolshevik-style coup like the Russian Republic. The Majority Socialists especially preferred orderly change under the leadership of the party to the spontaneous and difficult-to-control workers' and soldiers' councils that sprouted up in November 1918 following the Kiel mutiny.

of Modern History 73 (2001): 459–527; and Martin Kohlrausch, *Der Kaiser im Skandal: Die Logik der Massenmedien und die Transformation der wilhelminischen Monarchie* (Berlin: Akademie Verlag, 2005), 302–85.

The Provisional Government's loathing of revolution entailed yet another consequence. The expansionist ambitions that were so central to Germany's conduct of the war would not be discredited despite defeat and popular war weariness. Before the Constitutional Convention in February of 1919, Ebert complained that the peace negotiations then taking place in Paris had abandoned Wilson's Fourteen Points. Germany, he said, was being forced to cede territories that it occupied and the economic proposals of the peacemakers professed little more than "enslavement."[74] Moreover, thousands of soldiers left rootless by the armistice found a new purpose in the postwar "shatter zone" that was Eastern Europe. Led by their officers to whom they declared their sole allegiance, ex-soldiers coalesced into paramilitary units known as the Free Corps (*Freikorps*) and became hired guns who modeled themselves after the free booters of the Thirty Years War. In addition to giving an occupation to former soldiers after the collapse of the Second Empire, the Free Corps became anti-Marxist shock troops at home and abroad. Internally, the Majority Socialist Defense Minister Gustav Noske authorized the formation of paramilitary units on January 4, 1919, to assist the army in quelling the Spartacists and killing their leaders, Karl Liebknecht and Rosa Luxembourg. In the east, Free Corps units, often organized by Baltic Germans whom Ludendorff had placed as heads of local administrations during the final months of the war, took up arms against the Red Army, which, following the German Provisional Government's renunciation of Brest-Litovsk, pushed westward to reclaim the lost Russian territories. Wantonly spilling blood, Free Corps men adopted multiple identities. They imagined themselves variously as crusaders in the tradition of the Teutonic Knights' "drive to the East" (*Drang nach Osten*) or colonizers akin to European settlers who tamed the "wild West" and Africa. Acting out the drama of German nationalism, they envisioned themselves as the last heroic bulwark against the Bolshevik "flood" and certain annihilation. Should they succeed in destroying their enemy, the free booters would reap their reward, a huge expanse without borders open to them for conquest and settlement.[75]

---

74 Eric D. Wietz, *Weimar Germany: Promise and Tragedy* (Princeton and London: Princeton University Press, 2007), 32.
75 Lieulevicius, *War Land*, 227–46. On the obsessions of Free Corps men, Klaus Theweleit's, *Männerphantasien*, vol. 1, Frauen, *Fluten, Körper, Geschichte, and* vol. 2, *Männerkörper: Zur Psychoanalyse des Weissen Terrors.* (Frankfurt am Main: Verlag Roter Stern, 1977 and 1979) was pioneering. The English translation is *Male Fantasies*, vol. 1, *Women, Floods, Bodies, History*, and vol. 2, *Male Bodies: Psychoanalyzing the*

Noske, a member of the Social Democratic Party's imperialist wing that came of age in the decade before the war, grew decidedly uncomfortable with the violent and crass colonialism of the Baltic Free Corps units, who in his view, exceeded their assigned defensive mission.[76] Nevertheless, German and Entente interests converged in the desirability of blocking the westward expansion of Bolshevism. Unable to halt the invasion of the "Reds," the Entente materially underwrote Baltic independence movements and looked the other way as the Free Corps exploited the terms of the armistice agreement, which allowed German troops to remain in the east as an anti-Soviet bulwark. For its part, the Provisional Government saw the Free Corps as a useful bargaining chip in the ongoing peace negotiations in Paris.[77] Only the success of the Lithuanian and Latvian armies in pushing back the Free Corps into Prussian territory, after having themselves contributed to repelling the Bolshevik advance, brought about the Free Corps' demobilization. Even the signing of the Versailles Treaty in June of 1919 did not bring their eastern adventures to conclusion. The legacies of the Ober Ost, Brest-Litovsk, and the Free Corps, which fed directly into the putschism of the early Weimar Republic, would keep alive the annexationists' demands for *Lebensraum* in the east.

The Weimar Republic formally came into being in June of 1919 as a liberal democracy with constitutionally protected civil liberties, equal voting rights for all its citizens, equality between men and women, and ministerial responsibility to the Reichstag. Its constitution stipulated extensive social welfare provisions, arguably the most progressive in Europe, as entitlements.[78] Yet its ruling coalition was saddled with a double dilemma: the entrenchment of much of the Wilhelmine leadership and a treaty that ratified the termination of the Second Empire and its substitution by a territorially truncated republican nation state.[79] Signed under

White Terror, trans. Erica Carter and Chris Turner (Minneapolis: University of Minnesota Press, 1987 and 1989).

[76] See Noske's memoir, *Von Kiel bis Kapp: Zur Geschichte der deutschen Revolution* (Berlin: Verlag für Politik und Wirtschaft, 1920), 175–85.

[77] For the contributions of anti-Bolshevism to the postwar peace settlement, Arno J. Mayer's *Politics and Diplomacy of Peace-Making: Containment and Counterrevolution at Versailles, 1918–1919* (New York: Alfred A. Knopf, 1967) is indispensable. See esp. 284–343.

[78] See Weitz, *Weimar Germany*, 32–3.

[79] Philipp Ther, "Deutsche Geschichte als imperiale Geschichte: Polen, slawophone Minderheiten und das Kaiserreich als kontintales Empire," in *Das Kaiserreich transnational: Deutschland in der Welt 1871–1914*, eds. Sebastian Conrad and Jürgen Osterhammel (Göttingen: Vandenhoeck and Ruprecht, 2004), 145.

duress during the same month that the republic came to life, the Treaty of
Versailles was a catastrophe for most Germans, not just radical nationalists. It stripped Germany of 10 percent of its population and 13 percent of its territory, including Alsace and Lorraine, Northern Schleswig,
Memel, Posen, much of West Prussia, and Upper Silesia.[80] The Saarland
was placed under a fifteen-year mandate, while the Baltic port of Danzig
with its predominantly German population became a "free city" under
the League of Nations' supervision, surrounded by the new Polish state.
The Rhineland was demilitarized. Although the territorial adjustments of
Versailles paled in comparison to Brest-Litovsk and left the core of the
Bismarckian Reich intact, the forced decolonization of much Prussian
territory and the loss of Alsace on top of Lorraine entailed the diplomatic
negation of Prussia's long preunification history as a colonial power.

To add to those indignities, the treaty drastically reduced the size of
the German army, renamed the Reichswehr, to a 125,000-man defensive force with an officer corps of twenty-five hundred. To avoid turning over its ships to the British, the German admiralty scuttled much
of its navy in the Scapa Flow off the coast of Scotland. Despite the disintegration of the Austro-Hungarian Empire, the desire of the Austrian
National Assembly in Vienna to unite with Germany, and the Weimar
government's own desire for a merger of the two nations came to naught.
Refusing to heed the argument that the annexation of Austria would
legitimate the republic by rooting it in Germany's pre-1871 past,[81] the
Allies forbade it because the enlarged Germany would threaten France.
In addition to the cession of Prussian territory, Article 32 of the treaty
stripped Germany of its overseas colonies, which it placed under Entente
mandates. According to the victors, Germany's "uncivilized" conduct as
a colonial power had deprived it of the moral authority that defined a
"civilized" nation. Neither fully sovereign nor even "European" in the
eyes of the Entente, Germany had become in the eyes of many Germans
no more than a colony of the victors. The so-called "war guilt" clause of
the treaty, which provided the legal grounds for forcing Germany to pay
reparations, was but the last in a series of humiliations that removed it
from the ranks of the great powers. Although the Weimar cabinet recognized the Imperial government's role in starting the war based on its
examination of foreign office documents, Ebert and Scheidemann kept

[80] Strahan, *First World War*, 353.
[81] Gerwarth, *Bismarck Myth*, 35.

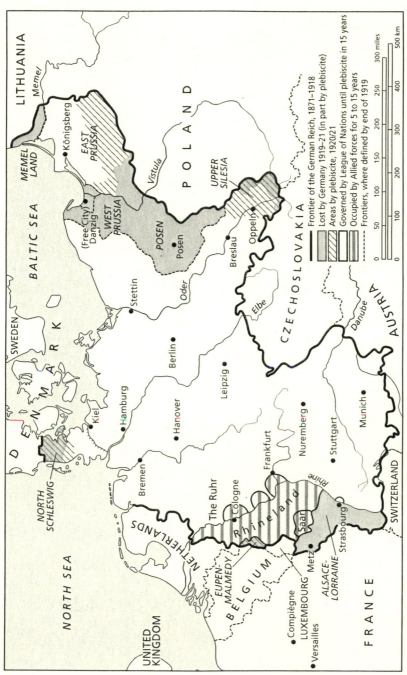

MAP 2.4. Germany after the Versailles Treaty. For most Germans, the Versailles settlement, or "dictated peace," represented the colonial subjugation of their country by the Entente.

Source: Richard J. Evans, *The Coming of the Third Reich* (New York: Penguin Press, 2004), 64.

Legend:

- Frontier of the German Reich, 1871–1918
- Lost by Germany 1919–21 (in part by plebiscite)
- Areas by plebiscite, 1920/21
- Governed by League of Nations until plebiscite in 15 years
- Occupied by Allied forces for 5 to 15 years
- Frontiers, where defined by end of 1919

0   50   100   150   200   250   300 miles
0   100   200   300   400   500 km

their reservations private so as not to alienate the army, the civil service, and middle-class opinion.[82]

The shock of the peace terms resulted from more than censorship, although it had concealed from popular view the extent of the German military's collapse on the western front and the weakness of its allies in the east and southeast. No doubt the naiveté of the German delegation to Paris led by Count Ulrich von Brockdorff-Rantzau, which believed that it would agree to terms consistent with Wilson's Fourteen Points, contributed its share to the German public's outrage.[83] The manner in which Versailles contradicted Germany's apparent success in achieving its imperialist designs proved to be even more important. The public adoration of Paul von Lettow-Vorbeck, who with the support of the German colonial administration in East Africa and native Askaris carried the war against the British, South Africans, French, Belgians, and Portuguese into Kenya, kept the vision of African colonies alive beyond Lettow-Vorbeck's sullen and begrudged surrender two weeks after the armistice. Sanctioned by the provisional government, Lettow-Vorbeck received a triumphal parade through Berlin's Brandenburg Gate in March of 1919. Challenging the Entente's accusation of an "uncivilized" Germany, he personified the courageous and unbowed masculine hero whose intrinsic gifts of heroic leadership won the loyalty of his African soldiers.[84] The Provisional Government's repudiation of Germany's one-time bonanza, the Treaty of Brest-Litovsk, had done nothing to discourage German commanders in the east from pursuing their dreams of colonization, especially because the government's priority, defeating Bolshevism, took precedence over renouncing colonialism. Upon their return from the Baltic, the seemingly disciplined Free Corps units visually sustained the myth of unconquered German men in arms betrayed by Marxist, Jewish, and pacifist "enemies" at home.[85] Tolerated for a time by the Entente as a bulwark against the westward march of Lenin's armies, the Free Corps' mission, simultaneously anti-Bolshevik and imperialist, would keep continental colonial ambitions alive under the Weimar Republic.

---

[82] Marcia Klotz, "Global Visions: From the Colonial to National Socialist World," *European Studies Journal* 16, no. 2 (1999): 57–9; Knox, *To the Threshold of Power*, 235–6.

[83] See Margaret MacMillan, *Paris 1919: Six Months that Changed the World* (New York: Random House, 2001), 460–67.

[84] Van Laak, *Imperiale Infrastruktur*, 197; Sandra Mass, *Weisse Helden, schwarzer Krieger: Zur Geschichte kolonialer Männlichkeit in Deutschland, 1918–1964* (Cologne: Böhlau, 2006), 34–9

[85] Liulevicius, *War Land*, 243.

FIGURE 2.2. General Paul von Lettow-Vorbeck leading his troops in the parade to celebrate his homecoming. Similar to the "triumph" at Brest-Litovsk, the seemingly unbowed East African protection forces under Lettow-Vorbeck's command sustained the myth of a militarily undefeated Germany.
Source: Bundesarchiv Koblenz, B145 Bild-008268.

The contradiction between "victories" seemingly won on the battlefield and the Entente's humiliating peace treaty hit especially hard because of the French occupation of the Rhineland. The deployment of some forty thousand French soldiers, which included French colonial troops from the Maghreb, French West Africa, Madagascar, and a few from Southeast Asia, appeared to overturn the "normal" hierarchies of Europeans over the colonized indigenes. Already an issue during the war when the British and French threw colonial troops against the German lines, which confirmed Germany's superiority over the west in the eyes of German intellectuals,[86] the presence of "subhuman beasts" on German soil signified the hideous degradation of German culture. Although the incidence of sexual assaults against German women usually involved white soldiers, the dread of sexual contact between French colonial troops and German women raised the specter of racial contamination infecting the very heart of the German family and nation, a contamination that overflowed the dykes of apartheid that undergirded German colonial

[86] Jelavich, "German Culture": 45–6.

FIGURE 2.3. "The Black Horror" (1918/1933). The terrified female victim and the looming black attacker in this poster depicting the French occupation of the Rhineland epitomized the Entente's colonial subjugation of Germany and the alleged racial "contamination" arising from it.
Source: Bundesarchiv Koblenz, Plak 002–012–030, Designer: Julius Ussy Engelhard.

policy.[87] The German press depicted the "black horror on the Rhine," as having unleashed "uncivilized hordes" and "savages" on the German population, in which German women especially appeared alternatively as victims of rape or the dangerous instigators of sexual degeneration. The outcry was not limited to the press, for it also emerged from women's groups, which extended from Social Democrats to the extreme right. While conspiratorial groups of citizens spied on their neighbors to monitor violations of German "honor," gangs of young men accosted women

[87] See Matthew P. Fitzpatrick, "The Pre-History of the Holocaust? The *Sonderweg* and *Historikerstreit* Debates and the Abject Colonial Past," *Central European History* 41 (2008), 477–503; and Jared Poley, *Decolonization in Germany: Narratives of Colonial Loss and Foreign Occupation* (Bern: Peter Lang, 2005), 151–247.

suspected of sexual dalliances, tearing their clothing, shearing their hair, and parading them through the streets to subject them to public mockery. Transgressed racial boundaries, or more precisely the perception of them, joined the personal with the political. The Entente's subjugation emasculated German men by rendering them unable to protect and defend their women and their nation. For the extreme right, that state of affairs represented nothing less than the "jewification" (*Verjüdung*) of Germany. "A Jewish-Marxist" revolution had capitulated to foreign enemies, who now threatened the integrity of the nation by racial mixing.[88]

Despite the Weimar Republic's turbulent birth, visions of a revived and expanded German empire, anchored in the experience of global war and the Entente's occupation policies, had little chance of being enacted. Because the most radical of them proposed a German-dominated, racially purified living space on the European continent, those visions could neither be achieved without war nor within the terms of the postwar peace settlement as long as the Entente enforced them and Weimar pragmatists played by the rules to revise them. In short, the Weimar Republic's collapse and the emergence of the radically imperialist National Socialists were not predetermined. There was the possibility that Germany would avoid the path of the Ottoman empire and later Turkey, where the wartime genocide and the huge postwar population transfers of Turks and Greeks superceded more traditional notions of imperial rule built upon the religious and ethnic diversity of peoples.[89] Nevertheless, the fragility of the postwar successor states in eastern and southeastern Europe, which turned ethnic Germans scattered throughout into minorities, the shaky global economy, which would impact Germany profoundly, and the declining threat of the Entente's intervention, would encourage the emergence of a movement bent on assaulting the European state system and substituting in its place a new racial order.

[88] Tina Campt, Pascal Grosse, and Yara-Colette Lemke-Muniz de Faria, "Blacks, Germans, and the Politics of Imperial Imagination, 1930–1960," in *The Imperialist Imagination: German Colonialism and Its Legacy*, eds. Sara Friedrichsmeyer, Sara Lennox, and Susanne Zantop (Ann Arbor: University of Michigan Press, 1998), 208–14; Wildt, *Volksgemeinschaft als Selbstsermächtigung*, 256–7; Gisela Lebzelter, "Die 'Schwarze Schmach': Vorurteile, Propaganda, Mythos," *Geschichte und Gesellschaft* 11, no. 1 (1985): 37–58. Mass, *Weisse Helden, Schwarzer Krieger*, 76–120, 198–9.

[89] On the precedent-setting significance of the Treaty of Lausanne in 1923, in which the Allies recognized the sovereignty of the Republic of Turkey and abrogated the earlier peace treaty with the Ottoman Empire, see Markus Leninger, *Nationalsozialistische "Volkstumsarbeit" und Umsiedlungspolitik 1933–1945* (Berlin: Frank and Timme, 2006), 9–10; and Eric D. Weitz, "From Vienna to the Paris System: International Politics and the Entangled Histories of Human Rights, Forced Deportations, and Civilizing Missions," *American Historical Review* 113, no. 5 (2008): 1313–43, and especially 1333–8.

3

From Colonizer to "Colonized"

The Weimar Republic 1918–1933

Germany's demotion from a great power with global aspirations to a republic saddled with defeat and decolonization underlay the instability of Weimar's first years. On March 13, 1920, Walther von Lüttwitz, a Reichswehr general serving in the defense ministry and Wolfgang Kapp, a Prussian landowner, state official, and cofounder of the annexationist Fatherland Party, launched a coup attempt against the Weimar government. Infuriated by the formal dissolution of the Free Corps, which the Social Democratic Defense Minister Gustav Noske reluctantly ordered under pressure from the Entente, the Kapp-Lüttwitz forces enlisted a diverse coterie of rebels for their endeavor. They included embittered Baltic fighters now lodged in military colonies in the eastern Prussian provinces, whose financial support came from sympathizers in heavy industry and estate agriculture, as well as dissident elements in the civil service and the military. General Erich Ludendorff, who helped saddle the Weimar coalition with the opprobrium of defeat, contributed significantly to planning the coup. Had the plotters succeeded, he would have become defense minister. In addition to mutinying against the Entente's "dictated peace" and the republic that had succumbed to it, the putschists sought to restore the authoritarian constitutionalism of the Bismarckian Reich, although they remained divided over who was to serve in the postcoup government.[1]

At first, the Weimar government seemed powerless to resist the counterrevolution. When the enigmatic Reichswehr chief of staff Hans von Seeckt

---

[1] See the introduction of Erwin Könnemann and Gerhard Schulze, eds., *Der Kapp-Lüttwitz-Ludendorff Putsch* (Munich: Olzog Verlag, 2002), xvii, and the extensive documentation that follows.

refused to fire on the soldiers who sided with the putschists, the government retreated first to Dresden, a long-time Social Democratic stronghold, and then to Stuttgart. As a result, Hermann Ehrhardt's Free Corps brigade accompanied by Ludendorff could safely occupy Berlin when Kapp gave the order. Yet the setback proved temporary as equally diverse constituencies converged to save the republic. Massive working-class demonstrations and armed resistance, a general strike invoked by the Socialist and Christian trade unions (the latter loosely affiliated with the Center), the refusal of noncommissioned officers and their troops in countless garrisons to follow their senior officers loyal to Kapp, and the threat of a French intervention in the west pulled the rug out from under the putsch. By reawakening fears of a popular revolution that forced the remnants of the Imperial government to dissolve the monarchy in the first place, the protests against the coup persuaded most of the ministerial bureaucracy, the Reich central bank, and especially the army to oppose the conspirators.[2] Unlike the Fascists' March on Rome two years later, when the Italian middle and upper classes united behind Mussolini as the "only" effective guarantor of their interests in the face of economic crisis and management-labor conflict, the relative strength of the left, the tactical divisions among counter-revolutionaries, and the threat of foreign intervention prevented the imposition of a radical nationalist and imperialist regime in Germany.[3]

Frustrated imperialist ambitions in the east exposed by the Kapp Putsch intensified the pressure on the Weimar coalition to contain revolution at home and resist the westward spread of Bolshevism. However inept, the Kapp Putsch might not have occurred at all had the Weimar coalition not deployed the Free Corps against the Spartacists and workers' and soldiers' councils, and against the Red Army in the Baltic. With Noske's tacit support, a coalition of counter-revolutionary Russians, known as "whites," Baltic Germans, and Free Corps units fighting under the Russian imperial flag and the leadership of the self-styled adventurer Pavel Bermondt-Avalov, attacked Riga in the fall of 1919. Pursuing the dream

---

[2] Hans Mommsen, *The Rise and Fall of Weimar Democracy*, trans. Elborg Forster and Larry Eugene Jones (Chapel Hill and London: University of North Carolina Press, 1996), 81–4; and Michael Geyer, *Deutsche Rüstungspolitik 1860–1980* (Frankfurt am Main: Suhrkamp, 1984), 129. As Könnemann and Schulze, *Kapp-Lüttwitz*, ix, point out, the putsch might well have succeeded had it not met with popular resistance.

[3] For a similar argument as to the significance of the threat of foreign intervention, see MacGregor Knox, *To the Threshold of Power: Origins and Dynamics of the Fascist and National Socialist Dictatorships*, vol. 1 (Cambridge: Cambridge University Press, 2007), 399.

of restoring conservative nationalist regimes in Germany and Russia, the counter-revolutionaries succumbed to Latvian and Lithuanian resistance and British aerial bombardment. The internment of Bermondt's forces, which deprived Kapp of additional manpower, affected the outcome of the putsch. Ironically, despite the failure of the Soviet armies to retake lands lost at Brest-Litovsk, the prospect of a joint German-Russian restoration died along with Bermondt's campaign. Although embroiled in a civil war at home and isolated internationally, Lenin's government survived because of the divisions among its counter-revolutionary adversaries and its own military effectiveness. Yet in Germany, the Kapp putschists and their allies would leave durable and poisonous legacies. Unleashing an orgy of violence against helpless civilians in the wake of the Bermondt disaster, Free Corps veterans, enraged by their failure to win the land promised to them, kept alive images of vast spaces for German colonization and practiced the politics of violence that, albeit on a more limited scale, would characterize Weimar in times of crisis.[4]

At home, counter-revolutionaries vented their hatred of the republic through brutality and propaganda, which included the dissemination of the infamous antisemitic forgery *The Protocols of the Elders of Zion*. That document, once confined to the conspiratorial imaginations of the Russian reactionaries before World War I, unveiled the secret plan of Zionist rabbis to secure world domination by fostering social conflict and revolution. After the war, the conspiratorial narrative of the *Protocols* appealed to a large audience as convincing explanation for social upheaval, economic instability, and the catastrophic dissolution of the Second Empire. The tract appeared in thirty-three German editions alone by 1933.[5] Although the Kapp putschists failed to maintain control of the national government in Berlin, they did succeed in upending the state government of Bavaria, over-throwing its Socialist Prime Minister Johannes Hoffmann. A new regime under the monarchist Gustav von Kahr allowed counter-revolutionary radicalism and antisemitism to flourish, enabling the emergence of new political movements, including the National Socialists.

[4] Michael Kellogg, *The Russian Roots of Nazism: White Émigrés and the Making of National Socialism, 1917–1945* Cambridge: Cambridge University Press, 2005), 78–108; Vejas Gabriel Liulevicius, *War Land in the East: Culture, National Identity and German Occupation in World War I* (Cambridge: Cambridge University Press, 2000), 227–46; Modris Eksteins, *Walking Since Daybreak: A Story of Eastern Europe, World War II, and the Heart of Our Century* (Boston and New York: Houghton Mifflin, 1999), 76–80.
[5] Saul Friedlander, *Nazi Germany and the Jews*, vol. 1, *The Years of Persecution* (New York: HarperCollins, 1997), 94.

The Reichstag elections of June 1920, the first since the Weimar Constitution came into effect, exposed the fragility of the center-left coalition despite its having survived the Kapp episode. Having triumphed in January of 1919 with over seventy-five percent of the vote in the elections for the assembly that would draft a new constitution, the "Weimar Coalition" composed of the Social Democrats, the reconstituted Progressives now known as the Democratic Party (DDP), and the Center dropped to a combined forty-eight percent. The parties that opposed the republic gained significantly. The Communists, together with the Independent Social Democrats won eighty-eight seats. On the right, the German National People's Party (DNVP), the postwar successor to the Conservative and Free Conservative parties, increased its number from forty-four seats in 1919 to seventy-seven in 1920. In addition to the visceral antisocialism that lay scarcely below the surface in the Center and Democratic parties, which pushed middle-class voters further to the right, the Versailles humiliation saddled the Weimar Coalition with the aura of defeat and the appearance of colonization by foreigners from which it never fully recovered.[6] Although the Weimar "system," as the opponents of the republic called it, would survive until 1933 when the Nazis backed by their conservative allies dismantled it, the noxious mix of economic hardship, social conflict, exclusionary nationalism, and unrequited great power ambitions would prove difficult to extinguish even in the best of times.

COLONIZATION AND CONFRONTATION: POLITICAL VIOLENCE AND ECONOMIC CRISIS

The battered Weimar economy, to which reparation payments only partially contributed, made it easy for Germans to attribute economic weakness to what they perceived as the Entente's colonial subjugation. In contrast to the price stability and high annual growth rates of the Kaiserreich, especially during the decade before World War I, the republic struggled with the consequences of the lost war and the peace settlement.[7] At the moment in which the constitutional guarantees of the new political

---

[6] On the elections and their significance, see Larry Eugene Jones, *German Liberalism and the Dissolution of the Weimar Party System 1918–1933* (Chapel Hill and London: University of North Carolina Press, 1988), 67–80.

[7] Niall Ferguson, "The German inter-war economy: political choice versus economic determinism," *Twentieth-Century Germany: Politics, Culture and Society, 1918–1990*, ed. Mary Fulbrook (London: Arnold, 2001), 38.

system expanded the opportunities for political expression, those same opportunities made it difficult for the republic to maintain its legitimacy. Having come into existence as the result of war weariness, military collapse, and popular frustration with the Imperial government's inability to meet the most basic material needs, the Weimar Republic would be given little leeway from a mobilized and expectant public. It also had to absorb the consequences of the loss of the Reich's peripheral territories, particularly important industrial regions such as Lorraine and ultimately the eastern third of Upper Silesia. The Saar, placed under the administration of the League of Nations for fifteen years, presented a double bind. Although French officials took control of German mines, they refused to pay out the accident benefits, pensions, and support for veterans and war widows, which remained the Weimar government's responsibility.[8] In addition, the republic contended with the precipitous decline in industrial and agricultural production that began during the war, as well as the disruption of commercial networks because of the loss of former German territories.

Inflation, the origins of which lay in the high indebtedness that the Imperial government incurred to fight the war, added to those burdens. In 1915 alone, prices rose more than in the previous forty-five years combined, and by the end of 1918 the Reichsmark, the national currency, had lost three-quarters of its 1913 value.[9] Military defeat removed the means by which Germany confidently intended to repay its debt, the exploitation of conquered territories and reparations imposed on its vanquished foes. Although it no doubt helped to create full employment, inflation spiraled out of control between 1920 and 1923. Aware of their tenuous legitimacy, Weimar governments refused to raise taxes to finance reparation payments and they increased salaries for public employees. The costs of pensions for disabled veterans and the widowed and orphaned dependents of deceased soldiers exploded, as did the tax incentives for employers to hire demobilized soldiers.[10] In January of 1923, French and Belgians troops occupied the Ruhr, Germany's leading industrial district, to confiscate its coal, having suspected that the Weimar government was

[8] David Blackbourn, *Marpingen: Apparitions of the Virgin Mary in a Nineteenth-Century German Village* (New York: Vintage Books, 1995), 332–3.
[9] Richard Bessel, *Germany after the First World War* (Oxford: Clarendon Press, 1993), 31.
[10] On inflation, the definitive work is Gerald D. Feldman's *The Great Disorder: Politics, Economics, and Society in the German Inflation 1914–1924* (New York and Oxford: Oxford University Press, 1997).

deliberately destroying the value of its currency to dodge its obligations. In response to the call from Berlin against cooperating with the occupation, passive resistance took on a life of its own, uniting Germans across class lines and even drawing in fifty thousand Polish miners. The continuing inflation and the punitive counter-measures of the occupiers, which included payroll seizures and customs barriers that blocked the importation of food from the surrounding countryside, took their toll in declining real wages, mounting malnutrition, and the anti-French solidarity itself. By September of 1923, passive resistance collapsed, and not only because the central government recognized that the spiraling inflation made its position untenable. Its accession to employer demands to lengthen the workday demoralized Ruhr workers, who had participated in the resistance to defend the republic.[11]

By December of 1923, the official exchange rate skyrocketed to 4.2 trillion marks to a single American dollar. The stabilization agreement between the Weimar government and the Reparations Commission of the Entente, known as the Dawes Plan after the American banker who brokered the deal, ended hyperinflation by linking the German currency to gold and by renegotiating reparation payments according to a new scale. In return, the French and Belgians withdrew their troops, depriving the French of the independent Rhineland buffer state that they had sought. Nevertheless, the hyperinflation left its demoralizing after-effects. It had a deleterious impact on shopkeepers and artisans, as well as undermining the livelihoods and cultural capital of the salaried employees and professionals who could not keep up with currency depreciation. It destroyed the modest savings of retirees and others on fixed incomes. By punishing creditors and rewarding debtors whether large or small, inflation upended the moral economies of borrowing and lending. It enabled some with the intestinal fortitude to gamble, such as the industrialist Hugo Stinnes, to acquire vast fortunes while wrecking havoc within the formerly solid and respectable middle class. Money lost its value as a medium of exchange and an expression of predictable social interaction, becoming instead the instrument of speculation for those who profited seemingly without effort.[12] Feelings of powerlessness and painful

---

[11] Conan Fischer, *The Ruhr Crisis 1932–1924* (Oxford: Oxford University Press, 2003), esp. 49–219.

[12] On the cultural impact of inflation, which has called into question recent revisions of the negative impact of inflation, see Bernd Wittig, *Culture and Inflation in Weimar*

FIGURE 3.1 A line of customers in front of a grocery shop in Berlin, 1923. Lines of anxious consumers queuing up to buy basic necessities before the value of their money declined further were commonplace during the hyperinflation that accompanied the occupation of the Ruhr. For many Germans, they were the consequences of an unjust peace and the weakness of the Weimar Republic.
Source: Bundesarchiv Koblenz, Bild 146–1971–109–42.

perceptions of social disintegration were palpable. The ever-multiplying zeroes, as the *Berliner Illustrirte Zeitung* put it, forced Germans to invest enormous energy in commonplace purchases before the value of their meager resources declined further. "There is not much to add. It pounds daily on the nerves: the insanity of numbers, the uncertain future, today, and tomorrow become doubtful once more overnight. An epidemic of fear, naked need: lines of shoppers, long since an unaccustomed sight, once more form in front of shops, first in front of one, then in front of all. No disease is as contagious as this one."[13]

Furthermore, the sudden deflation that resulted after the introduction of a new and more secure mark brought higher interest rates and taxes

Germany (Berkeley and Los Angeles: University of California Press, 2001); and Martin Geyer, *Verkehrte Welt: Revolution, Inflation und Moderne: München 1914–1924* (Göttingen: Vandenhoeck and Ruprecht, 1998), especially 319–28.

[13] Friedrich Groner, "Overwrought Nerves," *Berliner Illustrirte Zeitung*, August 26, 1923, in *The Weimar Republic Sourcebook*, eds. Anton Kaes, Martin Jay, and Edward Dimendberg (Berkeley, Los Angeles, and London: University of California Press, 1995), 63.

to many whom inflation had benefited. The impact on agriculture was especially pronounced, as the higher cost of borrowing and the need to pay taxes in hard currency eroded farmers' liquidity. Deflation encouraged employers to cut costs and impose other efficiencies under the rubric of "rationalization." The increasing concentration of industries in turn contributed to high structural unemployment, which hit young workers especially hard. The eight-hour day, which industrial workers won in 1918 as a provision of the Stinnes-Legien Agreement, was now a thing of the past. As early as the end of 1923, more than one-quarter of all trade unionists were out of work.[14] In actuality, the Weimar economy was no worse off than those of other European nations in the postwar period. Alternatively, it was somewhat stronger despite its territorial losses, because little fighting had taken place on German soil. Weimar governments avoided paying most of the reparations it ostensibly owed.[15] Despite German complaints about their colonial subjugation to the victors, neither the Weimar bureaucracy nor the Weimar political system were imposed from outside, nor was the legal status of German citizenship compromised. Yet, from the perspective of many Germans, the explanation for economic hardship could be reduced to a single, all-encompassing cause: the territorial punishments and financial exactions of the Entente and the Weimar "system's" craven capitulation to them. Although an "empire" by name (the Weimar Republic remained the German "Reich"), Germany had lost its overseas and continental colonial possessions. A comprador class of Marxists, liberals, pacifists, and especially Jews who did the bidding of the "colonizers" and who engineered and profited from the catastrophe of 1918, was now in power.

Wounded nationalism, thwarted imperialism, and economic crisis polarized the political climate and sharpened the propensity to extra parliamentary violence. Pitched battles occurred between Free Corps units and the left during and after the Kapp putsch as each side struggled for control of industrial cities. Nationalist veterans' associations, the "Steel Helmets" (*Stahlhelm*) having become the largest with 300,000 members, articulated the ugly antirepublicanism and antisemitism of former soldiers, while spinning off conspiratorial "combat leagues" that picked fights with political opponents. Although less extensive than the horrific battles between revolutionaries and counter-revolutionaries in Hungary

[14] Bessel, *Germany after the First World War*, 164.
[15] Doris Bergen, *War and Genocide: A Concise History of the Holocaust*, 2nd ed. (Lanham, MD: Rowman and Littlefield, 2009), 45.

or the Baltic region, political violence that had been unusual before World War I became routine afterward.[16] Conspiratorial right-wing groups targeted major political figures for assassination, notably those who were closely associated with Germany's "humiliation." The first to fall victim was Matthias Erzberger, the finance minister, leader of the Center party, and prewar imperialist. In August of 1921, the shadowy terrorist group "Operation Consul" murdered Erzberger because he had advocated a negotiated settlement to the war and signed the armistice in November, 1918. Because he supported Lithuanian independence in the last year of the Great War as the Center Party's leader in the Reichstag, Ober Ost administrators resented Erzberger's challenge to the plans for German protectorates and German lands for settlement.[17]

Moreover, the proliferation of right-wing "defense" units on Germany's redefined eastern borders, which enjoyed the undercover protection of the Reichswehr, personified the depth of hostility toward a newly independent Poland. The most contentious dispute arose in Upper Silesia, which was divided in 1921 after a plebiscite accompanied by a polarizing and bloody conflict between Polish nationalists and Free Corps units commissioned by the Weimar government.[18] Like the Free Corps, the "border protection" forces drew large numbers of men born between 1900 and 1910, who were too young to have fought in the war, but were old enough to have absorbed the martial values, imperial imaginings, and hostility of their elders toward the "November criminals," Marxists, Jews, and pacifists who stabbed Germany in the back.[19] Baltic Germans and White Russian émigrés continued their counter-revolutionary activities by associating with the former Kapp putschist, Hermann Ehrhardt. In June of 1922, Ehrhardt's Organization C assassinated the foreign minister Walther Rathenau in broad daylight. Two months earlier, Rathenau's negotiations with the Soviet Union resulted in the Rapallo Treaty, which, in addition to normalizing relations between the Weimar Republic and the Soviet government, renounced the territorial and financial claims of each signatory against the other. Rathenau's Jewishness, already an

---

[16] On the transnational counter revolution, see Robert Gerwarth, "The Central European Counter-Revolution: Paramilitary Violence in Germany, Austria and Hungary after the Great War," *Past and Present*, no. 200 (August 2008): 175–209.

[17] Liulevicius, *War Land*, 201, 209–10.

[18] James Bjork, *Neither German nor Pole: Catholicism and National Indifference in a Central European Borderland* (Ann Arbor: University of Michigan Press, 2008), 255–8.

[19] Michael Wildt, *Generation des Unbedingten: Das Führungskorps des Reichssicherheitshauptamtes* (Hamburg: HIS Verlag, 2002), 53–60.

issue for radical nationalists and antisemites during the war, became the explanation for his actions and the justification for his murder. The foreign minister, claimed the right, was imposing Bolshevism on Germany. Similar to their position in response to the murder of Erzberger, "respectable" right-wing circles that eschewed counter-revolutionary violence made no secret of their sympathy for the assassins.[20]

Paramilitary assaults ranged beyond those against political leaders such as Rathenau, or against prominent leftists such as Rosa Luxembourg, murdered in Berlin in 1919 by Free Corps units, and the leaders of the short-lived Munich republic such as Kurt Eisner and Gustav Landauer. Collectively, Jews became the targets of organized attacks whether polemical or violent, which in contrast to Imperial Germany, mushroomed into a mass phenomenon that did not evaporate after stabilization. Because the number of Jews skyrocketed as a result of the wartime decision to move skilled Jewish laborers to the capital to work in armaments industries, and the postwar influx of refugees from Poland and Russia, the Kapp putschists had called for a pogrom, which was prevented only by the intervention of groups of Jewish defenders. Hundreds of eastern European Jews found themselves interred and mistreated in concentration camps in the aftermath of the coup attempt. Although the Second Empire accorded Jews full legal equality, it was Weimar that facilitated their entry into prestigious careers in the civil service, diplomatic corps, and academia that prewar discrimination denied them. Jews appeared to benefit from the hated republic and thus personified defeat and foreign domination. Reiterating the connection between Jews and Germany's rivals that emerged during the Kaiserreich, the Leipzig antisemite Heinrich Pudor asserted that only pogroms would suffice to destroy a republic that he believed had been installed by "international Jewry." "Either German or Jewish English world domination!"[21]

Condemned as war profiteers and shirkers from military service during the war, Jews were now accused of profiting from economic distress.[22] In November of 1923, vicious attacks on eastern European Jews who were

---

[20] Kellogg, *Russian Roots*, 176–7; Eric D. Weitz, *Weimar Germany: Promise and Tragedy* (Princeton and Oxford: Princeton University Press, 207), 99–110.

[21] On Podor, see Dirk Walter, *Antisemitische Kriminalität und Gewalt: Judenfeindschaft in der Weimarer Republik* (Bonn: J.H.W. Dietz Nachf., 1999), 28.

[22] Frank Bajohr, "The 'Volk Community" and the Persecution of the Jews: German Society under National Socialist Dictatorship," *Holocaust and Genocide Studies* 20, no. 2 (2006): 185–6; Geyer, *Verkehrte Welt*, 280–8.

crowded into the Berlin ghetto, the Scheunenviertel, revealed the scape-goating outcomes of hyperinflation, as Jews became the outlets for the rage of the jobless, hungry, and disillusioned Berlin working classes, whose plight the Socialists in the city government failed to remedy. Unemployed Berliners perceived the eastern European Jewish immigrants as price gougers and profiteers despite the Scheunenviertel's general impover-ishment. They reacted to the pervasive stereotypes of postwar refugees, particularly Jews, as profligate consumers of scarce food and housing.[23] Beatings, lootings, and mass rioting exacerbated by the laggard response of the police exposed the utility of Jewish scapegoats for economic hard-ship and political frustration, even in a formidable leftist stronghold such as Berlin.[24] Yet violent antisemitic attacks surged throughout Germany, not just in Berlin. They resulted in the destruction of Jewish businesses, the theft of Jewish property, and the physical injury to countless Jews. The relatively high degree of Jewish integration of the prewar years was becoming a thing of the past.[25]

As the Scheuenviertel riots made clear, political violence was not con-fined to the secret and not-so-secret paramilitaries of the radical right. The Communists (KPD), a mass party of 350,000 members, which after the 1920 elections absorbed the majority of the Independent Social Democrats, attacked the republic from the left, condemning it as a bourgeois democracy that served the interests of large-scale capitalism. Believing in the efficacy of armed revolution following the Bolshevik model, its leaders despised the Majority Socialists for their collaboration with employers and the military, solidifying the split within the labor movement that first emerged during the war. The KPD's paramilitary force, the Red Front Fighting League, regularly staged local insurrec-tions in the streets of working-class neighborhoods and in welfare offices

---

[23] Trude Maurer, *Ostjuden in Deutschland 1918–1933* (Hamburg: Hans Christians Verlag, 1986), 128–33.

[24] David Clay Large, "'Out with the Ostjuden': The Scheunenviertel Riots in Berlin, November 1932," in *Exclusionary Violence: Antisemitic Riots in Modern German History*, Christhard Hoffmann, Werner Bergmann, and Helmut Walser Smith (Ann Arbor: University of Michigan Press, 2002), 123–40.

[25] See Michael Wildt, *Volksgemeinschaft als Selbstermächtigung: Gewalt gegen Juden in der deutschen provinz 1919 bis 1939* (Hamburg: Hamburger Edition, 2007), 72–80, and especially Till van Rahden, *Jews and Other Germans: Civil Society, Religious Diversity, and Urban Politics in Breslau, 1860–1925*, trans. Marcus Brainard (Madison: University of Wisconsin Press, 2008), 231–42, on the poisonous mix of antisemitism and border conflicts with Poland.

where it repositioned itself after its expulsion from factories, mines, and shop floors during the crisis of hyperinflation and the Ruhr occupation. Although the Communists' share of seats in the Reichstag declined steadily, its electorate surged after 1930 because of mass unemployment – an electorate drawn together by the common experience of deprivation, hunger, and the unending search for work. Exemplifying masculine toughness and the violent confrontation of enemies, the Communists shared one characteristic with their foes on the right, the attraction to military-style mobilization.[26] Yet working-class violence did not need the sanction of either the Socialist or Communist parties to erupt in spontaneous local outbursts over issues such as the protection of one's turf or the expression of one's masculinity, as economic hardship deprived working-class youths of the normal avenue of self respect, a job.[27]

The greater and more consistent threat, however, emerged from the higher civil service, the judiciary, the officer corps, and employers, whose members concluded an uneasy truce with the Weimar system as the only alternative to "Bolshevism." The largely Protestant parties, especially the German National People's Party and the German People's Party, spoke for their interests. Despite moving rightward after its defeat in 1920, the Democrats (DDP) steadily shrank into insignificance. Having performed well in the 1920 elections, the DNVP further expanded its delegation to ninety-five seats in 1924, making it the largest party except for the Social Democrats. In a series of "bourgeois" cabinets between 1924 and 1928, the DNP joined with the DVP and the Center with a parliamentary majority that could govern without the Socialists. However menacing the Communists appeared to the German middle classes, the military, business, and academically trained elite's position at the commanding heights of the economy and state assured it of abundant resources to protect itself against radicalism from the left. And although willing to play by the rules of parliamentary democracy, they tolerated violence if, in their view, circumstances warranted it. Thus, during and after the Kapp putsch, conservatives and radical nationalists created "Emergency Squads" fortified with broad discretionary police power to keep mines, factories, and large landed estates functioning during strikes. The Stahlhelm and other paramilitary units such the Young German Order became a form of middle-class "self-help" to clear the streets of leftists, indicative of the fact that the

[26] Eric D. Weitz, *Creating German Communism, 1890–1990: From Popular Protests to Socialist State* (Princeton: Princeton University Press, 1997), 100–279.

[27] Pamela Swett, *Neighbors and Enemies: The Culture of Radicalism in Berlin, 1929–1933* (Cambridge: Cambridge University Press, 2004), 232–85.

right would not leave it to the regular constituted police forces to protect their interests.[28] The tolerance for the use of extra-legal force extended to Jews as well. The DNVP publicly eschewed pogroms as the politics of the gutter, which resulted in the secession of its most extreme antisemitic and ethnic nationalist wing in 1922, yet its scarcely concealed delight over Rathenau's murder and its explicit targeting of eastern European Jews for expulsion blurred the distinction between violent and "nonviolent" antisemitism. The long-term effect of right-wing violence was to weaken public confidence in the republic's ability to keep order.[29]

The aristocracy and most notably the Junker nobility proved the most irreconcilable, arguably more so than employers, academicians, or civil servants. The passing of the monarchy, the terms of the peace settlement, and economic hardship cut to the core of noble identity. Even before 1914, the weakening economic position of east Elbian estate owners and the growing status division between Junkers and the grand seigneurs of the southwest who hobnobbed with the grand bourgeoisie in the salon and court culture of Berlin, yielded a hostility toward the "mammon-ism" and "materialism" of the "Jewish" industrial, financial, and educated bourgeoisie and the nobles who associated with it. Well before the war, many Junkers had grown disillusioned with the kaiser, whose conduct assaulted the values they claimed to hold. Wilhelm's association with Philipp Eulenberg especially affronted Junker notions of masculinity and martial bearing. The kaiser's refusal to sacrifice his life in battle at the head of his troops and his humiliating flight to the Netherlands left many rudderless. The November Revolution and the Versailles restrictions on the size of the army and its officer corps eliminated one of the primary careers for the Junkers, while nobles in general saw their foothold in the state service decline. The Weimar constitution abolished once legally vali-dated aristocratic privileges, including entailed estates. As a result, nobles played a prominent role in the putschism of the early Republic, either as estate owners who trained Free Corps troops and stockpiled weapons for the Kapp putsch, or as the experienced veterans of the "racial wars" in Africa and the bloody battles of the western and eastern fronts. Terrified by the Bolsheviks' assaults on the Russian and Baltic aristocracies and the execution of the tsar and his family, they rapidly joined Free Corps

---

[28] On Saxony as a prime example, see Dirk Schumann, *Political Violence in the Weimar Republic, 1918–1922: Fight for the Streets and Fear of Civil War*, trans. Thomas Dunlap (New York and Oxford: Berghahn, 2009), 2–107.

[29] Walter, *Antisemitische Kriminalität*, 41–51.

units and other armed formations. Anti-Bolshevik and antisemitic to the core, younger nobles became addicted to violence as the antidote to military defeat, the seeming cowardice of the kaiser, and "pacifist-Jewish-Bolshevik" republicanism. Unlike their elders, they abandoned monarchism for the hope of a revolutionary but authoritarian "Third Reich" built upon a charismatic leader and the "natural" superiority of the aristocracy, which they defined increasingly in racial and biological terms.[30]

If elites wavered between begrudged cooperation and antirepublican opposition, radical nationalist populism became the most distinctive and novel feature of Weimar politics. While the professional and commercial middle classes carried the banner of imperialism and anti-Marxism before the war, a more heterogeneous mix of middle- and lower-middle-class occupations and a peasantry mobilized in response to the Controlled Economy came to the fore afterward, radicalized by the war, defeat, and economic crisis. Bound to the bourgeois parties at the republic's beginnings, populists interests proved difficult to accommodate because they lacked influence with party leaderships and thus they could be easily dissatisfied. Moreover, the political significance of the left was crucial to the emergence of right-wing populism. Even when the Social Democrats did not hold cabinet portfolios as was the case between 1920 and 1928 when bourgeois coalitions governed, the SPD's leading role in the Prussian government and its standing in the Reichstag enabled the passage of social insurance legislation, unemployment compensation, and the extension of workers' rights on the shop floor.

The exclusionary nationalism and explicit imperialism of university students contributed significantly to the social diversity and potential explosiveness of antirepublicanism, the ironic consequence of the republic's democratization of higher education. Determined to broaden access to academic diplomas and university degrees for lower-middle- and working-class youth, Weimar's expansion of educational opportunities benefited precisely that cohort, that is, youths born between 1900 and 1910, who were raised with stories of wartime heroism and sacrifice, only to be embittered by the aftermath. Whereas in 1914, sixty thousand students populated Germany's universities, the number increased to 87,000 by 1921, jumping to 104,000

---

[30] Stephan Malinowski, *Vom König zum Führer: Deutscher Adel und Nationalsozialismus* (Frankfurt am Main: Fischer Taschenbuch Verlag, 2004), 198–282. Although not nearly as economically disadvantaged after 1918 as the Junkers, many among the high aristocracy rivaled the lesser nobility in their hostility toward Weimar. See Jonathan Petropoulos, *Royals and the Reich: The Princes von Hessen in Nazi Germany* (Oxford and New York: Oxford University Press, 2006), 50–96.

a decade later. The number of students pursuing law, the crucial route to civil-service positions, composed a disproportionate share of university enrollments. Growing numbers of university graduates became difficult to place in a weak national economy, which in turn frustrated ambitions to upward mobility. The radical nationalist proclivities of students became evident at the republic's beginnings, as students were among the first to join the Free Corps that put down the radical left in the cities, confronted Poles in Upper Silesia, and challenged the French in the Rhineland. Tropes of the Entente's "colonization" of Germany shaped the discourse of student radicals, such as Werner Best, the future deputy of Reinhard Heydrich in the Reich Security Main Office of the SS (Schutzstaffel or Protection Force) and agent of the German occupation in France and Denmark. In advocating armed resistance against the Ruhr occupation, Best drew upon the Irish resistance to the English occupation as his model. An armed "decisive struggle" against the occupiers, he insisted, would also mean an assault against the defeatists and traitors, who capitulated to the Versailles "dictated peace" and settled for passive resistance against the French and Belgians. Moreover, radical nationalist students imposed "Aryan paragraphs" in the constitutions of student groups, including that of their national union, the *Hochschulring*, as they re-formed according to putatively more democratic standards after the war. Committed to a *völkisch* ideology radicalized by the border adjustments of the postwar peace settlement, in which the immutable ties of biology and race mattered more than artificial political boundaries imposed by the Entente, right-wing students committed themselves just as fervently to excluding Jews whom they considered "alien" to Germans. Radical nationalist students became the bell weather of a future antisemitic dictatorship, when those affiliated with a movement whose roots lay in the postwar turbulence of southern Germany, the National Socialists, became the majority in national student associations.[31]

In the aftermath of the November Revolution, the Bavarian capital of Munich, surrounded by a state with a conservative and mainly peasant population for whom the "Jew" personified the evils of the Controlled Economy and political upheaval, became a major counter-revolutionary

---

[31] Wildt, *Generation des Unbedingten*, 72–89; Ulrich Herbert, *Best: Biographische Studien über Radikalismus, Weltanschauung und Vernunft 1903–1989* (Bonn: Verlag J. H. W. Dietz Nachf., 2001), 29–87. Best's analogy to the Irish is found on 75. See also Christian Ingrao, "Deutsche Studenten, Erinnerung aus den Krieg und nationalsozialistische Militanz: Eine Fallstudie," in *Nachrichtendienst, politische Elite, Mordeinheit: Der Sicherheitsdienst des Reichsführer SS*, ed. Michael Wildt (Hamburg: Hamburger Edition, 2003): 144–59.

center and a transnational magnet for Austrian, Hungarian, and German counter-revolutionaries.[32] Having spawned a more radical revolution than elsewhere, which by February of 1919 had evolved into a Soviet-style "council republic," Munich especially became a draw for rightists traumatized by the "Bolshevism" of urban leftists, many of whom were Jewish. Bavarian free booters and regular army units from Württemberg and Prussia ruthlessly suppressed the council republic by the late spring of 1919, murdering its leaders, Kurt Eisner, Gustav Landauer, and Ernst Toller. Nevertheless, Bavaria remained a hot bed of right-wing extremism, benevolently protected by the conservative Minister President, Gustav von Kahr, and the Reichswehr's patronage of radical nationalist agitators and counter-revolutionary paramilitary units.[33] The immigration of Jews from Eastern Europe aroused special ire, in which anti-semitism from below prompted punitive action from above. In 1920, the Kahr government decree the expulsion of Jewish newcomers or their containment in concentration camps until their expulsion could be arranged.[34]

From his perch in the Bavarian town of Bamberg, Heinrich Class and his Pan German lieutenants regrouped to initiate a "racial rebirth," one which the destruction of the "alien" democratic state and the expulsion of non-Germans, especially Jews, would realize. In addition to seeking the enlargement of the army and the annexation of Austria, the Pan Germans demanded the Baltic lands, western Hungary, and Alsace-Lorraine for German settlements. Asserting what would become an important theme of Weimar politics, the Pan Germans decried the stranding of millions of ethnic Germans as minorities in successor states dominated and mistreated by Slavic majorities. Deeming ethnic Germans as the bearers of German cultural and economic influence in the east, they insisted that Germany should act as their protectors until they could be reincorporated into the Reich.[35] Munich became a haven for veterans of the Kapp putsch, including Colonel Hermann Ehrhardt and General Ludendorff after his

---

[32] On antisemitism and the Bavarian peasantry's anger at Jewish cattle traders and alleged profiteers, see Benjamin Ziemann, *War Experiences in Rural Germany, 1914–1923*, trans. Alex Skinner (Oxford and New York, 2007), 186–91; and Geyer, *Verkehrte Welt*, 182–6. See e.g., Gerwarth, "Central European Counter-Revolution," 177.

[33] Geyer, *Verkehrte Welt*, 112–29.

[34] Walter, *Antisemitische Kriminalitätt*, 97–110.

[35] Werner Jochmann, *Nationalsozialismus und Revolution: Ursprung und Geschichte der NSDAP in Hamburg 1922–1933: Dokumente* (Frankfurt am Main, 1963). 10–24. For the Pan Germans under the republic, see Rainer Hering, *Konstruierte Nation: derAlldeutsche Verband, 1890 bis 1939* (Hamburg: Christians Verlag, 2003), 344–488.

brief exile in Sweden. The Pan Germans and their offspring, the German Nationalist Protection and Defiance Federation, and a host of other right-wing groups including the Thule Society, the National Socialists' predecessor, maintained a powerful presence as well. To a sympathetic public, they broadcast their platform of eastward expansionism, the recovery and extension of overseas empire, the eugenic purification of the *Volk*, and antisemitism.

The south German crisis opened the door to a permanent career for the decorated Austrian war veteran and staunch Pan German, Adolf Hitler, whose military service saved him from the frustration of vocational failure and social marginalization. Hitler would become the embodiment of the radical nationalist yearning to remedy the incompleteness of the Bismarckian Reich through an expanded German empire defined by the demonization of external and internal "enemies," and the exclusion of racial and biological "inferiors." Yet unlike the prewar leaders of radical nationalist pressure groups, Hitler could communicate more effectively with popular audiences, and he came from outside the Reich. In addition to his greater potential for appealing to ordinary Germans, he embodied the solution to the crisis of German ethnicity that Reich Germans perceived, evident among German minorities in the successor states of the "shatter zone" or among the citizens of a truncated and subjugated republic.

Hitler's early life testified to the centrifugal forces of ethnic and class divisions of the Austro-Hungarian Empire. As a child in elementary school, an illustrated history of the Franco-Prussian War, tales of the Boer War, and the adventure stories of the American west by Karl May became Hitler's passion, anchoring a fascination that he never abandoned. An aspiring artist and architect who could not win admission to the Vienna Academy of Fine Arts, Hitler struggled to earn a living by painting postcards for tourists. Simultaneously he emerged as a political animal. Adopting the creed of the Austrian Pan German Georg Ritter von Schönerer, which embraced antiliberalism, antisocialism, and especially antisemitism, Hitler shared Schönerer's hatred of the Habsburgs, who had presided over Austria's defeat in 1866 and its exclusion from the German Reich. He despised Austrian Social Democracy and the ethnic fractiousness of the Austro-Hungarian capital, which manifested itself in parliamentary debates conducted in a cacophony of languages worthy, in his view, of the Tower of Babel. The antisemitic Christian Socialist mayor of Vienna, Karl Lueger, most likely made the biggest impression. Although Lueger's Catholic piety and pro-Habsburg loyalties repelled

Hitler, Lueger's demagogic appeals to the "little people," in contrast to Austrian liberalism's clubby politics of notables, confirmed Lueger's ability to translate right-wing ideology into political success. The mayor's platform of social and political reforms to satisfy his constituencies transformed words into deeds. All told, Hitler's early life personified the resentment of German nationalists in prewar Austria-Hungary threatened by the expanded political, civic, and cultural rights of the Dual Monarchy's other subject peoples.[36]

A modest inheritance from his father's estate allowed Hitler to immigrate to Munich in 1913, which was in his view a true German city and a relief from the heterogeneous "Babylon of races" that had so troubled him in Vienna. Prior to enlisting in a Bavarian regiment at the outbreak of World War I, he peddled his postcards, voraciously consuming Social Darwinian and antisemitic literature, deepening prejudices that his years in Vienna had awakened in him. As a dispatch runner on the western front, Hitler served with distinction, receiving an Iron Cross first class. In November of 1918, while recovering in a military hospital from a mustard gas attack near the Belgian city of Ypres, Hitler learned of the armistice. As he later claimed in his political speeches and in his autobiography *My Struggle* (*Mein Kampf*), the Marxists, pacifists, and especially Jews who fomented revolution, acted as the Entente's fifth column. Returning to Munich after his release, Hitler worked as a propagandist and informer for the Reichswehr. His task? Hitler was assigned to indoctrinate Bavarian troops against "Bolshevism" and establish liaisons with right-wing organizations to determine which among them would receive financial backing from the military.

In the course of his duties, Hitler joined the fledgling German Workers' Party in the fall of 1919, which was founded by Anton Drexler, a locksmith who belonged to the Fatherland Party. Seeking to draw workers away from the left, the DAP's ideology melded militant nationalism and antisemitism with a "socialism" that, following the Pan German economist Gottfried Feder, attacked "interest slavery" and "mobile" or "unproductive" capital, while advocating imperialism. Hitler's success as a demagogic orator, the techniques of which he practiced assiduously, drew adherents to the party's meetings in beer halls. Specializing in attacks on "Jewish" capitalism that exploited workers through stock-market

---

[36] For Hitler's early life, see Brigitte Hamann, *Hitlers Wien: Lehrjahre eines Diktators* (Munich and Zürich: Piper, 1997), especially 337–503; and Ian Kershaw, *Hitler 1889–1936: Hubris* (New York: W. W. Norton, 1998), 3–105.

speculation and price gouging, Hitler's oratorical talents soon won him the leadership of the party, which changed its name in early 1920 to the National Socialist German Workers' Party (NSDAP). Consistent with its name, which fused radical nationalism and the "socialism" of the common bonds of ethnicity, the party's twenty-five-point program drawn up during the same year, the Nazi movement combined social reform and integration with imperialism. The platform called for an enlarged Germany with colonies, the denial of citizenship to Jews, protection for the middle class, the confiscation of war profits, land reform, the end of "interest slavery," profit sharing for wage earners, and a strong authoritarian government.[37] In addition to attacking the Versailles Treaty and justifying the German exactions at Brest-Litovsk, party rallies featured venomous attacks on Marxists and Jews, who putatively undermined the home front from within. Backing up their inflammatory rhetoric with their own paramilitary, the Storm Troops (SA), Nazi meetings became rowdy and frequently bloody occasions in which the party's thugs set upon political opponents. Often describing the NSDAP as a "movement" rather than a party because the latter smacked of ineffectual and effete parliamentarianism, Hitler's emergence was emblematic, postwar, radical nationalist politics. In addition to his populist appeals to the "masses," Hitler, like other new leaders of counter-revolution, emerged from outside the ranks of Germany's middle class and aristocratic elite.[38]

As his views took shape, Hitler's fusion of Jews and Bolsheviks into a single enemy overlapped with the connection he drew between the Jew and international mobile capital that lurked behind the machinations of the Entente. Reinforced by his conviction that Jews fueled the November Revolution, including the Munich Soviet,[39] the development of Hitler's antisemitism derived especially from his extended interaction with Baltic German refugees. They included Alfred Rosenberg and Max von Scheubner-Richter, members of the same dueling fraternity in Riga and veterans of the Latvian intervention who escaped to Munich following the Kapp putsch, and whose organization, Reconstruction (*Aufbau*), contributed both money and ideology to the Nazi movement. Hitler would reject Reconstruction's

---

[37] *Documents on Nazism: A History in Documents and Eyewitness Accounts, 1919–1945*, vol. 1 eds. Jeremy Noakes and Geoffrey Pridham (New York: Schocken Books, 1983), 14–16.

[38] Geyer, *Verkehrte Welt*, 105–6.

[39] See the notes of Hitler's speech in Munich of November 3, 1919 (no. 65) in *Hitler: Sämtliche Aufzeichnungen 1905–1924*, eds. Eberhard Jäckel and Axel Kuhn (Stuttgart: Deutsche Verlags-Anstalt, 1980), 92.

goal of collaboration between Russia and Germany following the overthrow of the Weimar Republic and the Soviet regime, because it would
sacrifice the German gains at Brest-Litovsk.[40] Nevertheless, Reconstruction
provided the Nazi leader with a conspiratorial and all-encompassing
explanation for Germany's current victimization, the international Jewish
conspiracy behind the twin evils of international finance capitalism and
Bolshevism. Derived largely, although not exclusively, from the antisemitic
tract, *Protocols of the Elders of Zion*, which anti-Soviet refugees brought
with them to Germany, the imaginings of the Baltic Germans and their
White Russian compatriots merged with Hitler's *völkisch* nationalism to
become the diagnosis of Germany's plight and the subsequent justification
for ridding the *Volk* of a parasitic, "culture-destroying" people. Imagined
as a powerful cosmic danger unmasked by the disorder of revolution, the
Jew personified the upheavals of war and its aftermath, the destruction
of the conservative land empires, Germany's enslavement by the Entente,
and the "stranding" of ethnic Germans in Slavic successor states.[41] As a
German from beyond the Reich's borders, Hitler and his Baltic associates
revealed the degree to which Germany would be imagined anew. He had no
intention of restoring the Bismarckian entity of 1871 despite his veneration
of Bismarck's boldness. Nor would his Germany be simply a nation-state
purified of its "others," particularly the Jews, although that was to be the
first step. Rather, the core of the new Germany would become a racially
purified empire with its center of gravity at Russia's expense. Unlike other
empires in history, this one would ensure its long-term survival via the
principle of ethnic homogeneity.[42]

Despite their reputations as populist rabble rousers, Hitler and the Nazi
movement developed contacts with Bavaria's elite. Led by Ernst "Putzi"
Hanfstaengel, the Harvard-educated scion of an upper-middle-class
art dealer, and the commercial adventurer, Kurt Lüdecke, who became
enraptured by Hitler's sense of mission, his ability to sway the masses,

---

[40] See Kershaw, *Hubris*, 247, and Geoffrey Stoakes, *Hitler and the Quest for World Domination* (Leamington Spa, Hamburg, and New York: Berg, 1986), 4–29 and 64–87.
[41] Scholars of genocide have increasingly focused on apocalyptic narratives that arise the intersections of collective psychopathology and acute social distress, the *Protokolls* as a prime example. See Mark Levene, *The Meaning of Genocide*, vol. 1, *Genocide in the Age of the Nation State* (London and New York: I. B. Tauris, 2005), 129–35.
[42] Kershaw, *Hubris*, 152–3; Kellogg, *Russian Roots*, esp. 109–65; Knox, *To the Threshold of Power*, 341–2; and Hitler, *Sämtliche Aufzeichnungen*, no. 450, 17 December 1922, 769–75. On the character of empires, see Charles S. Maier, *Among Empires: American Ascendency and Its Predecessors* (Cambridge, Massachusetts, and London: Harvard University Press, 2006), 19–111.

and his putatively common touch, Hitler won the financial backing of the Beckstein family, the Wagner circle in Bayreuth, the steel magnate Fritz Thyssen, wealthy Russian émigrés associated with Reconstruction, and other assorted aristocrats whose support, much of which was in hard currency, supplemented members' subscriptions and entrance fees to party meetings.[43] Although that combination of elite influence and popular following characterized the bourgeois parties generally at least until the late 1920s, the NSDAP differed significantly in two respects. First, Hitler's charisma drew well-heeled backers, despite the Nazi movement's plebeian roughness, who would otherwise have chosen another political home. Yet they rarely numbered among Hitler's closest confidants despite Hitler's ability to charm them with his love of Wagner and his pleasing antirepublicanism. Second, the Nazi Party's alliances with elites, which would become crucial after 1930, did not allow the latter to dictate the terms of their partnership. Influential enough to exploit Hitler's value as a weapon in the pursuit of common interests, conservatives were not powerful enough to accomplish what the NSDAP would later achieve, a broad-based movement that was strong enough to bid for power.

The Weimar government's decision in the fall of 1923 to call a halt to the passive resistance to the Ruhr occupation, a "surrender" in the eyes of radical nationalists, encouraged Hitler to risk a military-style putsch. In so doing, he emulated Benito Mussolini's march on Rome in October of the previous year and the Bolshevik coup of October 1917.[44] In November, on the anniversary of the hated Revolution of 1918, the Nazis launched an amateurish and disorganized coup attempt in alliance with an unstable 'combat league' composed of an assortment of right-wing bands and leaders. They included General Ludendorff, Max von Scheubner-Richter, and Count Rüdiger von der Goltz, whose Free Corps units joined Bermondt's attack on Riga. Unable to win the support of Kahr and the Reichswehr for a march northward to Berlin, the putsch collapsed after a bloody gun battle with the Bavarian police, which cost Scheubner-Richter his life. The disintegration of the putsch terminated as an antisemitic rampage. With address books in hand, the SA and other right-wing groups rounded up Jews from their residences and off the streets, confining them in the beer hall cellar as hostages.[45] Arrested and convicted for treason while his party was outlawed, Hitler drew a

[43] Kershaw, *Hubris*, 186–91; Fabrice d'Almeida, *Hakenkreuz und Kaviar: Das mondäne Leben im Nationalsozialismus, trans.* Harald Ehrhardt (Düsseldorf: Patmos, 2007), 30–46.

[44] See Kellogg, *Russian Roots*, 193–216.

[45] Walter, *Antisemitische Kriminalität*, 111–42.

curiously light sentence of five years in a minimum security prison, of which he served less than a year. Proclaiming his German patriotism as the motive for the putsch, his plea appealed to the sympathetic ear of a conservative judge and gained rapt national attention. The relatively gentle treatment that right-wing putschists received contrasted baldly with the swift and ruthless suppression of Communist uprisings in Hamburg, Saxony, and Thuringia in the same year, and the forced removal of legitimately elected Social Democratic-led governments in those states.

Regardless, the dismal failures of the Kapp and Munich coup attempts testified to the exhaustion of putschism in general. Due to the Entente's internal divisions, Germany's wartime enemies could not muster enough troops to occupy Germany and enforce the terms of Versailles directly, thus leaving Germany with room to maneuver in the conduct of its foreign and financial policy. Still the Ruhr intervention underscored Germany's acute vulnerability. The Ruhr occupation and the possibility of losing the Rhineland encouraged the Reichswehr to once again give its qualified support to the republic rather than to risk a civil war and further territorial dismemberment that it could not likely prevent. For his part, Hitler subsequently altered his tactics to bid for power. Despite the inherent ideological and tactical violence of the NSDAP, personified most clearly by its paramilitary SA, Hitler would pursue the reins of power by legal means. He would transform the Nazi Party into an electoral machine capable of winning a majority in the Reichstag, which would dismantle the Weimar "system." Placing a premium on party unity and the avoidance of coalitions that would crumble under the weight of internal disagreements and external pressure, major contributors to the failure of the Munich putsch, Hitler forbade Nazi Party members from belonging to other radical nationalist organizations. He would pursue alliances only from a position of strength. Although Hitler's Munich contacts had provided the Nazi Party with valuable exposure and financial support, Hitler's Munich experience underscored the merits of defining the terms under which he would accept support from elements outside the party.

Hitler's brief spell in the comfortable Landsberg fortress outside of Munich, which unlike regular prisons allowed inmates to receive unlimited visitors and avoid work assignments, granted him the leisure to dictate his life story and philosophy to his deputy Rudolf Hess, and codify his ideas as to the shape of a future German polity.[46] To some degree, Hitler

---

[46] Nicolaus Wachsmann, *Hitler's Prisons: Legal Terror in Nazi Germany* (New Haven and London: Yale University Press, 2004), 38.

continued to adhere to the Austrian Pan German ideas that he absorbed during his youth. Although harshly critical of the Dual Monarchy that in his view privileged dynastic ties over national ones, Hitler's wartime comments linked the occupation of the Netherlands, Belgium, and Yugoslavia, Belgrade in particular, with the early modern history of the Habsburg Empire. Annual Nazi Party rallies in Nuremberg adopted the city's insignia from the late-eighteenth century before Napoleon's dissolution of the Holy Roman Empire in 1806.[47] Moreover, his nocturnal musings during the Second World War revealed his admiration for the engineering feats of the Roman Empire and the political skills of the British, who ruled India with few administrators and officers of their own. Nevertheless, in his speeches before the putsch, in his autobiography *Mein Kampf*, and subsequently in his *Second Book*, which he wrote in 1928 but left unpublished,[48] Hitler demanded more than just the revision of Germany's postwar boundaries and he rejected the partnership between Germany and Russia that Baltic Germans and Russian émigrés envisioned before the Munich putsch. In contrast to the imperialism of the Second Empire, Hitler's expansionism unequivocally gave priority to living space in the east over the acquisition of overseas colonies.

In Hitler's view, Imperial German foreign policy after Bismarck, and the bourgeois imperialists who shaped it, including the Pan Germans, became fatally compromised by its alliance with a "corpse of a state," the "Slavic-Habsburg Empire," which had enabled the dilution of its German essence. Moreover, Germany tolerated the "growth of a new Slavic power on the border of the Reich," namely Russia, whose interests conflicted with Germany's moribund ally and drew Germany into a ruinous war. Imperial Germany's colonial and commercial policy, which Hitler derided as the "peaceful economic conquest of the world," a poor remedy to its encirclement by hostile powers, sacrificed what should have been its first objective. Rather than its tepid and unsuccessful attempts at inner colonization, it should have sought new lands in the east for the establishment of a "healthy peasantry" as a bulwark of Germanness and the preservation of the *Volk*. Misreading the motivations of prewar

---

[47] Brigitte Hamann, *Hitlers Wien*, 156–60. On the importance of the symbolism of the Holy Roman Empire to German history, see Russell Berman, "Colonialism and No End: the Other Continuity Thesis," in *Colonial (Dis)-Continuities: Race, Holocaust, and Postwar Germany*, eds. Volker Langbehn and Mohammad Salama (New York: Columbia University Press, forthcoming).

[48] *Hitler's Second Book: The Unpublished Sequel to Mein Kampf by Adolf Hitler*, ed. Gerhard Weinberg and trans. Krista Smith (New York: Enigma Books, 2003).

imperialism, Hitler complained that the Second Empire abandoned heroism for commercialism. It failed to replicate the time-honored Prussian
virtues of self-preservation and self-sacrifice that were most important
to determining national greatness, and it instead pursued the empty and
ruinous pursuit of economic prosperity detached from ethnic revitalization. As the self-appointed spokesman for Germans stranded beyond the
Reich, Hitler ridiculed demands for the restoration of Germany's 1914
borders and the return of its overseas colonies. Such limited ambitions
remained wedded to the failed policies of the past, furthered Germany's
internal decline, and ignored that which was essential to racial revitalization, new land in Europe itself. Following the model established by the
Teutonic Knights centuries before, who obtained "sod for the German
plow and daily bread for the nation" by the sword, Germany's expanded
territory would come at the expense of Poland and Russia.[49]

In his *Second Book*, Hitler continued to underscore the futility of prewar overseas colonialism. Because it benefited commercial interests and
ignored the survival of the German *Volk*, the maritime colonies of the
Second Empire had been too remote and climatically undesirable for permanent settlement. They also brought Germany into conflict with Great
Britain when the Imperial government lacked a navy of sufficient power
to deal with the consequences.[50] Alternatively, Hitler proposed an understanding with Britain that would divide the globe between the two powers. In return for Britain's acceptance of a German-dominated continent,
Britain would maintain its empire and rule the high seas. Unlike previous
cases of European settler colonialism that evolved from the logic of an
expanding global capitalist economy,[51] Hitler's vision of German colonization required the withdrawal from that interconnected economy, a
tendency that the Great Depression would later deepen. That vision also
accepted as a "given" that war would necessarily accompany the quest
for additional territory.

To be sure, as late as 1920, Hitler followed Heinrich Class in advocating the recovery of overseas colonies for settlements, markets, and raw
materials extraction, in addition to the pursuit of an enlarged Germany

---

[49] Adolf Hitler, *Mein Kampf*, trans. Ralph Manheim (Boston: Houghton Mifflin, 1971),
126–56.
[50] *Second Book*, 77–8.
[51] On the relationship between the murderousness of frontier settlers and the extension of
European dominion, see Patrick Wolfe, "Settler colonialism and the elimination of the
native," *Journal of Genocide Research* 8, no. 4 (2006): 387–409.

in Europe, especially in the east.[52] Moreover, the prewar experience of colonization in Africa partially and indirectly informed his conceptions. While in prison he became familiar with the geopolitical theories of the late-nineteenth-century, Pan German geographer Friedrich Ratzel. Having conceived of geography as the expression of the culture of peoples, Ratzel described political boundaries as inherently impermanent and unnatural. An expert in migration, Ratzel believed that continuous movement and the expansion of empires defined human history. The quest for space by higher cultures caused the destruction of inferior ones by undermining native traditions and societies. A devotee of Alfred Thayer Mahan, Ratzel advocated naval power as the means to obtaining living space and favored Southwest Africa as a site of German colonization consistent with his expectation that the white race would successfully spread around the globe at the expense of indigenous peoples. The African connection emerged as well through figures important to the early history of the Nazi movement, among them Hermann Göring, whose father was the first colonial governor of Southwest Africa. The Reichswehr commander in Bavaria, Franz Xaver Ritter von Epp, the so-called "liberator of Munich" for his role in the suppression of the Bavarian revolution who participated in the genocide of the Herero, originally hired Hitler as an army informant following the latter's release from the military hospital.[53] After the fall of France, Hitler would consider the acquisition of overseas colonies on strategic grounds.

Nevertheless, visions of the east as the font of German revitalization and expansion provided the more immediate inspiration, especially as Hitler grew obsessed by the threat of an expansionist Bolshevism against Germany.[54] Derived from the ongoing border tensions with Poland, the postwar obsession with the "marooning" of Reich Germans outside of the Weimar borders, and the historical myths of medieval German settlers and Teutonic Knights, Hitler's visions drank deeply from the popularity

---

[52] Stoakes, *World Domination*, 30–3; 54.

[53] Benjamin Madley, "From Africa to Auschwitz: How German South West Africa Incubated Ideas and Methods Adopted and Developed by the Nazis in Eastern Europe," *European History Quarterly* 35, no. 3 (2005): 432–5; 450–3; Helmut Smith, *The Continuities of German History: Nation, Religion, and Race across the Long Nineteenth Century* (Cambridge: Cambridge University Press, 2008), 182–8; Jan Rüger, *The Great Naval Game: Britain and Germany in the Age of Empires* (Cambridge: Cambridge University Press, 2007), 212–3.

[54] Stoakes, *World Domination*, 115–21.

of fiction on the American frontier, the annexationist dreams of wartime, the temporary bonanza of Brest-Litovsk, and postwar irredentism, which denied the independent existence of biologically and culturally inferior Slavic peoples. In this imagining, Ratzel's neologism, *Lebensraum,* the geographical space that peoples required for their continued health, became the central, academically legitimated, justification during the 1920s for the imperialist displacement of Slavic and Jewish populations of the east. The Versailles "humiliation," the Entente's colonization, the "black horror on the Rhine," and an ineffectual and alien liberal democracy would be replaced by a Germany liberated from the inconvenience of borders and the unfulfilled nationalist aspirations of the past. The expectation of continental living space contrasted noticeably to the skepticism of postwar *völkisch* racists toward overseas colonialism. Because colonies abroad placed superior and inferior races in close proximity, they increased the danger of racial mixing.[55]

The postwar Munich geographer Karl Haushofer, introduced to Hitler by his student Rudolf Hess and Nazism's agricultural expert Walther Darré, reiterated Ratzel's claim as to the malleability of political borders in the interests of the *Volk*'s need for living space.[56] The emergence of the United States as a world power during and after World War I provided powerful reinforcement for claiming continental *Lebensraum.* Explained Hitler, the size of European states was "absurdly small in comparison to their weight of colonies, foreign trade, etc.," in contrast to "the American Union which possesses its base in its own continent and touches the rest of the earth only with its summit. And from this comes the immense inner strength of this state and the weakness of most European colonial powers."[57] As he would argue several years later, Hitler averred that the colonization of the continental United States, which siphoned off the cream of the Nordic peoples of Europe, provided the closest model to the combination of a vast internal market, material prosperity, and biological reproduction that *Lebensraum* would offer Germany.[58]

[55] Dirk van Laak, *Über alles in der Welt: Deutscher Imperialismus im 19. Und 20. Jahrhundert* (Munich: C. H. Beck, 2005), 118–9.

[56] Liulevicius, *War Land,* 247–72; Michael Burleigh, *Germany Turns Eastward: A Study of Ostforchung in the Third Reich* (Cambridge: Cambridge University Press, 1988), 13–39. See also David Blackbourn, *The Conquest of Nature: Water, Landscape. And the Making of Modern Germany* (New York: W.W. Norton, 2006), 293–4. In contrast to Hitler, Haushofer wanted Germany to become a world power through peaceful means. See Stoakes, *World Domination,* 140–70.

[57] *Mein Kampf,* 129.

[58] *Second Book,* 107–9.

Hitler's imperialism, its fusion of racial cleansing, colonial expansionism, counter-revolution against "Jewish Bolshevism," and autarky, represented an amalgamation of radical nationalist revanchism in the postwar period. Having rejected the Habsburg's multiethnic creation and abhorring racial mixing as contrary to the laws of nature, neither the forced assimilation or "Germanization" of subject peoples, nor various means of cooptation or autonomy would satisfy Hitler, who envisioned nothing less than an expansion for the sake of racial homogeneity and the expulsion or destruction of racial inferiors. *Lebensraum* would be to Germany what the frontier was to America, the foundation of global power.[59] The demise of the Habsburg, Romanov, and Hohenzollern dynasties would provide the opportunity to achieve it. The acquisition of *Lebensraum* would also mean the destruction of the "culture-destroying" Jews, the agents of political and racial hybridity that destroyed the racial integrity of the *Volk* from within, whose transnational mobility allowed them to become parasites "in the body of other peoples. ... His spreading is a typical phenomenon for all parasites; he always seeks a new feeding ground for his race."[60] Nevertheless, the end of the Ruhr occupation, stabilization, and the bankruptcy of putschism provided enough stability to allow the republic's survival and postpone the implementation of grandiose schemes that would likely require a war to implement. To be sure, neither the minimalist goal of revising the Versailles settlement nor dreams of empire would be abandoned. Yet the preferred means of recovering Germany's prewar empire would be negotiation with Germany's former enemies. In turn, the broader context for negotiation would be Germany's reintegration in a liberal, international economic order.

REVISIONISM, COLONIALISM, AND GREAT POWER POLITICS: WEIMAR'S STABILIZATION, 1924–1930

The period between the end of hyperinflation and the beginning of the Great Depression, which extended to 1930 when the last cabinet with a parliamentary majority fell, provided but a tenuous respite. Despite the influx of American loans and investment that laid the foundation for

---

[59] Neil Gregor, *How to Read Hitler* (New York and London: W. W. Norton, 2005), 98. On the influence of the American west on German geographers, especially Ratzel, and National Socialists, see David Blackbourn, *The Conquest of Nature: Water, Landscape, and the Making of Modern Germany* (New York and London: Norton, 2006), 293–309.
[60] *Mein Kampf*, 302–5.

modest and episodic recoveries in 1924, 1925, and 1927, the Weimar economy remained saddled with serious structural problems, among them high unemployment, a weak primary sector, and low industrial productivity.[61] The reparations settlement encouraged industrialists and agrarians, as well as the parties that represented them, to support the republic by forming a series of bourgeois cabinets that excluded the SPD until 1928. Yet national elections produced a steady drift to the right in voter preferences and the subdividing of middle-class voters among smaller special-interest parties, the outcome of an uneven impact of the currency reform. In addition to weakening the Protestant bourgeois parties, the DNVP and the DVP, and to a lesser extent the Center, that fragmentation would radicalize their leaderships in an effort to broaden their constituencies.[62] The winner of the presidential elections of 1925 confirmed the rightward movement of the electorate. The successor to the Social Democrat Friedrich Ebert, who died suddenly while he was immersed in acrimonious libel suits against right-wing newspapers that had accused him of treason, was none other than the old field marshal and victor of the Battle of Tannenberg, Paul von Hindenburg. For some, he embodied Germany's imperial past. To many more, his status as a symbol of German identity transcended the Second Empire and the republic. Hindenburg was transformed into a charismatic führer (leader) who, in embodying the will of the *Volk*, stood above the congenitally competitive interests that characterized parliamentary politics.[63]

Nevertheless, stabilization did encourage many who were previously unreconciled to make their peace with the republic. The most aggressively antirepublication party, the DNVP, entered the government in 1925 and again in 1927 to advance the interests of its constituencies more effectively. Agricultural estate owners from the Prussian east, who readily deployed Free Corps veterans as scabs against their striking laborers,

---

[61] Harold James, *The German Slump: Politics and Economics 1924–1936* (Oxford: Clarendon Press, 1986), 110–61, 190–282.

[62] Heinrich-August Winkler, *Weimar 1918–1933: Die Geschichte der ersten deutschen Demokratie* (Munich: CH Beck, 1998), 285–305; Charles S. Maier, *Recasting Bourgeois Europe: Stabilization in France, Germany and Italy in the Decade after World War I* (Princeton: Princeton University Press, 1976), 481.

[63] Wolfram Pyta, *Hindenburg: Herrschaft zwischen Hohenzollern und Hitler* (Munich: Siedler, 2007), 461–76. On Hindenburg's electorate, see Noel D. Cary, "The Making of the Reich President, 1925: German Conservatism and the Nomination of Paul von Hindenburg," *Central European History* 23, no. 2–3 (1990): 179–204; and Jürgen Falter, "The Two Hindenburg Elections of 1925 and 1932: A Total Reversal of Voter Coalitions," *Central European History* 23, no. 2–3 (1990): 225–41.

backed bourgeois coalitions in which the DNVP participated. In return they won the restoration of grain tariffs at their prewar level and generous aid programs to offset structural weaknesses in eastern Prussian agriculture. Although willing to accept ministries in most Weimar cabinets, the German People's Party (DVP) did so only because its pragmatic leadership chose to pursue antisocialism and revisionism by less confrontational means, convinced that Germany's military weakness left no plausible alternative. Moreover, stabilization provided limited space for Germany's recovery as a great power. Diplomatic negotiation and compromise, albeit limited to rolling back the terms of the Versailles Treaty, now became central to preserving the unity of the Reich against further dismemberment. In addition, American economic intervention in the form of the Dawes Plan reduced the prospect of further foreign military intervention. Crucial in this respect was the transfer protection that the plan afforded. If Germany was to pay its reparations, it would only do so if the stability of the mark was assured. Yet transfer protection carried a hidden danger by encouraging Germans to borrow American capital to finance its recovery. In the end, facilitating imports and servicing commercial debt took precedence over reparations payments.[64] The influx of American loans and investment deepened aspirations to material consumption that those who had profited from the hyperinflation once personified. Mediated in many cases through American products and Hollywood films, consumption began to lose its early postwar association with "Jewish" speculation and profiteering, even though the acquisition of goods beyond the basic necessities was out of reach for most Germans. A future of possibility began to compete with the dominant experience of scarcity.

The DVP politician Gustav Stresemann became the principal actor during Weimar's recovery, first by heading the "great" coalition that extended from the DVP on the right to the SPD on the left, which formally ended the passive resistance to the Ruhr occupation and engineered the stabilization of the mark. After that cabinet fell because of the ill effects of stabilization on many middle-class constituencies, Stresemann served as foreign minister in subsequent bourgeois cabinets, which negotiated the rescheduling of reparations payments and secured American financial support, while doggedly pursuing the revision of the postwar peace

---

[64] Albrecht Ritschl, *Deutschlands Krise und Konjunktur 1924–1934: Binnenkonjunktur, Auslandsverschuldung und Reparationsproblem zwischen Dawes-Plan und Transfersperre* (Berlin: Akademie Verlag, 2002), esp. 120–7.

settlement. Stresemann's role in the stabilization of the republic was in many ways surprising. His relative moderation departed from his wartime support for the Fatherland Party and his subsequent condemnation of the Versailles Treaty. Consistent with the trope of Germany's colonization by its enemies, he described the victors as an Anglo-American "cartel" that effectively resulted in the "Egyptianization" of Germany. During the war, Stresemann had advocated the annexation of Belgium, the French coastline, Morocco, and extensive territory in the east to enable Germany to compete with the emerging power of the United States.[65] Nevertheless, the Kapp putsch and the unrest arising from the hyperinflation forced Stresemann to accept the Weimar Republic as the only alternative to a Marxist revolution, putschism, and civil war. Convinced of the impermanence of the postwar arrangements because of the social crises facing the victors, and the Allied fear of the Soviet Union that he believed Germany could exploit in its favor, Stresemann sought avenues to international cooperation that would expand Germany's room to maneuver and allow its return to the concert of European great powers. Germany's indispensability as the economic engine of Europe and its place among the top three industrial powers along with Britain and the United States also contributed to his belief that his country possessed leverage worth exercising.[66] Stresemann's acceptance of the Dawes Plan, which exploited the British unwillingness to support further harsh measures by the French and the American willingness to halt transfers of reparations payments if they jeopardized the stability of the mark, enabled the restoration of German sovereignty over the Rhenish-Westphalian industrial basin and forced the antirepublican DNVP into the government.

The Locarno Treaties of December of 1925 became Stresemann's most significant foreign policy achievement. In return for guaranteeing Germany's sovereignty and equality as a negotiating partner among western European nations, which paved the way for Germany' s admission to the League of Nations the following year, Germany declared its western borders as inviolable. To be sure, Locarno entailed painful compromises, notably the permanent loss of Alsace and Lorraine to France. Despite

---

[65] Adam Tooze, *The Wages of Destruction: The Making and Breaking of the Nazi Economy* (London: Allen Lane, 2006), 4.

[66] J.R.C. Wright, *Gustav Stresemann: Weimar's Greatest Statesman* (Oxford: Oxford University Press, 2002), 146–9; Tooze, *Wages of Destruction*, 3–8. For a reading of Stresemann that suggests that his republicanism was more principled than pragmatic, see Eric Kurlander, *The Price of Exclusion: Ethnicity, National Identity, and the Decline of German Liberalism 898–1933* (New York and Oxford: Berghahn, 2006), 262–3.

Stresemann's strenuous efforts, the agreement did not stipulate the evacuation of French troops from the Rhineland, which did not occur until
five years later. In any case, an immediate withdrawal would have done
nothing to assuage the bitterness over the "black horror," the irreversible legacy of which were the Afro-German children who personified
racial pollution imposed by the Entente.[67] Nevertheless, Locarno left in
place the treaty that Rathenau had concluded with the Soviet Union at
Rapallo in 1922. Under the cover of restored diplomatic relations, trade
agreements, and the abandonment of the reparation claims of each side
against the other, Rapallo allowed the Reichswehr to train in the Soviet
Union in violation of the Versailles limitations on Germany's offensive
military capability. Although Stresemann discouraged discussion of a
more far-reaching alliance with the Soviet Union against the Entente
because he feared that the Soviet army would export communism to
the West, the existing agreement weakened the prospect of an encircl-
ing Franco-Soviet entente. Moreover, Germany regained the tacit acceptance of its great power status, and left the door open to discussions
about the restoration of its overseas empire. The treaty withdrew the
presumption of Germany's moral unfitness as colonial power, the justification for Article 22 of the Versailles settlement. Although Germany
promised not to alter its boundaries with Poland and Czechoslovakia
by force, the Locarno agreement clearly left them open to future negotiations. As an indication of Germany's military weakness vis à vis its
neighbors and the counterproductivity of putschism, which threatened
more foreign intervention rather than less, Stresemann's pursuit of a
direct understanding with France departed significantly from the diplomatic practice of the Second Empire. Although vilified by the right as
an emblem of Germany's subordination to foreign powers, the Locarno
agreement provided a brief and uneasy respite from wartime and postwar antagonism.[68]

The possibility of future revision attached to the eastern boundaries
applied as well to Germany's maritime empire. Some observers, including
the sharp-eyed journalist and pacifist Carl von Ossietsky, recognized that
the loss of the colonies amounted to a blessing in disguise, for Germany did
not have to defend them against its enemies or confront the rising postwar
colonial national liberation movements that bedeviled other European

---

[67] Tina M. Campt, *Other Germans: Black Germans and the Politics of Race, Gender, and
Memory in the Third Reich* (Ann Arbor: University of Michigan Press, 2004), 58–60.
[68] Mommsen, *Rise and Fall*, 214–5.

FIGURE 3.2. Gustav Stresemann in Geneva on the occasion of Germany's formal admission to the League of Nations in 1926. From left to right are Stresemann, the British Foreign Secretary Austen Chamberlain, the French Foreign Minister Aristide Briand, and State Secretary Karl von Schubert of the German Foreign Office. Stresemann's conclusion of the Locarno Treaty and Germany's membership in the League signified a German willingness to negotiate revisions to the Versailles Treaty.
Source: Bundesarchiv Koblenz, Bild, 102–13209.

empires.[69] Nevertheless, the yearning to recover and expand Germany's overseas holdings attracted a vocal following. In 1918, former settlers and colonial officials founded the Reich League of German Colonists. Reorganized in 1920, the German Colonial Society (DKG) overcame its financial weakness during the hyperinflation to organize a congress in 1924 that commemorated the fortieth anniversary of the founding of Germany's overseas empire. By 1926, the DKG had 250 branches and over thirty thousand members. In addition to its Women's League, the DKG also organized its Youth Committee to spread the "colonial idea" among young people. Other colonial organizations sprouted as well, all of them converging under the umbrella of the Reich Colonial Task Force (*Kolonialen Reichsarbeitsgemeinschaft*, or KORAG). The Weimar colonial movement showcased a large number of former colonial officials

[69] Dirk Van Laak, *Imperiale Infrastruktur: Deutsche Planungen für eine Erschliessung Afrikas 1880 bis 1969* (Paderborn Ferdinand Schöningh, 2004), 213.

and financial interests with a stake in empire, including the ubiquitous Paul von Lettow-Vorbeck, whose luster derived, as it had immediately after the war, from having remained undefeated in the field at the signing of the armistice. Many who sought the recovery of Germany's overseas empire, however, increasingly recast their colonialism from the formal administration of territory to infrastructural and technological development through partnerships between private industry and government agencies. Together with the deployment of doctors who would eliminate tropical diseases, Germany's global influence and "civilizing mission" would be assured. The ambitions of colonialists did not stop there. They conceived of Africa as a venue of opportunity for the unemployed and even more grandiosely the means of Germany's and Europe's salvation. German engineers dreamed of building dams at Gibralter and Gallipoli to lower the level of the Mediterranean, a feat that would enable the construction of bridges to connect Africa to Europe. Such a project would enable the more efficient exploitation of resources and guarantee autarky, such that the danger of future blockades would recede.[70]

Although active, well organized, and articulate, the Weimar colonial movement had little mass appeal. Still, it maintained a strong presence in the Reichstag, cutting across all parties except for the Communists. Its center of gravity lay especially in the DVP, whose academic, commercial, and industrial middle-class constituencies were committed to colonial revisionism. The Inter-Party Colonial Union, the brainchild of the former governor of German East Africa Heinrich Schnee, who became the DVD's leading voice for colonialism, spanned from the DNVP to the SPD.[71] At the Berlin Colonial Week and Exhibition in 1925, Stresemann as the principal speaker conveyed his belief that Germany needed to expand because it lacked sufficient space.[72] Now favoring a liberal imperialism, commercial expansion overseas rather than the annexation of territory, Stresemann nonetheless sought to undermine France's "unnatural" hegemony on the continent through alliances with the new states of Eastern Europe and the revival of a German-dominated Central European "free

[70] Van Laak, *Über alles in der Welt*, 125–6; and, *Imperiale Infrastruktur*, 202–17, 237–42, and 248–53.

[71] Wolfe W. Schmokel, *Dream of Empire: German Colonialism, 1919–1945* (Westport, CT: Greenwood Press, 1964), 1–14; Lora Wildenthal, *German Women for Empire, 1884–1945* (Durham, NC and London: Duke University Press, 2001), 172–85.

[72] Sara Friedrichsmeyer, Sara Lennox, and Susanne Zantop, eds., *The Imperialist Imagination: German Colonialism and Its Legacy* (Ann Arbor: University of Michigan Press, 1998), 16.

trade" zone. Once British and American support for that objective was in place, Stresemann believed that the attainment of a German Central Africa would be possible.[73]

Germany's relative military and diplomatic weakness, the hostility to Versailles internally, and Stresemann's own predilections, defined his position toward Germany's postwar eastern borders. Having confidently assumed in the early twenties that Poland would not survive its own class and ethnic divisions, Stresemann had to be more accommodating after the coup d'état of the former general Josef Piłsudski as Poland's president in 1926 and the restoration of stability to Poland's domestic politics. Stresemann preferred to pursue German objectives through negotiation rather than confrontation and to use the League of Nations as his mediator. Yet his intervention on behalf of German minorities, which included supporting them financially, and lobbying for the return of Danzig and the northern half of the Polish Corridor to Germany, was unacceptable to the Poles who were equally determined to retain their western territories, polonize ethnic minorities, or coerce them into emigration. Pressured by the forced assimilation policies of the Polish government, an estimated 575,000 Germans emigrated to the Reich between 1918 and 1926, fearful of economic ruin and becoming stateless.[74] Although Stresemann considered compensating Poland for sacrificing those territories, his broader ambitions, an expanded German economic influence on the continent in which ethnic German communities would be crucial as a market for German manufactured goods and a source of raw materials, was not likely to be achieved in the tense ethnic conflicts of postwar central and east central Europe.[75]

Moreover, Stresemann's peaceful pursuit of his aims would become increasingly difficult to sell at home to those who saw that he played by

---

[73] Woodruff D. Smith, *The Ideological Origins of Nazi Imperialism* (New York and Oxford: Oxford University Press, 1986), 201–2.

[74] Mark Mazower, *Hitler's Empire: Nazi Rule in Occupied Poland* (London: Allen Lane, 2008), 37; Tammo Luther, *Volkstumspolitik des Deutschen Reiches 1933–1938: Die Auslandsdeutsche im Spannungsfeld zwischen Traditionalisten und Nationalsozialisten* (Stuttgart: Franz Steiner Verlag, 2004), 33.

[75] On Stresemann's policies, especially toward ethnic Germans, see Vladis Lumans, *Himmler's Auxiliaries: The Volksdeutsche Mittelstelle and the German National Minorities of Europe, 1933–1945* (Chapel Hill and London: University of North Carolina Press, 1993), 24–5; Luther, *Volkstumspolitik des Deutschen Reiches*, 34–5, Richard Blanke, *Orphans of Versailles: The Germans in Western Poland* (Lexington: University Press of Kentucky, 1993), 130–1, and most recently Carole Fink, *Defending the Rights of Others: The Great Powers, the Jews, and International Minority Protection, 1878–1938* (Cambridge: Cambridge University Press, 2004), 295–316.

the Entente's rules to accomplish Germany's return to the status of a great power. The Reichswehr, which under the terms of the Versailles treaty had to retool itself, became a smaller but more lethal offensive force envisioned by the general staff as capable of mobilizing a popular *levée en masse* against foreign enemies. It continued to develop its war planning against Poland throughout the 1920s, putting the recovery of the lost territories ahead of the return of the Saar, the annexation of Austria, and the remilitarization of the Rhineland. In effect, the army's planning amounted to a "first" rearmament plan once the Entente's on-site inspections ceased in January of 1927, well before Stresemann's death and well before economic collapse brought the demise of the liberal international order.[76]

Despite the lobbies that advocated the return of the overseas colonies, a noticeable clarification of priorities occurred. The searing experience of the wartime blockade and the loss of the overseas territories elevated the significance of a continental empire as an antidote, even as claims to Africa remained prominent. The popularization of geopolitics in the 1920s, an outgrowth of its position in German universities during the Weimar era, testified to the sentiment among the educated middle class for a German-dominated Europe. Overlapping with new fields, such as Eastern Studies (*Ostforschung*) and Native Peoples and Cultures Research (*Volks-und Kulturbodenforschung*), which imagined interconnected Germanic populations that putatively cried out for inclusion in an expanded Reich,[77] geopolitics carried sufficient political weight to limit Stresemann's room to maneuver, even had he been willing to accept the permanence of Poland and its postwar borders. While others continued to synthesize overseas colonies and eastern *Lebensraum*, prominent geopoliticians, Karl Haushofer among them, believed that present realities precluded risky attempts to reacquire Germany's lost colonies, preferring instead a continental

---

[76] Christian Leitz, *Nazi Foreign Policy, 1933–1941: The Road to Global War* (London and New York: Routledge, 2004), 63; Knox, *To the Threshold of Power*, 286–90. On the Reichswehr's conceptions of its mission during the interwar period to militarize society, see Geyer, *Deutsche Rüstungspolitik 1860–1980*, 118–53.

[77] Michael Burleigh, *Germany Turns Eastwards: A Study of Ostforchung in the Third Reich* (Cambridge: Cambridge University Press, 1988); Michael Fahlbusch, "*Wo der deutsche ... ist, ist Deutschland!": Die Stiftung für deutsche Volks-und Kulturbodenforschung in Leipzig 1920–1933* (Bochum: Brockmeyer, 1994), 49–263; and Wolfgang Wippermann, *Die Deutschen und der Osten: Feindbild und Traumland* (Darmstadt: Primus Verlag, 2007), 70–3.

bloc of revisionist powers that would resist "Anglo-Saxon" colonialism. Adhering to Social Darwinian visions of biologically determined competition among states for supremacy, they envisioned expansion as complementary to Germany's cultural and technological sophistication and its need for outlets for its overpopulation. Most geopolitical experts, however, were heavily invested in a vision of space as the expression of the unity of culture and race, and all produced the maps and academic studies that justified Germany's territorial claims against its neighbors. They were encumbered by the near-obsessive fear, made worse by the postwar peace settlement, of Germany's encirclement by its enemies, which in turn justified an aggressive and unilateral expansion. Finally, they maintained that Germany was destined to settle the putatively undersettled east while segregating the inferior races who lived there. Only a future that began with the elimination of Poland, the "unnatural" creation of Versailles, could Germany avoid being crushed by western capitalism on one side and Bolshevism on the other.[78]

Geopolitical theory cut across political boundaries to be sure, appealing to the DDP and even to some Social Democrats. It resonated among business leaders who were less interested in its ethnopolitical implications than in its possibilities for the creation of a German-dominated and integrated trade zone in central and southeastern Europe, which would be blockade resistant.[79] Yet the diffusion of geopolitics proved especially deep within the DVP, DNVP, and the Nazi Party which after 1928 grew more vociferous as the German economy weakened. Thus, in condemning the "German nationalist bourgeoisie" and Stresemann especially for their putative timidity, Hitler invoked the driving forces of space and struggle. Only "international Jewry," who not only caused the Great War but also profited from it, he said, welcomed a foreign policy based on bourgeois principles, diplomacy as the art of the possible, and the restoration of the impermanent borders of 1914. "The German borders of 1914," asserted Hitler in 1928, at the height of Stresemann's influence, "were borders that represented something just as unfinished as peoples' borders always are. The division of territory on the earth is always the momentary result of a struggle and an evolution that is in no way finished, but that naturally continues to progress. It is dumb to simply take the borders from any

[78] Liulevicius, *War Land*, 255; Burleigh, *Germany Turns Eastward*, 22–39; David Thomas Murphy, *The Heroic Earth: Geopolitical Thought in Weimar Germany, 1918–1933* (Kent, Ohio and London: Kent State University Press, 1997), 191–202, 218–23, 225–7.
[79] van Laak, *Über alles in der Welt*, 127–9; *Imperiale Infrastruktur*, 224–7.

given year in the history of a people and establish it as a political goal."[80]
If Hitler failed to appreciate Stresemann's past as a wartime annexationist, Hitler's worldview nonetheless differed fundamentally: Stresemann
sought to create an expanded continental market on the North American
model to enhance Germany's economic power, while using American
influence to restrain the British and French. North America influenced
Hitler in another way: Expansion would mean the removal of indigenous,
mainly Slavic and Jewish, peoples to make room for German settlers and
complete the project that had been left undone, a polity that embraced
all ethnic Germans. Unlike Stresemann, who believed that autarky would
amount to "economic death" for a nation that depended upon the export
of finished goods and imports of raw materials, Hitler saw *Lebensraum*
as the defense against the "economic death" that resulted precisely from
Germany's integration in a global economy, and the source of racial
revitalization.[81]

As Hitler's remarks revealed, visions of an enlarged Germany fed upon
myths of Germany's postwar victimization by the Entente that imperialist intellectuals furthered. Thus, Paul Rohrbach's lengthy and generously
illustrated volume *Germany in Crisis*, which he published in 1926, decried
the perilous position of millions of Germans in Europe beyond the Reich's
borders. Aiming to educate German youth, arouse Germany's educated
elites, and change opinion abroad, Rohrbach deplored the manner in
which the Versailles settlement prohibited Germans in Danzig and Austria
from returning "home to the Reich," while the remainder were abandoned
either to Bolshevism, as in the Soviet Union, or to minority status in the
successor states. Lacking effective representation and subject to relentless
measures designed to forcibly assimilate them and eliminate their culture,
ethnic Germans suffered from the misguided decisions of the peacemakers.[82] Yet, because the wounds of Versailles cut deeply, the popularization of imperialism was arguably broader than under the Second Empire,
beginning with the colonial nostalgia mediated through fiction. Easily the
most popular novel was Hans Grimm's *Volk ohne Raum*, first published
in 1926. By 1935, it had sold well over three hundred thousand copies.
Closely associated with the Colonial Society and the German National

[80] *Second Book*, 95–6, 121–2.
[81] Tooze, *Wages of Destruction*, 9. See Stresemann's remarks in *Gustav Stresemann: His
     Diaries, Letters, and Papers*, Vol. III, ed. and trans. Erich Sutton (New York: Macmillan,
     1940), 252–3.
[82] Paul Rohrbach, *Deutschland in Not! Die Schicksale der Deutschen in Europa ausserhalb
     des Reiches* (Berlin-Schmargendorf and Leipzig: Wilhelm Andermann, 1926).

FIGURE 3.3. Arrival of German refugees in the German border town of Bentschen, ca. 1920. Having fled the one-time eastern Prussian province of Posen, most of which was ceded to Poland in 1919, the new arrivals personified the unsettled status of ethnic Germans in the postwar successor states.

Source: Bundesarchiv Koblenz, Bild 137–001167. Photographer: Robert Sennecke.

People's Party, Grimm articulated through his characters Germany's mission to settle its *Volk* overseas, particularly in Africa, and supplant Great Britain as the world's dominant imperial power. The acquisition and settlement of living space would allow Germans to remake their social order. They would recover their spiritual and cultural values and, by providing opportunity for its surplus population, eliminate the class divisions that drew workers to socialism. Disturbingly, Grimm's retrospective novellas on prewar Southwest Africa, published in 1929, betrayed his approval of von Trotta's genocide as necessary to eliminate the contradiction of prewar settler colonialism between preserving apartheid and allowing male settlers to exercise dominion over native women.[83]

The Colonial Women's League and housewives associations that proliferated during the Weimar period marketed the household and

[83] Sara Lennox, "Race, Gender, and Sexuality in German Southwest Africa: Hans Grimm's *Sudafrikanische Novellen*, in *Germany's Colonial Pasts*, eds. Eric Ames, Marcia Klotz, and Lora Wildenthal (London and Lincoln: University of Nebraska Press, 2005), 63–75.

housekeeping as expressions of cultural and biological Germanness that cut across contemporary political boundaries. They imagined that ethnic Germans, whether trapped in Poland or Czechoslovakia or stranded in Southwest Africa under South African rule, maintained their identity through sparkling clean, linen-filled German households.[84] Nationalist women's associations affiliated with the DNVP and DVP, which were obsessed with the "niggerization" of the west, the "border struggle" in the east, and the rescue of fellow Germans trapped in Poland, promoted the creation of rural settlements as racially secure bulwarks against the "Polish flood."[85] Such efforts complemented those of the foreign office and numerous voluntary associations, the most prominent of which was the Association for Germandom Abroad (*Verein für das Deutschtum in Ausland*, or VDA), which championed the interests of roughly three million "Reich" Germans in the ceded territories and the millions of other ethnic Germans throughout Europe, especially in the non-German successor states.[86] Colonialist feature films, produced by commercial enterprises that involved retired colonial officials, supplemented popular fiction. Colonial revisionist groups collectively sponsored the 1926 UFA-produced film *World History and Colonial History* (*Die Weltgeschichte als Kolonialgeschichte*) to lobby for the return of Germany's empire, and thus reclaim Germany's standing as a "cultural people" (*Kulturvölker*), an agent of history and progress.[87] The continued commodification of colonial images was even more striking, whether as an expression of German superiority or German victimization. Thus, advertisements made prolific use of racialized stereotypes of blackness or, by contrast, chiseled Aryan whiteness, in marketing everything from cigarettes to soap to film. Possessing exaggerated lips, human bones as hairpins, and bare

[84] Wildenthal, *German Women for Empire*, 175–8; Nancy Reagin, *Sweeping the German Nation: Domesticity and National Identity in Germany, 1870–1945* (Cambridge: Cambridge University Press, 2006), 72–109.

[85] Elizabeth Harvey, *Women and the Nazi East: Agents and Witnesses of Germanization* (New Haven and London: Yale University Press, 2003), 23–43; Raffael Scheck, *Mothers of the Nation: Right-wing Women in Weimar Germany* (Oxford and New York: Berg, 2004), 121–5.

[86] Hans-Adolf Jacobsen, *Nationalsozialistische Aussenpolitik 1933–1938* (Frankfurt am Main and Berlin: A. Metzner, 1968), 161; Luther, *Volkstumspolitik*, 26–7; Markus Leniger, *Nationalsozialistische "Volkstumsarbeit" und Umsiedlungspolitik 1933–1945: Von der Minderheitsbetreuung zur Siedlerauslese* (Berlin: Frank and Timme, 2006), 24–5.

[87] Marcia Klotz, "Global Visions: From the Colonial to the National Socialist World," *European Studies Journal* 16, no. 2 (1999): 37–68.

feet, the cannibal emerged as the most frequently used image of Africans, cast in cartoonish form as to deflate such a character's inherent menace. Nevertheless, a rival image, that of the sexualized African, expressed the opposite or at least unsettling message. The emergence of mass culture carried with it the arrival of African and African-American entertainers, who even from the perspective of sympathetic observers, embodied unmediated primeval sensuality.[88] Commodifying the experience of the "black horror on the Rhine" during the French occupation, images of frightening black men raping German women expressed the colonization of Germany by the Entente and the unnatural reversion of racial hierarchy.[89] Such fear-ridden images of German victimization would not only grow more powerful during the Depression, they would also increase the emphasis on unilateralism, autarky, and expansionism at the highest levels of the state.

THE WEIMAR REPUBLIC UNRAVELS: ECONOMIC CRISIS, THE END OF "FULFILLMENT," AND THE RISE OF NAZISM

Stresemann's policy of "fulfillment," which was predicated on negotiation and incremental gains rather than unilateralism or military force, succeeded only as long as it bore fruit in the form of American loans and investment, and American protection of the mark. Moreover, it would endure only as long as that investment mitigated the weaknesses in the German economy, among them falling profits because of the lack of capital investment and high structural unemployment. In 1928, however, American investment and foreign lending began to decline. Both were shifted to domestic markets to take advantage of soaring stock prices and preserve gold reserves. In 1929, the introduction of the Young Plan, which under pressure from Germany's creditors rescheduled its reparations payments, benefited Germany by allowing it full economic sovereignty. Nevertheless, it removed transfer protection that, by forcing Germany to pay reparations even in periods of economic downturn, contributed to a debt service of eight percent of the German national income.[90] Wall Street's collapse that same year

[88] Ivan Goll, "The Negroes are Conquering Europe," *Die literarische Welt*, no. 2 (January 15, 1926): 3–4, in Kaes, Jay, and Dimendberg, *Weimar Republic Sourcebook*, 559–60.

[89] David M. Ciarlo, "Consuming Race, Envisioning Empire: Colonialism and German Mass Culture, 1887–1914" (Diss: University of Wisconsin, Madison, 2003), 418–27.

[90] Ritschl, *Deutschlands Krise und Konjunktur*, 128–41. See also Winkler, *Weimar*, 348.

terminated short-term loans altogether, which buttressed many of Germany's largest corporations, and removed the last support from Weimar's modest recovery. The combination of industrial stagnation, weak investor confidence, anemic industrial growth, and a crisis in agriculture arising from falling global commodity prices, could no longer be hidden, not least because their political consequences emerged with a vengeance. In 1928, employers in the heavy industries of the Ruhr locked out their workers. In an attack on binding arbitration and high social insurance costs, they refused to accede to their workers' wage demands, ominously forecasting the management-labor conflicts that would bring the collapse of a second "great coalition" in 1930. The bitter conflict between the SPD and DVD over the financing of one of Weimar's most noteworthy achievements, federal unemployment insurance, as well as the future of Weimar's social policy in general, resulted in the resignation of the Social Democratic chancellor Hermann Müller and in Hindenburg's appointment of steadily more authoritarian cabinets without majority support.

The agricultural sector proved most explosive. Because of higher taxes and interest rates that stabilization imposed, and serious structural problems that included the inefficient production and rural overpopulation in southern and western Germany, political disaffection expressed economic despair. In the thinly settled eastern Prussian border regions, the crisis was especially evident. Chronically low wage levels, the flight of workers to the industrial conurbations of the west, the modest successes of Weimar settlement projects, which were intended to restore economic health and ethnic vitality in the borderlands,[91] the lack of industrial investment and low levels of urbanization, and the lack of natural resources meant an over-reliance on a shaky primary sector. Even when measured against the low standards of popular commitment to the republic's survival, the predominantly Protestant agrarian regions of the east proved notably hostile. Its entrenched conservative landowning elite and the failure of Weimar's subsidy programs to stem alarmingly high rates of foreclosure intensified agrarian rage at the policy of Weimar governments to import food to the disadvantage of locally grown commodities. The loss of most of Posen and West Prussia and the eastern

---

[91] On the problems of settlement, see Heinrich Becker, *Handlungsspielräume der Agrarpolitik: Der Agrarpolitik in der Weimarer Republik zwischen 1923 und 1929* (Stuttgart: Franz Steiner Verlag, 1990), 269–304, and Uwe Mai, *"Rasse und Raum": Agrarpolitik, Sozial-und Raumplanung im NS Staat* (Paderborn: Ferdinand Schöning, 2002), 22–9.

third of Upper Silesia to Poland meant that anti-Slavism and hostility toward the Versailles settlement ran especially deep.[92]

Rural discontent surfaced well before the Depression, a legacy of government price controls and crop seizures during wartime and the ill effects of stabilization on the high indebtedness of farmers. In 1928, the Rural People (*Landvolk*) movement, which began in Schleswig-Holstein as an expression of peasant fury at high interest rates, the Republic's tariff policy, and high taxes that supported the Weimar welfare state, spread across northern and eastern Germany. In addition to refusing to pay taxes, peasants staged violent protests at farm foreclosures, often waving the flag of the rebellious peasants during the Peasants' War of the sixteenth century. The following year another rural protest surfaced in response to the Young Plan. Organized by the DNVP, the National Socialists, and the Stahlhelm, the National Rural League, the postwar successor to the Agrarian League, and splinter parties such as the Christian National Rural Peoples Party (CNBLP), the protest called for a referendum to block ratification of the agreement. Replete with the language of victimization, the extreme right's crusade against the Young Plan depicted a Germany exploited, enslaved, and colonized by foreigners. The chair of the Pomeranian DNVP, Georg Werner von Zitzewitz, claimed the Young Plan would reduce the German *Volk* to the status of a "helot *Volk*" without national sovereignty. The policy of fulfillment had yielded nothing but continued subjugation and misery.[93]

Election results from the eastern regions intensified the rightward movement of Weimar politics. From 1919 to January of 1928, the DNVP drew exceptionally well with local leaderships composed of large landowners and to a lesser extent peasants, Protestant pastors, and village school teachers, leaders who in turn composed the shock troops of the militantly conservative and demagogic National Rural League.[94] In the Reichstag elections of June, 1928, however, the DNVP's support declined markedly while special-interest splinter parties, such as the CNBLP,

[92] Richard Bessel, "Eastern Germany as a structural problem in the Weimar Republic," *Social History* 3 (1978) 199–218. On the political consequences of agrarian economic weakness, see also, Shelley Baranowski, *The Sanctity of Rural Life: Nobility, Protestantism and Nazism in Weimar Prussia* (New York and Oxford: Oxford University Press, 1995), 117–49.

[93] "Unser Kampf," *Pommersche Tagespost* 19, no. 223 (22 September 1929).

[94] Wolfram Pyta, *Dorfgemeinschaft und Parteipolitik 1918–1933: Die Verschränkung von Milieu und Parteien in den protestantischen Landgebieten Deutschlands in der Weimarer Republic* (Düsseldorf: Droste Verlag, 1996), 163–323.

became the primary beneficiaries of popular disillusionment. The DNVP's participation in government, its inability as a result to improve the economic viability of its constituents, and the correct perception that government aid programs to the east enriched estate owners had their effect. Even the DNVP's new leader, the Pan German media magnate Alfred Hugenburg, did not improve the party's electoral fortunes. In the elections of September, 1930, in which the NSDAP achieved its nationwide breakthrough to become the second largest party in the Reichstag, drew disproportionately well in the east and signified the DNVP's utter collapse in rural regions.

The economic crisis of the late 1920s radicalized the bourgeois parties in a permanently antirepublican direction. All sought at minimum to dissolve the Reichstag and reduce its powers, or at maximum to impose a dictatorship. Beset from defections that caused the shrinkage of two million votes and thirty Reichstag seats in the 1928 elections, the DNVP unceremoniously dumped its chair, Count Cuno von Westarp, who steered the DNVP's participation in government after 1924, in favor of Hugenberg. Determined to transform the party from a heterogeneous conservative coalition party into a unified radical nationalist bloc governed by what he termed the "iron brace of Weltanschauung," Hugenberg presided over a platform that fused authoritarianism at home and resistance to Germany's colonization by the Entente. It called for the "liberation" of Germany from "foreign domination" and asserted Germany's right to defend and protect Germans beyond the Reich's borders. It sought the restoration of the Hohenzollern monarchy and a reduction in the powers of the Reichstag. It further cried out for resistance to "the undermining, un-German spirit in all forms, whether it stems from Jewish or other circles," and "emphatically" opposed "the prevalence of Judaism in the government and public life, which has emerged ever more ominously since the revolution."[95] Insisting upon a muscular foreign policy as befitting a great power, the party demanded at minimum the revision of Versailles and the return of Germany's overseas colonies.[96]

---

[95] "German National Peoples' Party (DNVP) Program," in Kaes, Jay, and Dimendberg, *Weimar Republic Sourcebook*, 348–52.

[96] Richard J. Evans, *The Coming of the Third Reich* (New York: Penguin Press, 2004), 94–5; Larry Eugene Jones, "Kuno Graf von Westarp und die Krise des deutsche Konservatismus in der Weimarer Republik," in *'Ich bin der letzte Preusse:' Der politische Lebensweg des konservativen Politikers Kuno Graf von Westarp (1864–1945)*, eds. Larry Eugene Jones and Wolfram Pyta (Cologne, Weimar, and Vienna: Böhlau Verlag, 2006), 130–2.

In 1929, the DVP also moved sharply to the right with Stresemann's death, as its employer constituents, citing falling profits, mounted an aggressive attack on the Weimar welfare state, reflected especially in their objection to employer contributions to unemployment insurance. Nor was the Center spared as its party congress in December of 1928 chose the canon law professor and prelate Ludwig Kaas to be its new leader. The move strengthened the influence of the papal nuncio Eugenio Pacelli, who sought to revitalize the Center as the voice of Catholic interests and to achieve a concordat between Germany and the Vatican. It also signified the defeat of the party's left wing, which during the twenties sought to transform the Center into an interconfessional party backed by organized labor. The new leader's call for the abandonment of parliamentary democracy and the imposition of an authoritarian state that would destroy the influence of the left, meant that little remained of the Center that once formed part of the "Weimar coalition."[97] The shift to the right among Catholics paralleled that of Protestant clergy and most prominent laity, whose unceasing attacks on Weimar secularism, "mammonism," and "Jewish spirit" did much to fan the flames of antirepublicanism.

The collapse of the Great Coalition in March of 1930 mirrored Weimar Germany's profound social divisions. Because the resulting political fragmentation rendered the Reichstag increasingly unworkable, Reich President Hindenburg, a reluctant supporter of the "system" in the best of times, opened the door to a dictatorship in fact if not in name. By evoking Article 48 of the Weimar Constitution, which gave the president extraordinary powers in emergencies, the chancellors whom he subsequently appointed could rule by decree. Hindenburg's appointment of the Center Party politician, Heinrich Brüning as chancellor meant the installation of a devout monarchist who wanted to reduce the powers of the Reichstag and the Prussian minister president, so as to eradicate the remaining bastion of Social Democracy in Germany's largest state. Brüning's second goal was especially important to the Reichswehr because the Prussian government wanted to bring the military's alliance with right-wing combat leagues and illegal weapons depots under tighter republican control.[98] Although unable to persuade the Reich president to follow through on those measures, Brüning sharply curtailed the freedom of the press, granted the military more autonomy and a bigger budget, and effected draconian cuts in the salaries of civil servants and public expenditures generally, including

[97] Mommsen, *Rise and Fall*, 261.
[98] Ibid., 243.

unemployment insurance. "At heart," according to the historian Fritz Stern, whose converted Jewish family witnessed Weimar's decline with trepidation, Brüning was "a monarchist living in a different, unpolitical world. Austere, rigid, and untroubled by doubt, he assumed that people would accept prescribed hardships."[99] The Reichstag's refusal to endorse Brüning's austerity budget, which prompted the chancellor to call new national elections for September, accelerated the trend toward dictatorship. The Nazis, who regularly denounced the "Hunger Chancellor" during their campaign, significantly increased their share of the vote. They acquired 107 parliamentary seats, making the Hitler movement the second largest party in the Reichstag. Brüning's dependence on the toleration of the SPD in order to govern only compounded his problems. Hindenburg and the army leadership gradually wearied of him, believing that the Nazis would provide a more reliable mass base, and thus a more effective means of destroying the "pacifist" Social Democratic rank-and-file who, under Müller's chancellorship, had opposed funding a new generation of pocket battleships as the resurrection of Tirpitz's world policy. Finally, Brüning's decision to ban the SA interfered with the army leadership's desire to bring the Nazis into the government, while his proposal to eliminate government subsidies to estate owners in the eastern Prussian provinces infuriated the agrarian elite, whose influence on Hindenburg resulted in Brüning's firing in mid-1932.

Brüning's successor, the conservative Catholic landed aristocrat from Westphalia, Franz von Papen, dispensed with even the trappings of liberal democracy. With the backing of Reich President Hindenburg and General Kurt von Schleicher, the wily political voice of the Reichswehr, Papen appointed a thoroughly reactionary cabinet with no discernible popular support. It even lacked the backing of Papen's own party, the Center, which remained loyal to Brüning.[100] Nevertheless, the new cabinet continued the authoritarian trends of the Brüning era, as well as giving evidence of a more autarkic and unilateralist foreign policy. Unlike Brüning, who sought to preserve Germany's credit worthiness with the United States despite his government's reckless attempt to create a customs union with Austria to prepare the ground for the annexation of Austria, the Papen government abandoned multilaterialism altogether. Proposals for a German-dominated

[99] Fritz Stern, *Five Germanys I Have Known* (New York: Farrar, Strauss, and Giroux, 2006), 77.

[100] Larry Eugene Jones, "Franz von Papen, the German Center Party, and the Failure of Catholic Conservatism in the Weimar Republic," *Central European History* 39, no. 2 (2005): 191–217.

continental economic zone, which emphasized bilateral trade agreements with the southeastern states, supplanted what remained of liberal economic thinking among senior government officials, and industrial and agricultural trade associations.[101] Papen immediately lifted Brüning's ban on the SA following a bloody street battle between Nazis and Communists in the town of Altona near Hamburg. In addition to supporting the military's wish to deploy the Brown Shirts as a weapon against the Communists, Papen allowed the SA's recruitment as auxiliary troops in the Reichswehr's preparations for war. Enjoying Hindenburg's backing, Papen initiated what Brüning could not, a coup against the Social Democratic leadership of Prussia. He summarily removed the Minister President Otto Braun and the chief of the Prussian police Albert Grzesinski, citing a national emergency as his justification. Having undermined a bastion of Social Democracy since the Weimar Republic's beginnings, Papen's act enabled the transformation of the Prussian police into a resolutely anti-leftist strike force, facilitated especially by additional restrictions placed on the exercise of civil liberties. Central to the unconstitutional removal of the Prussian government was Papen's interior minister Wilhelm Freiherr von Gayl, the former Kapp putschist and Ober Ost interior minister, who after Brest-Litovsk became the architect of the Lithuanian border state that in addition to becoming an area of German settlement, would serve as a launching pad for a future German attack on Poland and Russia.[102] The Papen regime lasted only until the following December. Despite having called two national elections in its brief tenure, it could not cobble together a parliamentary majority that would support an authoritarian constitution without the risk of a civil war. Papen's counter proposal, the use of the Reichswehr to enforce a presidential dictatorship, infuriated the army, which could ill afford to deal with internal turmoil while preparing for war. Despite that, Papen's defeat of the Social Democrats in Prussia constituted a crucial way-station to the installation of a terrorist dictatorship after 1933, in which his assault against the left was hardly the only evidence. His cabinet even gave serious consideration to limiting the citizenship rights of Jews.[103]

The social consequences of economic disaster and political radicalization proved equally dangerous. The science of eugenics, the result of the

---

[101] Tooze, *Wages of Destruction*, 25. Eckart Teichert, *Autarkie und Grossraumwirtschaft in Deutschland 1930–1939: Aussenwirtschaftpolitische Konzeptionen zwischen Weltwirtschaftskrise und Zweiten Weltkrieg* (Munich: R. Oldenbourg, 1984), 100–4; 138–42; 177–9.

[102] Liulevicius, *War Land*, 202–3.

[103] Walter, *Antisemitische Kriminalität*, 231–6,

affiliation between biopolitics and expansionism, which emerged from Germany's first experience with colonialism and the scarcities of wartime, found even greater resonance during the Depression as the perception of an existential threat to Germany's survival mounted. The resources available to mitigate human misery declined sharply and the middle class's fear of the have-nots increased proportionately. Unemployment, which seemed to climb in inverse proportion to the shrinkage of federal and state budgets, the tightening of work rules in return for public assistance, and the frustration of welfare clients and case workers alike, emboldened eugenicists to define welfare recipients as burdensome "psychopaths," "degenerates," and "asocials." Similar language was applied to convicts, whose numbers increased dramatically as prosecutors sought higher sentences and judges were happy to grant them. Rather than assigning economic causes to the hardship before them, the many professions that hereditary science had influenced grew obsessed with the genetic origins of social problems, maladies that not only crippled the individual but also endangered the health of the *Volk*. Weimar social experiments, such as health insurance, municipal clinics, and prison reform were denounced as Marxist-inspired producers of namby-pamby humanitarianism, fiscal waste, sexual immorality, and the irresponsibility of social welfare programs, which sustained the "unfit" at the expense of the racially "valuable." To be sure, church-based welfare institutions, particularly the Catholic Caritas, rejected eugenics because it ignored the sanctity of the human personality. Although based on conservative and authoritarian premises and increasingly unsympathetic to the jobless, such organizations continued to advocate "self-help" and private support for the unemployed. Nevertheless, religious precepts gradually lost ground to racial and biological standards, which envisioned a different role for the state in the maintenance of public health and the distribution of welfare. Now the state was to promote "positive" eugenics; that is, the encouragement of large racially "fit" families. "Negative" eugenics, on the other hand, would restrict or deny the right of procreation of those designated "unfit," and withdraw public services from racial "undesirables." Like Papen's aggressive use of police repression against the left, academic and scientific debates during the last years of Weimar paved the way for the Third Reich's radical program of "racial hygiene," unencumbered by the constraints of either privacy or humanity.[104]

---

[104] David F. Crew, *Germans on Welfare: From Weimar to Hitler* New York and Oxford, 1998), 152–203; Young-Sun Hong, *Welfare, Modernity, and the Weimar State, 1919–*

Despite the fervent efforts of conservatives to sustain a presidential dictatorship and marginalize the Reichstag, the National Socialists became the principal beneficiaries of political fragmentation, social conflict, and economic crisis. In this there was no small irony. Hitler's "legal" strategy for taking power, which he had designed after the collapse of the Munich putsch, only partially contributed to the Nazi Party's success. Even its best national showing in the Reichstag elections of July, 1932, in which the party obtained 37.4 percent of the vote, the NSDAP came nowhere close to an electoral majority. In the November, 1932, national elections, the party's percentage declined sharply, leading to a crisis of confidence among Nazi leaders, including the party organization leader Gregor Strasser, who feared that the opportunity to take power had passed. Nevertheless, five factors converged to make Hitler chancellor, beginning with Hitler's charisma, which paradoxically combined personal initiative from the party's lieutenants and followers with obedience to the leader. Next there was the Nazi Party's ability to attract a socially diverse constituency drawn to its message of ethnic solidarity, national resurrection, and Hitler's calls for living space. The non-Nazi right's internal divisions and its inability to retain popular support contributed, as did the weaknesses of the German left, which the Depression grievously exposed. Finally, the threat of foreign intervention, which previously discouraged conservative elites from fully supporting putschism, declined as the economic crisis deepened.

During the "fallow" years between 1925, when the NSDAP was once again legalized, and 1930, when the party achieved its electoral breakthrough, the Nazis overcame internal divisions laid bare by the failure of the Munich putsch and Hitler's temporary imprisonment. Once Hitler imposed his will over ambitious and independent-minded party leaders, such as Joseph Goebbels and Gregor Strasser, who for a time advocated a "national Bolshevism" that favored anticapitalism and expropriation, the party built effective local organizations. Following the dictatorial "leader principal" (*Führerprinzip*) by which Hitler had come to identify himself as the messiah destined to lead Germany to greatness, local and regional party operatives took their marching orders from the top. Capitalizing on the widespread yearning for a "true" leader in the wake of the kaiser's

1933 (Princeton: Princeton University Press, 1998), 202–76; Elizabeth Harvey, *Youth and the Welfare State in Weimar Germany* (Oxford: Clarendon Press, 1993), 264–98; Paul Weindling, *Health, Race and German Politics between National Unification and Nazism 1870–1945 (Cambridge: Cambridge University Press, 1989)*, 441–88; Wachsmann, *Hitler's Prisons*, 46–63.

flight to the Netherlands in 1918, Hitler embodied the will of the *Volk*.[105]
The NSDAP attracted energetic, young, and overwhelmingly male, activists, who satisfied their idealism and ambition by carrying out Hitler's
intentions. Many of them had been born too late to have fought in the
war, but their mythic interpretation of the war and its aftermath – the
heroism and self-sacrifice of the battle front and their betrayal by republican politicians – motivated them to follow a leader, who rejected bourgeois politics and negotiated settlements to imperialist claims. For them,
Hitler was the alternative to Weimar parliamentarianism, the unreserved
enemy of "Juda" or "Jewish Marxism," and the epigone of Germany's
resurrection, and not just to its rightful position as a global power. Hitler
emerged as the true führer, the charismatic man of destiny, who would
embark on a sacred mission to achieve living space sufficient to resurrect
a defeated and demoralized *Volk*.[106]

The Nazi Party's restructure from top to bottom did not reap immediate benefits of course. The Hitler movement did not acquire a national
electorate until the fall of 1930 despite significant gains in state elections during the previous year, which might otherwise have discouraged
Brüning from calling new elections after the Reichstag refused to pass his
austerity budget. Nevertheless, the NSDAP's victories after 1930 could
not have occurred without the party's painstaking attention to structural
development at the local and regional levels, its sophisticated use of modern media and talent for spectacle, the commitment and organizational
skills of its local supporters, and its self-financed aid programs for the
poor and unemployed. In addition to constructing its electoral machinery, the party empowered the SA to demonstrate Nazism's commitment to
action instead of parliamentary debate. Whether attacking Communists
in working-class neighborhoods or viciously assaulting Jews before, during, and after Nazi Party rallies, the SA proved that the Nazi Party would
"do something" to contain the left, eliminate Jewish "influence," and
expose the Republic's inability to keep "order." Those achievements in
turn owed much to Hitler's ability to deliver what the leadership of other
parties could not, the successful, if potentially unstable, fusion of imperialism and authoritarianism with broad-based popular support.[107]

---

[105] Martin Kohlrausch, *Der Monarch im Skandal: Der Logik der Massenmedien und die
Transformation der wilhelminischen Monarchie* (Berlin: Akademie Verlag, 2005), 414–42.

[106] On the origins of the conservative führer cults and Hitler's relationship to them, see
Kershaw, *Hubris*, 180–5. Party members applied the title to Hitler as early as 1922.

[107] Local studies on the development of the Nazi party are legion. The first to appear,
William Sheridan Allen's *The Nazi Seizure of Power: The Experience of a Single German*

Apart from the Center, the social bases of which included the Catholic nobility and professionals, peasants, artisans, and workers united by confession, the NSDAP drew support from across the divides of class, religion, and region to a degree that other parties failed to achieve. The Hitler movement drew disproportionately from shopkeepers, peasants, civil servants, and artisans, and it performed especially well in the Protestant small town and rural regions of northern and eastern Germany. Yet it also attracted the urban upper-middle classes, Catholics, and even workers in greater numbers than any other nonleftist party had previously attained.[108] Moreover, the Nazi Party assumed no responsibility for Weimar's failures. Because it had never entered the government, it did not suffer the rage of voters whose interests successive bourgeois cabinets had frustrated, even during Weimar's so-called "golden years." As a result, the NSDAP could freely proclaim conflicting promises to diverse groups without a track record to contradict them. Yet even more important, the Hitler movement exploited the deeply felt desire for national unity and regeneration, a desire based on imaginings of the shared sacrifices and the comradeship of the mythical "front experience," and the yearning for a German resurrection after the catastrophe of 1918 and the "marooning" of ethnic Germans in hostile successor states. Unlike other bourgeois parties, the Nazis made their presence felt in the settings of everyday life, the pubs, market squares, and football fields, where ordinary Germans congregated.[109] Millions of war veterans cast their ballots in the fateful elections from 1930 to 1933 for a party that explicitly marketed the appeal to the *Volk* "community," a national and implicitly racial unity that would transcend the bitter social conflicts and the special interests that crippled all bourgeois parties. Nazism succeeded in embodying an

---

Town, 1930 to 1935 (Chicago: Quadrangle Books, 1965) is still indispensable. It subsequently went into a new edition, published by Franklin Watts in 1984. On the role of SA violence, see Walter, *Antisemitische Kriminalität*, 200–43, Wildt, *Volksgemeinschaft als Selbstermächtigung*, 87–100; and Dirk Schumann, *Political Violence*, 215–50.

[108] For the most comprehensive statistical analysis of the Nazi electorate, see Jürgen Falter, *Hitlers Wähler* (Munich: C.H. Beck, 1990). Thomas Childers, in his *The Nazi Voter: The Social Foundations of Fascism in Germany, 1919–1933* (Chapel Hill: University of North Carolina Press, 1983), was the first to identify the Nazi Party as a "catchall" protest movement that cut across class lines. On upper and upper-middle class support for Nazism, see Richard Hamilton's *Who Voted for Hitler* (Princeton: Princeton University Press, 1982), esp. 64–219.

[109] Peter Fritzsche, *Germans into Nazis* (Harvard University Press, 1998), 195; See the remarks of Kevin Cramer, *The Thirty Years' War and German Memory in the Nineteenth Century* (Lincoln and London: University of Nebraska Press, 2007), 224–31.

imagined nation that other parties could not convincingly approach.[110]
More to the point, Hitler's speeches at Nazi Party rallies conveyed his
blatantly expansionist intentions to the enthusiastic audiences. Although
generally silent as to specific territorial objectives, the führer repeatedly
averred that the purity and prosperity of the *Volk* depended on living
space in the east.[111] There was considerable overlap in the imperialism,
anti-Marxism, and exclusionary nationalism of National Socialism and
the non-Nazi right. Yet as the personification of youthfulness, determination, idealism, and energy, the party conveyed possibilities of revival and
transformation that conservatives could no longer muster.

The Nazi Party's ability to prosper at the expense of other parties, while
not sufficient to give it a majority, put it in a strong bargaining position
as three chancellors in succession, Heinrich Brüning, Franz von Papen,
and Kurt Schleicher, failed to generate enough support in the Reichstag
to create a dictatorship without Nazi backing. Before Nazism's electoral
breakthrough, the party did ally with conservatives to sponsor the referendum against the Young Plan in 1929. In October of 1931, it joined
with the DNVP, the conservative paramilitary veterans' organization, the
Stahlhelm, the National Rural League, the Pan German League, and the
United Patriotic Associations of Germany in the antirepublican Harzburg
Front of October, 1931, which campaigned for Brüning's removal. Yet,
consistent with his thinking after the Munich putsch, Hitler never allowed
conservatives to dominate the Nazi Party.[112] Thus, the führer repeatedly
made it clear that he would not accept a government in which he was not
chancellor, infuriating the DNVP leader Hugenberg, who pursued the
same ambition. Hitler's aloofness, the frequent conflicts between the SA
and the Stahlhelm, and the relentless attacks of Nazi propaganda against
"reactionaries" led to continuous debate among the elite over the desirability of bringing the Nazis into the government and on what terms. As
the avatar of the insecurities of Germans outside the Reich and able to
articulate the despair of millions of Germans inside, Hitler demanded
that the torch be passed from the Pan Germans of *kleindeutsch* Germany

---

[110] Richard Bessel, *Nazism and War* (New York: Modern Library, 2004), 29.

[111] For example, see Hitler, *Reden, Schriften, und Anordnungen: Februar 1925 bis Januar 1933*, ed. Institut für Zeitgesschichte (Munich and New York: K. G. Saur, 1992–2003), vol. 3/1, doc. no. 40, 27 October 1928, doc. no. 40, 29 October 1928, doc. no. 64, 10 December 1928; vol. 3/3, doc. no. 54, 6 June 1930, doc. no. 57, 11 June 1930, doc. no. 61, 19 June 1930, and doc. no. 86, 10 August 1930.

[112] Larry Eugene Jones, "Nationalists, Nazis, and the Assault against Weimar: Revisiting the Harzburg Rally of October 1931," *German Studies Review* 29, no. 3 (2006): 483–94.

with their roots in the Second Empire to the *"grossdeutsch"* Pan Germans of the future. Hitler would renovate the "spirit of 1914" as the expression, not of a tenuous "peace of the fortress," but of a new homogeneous and enlarged *Volk* community ready to purge its enemies from within and attack its foes without.[113]

The implosion of the bourgeois parties, which had once uneasily juggled leadership by elites with broad-based popular support, had obviously narrowed their options, a fact that Hitler was only too happy to communicate. In January of 1932, in a meeting arranged by the Ruhr steel magnate Fritz Thyssen, the führer reminded some 650 businessmen at Düsseldorf's Industry Club of the "millions of our German fellow countrymen" who had flocked to the Nazi movement, creating "something which is unique in German history. The bourgeois parties have had seventy years to work in; where, I ask you, is the organization which could be compared with ours?" While making no secret of his anti-Marxism, which no doubt reassured his audience, he spoke at length on the current crisis of industrial overproduction and high unemployment, and claimed that only a powerful state could create the conditions for a "flourishing economic life." Taking aim at the common bourgeois prejudice against the Nazi movement's rowdiness and violence, Hitler claimed that party enthusiasts represented a commitment to an ideal that transcended material interests, a faith in the future that would resurrect the German nation and save it from "Bolshevik chaos." In fact, relatively few employers joined the Nazi Party or openly sided with it before 1933. Yet if Hitler's speech did not encourage his audience to change its political affiliations, the meeting did reveal converging agendas, in which Hitler became impossible to ignore as the emerging voice of national resurgence and antileftism.[114] The führer concluded by summarizing what the Nazi Party's "idealism" had to offer, the energy to acquire *Lebensraum* and the development of a "great internal market," and the ruthlessness to suppress Germany's internal and external enemies.[115]

---

[113] See Sven Oliver Müller, "Nationalismus in der deutschen Kriegsgesellschaft 1939 bis 1945," in *Die Deutsche Kriegsgesellschaft 1939 bis 1945* Zweiter Halband, *Ausbeutung, Deutungen, Ausgrenzung*, ed. Jörg Echternkamp (Munich: Deutsche Verlags-Anstalt, 2005), 23–4.

[114] See the contrasting and bitterly contested positions of Henry A. Turner, Jr., *German Big Business and the Rise of Hitler* (New York and Oxford: Oxford University Press, 1985, and David Abraham, *The Collapse of the Weimar Republic: Political Economy and Crisis*, 2nd ed. (New York: Holmes & Meier, 1986), especially 271–318.

[115] "Address to the Industry Club, 27 January 1932, in Kaes, Jay, and Dimendberg, *Weimar Republic Sourcebook*, 138–41.

The Nazis' radical nationalism and imperialism won an enthusiastic response from the aristocracy, especially from economically hard-pressed or dispossessed Junkers, whose disillusionment had long caused them to abandon the monarchism of their elders. They were, to be sure, uncomfortable with the Nazis' "socialism," which seemingly threatened the private ownership of land to which they aspired, and they disliked the anti-Christian fulminations of some of the Nazi Party's leaders. Yet the hatred of socialism and Bolshevism, a bitter antisemitism and alienation from bourgeois culture, and an intense dislike of democracy, liberalism, and parliamentarianism, which had destroyed their career prospects and reduced their status, drew them to National Socialism. The Nazi plan to acquire living space in the east proved even more enticing to many young nobles. Not only did Nazi imperialism promise an enlarged army and the restoration of military careers in an expanded officer corps, it also held open the prospect of acquiring new landed estates beyond Germany's current borders as its answer to the catastrophic bankruptcies that dispossessed many Junkers. When once the estate owner-dominated Agrarian League advocated living space for peasant settlements to deflect radical nationalist criticism for hiring Polish labor, now living space would settle the impoverished high born.[116] Upper-class salons and personal contacts among aristocrats and leading Nazis, particularly the Crown Prince August-Wilhelm and Hermann Göring, lent increasing financial support and respectability to the party.[117] Those nobles who still owned their estates revealed the fluidity between the conservative and radical right. After 1928, the attacks of estate owners against the republic at the local level, where Junkers especially retained a strong influence in agricultural chambers and pressure groups, had the effect of encouraging agricultural laborers and peasants to give their votes to the Nazi Party.[118]

After increasing its share of the electorate after 1930, the Nazi Party's surprising electoral decline in the November 1932, Reichstag elections enabled the alliance of convenience that allowed Hitler to take power. Because of the resulting dispute between Hitler, who was unwilling to accept anything less than the chancellorship, and those such as the Reich Organization Leader Gregor Strasser, who was willing to settle for less,

---

[116] Malinowski, *Vom König zum Führer*, 476–552. On prewar conflicts between agrarians and radical nationalists, see Woodruff D. Smith, *Ideological Origins*, 83–94.

[117] Malinowski, *Vom König zum Führer*, 553–6; Petropoulos, *Royals and the Reich*, 97–135; d'Almeida, *Hakenkreuz und Kaviar*, 52–66.

[118] Baranowski, *Sanctity of Rural Life*, 145–76.

diehard monarchists, such as President Hindenburg, Franz von Papen, and Alfred Hugenberg, became convinced that Hitler would be more susceptible to their control if he were brought into the government at that moment. Nevertheless, conservatives could no longer pursue their agenda of dismantling the Weimar welfare state, establishing a dictatorship, suppressing the left, and conducting an aggressive foreign policy without the reliable mass base on the right that the NSDAP provided. The brief tenure of Kurt von Schleicher, Papen's successor who successfully schemed to remove him, presented to elites the worst possible alternative short of a Hitler chancellorship. Unable to entice Hitler to join his cabinet, Schleicher reached for the support of the SPD and the trade unions with proposals to repeal Papen's wage and benefit cuts and to nationalize the steel industry. Infuriating estate owners who had Hindenburg's ear, Schleicher dusted off one of Brüning's most controversial proposals, the elimination of subsidies to estate owners and the use of bankrupt estates for the settlement of peasants and unemployed workers.[119] Above all, the Reichswehr feared that without Hitler as chancellor, which would put the SA at its disposal to crush the Communists, it could not prevent a civil war. Adolf Hitler thus became the German Mussolini, whom the non-Nazi right believed could be managed. Yet he would be aggressive enough to carry out the agendas that they and the Nazis held in common, the destruction of the left, the creation of a dictatorship with broad popular support, and a foreign policy that would guarantee the resurgence of German power and enable expansion. Although the NSDAP had not taken power on its own, it had over the long term suffered less from its adaptation to republican politics than the conservative right. The Hitler movement reached its limits in amassing voters, but avoided the fate of the other parties, whose political compromises in governing coalitions cost them dearly among voters. Nazi street violence, which uneasily coexisted with its "legal" pursuit of power, further weakened confidence in the ability of republican authorities to maintain order in the eyes of middle-class Germans. For them, the threat from "Marxism" was far greater than that of the radical right.

The Depression was decisive in paving the way for the emergence of a German fascism. In addition to creating desperation in a population in which one in three workers was unemployed – a ratio that was even higher in heavy industrial regions such as Silesia and the Ruhr – it

[119] Evans, *Coming of the Third Reich*, 302–5.

fatally overwhelmed the ability of public welfare and unemployment compensation to cope. It especially undermined the ability of the left to resist. The unemployed who flocked to the KPD flaunted their solidarity and toughness in mass demonstrations and brutal street brawls with the Nazis, but KPD fighters were easily confined to working-class neighborhoods where the SA and the police regularly set upon them. For their part, the trade unions faced declining membership and ever-dwindling financial resources with which to mount an effective defense. The breach between the Socialists and Communists, which originated during the Majority Socialists' suppression of the radical revolution in 1919, had never been healed sufficiently to enable a united front. Although the Soviet Union withdrew its condemnation of Social Democrats as "social fascists," and called for a "popular front," that temporary accommodation failed to repair the division within the German left. And had the "popular front" lasted, even the Socialists and Communists together would not have been powerful enough to stop the right. As matters stood, the SPD was unable to resist Papen's coup in Prussia, weakened by the party's huge losses in the Prussian Landtag elections of April 1932.

Moreover, the Depression decisively transformed Germany's relationship with the victors of World War I. The global economic crisis effectively removed the threat of foreign intervention and further territorial losses, which between 1919 and 1924 had contained putschism and forced the Reichswehr to support the Weimar constitution. American economic intervention provided the foundations for stabilization and a modest recovery, as well as transfer protection until the United States ceased its lending altogether. The suspension of reparations through the Hoover Moratorium of 1931, although doing nothing to relieve the impact of deflation and the spiraling unemployment of the Brüning era, abandoned a crucial piece of leverage against Germany, indicative of the Depression's destruction of the interdependence of the global economy.[120] French pressure certainly prevailed upon Papen to fork over a final payment of three billion gold marks at Lausanne the following year. Entente exactions extended to other areas as well, as Papen reluctantly dropped his demand that the Versailles restrictions on German armaments be modified.[121] Yet, however humiliating those final measures, the resolution of the reparations question underscored the Entente's declining willingness to defend

---

[120] Tooze, *Wages of Destruction*, 23–4.
[121] Mommsen, *Rise and Fall*, 454.

the post–World War I settlement, as global economic collapse encouraged unilaterialism, economic nationalism, and ultimately appeasement. Dismissive of economic multilaterialism, which "world Jewry" manipulated at will to Germany's detriment, Papen's and Schleicher's more radical successor would provide the solution he had advocated since the mid-twenties, a war for *Lebensraum*.

4

The Empire Begins at Home

The Third Reich, 1933–1939

The government of "national concentration" that took power on January 30, 1933, with Adolf Hitler as its chancellor represented the consensus of the Nazi and non-Nazi right. Most portfolios went to ministers from the German National People's Party, beginning with its indefatigable leader Alfred Hugenberg, who won multiple appointments as the economics minister, the minister of agriculture, the Reich commissar in charge of the subsidy program for eastern Prussian agriculture, and leadership of the Departments of Social Policy and Labor. Five holdovers from Papen's "cabinet of barons," joined Hugenberg, including Konstantin von Neurath, the foreign minister, Lutz Graf Schwerin von Krösigk, the finance minister, and Franz Gürtner as the minister of justice. The unabashedly pro-Nazi general Werner von Blomberg became minister of the army, while the Stahlhelm leader Franz Seldte was installed as Minister of Labor. Franz von Papen, whose behind-the-scenes negotiations with President Hindenburg engineered Schleicher's removal and the formation of the new government, was now the vice-chancellor. Aside from Hitler, who for months insisted on being chancellor as the condition for participating in government, the National Socialists received only two positions. Two "old fighters" who had taken part in the Munich putsch, Wilhelm Frick and Hermann Göring, now respectively headed the national and Prussian ministries of the interior.[1]

---

[1] For recent accounts, see Richard J. Evans, *The Coming of the Third Reich* (New York: Penguin, 2004), 288–321; Hans Mommsen, *The Rise and Fall of Weimar Democracy*, trans. Elborg Forster and Larry Eugene Jones (Chapel Hill and London: University of North Carolina Press, 1996), 490–544; Heinrich-August Winkler, *Weimar, 1918–1933: Die Geschichte der ersten deutschen Demokratie* (Munich, 1993), 557–94; Hermann Beck,

Papen confidently expected that the coalition would discipline the Nazis and ensure the control of Germany's incumbent political class. In addition to speaking for powerful organized interests, especially big agriculture, Reich President Hindenburg thought of his own needs in agreeing to Hitler's appointment. He envisioned a partnership with Hitler as the logical outcome of the "spirit of 1914." The old field marshal believed that an authoritarian state with a charismatic leadership would create national cohesion and anchor Hindenburg's own place in history.[2] Yet Papen's and Hindenburg's confidence belied the significance of the positions that the National Socialists obtained. To the Nazi appointments accrued the responsibility for internal security, the poisonous consequences of which would soon become evident. Moreover, the conservatives in the cabinet were unlikely to put the brakes on nazification. They retained their misgivings about the Nazi Party's violent and uncouth methods, and even the least cautions among them, Alfred Hugenberg, prevailed upon Hindenburg to delay Hitler's oath of office when he learned to his dismay that Papen had agreed to new elections.[3] Nonetheless, conservatives would tolerate or encourage the destruction or marginalization of political and racial "enemies" at home and beat the drums for rearmament and an expansionism that would not be limited to undoing the Versailles settlement. Following on the heels of Ludendorff's vision during the Great War, the conservative-Nazi government assumed that only new territorial acquisitions would provide Germany with sufficient manpower and resources that would allow it to challenge British and American power. What conservatives did not appreciate was that the Nazis would unleash a radical dynamism at home that would compromise their own political standing.

The Fateful Alliance: German Conservatives and Nazis in 1933: The Machtergreifung in a New Light (New York and Oxford: Berghahn, 2008), 83–113; and Larry Eugene Jones, "Nazis, Conservatives, and the Establishment of the Third Reich, 1932–34," *Tel Aviver Jahrbuch für Deutsche Geschichte: Nationalsozialismus aus heutiger Perspektive* (1998), 41–64. Still valuable are Martin Broszat, *Hitler and the Collapse of Weimar Germany*, V. R. Berghahn, trans. (Leamington Spa, Hamburg, and New York: Berg, 1987), and especially Karl Dietrich Bracher *Die Auflösung der Weimarer Republik: Eine Studie zum Problem des Machtverfalls in der Demokratie*, 3rd ed. (Villingen and Schwarzwald: Ring Verlag, 1960).
[2] Wolfram Pyta, *Hindenburg: Herrschaft zwischen Hohenzollern und Hitler* (Munich: Siedler Verlag, 2007), 791–805.
[3] Beck, *Fateful Alliance*, 86–7. On Hugenberg's role in the negotiations to bring Hitler to power, see Larry Eugene Jones, "'The Greatest Stupidity of My Life:' Alfred Hugenberg and the Formation of the Hitler Cabinet, January 1933," *Journal of Contemporary History* 27 (1992): 63–87.

FIGURE 4.1. The German leadership at the National Opera in Berlin attending a ceremony honoring German soldiers killed in World War I, March 12, 1933. From right to left are Vice Chancellor Franz von Papen, Reich President Paul von Hindenburg, Reich Chancellor Hitler, and General Werner von Blomberg, the minister of defense. Combining the old right and the new, the government of "national concentration" that assumed power on January 30, 1933 pursued an aggressive foreign policy abroad and the containment of domestic "enemies," who undermined unity at home.
Source: United States Holocaust Memorial Museum (hereinafter cited as USHMM), photograph # 24538.

Within days of taking office, the führer met with the commanders of the various army districts to lay out his vision of the army's role in the Third Reich. His lengthy speech neatly fused foreign and domestic policy, imperialism abroad, and containment of "enemies" at home. Making no secret of his desire to destroy "Marxism" within Germany and the "poison" of Bolshevism without, Hitler promised a dictatorship instead of the Weimar democracy, the ruthless suppression of "treasonous" opposition, and the proper moral education of the *Volk*. That education would impart what Hitler considered the most basic law of nature, the struggle among races in which only the strongest would triumph. Repeating a theme of his since the early 1920s, Hitler argued that the salvation of the *Volk* depended not on exporting to markets in a global economy because of that economy's limited capacity for absorbing what Germany had to sell, but on acquiring living space beyond Germany's present borders for colonization by German settlers. Sounding a chord that echoed the long-standing desires of radical nationalists, his plans for settlement departed strikingly from those practiced by Bismarck in the 1880s and the attempts of successive Weimar governments to repopulate the eastern borderlands with unemployed workers and peasants. This time, Hitler averred, the "germanization of the population of annexed or conquered territories is not possible." Rather, one could "only germanize the soil. Like France and Poland after the War one must deport a few million people ..."

Despite their initial reserve toward Hitler, the army district commanders in attendance could only rejoice at the possibilities that the new chancellor provided. The Reichswehr had long wished for the elimination of the left, which included the Socialists, who by promoting redistributive social programs diverted resources from rearmament. Moreover, the National Socialists would perform the useful function of crushing the Socialists and Communists without the risk of a civil war, leaving the army to do its "real" job of preparing for an external conflict . Consistent with its operational planning during the 1920s, the Reichswehr coveted the prospect of launching an offensive war, especially against Poland. In addition to promising to enlarge the armed forces in preparation for war, Hitler assured his listeners that the army would be placed above politics to become the pillar of a militarized nation. It would have nothing to fear from the plebeian and rowdy SA.[4]

Conservative cabinet ministers, among them the hawkish foreign minister Neurath and army minister Blomberg, immediately served notice of the more militant tenor in German foreign relations. They demanded the restoration of Germany's overseas colonies and the incorporation of Austria into the Reich. They pushed for Germany's withdrawal from the League of Nations and its economic penetration of eastern and southeastern Europe. Although the western powers were willing to agree to a modest expansion of the German armed forces from 125,000 to 200,000 men, neither would allow a challenge to British and French military supremacy, nor would they tolerate the continued existence of the German paramilitaries. For his part, Hitler was inclined to cautious pronouncements as to Germany's peaceful

---

[4] Reinhard Müller, "Hitlers Rede vor der Reichswehrführung 1933: Eine neue Moskaue Überlierferung," *Mittelweg* 36, no. 1 (2001), 73–90. For an abbreviated English version and analysis, see Richard Bessel, *Nazism and War* (New York: Modern Library, 2004), 35–8.

intentions for fear of encouraging Allied sanctions or intervention, or arousing the anxieties of a German public that was skittish about the prospect of another war even as it desired a national resurgence. Nevertheless, the stalemated Geneva talks, which were postponed until June of 1933 and then to October, encouraged him to proceed in part as Neurath and Blomberg recommended. Following the second postponement, Hitler announced Germany's withdrawal from the League of Nations and the Geneva Conference. Although contradicting Hitler's claims as to Germany's desire to preserve the multilateralism of the "spirit" of Locarno, the British and French took no action. The lack of a response no doubt emboldened the führer to further assaults on the international order.[5]

Shortly afterward, Hitler demonstrated his independence from his conservative allies by opening negotiations over a ten-year nonaggression pact with Poland over the objections of the foreign office. Although implicitly antithetical to the führer's long-term goal of achieving living space, which all but presupposed Poland's obliteration, his tactical accommodation produced important benefits for each signatory. For Poland, the treaty provided a measure of protection now that the Entente had proven itself unable to achieve a disarmament settlement on its terms, stabilized the Polish-German border, and promised to end the Polish-German trade war of the Weimar era. For the Third Reich, the agreement allowed breathing space for rearmament and the expansion of the armed forces. If the regime had to tone down its rhetoric of re-annexing the "lost" eastern Prussian provinces and rescuing "stranded" ethnic Germans, the pact weakened the so-called "little Entente," the French-dominated system of alliances with eastern European nations that was designed to encircle Germany.[6] At home, Hitler capitalized on his triumphs by calling new Reichstag elections and a popular plebiscite for November, a gamble that added to his luster as a leader who could stand up to the Entente without war. Publicly assuring Germany's neighbors of its peaceful intentions while complaining of British and French intransigence, Hitler's gambit yielded an overwhelming popular majority in his favor and an exclusively Nazi Reichstag.[7] Having

---

[5] Christian Leitz, *Nazi Foreign Policy, 1933–1941: The Road to Global War* (London and New York, 2004), 40–1.

[6] Ibid., 62–70; and Philip T. Rutherford, *Prelude to the Final Solution: The Nazi Program for Deporting Ethnic Poles, 1939–1941* (Lawrence, KN: University of Kansas Press, 2007), 37–9.

[7] Ian Kershaw, *Hitler 1889–1936: Hubris* (New York and London: W. W. Norton, 1998), 490–5; Alexander B. Rossino, *Hitler Strikes Poland: Blitzkrieg, Ideology, and Atrocity* (Lawrence: University of Kansas Press, 2003), 2.

demonstrated its eagerness to exploit an international security system that crumbled in the face of a global economic crisis, the Hitler regime was pursuing with even greater alacrity political, social, and racial policies at home that it deemed as the essential preconditions for war.

PREPARING FOR LEBENSRAUM: REPRESSION, REARMAMENT, AND "RACIAL HYGIENE"

The domestic component of the Nazi imperialist agenda commenced with its strike against the left, which, in the regime's view, undermined the domestic cohesion that was essential to waging war. The semi-constitutionalism of Imperial Germany had provided room for an opposition to imperialism, or at least to some of its most extreme outcomes. The Third Reich eliminated that space altogether. The suppression of domestic enemies, especially the Socialists and Communists, became the mechanism by which the Nazi regime's political and racial repression would fuse. It invoked draconian measures that made Bismarck's Anti-Socialist law seem tame by comparison. Within days of Hitler's appointment, the Reich Chancellery issued emergency degrees that sharply curtailed the freedoms of assembly and the press beyond the restrictions that Brüning and Papen had already imposed. On the night of February 27th, the itinerant Dutch construction worker and former communist, Marinus van der Lubbe, who was given to impulsive acts of protest, set fire to the Reichstag building. Although the perpetrator acted alone, the Reichstag fire provided seemingly irresistible evidence of a Communist insurgency and presented the regime with a golden opportunity to declare a state of emergency.[8] In addition to suspending the civil liberties guaranteed by the Weimar constitution, the Reich government assumed the right to impose decrees directly on the states. Hermann Göring and Wilhelm Frick, acting from arrest lists compiled well in advance, made ample use of the powers assigned to them.[9] They decreed the end of police surveillance of Nazi organizations and transformed the SA and SS into police auxiliaries, ostensibly for the purpose of restoring "order" against the "threat" of a Bolshevik revolution in Germany.

Throughout the spring and summer of 1933, the Nazi Storm Troops ruled the streets, eager for the opportunity to unleash their vengeance against the left. They beat up and arrested Socialists and Communists,

---

[8] On van der Lubbe, see Evans, *Coming of the Third Reich*, 328–9.
[9] Beck, *Fateful Alliance*, 187–8.

ransacked their offices and those of the trade unions, and completely
routed an opposition with few reserves left to protect itself against a savage
repression backed by the government and tolerated by broad swaths of
middle-class opinion. Although the regime permitted the Communist
Party to campaign for Reichstag seats in the March elections, a tactical
move that would prevent the Socialists from absorbing the votes of KPD
constituents, emergency decrees justified as necessary to combat "treason"
led to the arrest of KPD delegates before they could take their seats. By
June of 1933, thousands of Communists and Socialists had either fled the
country or were crowded into jails and concentration camps. With the
blessing of the national and state governments, the SA and the National
Socialist Factory Cell Organization (NSBO) confiscated the treasuries and
other assets of the Communists, Socialists, and trade unions. Much of the
confiscated booty subsidized the party's new creation, the German Labor
Front (DAF), under the leadership of the successor to Gregor Strasser as
the party organization leader, Robert Ley. Although claiming to "honor"
workers in the new Reich by incorporating them into the Labor Front,
a mass institution that the regime promised would mediate between the
interests of employers and employees, the DAF ended once and for all
the republic's factory arbitration committees and collective bargaining.
Under the guise of creating a harmonious shop-floor environment that
would eliminate class struggle, the DAF gave employers more power to
manage their workplaces as they saw fit and to enhance their profitability
without the burden of wage increases.

Despite its unrelenting intimidation of political opponents and a
propaganda barrage that whipped up voter anxiety over the "Marxist
threat," the Nazi Party obtained a majority in the new Reichstag of
March, 1933, only by means of its electoral alliance with the DNVP.
Although the Nazi Party obtained 43.9 percent of the vote on its own, a
significant increase over its Weimar high of July, 1932, only its coalition
with the German Nationalists would have kept the Hitler government in
power had the Communist delegates been allowed to take their seats.[10]
As a consequence, the ceremony that opened the new Reichstag session
on March 21, 1933, at the Potsdam Garrison Church sacralized the
partnership between the Nazi and non-Nazi right as Protestant pastors
bestowed their blessings upon Hitler and Hindenburg before the vault
of Frederick the Great and his father Frederick Wilhelm I. When it came
their turns to speak, the president and chancellor each underscored the

---

[10] Ibid., 119.

revivalist core of the current "national awakening," which would lead the German resurgence and put an end to the humiliation of the past fifteen years. Nevertheless, the Hitler movement's disappointing result belied the willingness of the conservative and Catholic right to legislate ever-more authoritarian and dictatorial solutions to the current crisis. Thus, the passage of the Enabling Law on March 24th gave Hitler "emergency" legislative powers that required neither the approval of the Reichstag, nor even the consent of the Reich president. The votes of the Center Party proved crucial to the passage of the law, the result of its leadership's Faustian bargain with the regime. In return for supporting the legislation, the Center won the Nazis' flimsy assurances that the legal position of the Catholic Church and the federal powers of the Catholic-dominated states of the south would be protected. Unlike the Second Empire, in which the minority status of Catholics moved the Center Party to defend civil liberties, restrict clerical oversight of its operations, and protest the arbitrary exercise of power at the top, the Center leadership's loathing of the left and its determination to protect the interests of a church obsessed by the specter of "Bolshevism" testified to the party's rapid capitulation to a dictatorship that would not live up to its promises. Having sought a concordat similar to its Lateran Agreements with the Italian Fascist dictator Benito Mussolini, the Vatican all but undermined the Center's reason for being. It accepted the regime's condition that it be allowed to ban the Catholic clergy's political activities.[11]

Without a KPD delegation in the Reichstag, only the Socialists voted against the Enabling Law. The subsequent self-dissolution of all bourgeois parties except for the Nazis during the summer of 1933 merely confirmed what the Enabling Law had made evident: the total collapse of parliamentary government. The demise of the DNVP proved especially ignominious. Having lost many of its members and much of its electorate to the Nazis, Hitler ordered the absorption of the Stahlhelm into the SA during the month following the Enabling Law's passage. Moreover, Alfred Hugenberg, the DNVP Economics Minister and one of the original founders of the Pan German League, embarrassed himself at the World Economic Conference in London in June, which resulted in his hasty

---

[11] Rudolf Morsey, *Der Untergang des politischen Katholicismus: Die Zentrumspartei zwischen christlichem Selbstverständnis und 'Nationaler Erhebung' 1932/33* (Stuttgart: Belsier Verlag, 1977), 115–222; Klaus Scholder, *The Churches and the Third Reich, vol. 1, Preliminary History and the Time of Illusions 1918–1934*, trans. John Bowden (Philadelphia: Fortress Press, 1988), 237–53; 381–414.

resignation from Hitler's cabinet. In contrast to Hitler's then publicly cautious line, Hugenberg not only condemned global economic liberalism and demanded the return of Germany's colonies, he also insisted upon Germany's right to land in the east for German settlement as essential to its economic recovery.[12] Once convinced that he could engineer a cabinet of the right with himself as chancellor, Hugenberg's declining influence personified the triumph of a more ruthless, more violent, and more populist counter-revolution that would not hesitate to destroy its allies, much less its enemies. Unlike the governments of the Second Empire, which could neither dispense with support in the Reichstag nor eliminate opposition to the policies of the government, whether it came from the right or left, the disintegration of all vestiges of parliamentary government ensured that the Third Reich faced no such liabilities.

Hitler's "emergency" powers lent legal legitimacy to the ongoing "synchronization" (*Gleichschaltung*) of the federal states in the interests of consolidating power at the top, in which Papen's removal of the SPD-dominated government of Prussia in July of 1932 had already set a valuable precedent. That process, facilitated by the compliance of conservative state governments and the pressure of SA mass demonstrations and intimidation, allowed the Reich government to overrule powers reserved to the states and to centralize decision making from the Reich Chancellery in Berlin. To check the power of the highest state officials, the minister presidents, Hitler appointed rival Reich governors drawn from the senior party leaders of each state. In addition to ending the semisovereignty of the states that had existed under the Second Empire,[13] the destruction of Weimar's federal system contributed significantly to the regime's radical campaign against the left, the extensiveness of which soon required new and more lethal means of police regulation.

The southern state of Bavaria, that bastion of Catholic conservatism and long-time incubator of the radical right, not only revealed the shallowness of Nazi guarantees to the Catholic Church, the Center, and its regional sister party, the Bavarian People's Party, it also became a laboratory for perfecting the means of repression. Even before the March 5th Reichstag elections, the Reich Interior Minister Frick appointed Adolf Wagner to the Bavarian ministry of the interior, who in turn named the leader of the Nazi "Protection Force" (*Schutzstaffel*) or SS, Heinrich

---

[12] Hugenberg's memorandum is found in *Documents on German Foreign Policy*, Series C, vol. 2, 30 January to 14 October, 1933 (London and Washington, 1957), 562–7.
[13] Beck, *Fateful Alliance*, 257–8.

Himmler as Provisional Police President. In Frick's opinion, an ironic one in light of its long-standing tolerance of counter-revolutionary putschism, the Bavarian state government was not ruthless enough in cracking down on the Communists despite banning the party's press and prohibiting its public assemblies. In Himmler, Frick found the appropriate antidote. An agronomist by training with ties to the right-wing Artaman League, an anti-urban, anti-Slavic, and antisemitic organization that promoted German settlement in the eastern borderlands as the remedy for racial degeneration,[14] Himmler gravitated to the NSDAP and SA after service in the Free Corps. During the Munich putsch, he became the standard bearer for Ernst Röhm, the SA leader he would later have a hand in murdering. Selected in 1929 to head the SS, then Hitler's personal bodyguard unit, Himmler proceeded over the next four years to increase the SS membership, separate it from the SA, and create the SS Security Service (SD) under the authority of his deputy, Reinhard Heydrich. Himmler's dragnet in 1933, which corralled thousands of the regime's "enemies" and continued the settling of scores that dated back to the Munich Soviet, soon exceeded the available space for their incarceration.

By June of 1933, the number of prisoners in "protective custody" stood at twenty thousand, most of them victims of denunciation, whom existing jails could not accommodate. To absorb the huge number of prisoners, a vacant World War I munitions factory in the town of Dachau not far from Munich, became the nucleus of the first of the Third Reich's "concentration camps," a term with a long imperialist pedigree.[15] Created by the British as detention centers during the Boer War, the German military constructed similar structures during the Herero and Nama Wars in Southwest Africa, wherein most prisoners died by starvation and disease. Even if it is difficult to claim the Herero War as *the* precedent for the genocidal practices of the Third Reich, the Namibian camps, as sites of slow death through forced labor, became part of the broader imperial experience in the organization and utilization of prisoners.[16] Yet Dachau and similar camps represented a significant departure, for now

---

[14] Uwe Mai, *"Rasse und Raum": Agrarpolitik, Sozial-und Raumplanung im NS-Staat* (Paderborn: Ferdinand Schöningh, 2002), 29–30. On Himmler's early career, see Peter Longerich, *Heinrich Himmler: Biographie* (Munich: Siedler Verlag, 2008), 17–125, and 157–65.

[15] Evans, *Coming of the Third Reich*, 345–6.

[16] Benjamin Madley, "From Africa to Auschwitz: How German South West Africa Incubated Ideas and Methods Adopted and Develop by the Nazis in Eastern Europe," *European History Quarterly*, 35, no. 3 (2005): 446–50.

they would be used to incarcerate Germany's citizens, not colonial subjects.[17] As such, they owed more to the specifically German and European context, namely the social and political polarization of Europe between the world wars, which entailed the transformation, rather than the mere imposition, of an overseas colonial precedent. As Europe's largest and most deeply organized labor movement, the German left "necessitated" the scale of the Nazi regime effort to destroy it. The attack on it in turn laid the foundations for the extension of camps to other "enemies." It was in Dachau where shaved heads, forearms tattooed with numbers, and filthy blue-striped uniforms became standard operating procedure, giving license to barbaric and dehumanizing treatment to victims deprived of their liberty and identities. Moreover, Dachau enabled the SS, which assumed supervision of the camp because the regular Bavarian police was stretched too thin, to expand its influence rapidly at the SA's expense.[18] As the catalyst for the growth of the institutional empire that would spearhead the Nazi empire to come, Dachau's role in the regime's destruction of its opposition became emblematic of the manner in which the Third Reich linked the success of its long-term goals with the elimination of its domestic enemies.

As significant as the concentration camp system became, however, the Nazi regime's successful appropriation of the regular judiciary and penal system provided an indispensible component of its reign of terror. Armed with sweeping powers of indefinite detention and stricter sentencing, state prosecutors and judges, the vast majority of them right-wing and antirepublican, had little difficulty conforming to the regime's dictum that the protection of the "racial community" and the survival of the state took precedence over the rule of law. In addition to ruthlessly targeting social "deviants" and the instigators of other crimes, the courts went after political opponents with a vengeance, beginning with the Socialists and Communists. The number of inmates in prisons rose dramatically. By the summer of 1934, the prison system throughout Germany reached 100,000 inmates and by the winter of 1937, over 120,000 inmates, far exceeding the number of prisoners in the concentration camps. If prison conditions during the Weimar Republic rarely enacted the less-draconian practices envisioned by penal reformers, they amounted to paradise

---

[17] Birthe Kundrus, "Kontinuitäten, Parallelen, Rezeptionen": Überlegungen zur 'Kolonialisierung' des Nationalsozialismus," *WerkstattGeschichte* 15, no. 43 (2006): 58.

[18] Hans-Günter Richardi, *Schule der Gewalt: die Anfänge des Konzentrationslagers Dachau: eine Dokumentarischer Bericht* (Munich: C. H. Beck, 1983), 26–87.

FIGURE 4.2. The Reichsführer SS Heinrich Himmler scrutinizing a prisoner on an inspection tour of Dachau, May 8, 1936. As the first Nazi concentration camp, opened in the spring of 1933, Dachau provided leverage for the subsequent expansion of the SS and the use of colonial practices to contain the German left.
Source: Bundesarchiv Koblenz, Bild 152-11-12. Photographer: Friedrich Franz Bauer.

compared to those of the Third Reich, in which repression, forced labor, corporal punishment, an exaggerated and fetishized military discipline, and the provision of food and medical care that can charitably described as minimal, became routine.[19]

The eruption of ethnic hatreds overlapped with the violent expression of political animosities. Terror from below, which the SA often initiated in broad daylight, claimed countless victims, starting with Jewish citizens from other nations and eastern European Jews, who had lived in Germany for decades without receiving citizenship.[20] Although disappointing because it neither won popular compliance nor silenced foreign criticism of the SA's antisemitic actions following the "seizure" of power, a

[19] See Nikolaus Wachsmann, *Hitler's Prisons: Legal Terror in Nazi Germany* (New Haven and London: Yale University Press, 2004), 67–101. The statistics on the numbers of inmates are found on pp. 70–1.
[20] Beck, *Fateful Alliance*, 182–4.

one-day boycott of Jewish businesses during the first week of April served notice that antisemitism was now "official" policy, even though the party and not the government ministries had taken the initiative. Responding to boycotts throughout Germany organized by local party and SA leaders, Hitler assented to a national boycott to ensure a more "rational" and "orderly" offensive. To be sure, professional civil servants disapproved of the "gutter" antisemitism of the SA. Many German consumers ignored the boycott out of self-interest or loyalty to Jewish shopkeepers. Foreign outrage threatened to unleash a severe economic backlash against Germany. Yet the national boycott's failure belied the "legal" impositions on Jews that became a staple of daily life in the Third Reich, as did the street violence of the SA against Jews and Jewish-owned property. The Law for the Restoration of the Civil Service, which was promulgated during the same month, resulted in the dismissal of "non-Aryans" as well as political opponents, the only exception being Jewish war veterans, who benefited temporarily from President Hindenburg's intercession. Subsequent legislation curtailed the admission of Jews to the legal profession and prohibited Jewish doctors from treating national insurance patients. Jews were summarily dismissed from the major cultural institutions and the arts as befitting the carriers of a putatively "un-German spirit." Other measures decreed during that spring imposed quotas on the admission of Jews to German universities and the withdrawal of citizenship of Eastern European Jews who had immigrated to Germany after World War I. Denaturalization, which a law in mid-July 1933 codified, became a key means of confiscating Jewish property once the regime developed subsequent legislation to deprive native-born Jews of citizenship.[21]

Together, the pogroms and "legal" antisemitism represented the most determined attempt yet to undermine the civic, political, and economic status of Jews. Legal initiatives from above complemented extralegal Nazi attacks at the local level, including boycotts, the destruction of homes and businesses, and the physical injury or murder of Jewish victims. The antisemitism of the Second Empire was corrosive enough, more so was its radical and violent expression under the Weimar Republic, which warranted in most cases minor sanctions from the largely conservative judiciary.[22] Yet it enjoyed nowhere near the legal or official status

---

[21] Martin Dean, *Robbing the Jews: The Confiscation of Jewish Property in the Holocaust, 1933–1945* (Cambridge: Cambridge University Press, 2008), 33.

[22] Dirk Walter, *Antisemitische Kriminalität und Gewalt: Judenfeindschaft in der Weimarer Republik* (Bonn: J.H.W. Dietz Nachf., 1999), 151–99.

FIGURE 4.3. Three Jewish businessmen are paraded down Breuhl Street in central Leipzig, carrying signs that read: "Don't buy from Jews; Shop at German stores!" (1937). Despite the negative international reaction and tepid domestic response to the April 1933 boycott, SA-led assaults on Jewish property and livelihoods became routine, as the date of the photograph makes clear.
Source: USHMM, photograph #20210, courtesy of William Blye.

that it occupied under Nazism, a state-sanctioned hatred that spawned countless acts of anti-Jewish violence from ordinary Germans, especially in staunchly Nazi strongholds such as the northern Bavarian region of Franconia, the largest city of which, Nuremberg, served as the site for annual Nazi Party rallies.[23] The distinctiveness of Nazi antisemitism was evident from the beginning to Victor Klemperer, the philologist and convert from Judaism to Protestantism, who recorded his fears in his diary. "The pressure I am under is greater than in the war, and for the first time in my life I feel political hatred for a group (as I did not during the war), a

[23] See Peter Longerich, *'Davon haben wir nichts gewusst!' Die Deutschen und die Judenverfolgung1933–1945* (Munich: Siedler Verlag, 2006), 55–73; Hans Mommsen and Dieter Obst, "Die Reaktion der deutschen Bevölkerung auf die Verfolgung der Juden 1933–1943," in *Herrschaftsalltag im Dritten Reich: Studien und Texte*, ed. Hans Mommsen and Susanne Willems (Düsseldorf: Schwann, 1988), 374–421; Volker Ullrich, "'wir haben nichts gewusst.' Ein deutsches Trauma," *1999: Zeitschrift für Sozialgeschichte des 20. Jahrhunderts* 6 (4) (1991): 11–46; Michael Wildt, "Violence against Jews in Germany, 1933–1939," in *Probing the Depths of Antisemitism: German Society and the Persecution of the Jews*, ed. David Bankier (New York and Oxford: Berg, 2000), 181–209; and Wildt again, *Volksgemeinschaft als Selbstermächtigung: Gewalt gegen Juden in der deutschen Provinz 1919 bis 1939* (Hamburger: Hamburger Edition, 2007), 101–218.

deadly hatred. In the war I was subject to military law, but subject to law nevertheless; now I am at the mercy of an arbitrary power."[24]

Local party initiatives and the tolerance of non-Jewish Germans, which arose from motives that ran the gamut from the advancement of personal interest to ideological commitment, deepened the impact of antisemitism, leaving few sites of social interaction, public or private, ordinary or extraordinary, untouched. Local party harassment encouraged non-Jewish Germans to shun Jewish acquaintances for fear of being declared "a friend of the Jews," while Jewish Germans in turn avoided their neighbors so as not to cause trouble. Insidious forms of behavioral segregation did not just affect the schools or workplaces; rather, they extended to leisure venues as well, as the regime's influence on the tourism industry made clear. The "synchronized" National Socialist tourism board declared Jewish vacationers as "undesirable" guests in German spa towns and resorts, excluding Jews from a popular bourgeois practice and ruining the livelihood of Jews in the tourism industry. Vacation hotels and tourism sites were among the first to use a phrase that would become common currency by proudly announcing their status as "Jew-free."[25] In turn, the ability or inability to participate in pleasurable leisure pastimes had an impact on how Germans experienced the Third Reich, which deepened the experiential divide between those who suffered from the regime's depredations and those who benefited from its ethnic inclusivity.

Still more ominously, the Nazi regime's linkage of Jews with "Marxism" became explicit in camps such as Dachau, where prisoners who had the misfortune of being both Communist and Jewish received the harshest treatment in a setting that continually reaffirmed its reputation for sadistic brutality. The horror of the early months of Nazi rule, however, was not limited to the construction of concentration camps and the uncontrolled violence of the SA. It lay also in the willingness of the Nazis' conservative allies to encourage the "get tough" punishment of "Marxism" and to push for "legal" measures of exclusion, believing that Jews had long enjoyed a "disproportionate" influence in German

---

[24] Victor Klemperer, *I Will Bear Witness: A Diary of the Nazi Years 1933–1941*, trans Martin Chalmers (New York: Random House, 1998), entry of April 7, 1933, 12.

[25] See especially Frank Bajohr, *"Unser Hotel ist judenfrei": Bäder-Antisemitismus im 19. Und 20. Jahrhundert* (Frankfurt am Main: Fischer Taschenbuch Verlag), 116–41. On the "de-Jewification" of the German tourism industry as well as seaside resorts, see Kristen Semmens, *Seeing Hitler's Germany: Tourism in the Third Reich* (Houndsmills, Blasingstoke, Hampshire: Palgrave Macmillan, 2005), 17–8, 33–4, 95–6, 147–8.

society and culture. Moreover, despite the tepid or hostile public reaction to the boycott, which disrupted everyday commercial interactions, ordinary Germans did not disagree with the regime's exclusionary practices. In fact, the press, now purged of "non-Aryan" editors and Socialist and Communist papers, regularly reported on the regime's decrees, its arrest of thousands of prisoners, and its construction of concentration camps, placing the Nazi dragnet in the public eye. Although increasingly centralized and tightly controlled by the Propaganda Minister Joseph Goebbels and his press chief Otto Dietrich, the press helped to forge a consensus between the regime and its citizens based on the conviction that, however unfortunate, the violent campaign against "undesirables" was necessary to the restoration of "order" and the preservation of community values. Propaganda posters, an essential means of communication with a public reliant on public transportation, bicycles, and ambulation, accustomed the public to the regime's steady assault on Jews.[26]

The destruction of the left and "synchronization" provided the context for the unfolding of a complementary and equally insidious dimension of Nazi racial policy, the imposition of "racial hygiene." As the state-imposed regulation of the genetic health of the *Volk*, "racial hygiene" linked moral revolution with ethnic revival, in that ridding the *Volk* of threats to its existence was to take precedence over individual well-being.[27] Within six months of taking power, the regime had laid the foundations of an aggressive campaign to mutilate the carriers of "undesirable" genetic traits, which threatened to pollute and weaken the "*Volk* body" (*Volkskörper*) such that it could not fulfill its historical and biological destiny as an expansionist "master race." The Law for the Prevention of Hereditarily Diseased Offspring, which was drafted in the ministry of the interior and announced on July 14, 1933, ordered the compulsory sterilization of those with congenital feeble-mindedness or psychoses. Those with physical disabilities or hereditary maladies such as Huntington's chorea would also be targeted, as would epileptics, deaf mutes, and alcoholics. Social deviants, such as beggars, pimps, prostitutes, and the Sinti and Roma, derogatorily referred to as "gypsies," rounded out the list of potential victims. As such, the law was more radical than the draft

---

[26] Robert Gellately, *Backing Hitler: Consent and Coercion in Nazi Germany* (Oxford: Oxford University Press, 2001), 34–69; Jeffrey Herf, *The Jewish Enemy: Nazi Propaganda during World War II and the Holocaust* (Cambridge, MA and London: Harvard University Press, 2006), 17–49.

[27] Claudia Koonz, *The Nazi Conscience* (Cambridge, MA: Belknap Press of Harvard University Press, 2003), 103–4.

legislation presented to the Prussian government in July of 1932 after Papen's coup, which envisioned "only" voluntary sterilization. Attracting willing health care professionals, social and welfare workers, lawyers, and scientists who either referred cases to, or mediated cases before, the nearly two hundred specially established "Hereditary Courts," the new legislation brought to fruition the desires of racial hygienists that had grown more insistent and anxious during the Depression. Public funding, announced Minister of the Interior Wilhelm Frick, would go to support only the racially and genetically sound, while those who did not meet that standard would be subject to ruthless and irreversible bodily intervention to protect the *Volk* from the genetically "unfit." In each of the first four years of the sterilization law's existence, over fifty thousand people were sterilized, the vast majority of them involuntarily following unsuccessful appeals through the Hereditary Courts. By the end of the Third Reich, 360,000 sterilizations had occurred, most of them before the outbreak of war in 1939. The majority of the sterilized were inmates of mental hospitals, who were helpless in the hands of doctors who saw the program as a way to discharge patients and cut expenditures.[28] At the same time that Hitler sought to channel the Nazi "revolution" into more orderly, efficient, and bureaucratic procedures, public health offices and hereditary courts carried out the regime's determination to remake Germans.[29]

The July sterilization law was only the foundation for additional, more encompassing, and too numerous to list, decrees that revealed the link between criminality and hereditary illness in the minds of racial hygienists. The following November, legislation was introduced that expanded the power of the police and the courts to lengthen the confinement of "habitual criminals," remand "asocials" (i.e., petty criminals and prostitutes) to state hospitals, and order the castration of convicted sexual offenders, most for assaults on children or indecent exposure.[30] In October of 1935, the Marriage Health Law and subsequent ancillary decrees demanded the screening of couples seeking marriage licenses so as to discourage the union of persons deemed as carriers of hereditary

---

[28] On sterilization, see Robert Proctor, *Racial Hygiene: Medicine under the Nazis* (Cambridge, MA: Harvard University Press, 1988), esp. 95–117; Gisela Boch, *Zwangssterilisierung im Nationalsozialismus: Studien zur Rassenpolitik und Frauenpolitik* (Opladen; Westdeutscher Verlag, 1986); and Christian Ganssmüller, *Die Erbgesundheitspolitik des Dritten Reiches: Planung, Durchführung und Durchsetzung* (Cologne: Böhlau Verlag 1987), 34–115.

[29] Peter Fritzsche, *Life and Death in the Third Reich* (Belknap Press of Harvard University Press, 2008), 89–90.

[30] Wachsmann, *Hitler's Prisons*, 142.

degeneration. The laws governing "racial hygiene" rested on the argument that individual choices and supposedly private decisions regarding marriage and procreation had no place in the Third Reich, where biological health and the survival of the *Volk* took precedence over individual rights and personal privacy.

Racial hygiene exposed the indissoluble ties between the long-debated "social question," that is, the debate over how to discipline and integrate the working class, and racial interventionism. Having originated in the last quarter of the nineteenth century, the eugenics movement articulated the bourgeois fear of the impact of Germany's rapid economic growth and urbanization, especially the emergence of a politically autonomous and restive proletariat crammed into urban ghettos that allegedly fostered moral and familial disintegration. Working-class women, who worked in defiance of their duty to reproduce, gave rise to state intervention to ensure the biological health of the *Volk* and the enlargement of the population in an era that equated military strength with population size.[31] In addition, the reinstatement of the death penalty in the late 1880s and early 1890s, which received its justification from theories of criminality that assumed social deviance was inborn, was explicitly directed against the "threat" of a socialist revolution and the Marxist view of criminal behavior as environmentally grounded.[32] The catastrophic battlefield losses and domestic privations of World War I, military defeat and revolution, and the postwar inflation emboldened the proponents of "negative" eugenics, or the aggressive prevention of procreation by the "unfit." The Depression exacerbated that trend as welfare agencies struggled to cope with an influx of uncooperative clients, seemingly incorrigible working-class youths, and the chronically unemployed.

It was no accident that the majority of the sterilized came from proletarian backgrounds. Their poverty, joblessness, fractured families, and suspicious politics attracted official attention from police, case workers, and medical personnel already predisposed to consider behavior that deviated from bourgeois norms as congenital. Thus, the teenager Karl Himmel, the illegitimate son of a housemaid who hailed from a small industrial city in western Germany, became the sort of case that from the official point of view merited sterilization. Following his mother's

---

[31] Kathleen Canning, *Languages of Labor and Gender: Female Factory Work in Germany, 1850–1914* (Ithaca and London: Cornell University Press, 1996), 85–217.

[32] Richard J. Evans, *Rituals of Retribution: Capital Punishment in Germany, 1600–1987* (Oxford: Oxford University Press, 1996), 433–4.

marriage to his stepfather and the birth of his legitimate half brother, Himmel's growing alienation from his family and his poor performance in school led to his eviction from the household. A series of trade schools and jobs did not compensate for his feelings of rejection. As a resident in a shelter, Himmel was reported to the local hereditary health court in 1936. After an intelligence test and an examination by doctors, the court ordered that he undergo a vasectomy in January of 1937 because of his inability to adhere to socially acceptable behavior. Himmel's conviction that his refusal to answer questions on the intelligence test that would have betrayed his communist sympathies, which he later revealed in an interview for an oral history, underscored the manner in which eugenics and social polarization converged in each side's view as to how the fate of candidates for sterilization were determined.[33]

Although the connection between concentration camps and Germany's prior colonial experience was indirect, "racial hygiene" belonged to a longer history, the difficult management of the overseas empire prior to World War I and the imposed decolonization of Germany afterward. Both allowed the "race question" and the "social question" to intersect. In the face of "native" resistance and global economic integration, which put a premium on labor efficiency at home and abroad, eugenics became the justification for banning miscegenation, segregating natives while simultaneously exploiting their labor, and pushing for higher-quality, less-proletarianized settlers who would not "go native." Imperialism linked the two bourgeois phobias of socialism and racial mixing, in which workers were imagined much like "natives," unclean, insubordinate, and dark. Although the Second Empire's citizenship law of 1913 was less exclusionary than radical nationalists preferred, the loss of colonies and the "Black horror on the Rhine" provided support for the argument that citizenship should be to the hereditarily fit, those who did not require eugenic intervention. Instead of the right to privacy, including privacy in sexual matters, the specter of miscegenation increasingly dictated the restraint of sexual freedom and the exclusion of those who embodied racial endangerment from the *Volk* body. Biology would indeed become destiny.[34]

---

[33] See Ulrike Jureit, *Erinnerungsmuster: Zur Methodik lebensgeschichtlischer Interviews mit Überlebenden der Konzentrations-und Vernichtungslager* (Hamburg: Ergebnisse Verlag, 1999), 194–233.

[34] Pascal Grosse, *Kolonialismus, Eugenik und bürgerliche Gesellschaft in Deutschland 1850–1918* (New York: Campus Verlag, 2000), 233–8.

Moreover, as the career of the anthropologist Eugen Fischer demonstrates, continuities in personnel existed between Imperial Germany and the Third Reich. In 1913, after having conducted field research in German Southwest Africa after the Herero War, Fischer published a study of the Afrikaans-speaking Rehoboth Basters, the offspring of African women and Boer, British, and German men, which established his reputation. Although ambiguous in its findings, Fischer's study concluded that miscegenation endangered whites. It also argued that racial inferiors deserved to live only if they could prove their utility to their racial superiors. If that condition were not met, racial "inferiors" could legitimately be eliminated. Fischer's postwar prestige as director of the Kaiser Wilhelm Institute for Anthropology, Human Heredity, and Eugenics, which allowed him to undertake an expanded program of racial science and which trained Nazi luminaries such as the Auschwitz doctor Josef Mengele, elevated him to significance during the Third Reich. In addition to playing a key role in the sterilization of the mixed-race children of German women and the French colonial troops who occupied the Rhine, Fischer's work on mixed marriages helped to create the broader "scientific" underpinnings of the Nuremberg Laws.[35]

Nevertheless, the Nazi regime's emerging racial policy did not simply evolve from earlier precedents. Structurally its reconstitution of police power into outright terror entailed a violent rupture with important implications for the practice of health care and public welfare. In addition to destroying the institutional foundations of the working-class movement and its parties and trade unions, it also suppressed those who held the greatest potential for inhibiting Nazism's deployment of eugenics, not to mention the rapid expansion of the SS, which became the institutional embodiment of "racial hygiene." In many cases Jewish and sympathetic to the left, public health care and welfare professionals, who challenged hereditarian science or affirmed individual autonomy in family planning, were purged, exiled, or arrested. Even if the most conservative of Weimar's diverse social service agencies had moved dangerously close to Nazi welfare ideology, they neither totally eliminated individual choice nor adhered to the criterion for public support that Nazis saw

---

[35] See Henry Friedlander, *The Origins of Nazi Genocide: From Euthanasia to the Final Solution* (Chapel Hill and London: University of North Carolina Press, 1995), 11–14; Alan E. Steinweis, *Studying the Jew: Scholarly Antisemitism in Nazi Germany* (Cambridge, MA and London: Harvard University Press, 2006), 46–54; Madley, "From Africa to Auschwitz," 453–6.

as essential, the individual's "value" to the community. Yet after 1933, the arrest and imprisonment of Socialists narrowed the field considerably. The regime's attack on the left, coupled with its determination to concentrate political power at the top, enabled eugenics, especially negative eugenics, to become deadlier in Germany than in other industrialized nations where it was practiced.[36]

To be sure, sterilization measures in California started in 1909 constituted an important model for the German sterilization law of 1933, indicating the degree to which eugenics had become a transnational movement that involved the sharing of important information and precedents. Ultimately, however, German eugenicists pointed to the superiority of the Nazi approach. A nationwide law, the execution of which lay in a system of hereditary courts, was in their view a more effective and rational course of action than the federalized, inconsistent, and presumably chaotic approach of the United States.[37] Nazi eugenics not only reached extremes unachieved elsewhere, its racial policy also rested on an assumption that no other imperialist power ever acted upon. As the assault against the left and the sterilization law made evident, the regime's imposition of "racial hygiene" did not just accompany imperialism. Rather, the regime considered it necessary to impose "cleansing" in advance of the war for empire. Only a nation unencumbered by social conflict and the expensive ballast of "inferiors," as well as cleansed of "undesirable" genetic material could expand and prosper. To that end, the *Volk* required instruction to overcome deep-seated moral prohibitions whether liberal individualist or Christian, not only to sanction the new practices of medical professionals, but also to harden themselves for the apocalyptic battle ahead. Despite the indirect and direct contributions to the racial policy of the Third Reich of Eugen Fischer and others, they would have been impossible had not the Nazi regime placed the destruction of "Marxism" as the first priority in its agenda. The elimination of organized labor ensured

[36] Atina Grossmann, *Reforming Sex: The German Movement for Birth Control and Abortion Reform 1920–1950* (New York and Oxford: Oxford University Press, 1995), 136–65; David L. Hoffmann and Annette F. Timm, "Utopian Biopolitics: Reproductive Policies, Gender Roles, and Sexuality in Nazi Germany and the Soviet Union," in Michael Geyer and Sheila Fitzpatrick, eds., *Beyond Totalitarianism: Stalinism and Nazism Compared* (Cambridge: Cambridge University Press, 2009), 94–5.

[37] See Stefan Kühl, *The Nazi Connection: Eugenics, American Racism, and German National Socialism* (New York and Oxford: Oxford University Press, 1994), 37–63, on what German eugenicists learned from the United States; and Friedlander, *Origins*, 9–10. As university scientists, German eugenicists enjoyed greater prestige than their American counterparts, which obviously elevated their influence.

that its racial agenda would receive no effective opposition. Moreover, that agenda would further build upon the regime's elimination of the Socialist and Communist "threat" and the compulsory sterilization of the hereditarily "unworthy."

If immediacy characterized the suppression and exclusion of domestic "enemies," it also characterized developments in the German economy in keeping with the radical nationalist and imperialist foreign policy that united the Nazis with their conservative enablers. Early in the second week of February 1933, Hitler announced to his cabinet that rearmament would be undertaken immediately and economic policy would serve as its handmaiden. Only rearmament, according to the führer, would make military conquest possible. In turn, only military conquest would provide the living space that would assure the biological survival and material prosperity of Germans. Thus, the armed forces received its own budget from resources diverted from the economic recovery program instituted in late 1932 by the then chancellor Kurt von Schleicher to boost the production of ships, planes, artillery, tanks, and other essential hardware. To finance rearmament, the Finance Minister Hjalmar Schacht, a National Liberal before the war who by the late 1920s had become a radical nationalist with strong pro-Nazi leanings, created a consortium that issued a new currency called "Mefo bills" guaranteed by the state and discounted by the Reichsbank. All told, the government pledged to commit thirty-five million Reichsmarks over eight years to rearmament for an average of 5–10 percent of the German GDP each year. Not only did this expenditure exceed the military spending of the western powers by two to three times, the proportion of the Reich's budget devoted to rearmament in peacetime was not achieved by western nations until the Cold War.[38]

Because of the profound impact on the Nazi consciousness of the Entente's blockade during World War I, the key to rearmament over the long term was not the deficit spending that the Mefo bills barely disguised, but economic self-sufficiency. Autarky would relieve Germany's dependence on food imports, create currency reserves that could be used to purchase critical raw materials, and foster bilateral trade agreements with the successor states of southeastern Europe. In turn, economic dependency would pave the way for their incorporation into a German empire, transforming what had been a export-based German economy

[38] Adam Tooze, *The Wages of Destruction: The Making and Breaking of the Nazi Economy* (London: Allen Lane, 2006), 54.

into a self-contained one. In fact, in June of 1933 at Schacht's urging, the Nazi regime unilaterally declared a moratorium on its repayment of its long-term foreign debt, especially to the United States. In so doing, the regime completed what Brüning and Papen began, the abandonment of a practice that Weimar governments between 1924 and 1929 had considered essential, the use of American leverage to alleviate reparations pressures from Britain and France and to secure markets for German exports.[39] Unlike previous European colonial wars, which imperialist powers waged in part to integrate their colonies in a global economy, the Nazi regime linked the resurgence of the Reich with the pursuit of autarky.[40]

Improving the chronically parlous state of German agriculture was equally crucial to achieving economic self-sufficiency and racial revival. Significant increases in domestic food production would compensate for the loss of imports and insulate Germany from the consequences of a probable enemy blockade. Yet low rural living standards and the practice among peasant families in the south and west to divide holdings among multiple siblings, which resulted in farms that were too small to achieve a decent economy of scale, were major problems that had to be overcome. The emigration of landless laborers and peasants only compounded the difficulties. The need to produce more food internally to reduce Germany's dependence on imports was not the only justification for agrarian "reform." Consistent with the premise of the sterilization law to prepare the *Volk* biologically for the struggle ahead, the regime's measures in agriculture infused economics with race. Through the legal and biological restructuring of inheritance, an economically and racially healthy peasantry would become the core of a revitalized *Volk*

To that end, the regime instituted two programs that signified the complete abandonment of a liberal economy in agriculture and the imposition of racially based property rights that anticipated the redefinition of citizenship that would occur as a result of the Nuremberg Laws. The first, the Reich Entailment Law promulgated in 1933, protected peasant holdings from foreclosure while doing away with the right of owners to sell their farms or use them as security against mortgages. Designed to force peasants into a rigid system of primogeniture and eliminate partible

---

[39] Ibid., 55.

[40] See Dierk Walter, "Warum Kolonialkrieg?", in *Kolonialkriege: Militärische Gewalt im Zeichen des Imperialismus*, eds. Thoralf Klein and Frank Schumacher (Hamburg: Hamburger Edition, 2006), 19–20.

inheritance, the right to inherit property excluded women, as well as men with Jewish or "colored" ancestry. Peasants found to be deficient by the hereditary health courts were excluded as well. Initially the law expected entailed estates to manage their debt burden cooperatively. Because the law proved more effective in principle than in practice, the ministry of agriculture resorted increasingly to extending credits or loans to peasants to ensure their cooperation and weaken their resistance to the new standards of inheritance.

The second law created the Reich Food Estate, which established price and output controls to raise farm incomes and improve rural living standards so that rural dwellers would be less inclined to leave. Both programs originated with Hugenberg's replacement as Minister of Agriculture, the committed Nazi Walther Darré, and his deputy Herbert Backe. Both advocated a thorough agrarian protectionism and a virulent hostility to what he termed the "Jewish" doctrine of free trade. Economic liberalism, they determined, was the foundation of a soulless urbanism, which sacrificed the backbone of German culture, the peasantry. It mocked the principal value to which peasants adhered, rootedness to the land. Both maintained that a "return" to core German values of blood and soil depended on a radically enlarged living space that would permit larger, more efficient, and more modern farms. Significantly, neither Darré nor Backe had been born and raised in Germany. Darré hailed from Argentina. Backe's ethnic German ancestors had settled in Georgia during the nineteenth century, but his immediate family had fled the Bolshevik Revolution. As so-called *Volksdeutschen* (ethnic Germans who were not Reich citizens), the prominence of the two signified not only the Nazi movement's magnetic attraction for some of those it claimed to benefit, Germans from beyond the Reich's borders, but also that Nazi agricultural policy would not be confined within Germany's present boundaries. Although during the war the goals of settlement as pursued by the SS would move further afield from the Reich Food Estate's peasant-centered agenda, territorial expansion was from the beginning envisioned as the panacea that would seamlessly integrate economic health and ethnic revival.[41]

---

[41] The literature on Nazi agricultural policy is substantial. See Tooze, *Wages of Destruction*, 166–99; Gustavo Corni, *Hitler and the Peasants: Agrarian Policy in the Third Reich, 1930–1939*, trans. David Kerr (New York: Berg, 1990); and Gustavo Corni and Horst Gies, *Brot, Butter, Kanonen: Die Ernährungswirtschaft in Deutschland unter der Diktatur Hitlers* (Berlin, 1997). See especially Uwe Mai, *"Rasse und Raum": Agrarpolitik, Sozial- und Raumplanung im NS-Staat* (Paderborn: Ferdinand Schöningh, 2002), 48–76.

Compared to the hyper-rearmament that took off after 1936, the investment in military production beforehand was modest. Still the regime's
initial measures signified major shifts in priorities. Those included limitations on dividends that joint-stock companies could pay their sharehold-
ers in order to redirect investors to the purchase of government bonds,
and the increasing discrimination against the production of goods with
little military application.[42] Although Hitler appreciated the German
population's attraction to an emergent consumerism, he never deviated
from his belief in delayed gratification until empire was achieved. Even
job creation programs, which Hitler only began to address in late May
of 1933, and which in the beginning drew upon funds already budgeted
by Schleicher, developed less from the need to return the unemployed to
work than to their utility as a stopgap measure until rearmament took
hold. Investment in public works projects, which never came close to
that for military spending, would serve as camouflage for remilitarizing
Germany, keeping the Entente off guard until the Reich was fully prepared. The most attention-grabbing job creation projects, the construction
of superhighways (*Autobahnen*) and the production of the Volkswagen
that would be priced low enough for workers to afford, were themselves
closely linked to rearmament. If ultimately useless to the military because
of its vulnerability to enemy air attack and left unfinished once war came,
the Autobahn originated in the belief that it would serve military needs.
Hitler's fascination with Henry Ford's mass-produced cars, which the
Volkswagen ultimately embodied, resulted not only from the regime's
wish to "motorize the masses" and win the loyalty of "lesser earning"
Germans, but also from the recognition that automobile factories could
be easily converted to the production of military vehicles.[43]

Even Hitler's desire to halt further "revolution" by curbing the SA's
orgy of vigilante "excesses," which he expressed in July of 1933 following the defeat of the left and the implementation of *Gleichschaltung*,
resulted in a further radicalization. Faced with the mounting restiveness
of government ministries and the military, the Nazi leadership decided

---

[42] Dean, *Robbing the Jews*, 50.

[43] On the regime's job creation programs, see Dan P. Silverman, *Hitler's Economy: Nazi
Work Creation Programs, 1933–1936* (Cambridge, MA and London: Harvard University
Press, 1998). On the Autobahn and the Volkswagen see Richard J. Overy, "Cars, Roads,
and Economic Recovery in Germany, 1932–1939," in Overy, *War and Economy in
the Third Reich* (Oxford: Clarendon Press, 1994), 68–89; and Hans Mommsen and
Manfred Grieger, *Das Volkswagenwerk und seine Arbeiter im Dritten Reich*, 3rd ed.
(Düsseldorf: Econ Verlag, 1997), 51–113.

to curb the SA's auxiliary police powers and reduce its role strictly to the political mobilization of the masses. As long as the SA terror primarily targeted Communists and Socialists, conservatives had voiced few objections. Once the left was contained, however, the Brown Shirts took to assaulting foreign diplomats, government offices, and workplaces. Initial measures to restrain the SA did nothing to contain the resentment of the organization's "old fighters," who disliked the influx of huge numbers of new members after January of 1933 and Hitler's tacit promises to the regular army that the "brown battalions" would not compete with it. The Brown Shirts wore their ambition to replace the Reichswehr as the true national militia on their sleeves. In addition to their continuous brawling, they demanded a "second revolution" that would put aside the compromises that brought Hitler to power, and eliminate the conservative establishment.

Although wavering for months because he was unwilling to lose face with party "old fighters," Hitler temporized until Vice-Chancellor Papen's alarming speech at the University of Marburg in mid-June, 1934. Betraying his dismay that the authoritarian and elitist system that he hoped Hitler would support was now under threat, Papen vigorously condemned the "second revolution" and the "false personality cult" that surrounded the chancellor. Shortly thereafter, Hindenburg threatened to invoke martial law and place the government in the hands of the army. With his back to the wall, Hitler acted. On June 30, 1934, Göring, Himmler, and Himmler's deputy Reinhard Heydrich engineered the arrest and murder of the SA's leadership, including its commander Ernst Röhm, who had been one of Hitler's closest associates since the party's beginnings in Munich. The army command, which provided the SS with transport and weapons, was relieved by the destruction of its most dangerous rival and reassured by the guarantees that Hitler had bestowed on the military initially after taking power. Although the "Night of the Long Knives," as the Röhm Purge came to be known, unfolded with a cascade of violence worthy of the paramilitary that was now being brutally chastened, public opinion praised Hitler's decisiveness in restoring order against SA bullies and in taking on party "bosses" who had grown too big for their breeches.[44] Because many Germans separated Hitler from the actions of his party, his popularity had hardly suffered, according to informants for the Social Democratic Party in Exile (*Sopade*). In some

---

[44] Ian Kershaw, *The 'Hitler Myth': Myth and Reality in the Third Reich* (Oxford: Clarendon Press, 1987), 84–95.

circles it had actually increased.[45] Neither the Protestant nor the Catholic Church raised its voice, perhaps a sign of the effectiveness of Hitler's justifications for the purge, the SA leadership's homosexuality, drunkenness, corruption, and debauchery. Already compromised by emergency decrees and antisemitic legislation to which it had acceded, the legal profession found nothing to object to either.

The army's palpable relief was premature, however, for the regime sought a broader settling of scores that affected the old elite as well. The "Night of the Long Knives" did not simply target the SA leadership, it also engulfed prominent conservatives who were murdered in acts of revenge. Papen's aide, Edgar Jung, who wrote the vice-chancellor's Marburg speech, was killed, as was Hitler's immediate predecessor Kurt von Schleicher, who had tried to block a Hitler chancellorship. A leading Catholic politician, Erich Klausener, was gunned down as a warning to Heinrich Brüning, who having gotten the message, hastily escaped the country. Gustav von Kahr, the staunchly monarchist Minister President of Bavaria, who despite his hospitality to the radical right after the Kapp putsch did not go along with the Munich uprising in 1923, met his violent demise. The purge also finished off a leading general, Erich von Bredow, who was suspected of publishing criticisms of the regime abroad. Gregor Strasser, once the Nazi organization leader, who in defiance of Hitler had sought a position in Schleicher's cabinet, was coldly executed by order of Göring and Himmler. Commenting on the demise of leading conservatives in the purge, the writer Thomas Mann, a qualified supporter of the republic, who once championed the war against the Entente, acidly pronounced a plague on both houses. "I feel no sympathy for these people who paved the way for this misery any more than I do for those thugs [the Nazi chief of police in Breslau Edmund] Heines and Röhm, and yet their blood will also be on the 'head' of this revolting swindler and murderous charlatan one day, a hero of history such as the world has never seen before, beside whom Robespierre seems downright honorable."[46]

Mann's warning was prescient. The Röhm Purge significantly enhanced the position of the SS, enabling Himmler to assume management of all concentration camps in addition to Dachau, and it anchored its place as the emerging racial elite of the Third Reich. Two months before the

---

[45] *Deutschland-Berichte der Sozialdemokratischen Partei Deutschlands (Sopade)* (hereinafter cited as *Sopade*) (Frankfurt am Main: Verlag Petra Nettelbeck, 1980), June/July 1934, 249.

[46] Thomas Mann, *Diaries 1918–1939*, trans. Richard and Clara Winston (New York: Henry N. Abrams, 1982), 216.

purge, after Himmler had already assumed command of the police in a number of other German states in addition to Bavaria, Göring authorized his command of the Prussian police who would be essential to the coming crackdown on the SA. Despite Interior Minister Frick's objections to Himmler's expanding empire, Himmler exploited his personal connection to Hitler to expand the indiscriminate use of "protective custody" without judicial review. From now on, the SS, an organization that had begun modestly during the 1920s as Hitler's personal bodyguard, would be responsible to Hitler alone.

In addition to its widening police powers, the SS embodied the fusion of racism and expansionism to a degree that was exceptional in the history of European imperialism. It personified the regime's commitment to purification as a crucial antecedent to war. Having expelled sixty thousand "undesirable" members of the SS between 1933 and 1935, Himmler imposed new regulations that involved extraordinary scrutiny of the private lives of SS initiates. In addition to specifying the appropriate height, physical appearance and bearing, athletic accomplishment, and intelligence, he demanded that candidates for admission prove Aryan ancestry back to 1750 for officers and 1800 for enlisted men. Senior SS leaders had to prove a racially unobjectional ancestry back to 1650. Moreover, SS men could not marry unless their brides-to-be submitted to the screening of their racial suitability, a policy initiated by Walther Darré before the Nazi takeover, whose close relationship to Himmler and membership in the organization allowed him to put his theories of racial selection into practice.[47] Although ordinary Germans were also expected to present genealogical evidence of their racial acceptability, the threshold was lower than that expected of the regime's racial elite.[48] As older SS members retired, many of them veterans of Free Corps campaigns, the SS attracted legions of highly educated younger initiates. The new recruits, many of whom like Himmler himself held doctorates, and whose counter-revolutionary radicalism had been fanned at the universities,[49] would define the enormous scale and lethality of Nazi imperialism by infusing its apocalyptic racism with the weapons of a highly developed economy and culture.

[47] Longerich, *Himmler*, 310–22; 365–95.

[48] Eric Ehrenreich, *The Nazi Ancestral Proof: Geneology, Racial Science and the Final Solution* (Bloomington and Indianapolis: Indiana University Press, 2007), 58–77.

[49] Isabel Heinemann, *"Rasse, Siedlung, deutsches Blut:" Das Rasse-und Siedlungsamt der SS und die Siedlungshauptamt der SS und die rassenpolitische Neuordnung Europas* (Göttingen: Wallstein Verlag, 2004), 49–62.

For Himmler and Darré, the Teutonic Order served as a model for the SS in many ways – its vows of obedience, its military prowess, its aristocratic composition, and its organizational efficiency. Since the early 1920s, the east had captivated Himmler as the space for fulfilling Germany's imperial destiny after he heard a speech by the Free Corps commander and Baltic fighter, Rüdiger von der Goltz.[50] Yet Himmler was not interested simply in the restoration of a medieval precedent, but rather that precedent's modernization and renovation. In addition to rejecting the Teutonic Order's rule of celibacy, which putatively led to "a dissipation of the blood," and proclaiming a "new" aristocracy based on "achievement" and "efficiency," the Order's version of colonialism, which brought the imposition of Germanic laws and language, was lacking. Instead, the SS would mean colonization by German blood.[51] Despite the conflict that developed between Himmler and Darré, the relationship between the SS and the party's agrarian wing, especially Herbert Backe, jointly affirmed the colonization in the east as the solution to Germany's food problem and, more important, the protection of German ethnicity against the multiple threats to its existence.[52]

The death of Reich President Hindenburg during the first week of August, 1934, allowed Hitler to assume the powers of that office, while simultaneously changing his title to führer and Reich chancellor. In fact, Hitler did not even wait for the announcement of the old field marshal's passing to demand that his ministers sign a document that transferred the powers of the president to the führer at Hindenburg's death. Subsequently ratified in a national plebiscite, Hitler's action, backed up by Blomberg, allowed him to become Supreme Commander of the Armed Forces. Because Hitler was now head of state as well as the head of government, the military was forced to swear a new oath of loyalty of unconditional obedience to the man Hindenburg had once disdained as the "Bohemian corporal." A similar oath was required of civil servants. The government of "national concentration," which had converged on the "need" to destroy "Marxism" and the liberal democratic system that preserved it, solidified a dictatorship that mocked Papen's once-confident assurance that Hitler and the Nazi Party would be subservient to conservatives and rein in its populist radicalism. "The people hardly notice this complete

---

[50] Longerich, *Himmler*, 60.

[51] Michael Burleigh, *Ethics and Extermination: Reflections on Nazi Genocide* (Cambridge: Cambridge University Press, 1997), 22–4; Longerich, *Himmler*, 283.

[52] Tooze, *Wages of Destruction*, 171.

coup d'état," complained the well-informed Victor Klemperer, "it all takes place in silence, drowned out by hymns to the dead Hindenburg."[53]

The stunning rapidity with which the Nazi regime consolidated its power, outflanking conservatives and trouncing the left, belied the evidence of popular dissatisfaction with the regime's economic and religious policies. The Nazi government's work-creation programs in 1933 and 1934, those that it initiated on its own such as the Autobahn and those it carried over from its predecessors, temporarily reduced unemployment in the countryside where unskilled labor was plentiful. Yet they did relatively little for unemployed skilled workers in urban areas. The "credit" for reducing unemployment, which became evident by 1936, belonged to rearmament. Nevertheless, popular disaffection became evident by the spring of 1935. Food shortages arising from a poor harvest and rising prices for basic necessities, to which the rearmament-generated inflation contributed, had clearly begun to dampen popular enthusiasm for the regime. Wages remained lower than the levels of 1928, the last pre-Depression year. Hjalmar Schacht's "New Plan," which he introduced in the fall of 1934 to place strict controls on the use of foreign exchange for imports and increase bilateral agreements that would exchange raw materials for finished goods, did nothing to relieve the burden that rearmament imposed on consumers. Importing foodstuffs to relieve shortages and reduce prices was incompatible with an armaments industry dependent on the import of raw materials. That dilemma led to Schacht's own desperate recommendation less than two years later to slow the pace of rearmament so that shortages of raw materials and foodstuffs could be mitigated and popular opinion assuaged.

The regime's treatment of the Protestant and Catholic Churches proved nearly as unsettling to the public, especially in regions where religious commitment remained firm. Despite Hitler's assurances upon taking power that the regime would respect the social, cultural, and legal position of the churches, and the sincere if unorthodox Christianity of the Nazi leadership, the practices of local and regional party militants undermined such guarantees.[54] On the Protestant side, the German Christians,

---

[53] Klemperer, *I Will Bear Witness*, entry of August 4, 1934, 80.

[54] Richard Steigmann-Gall, *The Holy Reich: Nazi Conceptions of Christianity, 1919–1945* (Cambridge: Cambridge University Press, 2003), 114–89. On the German Christians, see Doris Bergen, *The Twisted Cross: The German Christian Movement in the Third Reich* (Chapel Hill: University of North Carolina Press, 1996). The most comprehensive study of the churches is that of Klaus Scholder, *The Churches and the Third Reich*, vol. 1 already cited (n. 11), and vol. 2, *The Years of Disillusionment: 1934 Barmen and Rome*. Volume 3,

pro-Nazi insurgents who wanted to reform the federal structure of the Protestant Church according to the leadership principle and remove pastors and laity with Jewish ancestry, succeeded by the end of 1933 in creating a more centralized Reich church with a new Reich bishop, Ludwig Müller. By the summer of 1934, Nazi Party leaders in the states of Bavaria and Württemberg removed the Protestant bishops in both states, placing them under house arrest. Yet the German Christian campaign to nazify the church structure and incorporate the Aryan Paragraph from the Civil Service Law into the church constitution spawned the Confessing Church, a vocal and well-connected counter insurgency of prominent clergy and lay persons. Although many Confessing Church members sympathized with the Nazi assault on "Marxism," the "excessive" influence of Jews in German life, and the regime's commitment to national and moral renewal,[55] they rejected the unchristian imposition of the "secular" standards of the Nazi movement and condemned the German Christian Reich Church as an apostasy. Moreover, the removal of the southern German bishops infuriated ordinary parishioners, including many Nazi Party members who turned in their membership cards in protest. To calm the tempest, the regime removed the Reich bishop and created a ministry for church affairs to mediate among the different factions. More centralized and hierarchical than the Protestant Church, the Catholic Church experienced no comparable insurgency. Nevertheless, the regime exploited the ambiguities in the Concordat to ban Catholic periodicals, confiscate the assets of Catholic lay organizations, impugn the "morality" of priests, and force the dissolution of Catholic youth groups, measures that poisoned morale among Catholic parishioners.

Despite the rifts in the "racial community," which exposed the fallacy of the Nazi regime's dream of a society free of social and religious

---

Die Kirchen und das Dritte Reich: Spaltungen und Abwehrkämpfe (Frankfurt am Main, Berlin, Vienna: Ullstein, 2001) remains untranslated. On the regime's surveillance and intervention, see Wolfgang Dierker, *Himmlers Glaubenskrieger: Der Sicherheitsdienst der SS und seine Religionspolitik 1933–1941* (Paderborn: Ferdinand Schöningh, 2003), 335–490.

[55] On the antisemitism in the Confessing Church, see Wolfgang Gerlach, *Als die Zeugen schwigen:Bekennende Kirche und die Juden* (Berlin: Institut Kirche und Judentum, 1987), and Susannah Heschel, *The Aryan Jesus: Christian Theologians and the Bible in Nazi Germany* (Princeton and Oxford: Princeton University Press, 2008), 5, 7, 112, 161, 247, and 286. On the positions of the Protestants at the parish level, see Kyle Jantzen, *Faith and Fatherland: Parish Politics in Hitler's Germany* (Minneapolis: Fortress Press, 2008), and Manfred Gailus, *Protestantismus und Nationalsozialismus: Studien zur nationalsozialistischen Durchdringung des protestantischen Sozialmilieus in Berlin* (Berlin: Böhlau, 2001).

divisions, the Third Reich faced no serious threat to its survival. And, despite the potential for deepening repression, to which Germany's mushrooming prison population and Himmler's expanding power base testified, the number of prisoners in concentration camps dropped significantly after the initial dragnet against the Communists and Socialists. In part, Hitler's stunning foreign policy successes undermined the potential for discontent. At minimum, most Germans wanted the restoration of their nation to great power status, the destruction of Versailles, and the return of the ceded territories, including Germany's overseas colonial empire. The withdrawal from the League of Nations and the disarmament talks, the return of the Saar to Germany following a successful plebiscite, and Hitler's announcement of universal military conscription in March of 1935 – all undertaken without western intervention or resistance – greatly enhanced the führer's prestige. The rapid expansion of the Wehrmacht provided the opportunity for upward mobility to thousands of young men from modest social backgrounds and educational attainment to become officers and NCOs.[56]

To be sure, the clumsy attempt by Austrian Nazis in June of 1934 to overthrow the Austrian chancellor Engelbert Dollfuss, with Hitler's tacit blessing, ended in disaster and contributed to Mussolini's overtures to the British and French to secure Italy's interests in Austria. Further disturbed by Hitler's announcement of universal military conscription in March 1935, Mussolini convened a summit with the British and French in the Italian town of Stresa. In a pointed attack on the Third Reich, the conference reaffirmed the 1925 Locarno Treaty and Austria's territorial integrity. Nevertheless, Germany's conclusion of a naval agreement with Britain two months later, which allowed it to build a navy to 35 percent of the size of the British navy, showcased Hitler's ability to exploit the disagreements between Britain and France. Mussolini's subsequent abandonment of the Stresa agreement only six months later when Italy invaded Ethiopia, provided additional testimony to the death of the international security apparatus put into place after World War I. Hitler's daring gamble in March 1936 to remilitarize the Rhineland, which he undertook against the advice of the high command of the armed forces (*Wehrmacht*), with an eye on its potential for firming up his public support, removed a crucial Versailles restriction on Germany's offensive military capability. At

---

[56] MacGregor Knox, *Common Destiny: Dictatorship, Foreign Policy, and War in Fascist Italy and Nazi Germany* (Cambridge: Cambridge University Press, 2000), 207–25.

home, Germans across class lines greeted Hitler's move with rapturous enthusiasm, as the führer's triumph had come without a war.[57]

The convergence of repression at home and diplomatic success abroad gave the Nazi regime sufficient power to expand its campaign for racial purification, an insidious web of repression and exclusion that functioned effectively precisely because it privileged the majority of Germans while ruthlessly punishing leftists, minorities, and the socially deviant. Hitler's decree of June 1936 allowed the SS to incorporate the professional police throughout the Reich into two main offices, the Order police headed by Kurt Daluege, and the political police, which included the Gestapo (political police) and Kripo (criminal police), under the aegis of the leader of the SS intelligence service, the SD, Reinhard Heydrich. Having served in the war, Daluege was older than most SS officers. Yet he possessed impeccable radical nationalist and imperialist credentials that included service in the Free Corps and the anti-Polish Upper Silesian "protection" force before joining the Nazi Party in 1922. Heydrich closely fit the profile of the younger men whom the SS drew to its ranks. Born in 1904 to an upper-middle-class family, headed by a father who founded the musical conservatory in Halle, Heydrich enlisted in the Free Corps at sixteen before becoming a naval officer. Forced to resign his commission in 1931 because of his numerous affairs, Heydrich joined the Nazi Party and the SS where his administrative skills and utter ruthlessness could be more fully appreciated. With the police and concentration camps under its control, the SS devoted itself to rooting out not only the agents of "Jewish Bolshevism," but also those whose allegedly disintegrative effect had no place in the "racial community." Their numbers included Free Masons, Jehovah's Witnesses, Seventh-Day Adventists, homosexuals, especially gay men, the "work shy," that is, beggars and the chronically unemployed, and the otherwise "asocial," which included "habitual criminals." Operating independently of the ministry of the interior and the courts, the SS faced few restrictions on its power.

In addition to the restiveness of SA men, who expected compensation for their reduction in status in the wake of the Röhm Purge, increasing prices and stubbornly high unemployed fueled an upswing in antisemitism in 1935.[58] The continued local boycotts and vandalizing of Jewish-owned

---

[57] On the führer's diplomatic gambits, see Leitz, *Nazi Foreign Policy*, especially 43–5, and Kershaw, *Hubris*, 529–91, which especially emphasizes the domestic impact of Hitler's initiatives.

[58] See Longerich, '*Davon haben wir nichst gewusst!*', 75–7; Wildt, *Volksgemeinschaft als Selbstermächtigung*, 232–66.

businesses, attacks by the SA and Hitler Youth against Jews in many cities and towns, public humiliation and imprisonment of Jews and non-Jews suspected of sexual contact or "racial defilement" (*Rassenschande*), and countless other acts of discrimination built momentum toward the eradication of "Jewish influence" once and for all. Although local boycotts proved strikingly effective in forcing the liquidation of Jewish-owned businesses,[59] the dismay of conservatives and broad swaths of popular opinion at the economic disruption and the crudeness of party radicals demanded more orderly procedures to purify the *Volk* of "alien races." Thus, the ministries of the interior and justice completed anti-Jewish legislation, in preparation since 1933, that went well beyond the removal of Jews from the universities, the civil service, or the professions. This legislation, the culmination of fears that had mounted since the Great War, would address the deepest phobia of racists and antisemites, the contamination of the *Volk* by "racial mixing."

For maximum effect, the Reichstag passed the legislation at the September 1935 Nazi Party rally in Nuremberg, the one-time imperial capital of the Holy Roman Empire that had grown into a Nazi bastion during the 1920s. Located in Middle Franconia, the city and its parade grounds lay in one of the most antisemitic regions in Germany. The Nuremberg Laws fused two strands of Nazi racial theory, the eugenic emphasis on eliminating genetic impurities to ensure racial revitalization and the virulent antisemitism of the postwar *völkisch* movement, which drew from Artur Dinter's theory that sexual relationships with Jews would result in the degeneration of Germans. Crucial to blending engenics and antisemitism was the widely disseminated work of the anthropologist Hans J. K. Günther, which determined that Jews were the product of the fusion of Near Eastern and Oriental races, and thus radically different from Europeans.[60] The Nuremberg Laws and their supplementary decrees "scientifically" codified the radical otherness of Jews that justified their separation from German society. In addition to depriving Jews of full citizenship as Germans, the laws forbade Jews from flying the swastika, now officially the flag of the Third Reich, banned intermarriage and extramarital sexual relationships between Jews and non-Jews, and prohibited Jews from employing German women as servants under the

[59] See Dean, *Robbing the Jews*, 47–8, for a summary of research on this issue.

[60] On Günther, see Steinweis, *Studying the Jew*, 41–6. On the complexities of Nazi racial theory and the development of the Nuremberg Laws, see Cornelia Essner, *Die "Nürnberger Gesetze" oder die Verwaltung des Rassenwahns 1933–1945* (Paderborn: Ferdinand Schöningh, 2002), 76–112.

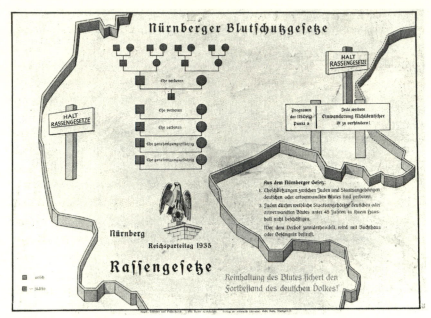

FIGURE 4.4. Eugenics poster entitled "the Nuremberg Laws for the Protection of Blood and German Honor." One of a series of advertisements, this stylized map of central Germany defines borders against the immigration of non-Aryans and the text of the Law for the Protection of German Blood. The text at the bottom reads, "Maintaining the purity of blood insures the survival of the German *Volk*." *Source*: USHMM, photograph #94188, courtesy of Hans Pauli.

age of forty-five. The ostensible justification for such measures, according to the führer's prefatory speech to the rally, was "Bolshevik agitation" arising from the disputed Lithuanian territory of Memel with its large ethnic German population, the work of "almost exclusively Jewish elements" that spread animosity and confusion.[61]

Despite such fundamental transformations in the law governing citizenship and civil marriage, the definition of a "Jew" was far from clear. Thus, a succession of implementation decrees would be introduced subsequently to achieve precision and forestall the proliferation of murky cases where determining ancestry proved difficult to determine. Having three full-Jewish grandparents or two Jewish grandparents and marriage

---

[61] Max Domarus ed. *The Complete Hitler: A Desktop Reference to His Speeches and Proclamations 1932–1945* (Wauconda, IL: Bolchazy-Carducci Publishers, 2007), vol. 2 (German version), 15 September 1935, 536.

to a Jewish spouse labeled one a Jew, yet identification with the "Jewish religious community" could also determine Jewishness rather than blood. Much to the dismay of antisemites, who wanted to define as Jews those with only partial Jewish ancestry, the first implementation decree created a separate class of "mixed-race" (*Mischlinge*) people, roughly 200,000 Germans who met the criteria,[62] whose status was defined by one or two full-Jewish grandparents, or by having simply married a full Jew. Nevertheless, the Nuremberg Laws provided the framework for future decrees, which would infiltrate the private, indeed intimate, decisions of individuals, impose new identities on individuals against their will, and intensify the exclusion of those defined as "Jewish." Already hellish for those labeled political or racial enemies, the Nuremberg Laws added significantly to the elevation of Nazi Germany, like the U.S. South under Jim Crow, to the status of an "overtly racist regime," in which the official state ideology, legalized social discrimination, and the outlawing of miscegenation stigmatized and marginalized its victims.[63]

To some degree the Nuremberg Laws inherited concepts from pre-war debates as to the consequences of colonial contact, that is, mixed marriages. The notion of "alien races" unworthy of German citizenship was in fact a Pan German neologism. Although his theories as to the outcomes of racial mixing were ambiguous in their implications, Eugen Fischer claimed as a result of his study of the Rehoboth Basters that hereditary and racial traits were one and the same. His work thus supported subsequent attempts to combine eugenic and antisemitic strands of racism. Yet even in this case, the Nazi regime radicalized Imperial German practice, and not just because, as a dictatorship, it could alter citizenship and marriage law with far less difficulty than its predecessor. Rather, Germany's forced decolonization after World War I, as well as the wartime and postwar surge of biological antisemitism, obliterated the distinction between colonial and metropolitan law, and encouraged more desperate and virulent fears of racial mixing to arise. At one time sexual contact between German males and "native" women prompted antimiscegenation measures in the colonies, but the colonies were distant then and absent now. Even worse measures would be imposed at home

---

[62] Saul Friedlander, *Nazi Germany and the Jews*, vol. 1: *The Years of Persecution* (New York: HarperCollins, 1997), 151.

[63] George Frederickson, *Racism: A Short History* (Princeton: Princeton University Press), 2002), 101–2.

against a more proximate threat, the Jews, whose markers of difference were often not obvious and thus more dangerous.[64]

The Nuremberg Laws also affected Sinti, Roma, and mixed-race Germans because they denied full citizenship rights to "persons of alien blood," in addition to Jews. By the beginning of 1935, the regime extended mandatory sterilization to the offspring of unions between French colonial soldiers and German women during the occupation of the Rhineland. Although not legally covered by the Law for the Prevention of Hereditarily Diseased Offspring because racial specialists found it difficult to prove that "blackness" resulted in hereditary illness, the regime nonetheless sterilized over half of the mixed-race children by 1937, some six to eight hundred in number, in a secretive affair that even circumvented the hereditary courts.[65] The Nuremberg Laws, however, were imposed less rigorously on mixed marriages that did not involve unions between non-Jewish Germans and Jews. Although marriages between Africans and Germans were obviously stigmatized, they were not punishable under the law, nor were sexual relationships between Germans and "gypsies" or blacks punished as "racial defilement."[66] The relatively small number of Sinti, Roma, and Afro-Germans as compared to Jews helps to account for the difference in treatment.

The overlap of racism and imperialism informed the regime's position toward Afro-Germans and Africans. Because the so-called "Rhineland bastards" personified Germany's colonization by the Entente and the resulting defilement of German "blood," their eventual sterilization would mean the bodily rejection of foreign conquest literally and figuratively. Yet for Africans who migrated to Germany from Germany's

---

[64] Cornelia Essner, "'Border-line' im Menschenblut und Struktur rassistischer Rechtsspaltung: Koloniales Kaiserreich und 'Drittes Reich'", in *Gesetzliches Unrecht: Rassistisches Recht im 20. Jahrhundert*, eds. Micha Brumlik, Susanne Meinl, and Werner Renz (New York: Campus Verlag, 2005), 57–60.

[65] Tina Campt, *Other Germans: Black Germans and the Politics of Race, Gender, and Memory in the Third Reich* (Ann Arbor: University of Michigan Press, 2004), 63–80; Clarence Lusane, *Hitler's Black Victims: The Historical Experiences of Afro-Germans, European Blacks, Africans, and African Americans in the Nazi Era* (New York and London: Routledge, 2003), 129–43; Rainer Pommerin, *Sterilisierung der Rheinlandbastarden: das Schicksal einer farbigen deutschen Minderheit* (Düsseldorf: Droste Verlag, 1979), 77–87; Sandra Mass, *Weisse Helden, Schwarzer Krieger: Zur Geschichte kolonialer Männlichkeit in Deutschland 1918–1944* (Cologne/Weimar/Vienna: Böhlau Verlag, 2006), 277–99.

[66] Birthe Kundrus "Von Windhoek nach Nürnberg? Koloniale 'Mischehenverbote' und die nationalsozialistische Rassengestzgebung," in *Phantasiereiche: Zur Kulturgeschichte der deutschen Kolonialismus*, ed. Birthe Kundrus (Frankfurt and New York: Campus Verlag, 2003), 114–16.

former colonies, and who either possessed German citizenship or had served in Lettow-Vorbeck's campaign during the war, the cold calculation of utility coexisted with anti-black racism. Even as the regime put blacks under tighter surveillance than was the case under the republic, it also found uses for them.[67] Thus, while confined to working in "Africa shows" that displayed "native primitiveness" to Germans as entertainment while keeping blacks segregated, blacks reminded Germans of their colonial past until a restored and expanded German empire in Africa would enable their return as ambassadors who could proclaim the blessings of German culture. By 1940, "inappropriate mixing" between black entertainers and German women shut down the shows, consigning many blacks to a violent end in concentration camps. Yet the Third Reich could not arrive at a consistent policy toward blacks, including in some cases the "Rhineland bastards."[68] The status of Jews was far less ambiguous in the Nazi universe, for "Juda" embodied the fear that lay at the root of German nationalism, the possibility that Germany would be destroyed from within and without. Jews personified global capitalism, or the highly developed economies of Germany's rivals and the insidious contamination of Bolshevism.

The Nuremberg Laws testified to the increasing systemization of legal discrimination and the increasing precision, or at least the attempt at it, in identifying "others" whose racial unsuitability excluded them from the Nazi *Volk* "community." Despite the inconsistent and arbitrary application of the means of exclusion, lives were irrevocably changed as Nazi categories forced individuals to reconsider their life choices and, indeed, their very identities under a regime determined to eliminate other forms of allegiance and replace them with race. For full Jews, the force of exclusion was unambiguous. For those "mixed-race" Germans in between (*Mischlinge*), the ambiguity of their position brought its own form of anxiety. As the children of marriages between Jews and Christians, most of them arose from the solidly law-abiding and nationalistic middle classes who wanted nothing more than to prove their

---

[67] Heiko Möhle, "Betreung, Erfassung, Kontrolle: Afrikaner aus den Deutschen Kolonien und die 'Deutsche Gesellschaft für Eingeborenenkunde' in der Weimarer Republik," in *Die (koloniale) Begegnung: AfrikanerInnen in Deutschland 1880–1945, Deutsche in Afrika 1880–1918*, eds. Marianne Bechhaus-Gerst and Reinhard Klein-Arendt (Frankfurt am Main: Peter Lang, 2003), 225–36; Mass, *Weisse Helden*, 280–1.

[68] Elisa von Joeden-Forgey, "Race Power in Postcolonial Germany," in *Germany's Colonial Pasts*, eds. Eric Ames, Marcia Klotz, and Lora Wildenthal (Lincoln and London: University of Nebraska Press, 2005), 167–88.

value to the "community." For some, rediscovering one's Jewish heritage became the answer; for others, the solution lay in exploiting the legal loopholes to deny the paternity of a Jewish father with the heavy emotional price that went along with it. Few could bring themselves to consider emigration. All wavered between the extremes of hope that their personal and family circumstances would allow them to escape the impact of antisemitic legislation and the fear that exceptions would never fully protect them from social marginalization, impoverishment, arrest, and death.[69]

For the majority who were neither politically nor racially marginalized, Nazi policies elevated them into a realm where previous markers of social distinction, although those hardly disappeared, would not matter. Nazi social policy, the execution of which the regime's racial categories obviously defined, aimed to transcend all manner of local identity, privilege, and social distinction, thereby eliminating previous barriers to an integrated nation. It would unite all Germans around their common racial superiority. It aimed to teach Germans how to behave in preparation for their future role as a superior race and as the executors of global power: with generosity toward their own and hardness toward their enemies. Some found it difficult to abandon those friends and acquaintances now condemned as unacceptable. Yet if they had not already researched their families' genealogies, a practice that was popular well before the coming of the Third Reich, many Germans now took up "kinship research" (*Sippenforschung*) with a vengeance in order to prove their worthiness of the regime's "racial passport" (*Ahnenpass*). Proof of an acceptable Aryan lineage would grant them access to the privileges of citizenship, be they tax benefits and interest-free loans for Aryan marriages, subsidized health care, or inexpensive vacation trips.[70] Indeed the regime's racial and social programs infiltrated everyday life, playing at least as significant a role as racial policy in segregating acceptable Germans from the unacceptable. Not surprisingly, the claims of rearmament etched the contours of social policy. Even as the regime insisted that it was raising the living standards of its population, the messages of delayed gratification and present sacrifice hovered just below the surface.

---

[69] For moving examples, see Beate Meyer, *"Jüdische Mischlinge:" Rassenpolitik und Verfolgungserfahrung 1933–1945* (Hamburg: Dölling Verlag, 1999); and Thomas Pegelow Kaplan, *The Language of Nazi Genocide: Linguistic Violence and the Struggle of Germans of Jewish Ancestry* (Cambridge: Cambridge University Press, 2009), 141–59.

[70] Fritzsche, *Life and Death*, 76–82; Ehrenreich, *Nazi Ancestral Proof*, 58–77.

The first major social endeavor of the Third Reich, Winter Aid, began as an emergency relief program for the millions of unemployed, whom the regime could not afford to ignore, that built upon the relief schemes of regional party leaders already in place.[71] Yet by 1939, under the auspices of Goebbels' propaganda ministry, Winter Aid mushroomed into a vast state-initiated repository of donations and support services subsumed under the National Socialist People's Welfare. It included nurseries and vacation homes for mothers, which were administered by millions of volunteers. Although facing the competition of private welfare organizations, including those of the churches, Winter Aid became dominant with the coercion of the state behind it. Contributions were supposed to be "voluntary," yet compulsion became the rule as the Social Democratic Party in Exile extensively documented on the basis of its underground situation reports. In addition to Hitler Youth and representatives of other party organizations, SA men appeared in theaters, shops, on street corners, and on front door steps to intimidate pedestrians and residents into parting with their money.[72] The Collection Law of November 1934 gave the Interior Ministry the authority to suspend charities that competed with the Nazi-run organization. Furthermore, Interior Ministry directives made clear that selectivity determined who would receive food, clothing, and other services. Disparaging Christian concepts of charity, Winter Aid would go only to racially "valuable" Germans, excluding those who fell into the ever-more capacious category of "undesirable," including Jews who after the Nuremberg Laws were eliminated as donors and recipients. Thus, because welfare spending was selectively awarded to the racially and politically deserving, it revealed the two sides of the regime's war preparations: It excluded those whom the *Volk* could not be expected to sustain, and allowed the regime to divert tax-generated income to rearmament. Nevertheless, Winter Aid proved popular with Germans whose heritage was sufficiently unobjectionable to elude its racial interventionism. Not only did it dispense necessities to those in need, it also lent material support to a vision that united the regime and most Germans – that of a transcendent *Volk* "community," which eliminated the regional particularism and social fractiousness of the past.

Even housekeeping was fair game for determinations as to who could and could not belong to the "community." Domesticity and motherhood,

---

[71] Richard J. Evans, *The Third Reich in Power 1933–1939* (New York: Penguin Press, 2005), 485–92.
[72] *Sopade*, vol. 4 (1937), 718–43.

although mythologized as the "private sphere," in which women remained sheltered from the public realm, also operated as a site of intervention and exclusion. Shared sacrifice to meet the needs of the *Volk* and housewifely competence divided "German" home management from that of the racially and genetically "unacceptable." Before World War I, a German housewife's duty to provide a proper home became a badge of German superiority over rival European nations, and in the colonies it was a symbol of German domination over, and segregation from, natives.[73] Nazi women's organizations and social workers, however, exercised considerably more coercion and intimidation than their Imperial and Weimar predecessors. Women considered to have been slovenly housekeepers, inattentive caregivers to their children, and wasteful spenders unwilling to economize, were denied the few awards bestowed on women, particularly the Mother Cross. The most incorrigible of them were sent to special camps, such as the Hashude Educational Settlement, to rid them of their "asocial" deficiencies. Confined to small homes surrounded by barbed wire and subject to unrelenting surveillance, they would learn proper domestic skills that would allow them to become fully German. Failure to achieve an acceptable standard meant transfer to concentration camps. For "acceptable" women, keeping household consumption under control in the interests of autarky while maintaining the standards of the proper German home assured the survival of the family and furthered the drive for empire.[74]

Although deeply affected by the diversion of resources to rearmament, consumption also determined membership in the "community." Certainly the regime's loudly advertised "*Volk* products," such as the Volkswagen and radio, remained either limited in sales or, in the case of the Volkswagen, merely a mechanism to soak up the savings of potential buyers.[75] Yet other types of consumption more successfully interwove consumer desires with military and racial ends. Thus, the National Socialist Motor Vehicle Corps (NSKK) provided the thrill of motorcycle and auto

[73] Nancy R. Reagin, *Sweeping the German Nation: Domesticity and National Identity in Germany, 1870–1945* (Cambridge: Cambridge University Press, 2007), 49–71.

[74] Lisa Pine, *Nazi Family Policy, 1933–1945* (Oxford and New York: Berg, 1997), 8–87, 117–46. On the continuities and discontinuities between the Weimar Republic and Third Reich, see Michelle Mouton, *From Nurturing the Nation to Purifying the Volk: Weimar and Nazi Family Policy* (Cambridge: Cambridge University Press, 2007), esp. 272–82.

[75] On the limited impact of "*Volk* products" see Wolfgang König, *Volkswagen, Volksempfänger, Volksgemeinschaft: "Volksprodukte" im Dritten Reich: Vom Scheitern einer nationalsozialistischen Konsumgesellschaft* (Paderborn: Ferdinand Schöningh, 2004), esp. the summary on 258–62.

racing to its large, male, middle- and working-class membership, Jews excluded of course, while training the young men of the Hitler Youth in the essential skills of motorized and mechanized warfare.[76] Tourism also embraced the themes of race, rearmament, expansion, and community in what was arguably the Nazi regime's most popular institution, "Strength through Joy" (*Kraft durch Freude*, or KdF). Founded in November of 1933 as a subsidiary of the German Labor Front, KdF originally sought to raise the status of workers by improving the aesthetics and health of the workplace, and by providing respite through sports, tourism, and cultural outings to the opera, theater, and symphony. Using its size to negotiate bargain rates for its activities, KdF claimed to raise the standard of living for ordinary Germans and mitigate class differences by giving wage earners access to middle-class practices. By the outbreak of war, however, KdF had evolved into more than cultural programs for workers, although that remained its stated mission. If it indeed drew workers to its activities, many its participants were middle-class, particularly white-collar workers and civil servants, who could afford its most expensive tours and cruises.[77] KdF owned or leased twelve ships for cruises to exotic ports of call, evocative of the Germans' deserved status as a "world people" (*Weltvolk*). Construction was underway on a huge resort on the Baltic island of Rügen and four others were in the planning stages. KdF organized hundreds of inland cultural events and tours that, like Winter Aid programs, lent a grain of truth to the regime's promises of community. Beyond the explicit appeal to commonalities among Germans, KdF normalized racial privilege and exclusion. Its "Beauty of Labor" program, which pressured employers to improve the safety and appearance of the shop floor, attempted to educate wage earners in the signifiers of racial superiority, neatness, cleanliness, and an appreciation for aesthetics. The financing of KdF programs, which combined the stolen assets of the trade unions, the achievement of economies of scale, the promotion of weekly savings plans, and employer contributions, all of them entailing more than a little coercion, allowed the regime to satisfy consumer desires without diverting revenue from rearmament. It gave to its thousands of

---

[76] Dorothee Hochstetter, *Motorisierung und "Volksgemeinschaft": Das Nationalsozialistische Kraftfahrkorps (NSKK) 1931–1945* (Munich: Oldenbourg, 2005), esp. 231–329.

[77] See Hasso Spode, "Arbeiterurlaub im Dritten Reich," in *Angst, Belohnung, Zucht und Ordnung: Herrschaftsmechanismen in Nationalsozialismus*, eds. Carola Sachse et al. (Opladen: Westdeutscher Verlag, 1982), 296–305; Wolfhard Buchholz, "Die Nationalsozialistische Gemeinschaft 'Kraft durch Freude': Freizeitgestaltung und Arbeiterschaft im Dritten Reich" (Diss: Munich, 1976), 356–73.

FIGURE 4.5. Vacationers at the swimming pool on the Strength through Joy cruise ship, "Wilhelm Gustloff." Indicative of the benefits bestowed on racially accept-able Germans, Strength through Joy's tourism embodied the promise of a harmo-nious "racial community" and Germany's future as a world power. Bundesarchiv Koblenz, Bild 146–1988–107–05. Photographer: Anne Winterer.

participants a taste of the prosperous future that would be permanently realized once Lebensraum was obtained.[78]

---

[78] For the details, see Shelley Baranowski, *Strength through Joy: Consumerism and Mass Tourism in the Third Reich* (Cambridge: Cambridge University Press, 2004), 118–98.

IN HIGH GEAR: THE FOUR-YEAR PLAN, RACIAL
VIOLENCE, AND THE APPROACH OF WAR

The ironic combination of effective diplomatic brinksmanship and approaching economic collapse pushed Hitler to greater extremes. In addition to increasing the prospects for the twentieth century's second global war, the Nazi regime accelerated its effort to "purify" the "racial community," both of which were derived from the ideologically grounded consequences of rearmament. By 1936 armaments production had produced shortages of essential raw materials and foreign exchange reserves. The spiraling international arms race that Germany had itself initiated pushed the regime's own military budgets higher still. By the same year, rearmament in Germany had brought full employment. Yet labor shortages fueled thereafter by the insatiable demand of war-related industries only exacerbated the need for expansion. Conquered territories would provide subject peoples whose labor could be exploited.[79] When confronted with the dilemmas that Schacht's New Plan could not solve, Hitler turned to Hermann Göring, then the head of the Luftwaffe, to administer a solution that depended unambiguously on expansion to the east. Carl Goerdeler, the Reich commissioner for price controls, argued for an alternative solution, bringing the military expenditures under control and devaluing the Reichmark to encourage German exports. He was ruled out of court.

The Four-Year Plan, which the führer announced in September of 1936 at the annual party rally in Nuremberg, instituted the centralized production and distribution of raw materials, the allocation of labor, and the imposition of price and foreign exchange controls. The plan also aimed to stimulate the production of synthetic fuels and rubber to eliminate Germany's dependence on imports. Consumers would suffer more than ever, for the program ratcheted up the pace of rearmament to the point where the Four-Year Plan would claim in excess of 20 percent of the national income.[80] As Germany's enlarged living space, east-central and eastern Europe would settle its raw material, labor, and food needs permanently. The Four-Year Plan testified to Hitler's inflexible and long-standing ideological predilections, and it would further weld together his war for empire and the war against the Jews. The timing of the führer's announcement, however, came at the point when the economy at home

---

[79] Tooze, *Wages of Destruction*, 203–43.
[80] Ibid., 255.

forced his hand, and when developments abroad gave vent to a phobia that extended back to the early 1920s: Bolshevism.

Even as early as 1933 when Hitler prepared to sign the nonaggression treaty with Poland, the German government broke decisively from Weimar practice. During the 1920s, the Republic and the Soviet Union met on the common ground of revisionism to promote trade, and more important, cooperation between the Reichswehr and the Soviet Army. The Rapallo Pact of 1922 gave the Reichswehr cover to engage in maneuvers and test new weaponry in the Soviet Union. Nevertheless, negotiations to maintain economic ties foundered and Germany rejected a Soviet-sponsored guarantee of the independence of the three Baltic states. Hitler's virulent hostility to Bolshevism, which he believed had been the creation of Jews, and the increasingly anti-Soviet line of cabinet conservatives, disrupted ties that even Stalin was prepared to continue despite the Nazi regime's repression of German communism. Antisemitism and anti-Marxism merged seamlessly with lust for the Soviet Union's vast agricultural and mineral resources, especially oil, and its territory for future German settlement. By mid-1936, Hitler's memorandum to Göring and Blomberg, which preceded his September announcement, asserted that the global racial struggle had reached a new level with the triumph of Bolshevism in the Soviet Union, a specter so menacing that it promised Germany's destruction and the final victory of "world Jewry" if the plan was not undertaken. A Soviet victory, stated Hitler, would produce an outcome worse than the Versailles Treaty, "the annihilation of the German people."[81] The rapid industrialization of the Soviet Union, which resulted from Stalin's Five-Year Plans, as well as the Soviet Union's intervention in the Spanish Civil War on the republican side, necessitated the equally rapid expansion and provisioning of the German armed forces. In addition to pleasing the high command of the Wehrmacht, which objected to cutting back on rearmament, the anti-Bolshevik presupposition s of the plan decisively undermined Schacht and his allies.

The urgency to expand grew even clearer in the following year. In a meeting in the Reich Chancellery on November 5, 1937, Hitler again reiterated the need for living space in the east. He alluded as well to the likelihood of further colonization overseas within a few generations, colonization that in his view would capitalize on the collapse of the British Empire.

---

[81] Jeremy Noakes and Geoffrey Pridham, eds., *Nazism 1919–1945: A History in Documents and Eyewitness Accounts*, vol. 1 (New York: Schocken Books, 1983), 281–2.

In fact, during the previous spring, Hitler had ordered a significant increase in naval construction to multiply the number of large battleships and cruisers. Global domination over the long term, however, depended on acquiring raw materials and labor within Europe itself. Thus, Hitler noted, Germany's immediate space problem would have to be resolved by 1943 or 1945 at the latest. If domestic conflicts in France weakened that nation sufficiently, then Germany would declare war even earlier. In either case, Germany would first absorb Austria and Czechoslovakia, which piteously enough would entail the forcible removal of millions in order to free up food supplies for Germans.[82] Unwilling to recognize their own complicity in the regime's radicalization, a nervous Foreign Minister Neurath and the army command objected, not to the goal but to the pace of Hitler's proposals, believing that another world war would result in Germany's destruction. Subsequent pleas from the Finance Minister Lutz Schwerin von Krosigk and others to slow rearmament and restore fiscal sanity fell on deaf ears. By 1938, the führer had sacked the remaining conservatives in his cabinet. Following the convenient exposure of skeletons in their closets, which compromised war minister Blomberg and Wehrmacht chief-of-staff Wilhelm Fritsch, the führer assumed supreme command of the Wehrmacht himself.

To be sure, the Reich Chancellery meeting did not produce a strict blueprint of Hitler's plans nor his precise moments of attack, the execution of which depended on external circumstances over which he had minimal control. Nevertheless, Hitler wasted little time in turning his attention to the former territories of the Austro-Hungarian Empire, beginning with his native Austria. Seeking to exploit Austria's strategic position and material resources, and to assert his protection over a vociferous Austrian Nazi movement that roiled an already conflict-ridden body politic, he would make good on the Pan German fantasies of his youth and end Austria's independence as a precarious rump state that was once denied its rightful incorporation in a greater Germany. Hitler assigned the task of incorporating the economies of soon-to-be captured territories, particularly their iron ore and foreign exchange reserves, to Göring, who used the occasion to add to his industrial conglomerate, the Reichswerke Hermann Göring.[83] Using diplomatic pressure simultaneously against the British,

---

[82] See the Hossbach Memorandum, 10 November 1937 at the Avalon Project's extensive documentation arising from the International Military Tribunal at Nuremberg: http://www.yale.edu/lawweb/avalon/imt/hossbach.asp. Accessed April 27, 2010.

[83] On Göring's growing importance in the Nazi economy, especially in conjunction with the Four-Year Plan and after, see Richard Overy's essays, "Heavy Industry in the Third

the Italians, and Austria's unpopular Chancellor Kurt Schuschnigg, and egged on by Göring who deemed the absorption of Austria as crucial to the Four-Year Plan, Hitler engineered the forced merger in March of 1938. Despite Pan German efforts to promote solidarity among Austrian Germans, which carried over after the fall of the Habsburg Empire, relatively few Austrians wanted annexation to the German Reich. Yet in the context of the present political and economic crisis, the Third Reich appeared to offer a lifeline.[84] Greeted by unrestrained adulation as he toured Vienna, Linz, and his birthplace, Braunau-am-Inn, by Austrians who feared that their Depression-hobbled nation could no longer survive as an independent state, the British and French mounted no resistance.

The radicalism of the Anschluss went beyond the conquest of a sovereign state. In addition to the regime's publicly stated grounds, that Austrians belonged to Germany and had been denied the right to join it after World War I, the annexation ushered in a precedent-breaking solution to a problem that troubled relations between Germany and Fascist Italy, the status of the Germans of South Tyrol. For Hitler and Himmler, securing Italy as an ally and resolving a severe shortage of labor, especially in agriculture, was more important than preserving and supporting a German-speaking community in Italian territory. For Mussolini, the irredentism of the South Tyrolean Germans, which the Anschluss exacerbated, the abject failure of Fascist attempts at forced assimilation, and the collapse of the Stresa Front after the invasion of Ethiopia, increased the desirability of a population transfer as a permanent solution. Although the resettlement agreement concluded between Germany and Italy resulted in the transfer of less than half of the South Tyrolean Germans by the end of 1942, the Third Reich had managed to engineer a population policy over the heads of the people affected, and decisively broke with the Weimar practice of keeping ethnic Germans where they resided as a justification for border revisions. The resettlement of South Tyrolean Germans would become a model for the future.[85]

Reich: the Reichswerke Crisis," and "The Reichswerke 'Hermann Göring': A Study in Economic Imperialism," in Overy, *War and Economy in the Third Reich*, 93–118 and 145–74.

[84] Pieter Judson, "When Is a Diaspora Not a Diaspora? Rethinking Naition-Centered Narratives about Germans in Hapsburg East Central Europe," in *The Heimat Abroad: The Boundaries of Germanness*, eds. Krista O'Donnell, Renate Bridenthal, and Nancy Reagin (Ann Arbor: University of Michigan Press, 2005), 219–47.

[85] Markus Leniger, *Nationalsozialistische "Volkstumsarbeit"und Umsiedlungspolitik 1933–1945: Von der Minderheitenbetreuung zur Siedlerauslese* (Berlin; Frank & Timme, 2006), 34–51; Valdis O. Lumans, *Himmler's Auxiliaries: The Volksdeutsche Mittelstelle*

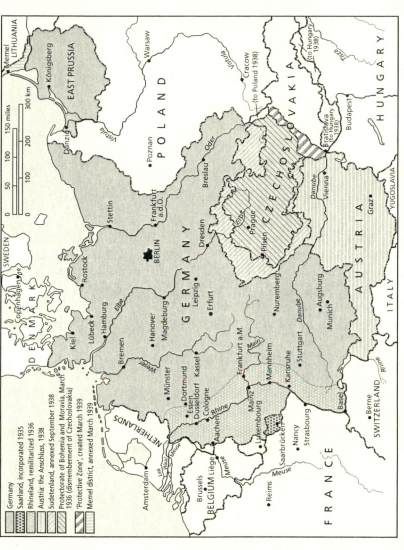

MAP 4.1. German expansionism, 1935–1939. Prior to annexing Austria and the Sudetenland, Germany won the return of the Saar by plebiscite and remilitarized the Rhineland. Following the creation of the Protectorate in the spring of 1939, the Reich secured the dependence of a nominally independent Slovakia with a "protection zone" occupied by the Wehrmacht. It also won the return of the Memel district from Lithuania.

Source: Germany and the Second World War, vol. 1, *The Build-up of German Aggression*, eds. Wilhelm Deist, Manfred Messerschmidt, Hans-Erich Volkmann, and Wolfram Wette, trans. P.S. Falla, Dean S. McMurry, and Ewald Osers (Oxford: Clarendon Press, 1990), front endpaper.

Hitler's success in Austria emboldened him, again with Göring's support, to seek the destruction of Czechoslovakia. In addition to making good on his deep loathing of Czechs stemming from his years in Vienna,[86] Czechoslovakia's substantial industrial base, significant foreign exchange reserves, and strategic position as a launching pad for eastern expansion made an invasion attractive to a regime starved of the resources to keep its war machine going. Here, too, Hitler exploited the economic hardship and the perceived oppression by Slavs of the Germans of Bohemia, Moravia, and Austrian Silesia in a crucial border region, the Sudetenland.[87] There the Ethnic German Liaison Office (*Volksdeutsche Mittelstelle*) of the SS, which had "synchronized" the conservative-national organizations of Weimar that sought to protect the Czech German minority, had already deputized the local Nazi Party and its leader Konrad Henlein as the spokesman for Sudenten German interests. The presumed artificiality of the postwar successor states would not stand in the way of the acquisition of living space and the Reich's protection of Germans drowning in a sea of Slavs.[88] This time, however, Czechoslovakia's alliances with France and the Soviet Union raised the serious prospect of war if Germany violated its territorial integrity. Moreover, the looming conflict over Czechoslovakia raised the anxiety of Reich Germans and even Hitler's generals, who remained unconvinced that Germany's present state of rearmament was sufficient to tackle a well-fortified, well-armed, and mountainous nation. The prospect of British, French, and Soviet interventions added to those fears. Nevertheless, the unwillingness of Britain to risk a war because of its insufficient military readiness and "because of a quarrel in a far-away country between people of whom we know nothing," in the words of the British Prime Minister Neville Chamberlain,[89] ultimately turned the tide in Hitler's favor. Although forced into a peace conference in Munich where he had to settle for "only" the annexation of the Sudetenland, Hitler's rage at this setback could not

---

und the German National Minorities of Europe, 1933–1945 (Chapel Hill: University of North Carolina Press, 1933), 154–7.

[86] Brigitte Hamann, *Hitlers Wien: Lehrjahre eines Diktators* (Munich and Zurich: Piper Verlag, 1997), 462–6.

[87] Ronald M. Smelser, *The Sudenten Problem 1933–1938: Volkstumspolitik and the Formulation of Nazi Foreign Policy* (Middletown, CT: Wesleyan University Press, 1975), 6–10.

[88] Lumans, *Himmler's Auxiliaries*, 80–1.

[89] Chamberlain's radio broadcast, 27 September 1938, www.st-andrews.ac.uk/~pv/munich/czdoc09.html, accessed April 27, 2010.

long disguise Czechoslovakia's vulnerability. Preyed upon by Hungary and Poland, which seized the opportunity to claim Czech territories they deemed as theirs, and beset by bitter internal divisions between Czechs and Slovaks, Czechoslovakia succumbed to a German invasion in March of 1939. Reminiscent of European overseas interventions in the affairs of nominally independent states, a Hitler decree claimed Bohemia and Moravia as "protectorates."[90] Having apparently won its independence of the larger postwar successor state, Slovakia became, for all intents and purposes, a German puppet under the leadership of the Roman Catholic Monsignor Josef Tiso.

In addition to acquiring a nation with a substantial heavy industrial base, which included a formidable armaments industry, mineral resources, and a significant banking industry, the Protectorate provided the Reich with foreign exchange reserves, a sizeable skilled labor force, and a strategic launching pad for a subsequent invasion of Poland. Similar to the cases of Austria and Czechoslovakia, Hitler once more proclaimed the right of the Third Reich to protect ethnic Germans as the cover for the pursuit of broader population and imperialist aims. The predominantly German city of Danzig, surrounded by Polish territory and cut off from the Reich, became the excuse of renouncing the 1934 nonaggression pact with Poland, as well as the 1935 naval agreement with Britain. In late April of 1939, Germany and Italy signed the "Pact of Steel" to isolate Poland further. Despite the British government's pledge to come to Poland's aid militarily in the event of a German attack, Germany neutralized the impact of the British decision with a stunning surprise of its own. Seemingly negating the anti-Soviet assumptions that had defined Hitler's foreign policy since taking power, the German government and the Soviet Union concluded a nonaggression pact following protracted negotiations throughout the summer.

The Nazi-Soviet pact spared Germany of a two-front war if the western powers actually came to Poland's defense. It also promised to relieve Germany's raw materials shortages that had forced the sudden reduction in armaments production during the previous spring.[91] In addition to showcasing the complete breakdown of collective security negotiations between the Soviet Union and the west, the pact demonstrated why both sides pragmatically suspended their hostility to the other. Under its

[90] Mark Mazower, *Hitler's Empire: Nazi Rule in Occupied Europe* (London: Allen Lane, 2008), 59–60.
[91] Tooze, *Wages of Destruction*, 318–21.

terms, the Soviet Union acquired all of Poland east of the Vistula, Narew, and San rivers, or roughly half of Poland's post-1918 territory. As well as allowing time for Stalin to rebuild the armed forces and expand the Soviet industrial base, the agreement presumed Stalin's right to annex the Baltic states, Lithuania, Latvia, and Estonia. He also claimed portions of Belorussia and Ukraine east of the Curzon Line, once proposed during the Russo-Polish War of 1919–1920 as the Soviet boundary and subsequently rejected to Poland's territorial benefit. Hitler, on the other hand, secured the delivery of foodstuffs and raw materials from the Soviet Union and a green light to attack a state that even his generals, who had been troubled by the führer's gambles in the Rhineland, Austria, and Czechoslovakia, had long wanted to destroy.[92]

The approach of war and the radicalization of Nazi racial policy became a lethal symbiotic relationship. Hitler's memo to Göring in August of 1936, which charged him with the responsibility for executing the Four-Year Plan, cast the confrontation with Bolshevism as a final reckoning with "international Jewry," the prime mover behind all the social upheavals since the French Revolution. The expropriation or "aryanization" of Jewish property, which accelerated with the promulgation of the Nuremberg Laws, was to finance Germany's war preparations. Measures included laws to criminalize the transfer of Jewish assets abroad and block private bank accounts, as well as increases in the "flight tax" for Jews attempting to emigrate.[93] An autobiographical novella by the American writer Thomas Wolfe captured the human tragedies that arose from the fusion of antisemitism and financial desperation. On a train from Berlin to Paris in the fall of 1936, Wolfe's main character Paul Spangler witnesses the arrest of a Jewish lawyer, one of several travelers in his compartment, for his attempted escape from Germany in violation of the regime's currency regulations. Despite the temporary companionship that the travelers established on the long ride between Berlin and the border city of Aachen, the antisemitic outburst of one of the travelers ("These Jews!" she cried, "These things would never happen if it were not for them! They make all the trouble. Germany has had to protect herself. The Jews were taking all the money from the country.") disrupts

---

[92] On the debate surrounding the Nazi-Soviet pact, see Leitz, *Nazi Foreign Policy*, 84–7; and Klaus Hildebrand, *Das Dritte Reich*, 6th ed. (Munich: Oldenbourg, 2003), 261–3.

[93] Peter Longerich, *The Unwritten Order: Hitler's Role in the Final Solution* (The Mill, Brimscomb Port, Stroud: Tempus, 2005), 54–5; and Martin Dean, *Robbing the Jews*, 54–93.

the bonds of humanity between the travelers and the arrested man. As the train departs, Paul and the terrified Jew exchange glances as the police drag their victim away: "And in this silent glance lies the deep, deathly fear of a man."[94]

The bellicosity of Germany's aggression against Austria and Czechoslovakia followed logically from Hitler's racially saturated vision of *Lebensraum* and with it plans for ridding their populations of "undesirable" elements. Thus, it meant the encouragement of antisemitic violence and the imposition of Reich legislation into the newly acquired territories. But it also meant worse outbreaks in the "Old Reich," exacerbated by popular fears of war, in which the "Jew" became the scapegoat for the mounting international tensions.[95] In addition to incorporating the Austrian economy into the Four-Year Plan, gobbling up numerous Austrian businesses, and introducing a forced-labor draft, the German occupiers introduced the Civil Service and the Nuremberg Laws. In order to bring under control the "wild" looting and vandalizing of Jews by Austrian Nazis orchestrated by the newly appointed Gau leader of Vienna, Odilo Globocnik, Reich authorities appointed by Göring, undertook the systematic registration of Jewish property, blocked Jewish bank accounts, and applied the Reich's currency laws to prevent Jews from transferring their assets abroad. The aryanization or liquidation of Jewish property proceeded apace. By the end of 1940, 11,357 Jewish-owned craft-trading firms were shut down and an additional 1,689 aryanized out of a total of 13,046. Of 10,992 Jewish-owned trading firms, 9,112 were closed and an additional 1,870 aryanized. Austrian Nazis became the principal beneficiaries.[96] The SD contributed its share to the confiscation of Jewish wealth. Under the leadership of the ambitious Pan German and Linz native, Adolf Eichmann, who since his entry into the SD in 1934 had established himself as the foremost expert in the SS on the "Jewish question," the Central Agency for Jewish Emigration processed Jewish applications, confiscated assets, and through indirect means extracted help from foreign aid organizations to finance the removal of Jews.[97]

---

[94] Thomas Wolfe, "I have a thing to tell you ...", excerpted in *Reisen ins Reich 1933 bis 1945: Ausländische Autoren berichten aus Deutschland*, ed. Oliver Lubrich (Frankfurt am Main: Eichborn Verlag, 2004), 140–67.

[95] Wildt, *Volksgemeinschaft und Selbstmächtigung*, 301–19.

[96] Dean, *Robbing the Jews*, 84–111. The statistics are found in Harold James, *The Deutsche Bank and the Nazi Economic War Against the Jews: The Expropriation of Jewish-Owned Property* (Cambridge: Cambridge University Press, 2001), 137.

[97] Dean, *Robbing the Jews*, 102–3.

After the annexation of the Sudetenland and the rest of Czechoslovakia, Jews there found themselves subjected to similar treatment. On top of the trauma of antisemitic pogroms, Jews quickly lost their homes and property, which was "aryanized" through sale mainly to Reich companies and banks eager to get in on the spoils.[98]

In addition to the continuing, and increasingly dire, need for assets to finance rearmament and assuage Germany's mounting debt to sustain it, the incorporation of 200,000 Austrian Jews through the Anschluss increased the pressure at home to force the emigration of those classified as racially Jewish. Jews previously discouraged from emigrating because of the Reich's stringent currency controls and confiscatory "flight tax" would now be forced to leave through physical terror and the destruction of property, if their remaining assets and connections allowed them. In early November of 1938, a seventeen-year-old Polish Jew Herschel Grynspan, distraught by the news that the Reich had deported his parents back to Poland, murdered a low-level German diplomat in Paris, Ernst von Rath. Grynspan's revenge provided the excuse for restive Nazi Party radicals to ratchet up their assaults against German Jews even beyond the scores of attacks that had accompanied the Sudeten crisis.[99] The regime publicly and piously claimed that the pogrom of November 9 and 10, 1938, subsequently named "Crystal Night" for the sound of broken glass from the windows of synagogues, was the expression of the "people's rage" against Jews. Indeed, foreign reporters and other contemporary observers described the event as the act of mob violence, often comparing it to the revolutionary upheavals in Russia.[100] "The English and American press declare that events in Germany no longer conform to Western European norms, but must be compared to what took place during the Russian Revolution. (This after six years!)," remarked the now-exiled, anti-Nazi writer Thomas Mann. Yet it was the Reich's senior leadership that authorized the nationwide event, again with the intention of forcing Jews to leave and pressuring other nations that had been critical of Nazi

---

[98] Chad Bryant, *Prague in Black: Nazi Rule and Czech Nationalism* (Cambridge, MA and London: Harvard University Press, 2007), 82–4. On the Sudetenland in particular, see Jörg Osterloh, *Nationalsozialistische Judenverfolgung im Reichsgau Sudetenland 1938–1945* (Munich: Oldenbourg Verlag, 2006), 185–482.

[99] Peter Longerich, *The Unwritten Order: Hitler's Role in the Final Solution* (The Mill, Brimscombe Port, Stroud, Gloucester, 2005), 63–4.

[100] Mann, *Diaries*, entry for November 13, 1938, 312. See also Peter Gay's recollections in his memoir, *My German Question: Growing Up in Nazi Berlin* (New Haven and London: Yale University Press, 1998), 131–7.

antisemitism to take them. Reich leaders quietly delegated anti-Jewish attacks to local party leaders, such as the infamous Jew-baiter Julius Streicher who, after a inflammatory speech to his SA men in Nuremberg, assigned teams of them to the city's neighborhoods to set upon Jews and smash their property.[101] Although some disapproved of the violence and destruction of property, many Germans either actively participated in the pogrom or remained complicit bystanders, perhaps cowed by the pervasive contamination of public spaces by young Nazi Party militants, but also inclined to accept the validity of a Jewish "threat."[102]

The pogrom burned scores of synagogues in Germany and Austria, destroyed Jewish-owned shops and homes, killed over ninety Jews while imprisoning hundreds of others. It set in motion the final aryanization of Jewish assets in what was now termed the "Old Reich," Germany within its pre-1938 borders. Although non-Jewish, German competitors had regularly denounced Jewish-owned firms since the April, 1933, boycott, using state-sanctioned antisemitism to advance their material interests, the "night of broken glass" accelerated "… the single greatest exchange of property in modern German history," in which nearly 100,000 Jewish firms were liquidated. Banks in particular profited handsomely by extending credit to Aryan buyers so that they could purchase Jewish property for a song. So did the state by raking in revenue from flight taxes, the transfer of Jewish assets, and "atonement" payments cynically levied against Jews for the damages inflicted upon them.[103] Fighting tooth and nail against Göring's order that claims be paid either to Aryans who suffered damage to their property or to the state in the case of Jewish policy holders,

---

[101] René Juvet, "Reichsscherbentag," 8 November 1938, in *Reisen ins Reich*, ed. Lubrich, 191.

[102] Longerich. "*Davon haben wir nichts gewusst!*", 143; Wildt, *Volksgemeinschaft und Selbstermächtigung*, 319–34; and Alan E. Steinweis, *Kristallnacht 1938* (Cambridge, MA and London: Belknap Press of Harvard University Press, 2009), 56–98.

[103] Frank Bajohr, "The 'Folk Community' and the Persecution of the Jews: German Society under National Socialist Dictatorship, 1933–1945," *Holocaust and Genocide Studies* 20, no. 2 (2006): 102. See also Frank Bajohr, "*Aryanization" in Hamburg: The Economic Exclusion of the Jews and the Confiscation of Their Property* (New York: Berghahn Books, 2002), 142–272; and Götz Aly, *Hitler's Beneficiaries: Plunder, Racial War, and the Nazi Welfare State*, trans. Jefferson Chase (New York: Metropolitan Books, 2007), 41–51. On the role of German banks, see James, *Deutsche Bank*, 43–126, and Ludolf Herbst and Thomas Weihe, eds., *Die Commerzbank und die Juden 1933–1945* (Munich: C.H. Beck, 2004), particularly the essays of Herbst, "Banker in einem Prekären Geschäft: Die Beteiligung der Commerzbank an der Vernichtung jüdischer Gewerbunternehmen im Altreich (1933–1940)," 74–137 and Hannah Alheim, "Die Commerzbank und und die Einziehung jüdischen Vermögens," 138–72.

FIGURE 4.6. The Vienna Boys Choir assembled under a banner that reads, "We sing for Adolf Hitler," salute Hitler and his entourage during his first official visit to Vienna after the Anschluss, May 13, 1938.
Source: USHMM, photograph #00410, courtesy of the National Archives and Records Administration, College Park, Maryland.

insurance companies, notably Germany's largest Allianz, negotiated with the regime to reduce its required payouts to the state to cover Jewish claims.[104] Numerous other decrees, which denied Jews the right to occupy public spaces, took away their drivers' licenses, and crowded them into "Jew houses," completed their marginalization. Jews with sufficient wherewithal, foreign connections, language skills, and willingness to do low-wage jobs who had not to that point emigrated, struggled to do so against the at-best tepid willingness of other nations to accept refugees. Thousands who were either too old, too unconnected, or two poor to leave, could not. "No reply to the many applications," rued the increasingly desperate Victor Klemperer in early February of 1939, after his strenuous attempts to emigrate with his wife Eva had come to naught.[105]

[104] Gerald Feldman, *Allianz and the German Insurance Business, 1933–1945* (Cambridge: Cambridge University Press, 2001), 190–235.
[105] Klemperer, *I Will Bear Witness*, entry of February 5, 1939, 293; Debórah Dwork and Robert Jan van Pelt, *Flight from the Reich: Refugee Jews, 1933–1946* (New York and London: W. W. Norton, 2009), 119–84.

FIGURE 4.7. Germans pass by the broken shop window of a Jewish-owned business in Berlin that was destroyed during Crystal Night, November 10, 1938. Designed to frighten the remaining Jews in Germany to emigrate, the pogrom accelerated the aryanization of Jewish-owned property.
Source: USHMM, photograph #86838, courtesy of National Archives and Records Administration, College Park, Maryland.

Antisemitic outrages were not the only evidence of the symbiosis of racial policy and war. In addition to tightening the noose around the livelihoods and social relationships of Sinti and Roma, the involuntary sterilization campaign had by 1937 affected over half of Afro-Germans, the offspring of consensual relationships between German women and French colonial troops in the Rhineland.[106] By the winter and spring of 1938, however, sterilization would no longer suffice to rid the *Volk* permanently of unwanted genes. Having long admired the martial state Sparta for killing sickly infants, while disparaging "modern fuzzy humanitarianism" (*Humanitätsduselei*) that prevented the elimination of the mentally and physically disabled, Hitler ordered the murder of handicapped

---

[106] Pommerin, *Sterilizierung der Rheinlandbastarden*, 77–87.

children.[107] The occasion for his decree, the direct request to the führer in February of 1939 from a father of a severely handicapped infant, was as good an example as any of the plebiscitary relationship that Hitler envisioned between the *Volk* and himself. Hitler's order that the infant be killed set in motion a more encompassing "euthanasia" action that the regime would launch after the outbreak of war. Unwilling to risk such an initiative in peacetime for fear of the controversy that would arise, Hitler believed that war would provide the perfect cover to accomplish long-standing ideological aims.

Indeed the killing of the incurable had been discussed since the beginnings of the Third Reich, as ministries put the Nazi penal code into place and party institutions discussed internally. The discourse that rendered such a policy acceptable followed the cruel logic of Social Darwinism and the pitilessness of cost-benefit analysis. Thus, a reader of the SS newspaper, *The Black Corps*, complained in a letter to the editor about a relative whose fifth child had been born "an idiot" and whose costs to keep it alive constituted an undue burden on its parents, its four siblings, and the racial community. According to the laws of nature, the reader continued, such a child would have starved to death. Now "we can be more humane and give it a painless mercy death," which would be "a hundred times more noble, decent, and humane than that cowardice which hides behind a sentimental humanitarianism" that imposes unjustifiable burdens on those assigned to its care.[108] Nevertheless, the regime's fear of opposition from the churches, real enough in light of the ongoing conflicts between the party and the Protestant and Catholic clergy, declined with the approach of war.

The plebiscitary adulation accorded to Hitler was real enough, but it did have its limits, limits that revealed themselves apart from the negative public view of Nazi Party "bosses."[109] In addition to the periodically low morale arising from shortages, poor-quality consumer goods, rising prices, harsher working conditions, and increased taxation, most Germans dreaded the prospect of another war. Their joy at the results of Hitler's diplomatic panache, which overturned a hated treaty and

---

[107] Adolf Hitler, *Reden, Schriften, Anordnungen: Februar 1925 bis Januar 1933*, eds. Institute für Zeitgeschichte (Munich and New York: K.G. Saur, 1992–2003), vol. 3/2, 4 August 1929, doc. 64, 348.

[108] *Das Schwarze Korps*, 18 March 1937, in Jeremy Noakes and Geoffrey Pridham, eds., *Nazism 1919 to 1945: A History in Documents and Eyewitness Accounts*, vol. 2: *Foreign Policy, War and Racial Extermination* (New York: Schocken Books, 1988), 1003.

[109] Kershaw, "*Hitler Myth*," 96–104.

reestablished Germany as a great power, betrayed more than a little relief that armed conflict had been avoided. If the führer's territorial ambitions could scarcely have been a secret in light of Hitler's numerous public statements attesting to them, Germans seemingly clung to his image as a "peacemaker," one cultivated assiduously by Goebbels.[110] Many Germans abhorred the physical violence visited upon Jews and particularly the wanton destruction of property that accompanied the Crystal Night pogrom. Yet contrary to the moving stories of rescue and solidarity that Social Democratic informants relayed to the SPD leadership in exile in Prague, few Germans questioned the premises that lay behind the assault. Common denominators of agreement bound the regime and its racially unobjectionable population together. They rendered most Germans vulnerable to the regime's propaganda and unwilling to question it. Having thus agreed that a Jewish "question" or "problem" existed in the first place, an assumption reinforced by the regime's own discourse, Germans could be easily seduced by the "justice" of legal exclusion or the material benefits that aryanization provided them, while attributing the crassest actions to party "bosses," who (putatively) lacked the führer's approval.[111] For others, such as the teenage diarist Lore Walb, the pogrom did not even register as a topic worthy of inclusion in her daily entries despite her normally lively attention to political developments.[112] Nor was the quiet tolerance limited to antisemitism. Involuntary sterilization, the incarceration of homosexuals, and the persecution of the Sinti and Roma met with little objection, except for the relative few whose personal relationships with the marginalized and excluded were deep enough to allow human compassion to transcend the fear of contact.

Furthermore, the führer's ability to diffuse popular dissatisfaction with diplomatic "achievements" rested on the at least tacit acceptance of Germany's imperial destiny, the fulfillment of which the Entente had illegitimately blocked. In addition to assuming the justice of the restoration of Germany's overseas colonies, few Germans accepted the territorial integrity of Poland or Czechoslovakia, especially when Nazi propaganda

[110] Ibid., 121–47.
[111] *Sopade*, November 1938, 1180–211; David Bankier, *The Germans and the Final Solution: Public Opinion under Nazism* (Oxford, UK and Cambridge, MA: Blackwell, 1996), 85–8. For the most recent summary, see Frank Bajohr and Dieter Pohl, *Der Holocaust als offene Geheimnis: Die Deutschen, die NS-Führung und die Allierten* (Munich: C.H. Beck, 2006), esp. 37–45.
[112] Lore Walb, *Ich, die Alte: Ich, die Junge: Konfrontation mit meinen Tagebüchern 1933–1945* (Berlin: Aufbau Taschenbuch, 1998), 119–20.

repeatedly reminded their listeners and readers of the "victimization" of ethnic Germans, be they in the Sudetenland or Danzig. "For the populace on the front pages of the German press," Victor Klemperer commented after the Munich agreement, "it is of course the absolute success of Hitler, the prince of peace and brilliant diplomat. And truly it is indeed an unimaginably huge success."[113] In contrast to the party elite, most Germans did not expend much energy fantasizing about *Lebensraum* in the east, even though few objected to the regime's repeated promises to acquire it. Yet they wanted to see the rescue of ethnic Germans and they accepted their nation's resurgent great power ambitions while continuing to hope they could be acquired on the cheap. They applauded the annexation of Austria as the fitting and logical end to the "incomplete" Bismarckian unification of 1871 and the Weimar Republic's failure to negotiate its inclusion after World War I. Nazism accomplished what even the Socialists desired but could not get.

Finally, the Nazi regime's ostensibly "positive" message of ethnic unity contributed to the containment of dissent. Instead of regional, religious, and class divisions, which Weimar's combustible mix of economic hardship and political fractiousness intensified, Nazism summarily dispensed with the disorder of parliamentary politics and social conflict, and the regime had put Jews and other "undesirables" in their place.[114] It declared the end of social division through the *Volk* "community," all while ending unemployment and raising Germany's global profile. It represented the triumphant resurrection long embedded in German nationalism, which this time seemed capable of permanently eliminating the threat of division and dissolution. That the regime's "achievement" came with a high price tag – a nasty dictatorship with a minacious and cancerous police network, an economy that while providing jobs required long hours, frozen wages, and few outlets for consumption, and finally, the likelihood of war – did not suffice to challenge the crucial point. By and large, the Third Reich "limited" its violence to the Communists and Socialists, the socially "deviant," and widely disliked minorities while creating visions of future prosperity and well-being for the majority. In contrast to the Soviet Union at the same time, where the Communist Party's fear of, and

---

[113] Klemperer, *I Will Bear Witness*, entry of October 2, 1938, 269.

[114] Sven Oliver Müller, "Nationalismus in der deutschen Kriegsgesellschaft 1933 bis 1945," in Jörg Echternkamp, ed., *Die Deutsche Kriegsgesellschaft 1939 bis 1945*, Zweiter Halbband. *Ausbeutung, Deutungen, Ausgrenzung* (Munich: Deutsche Verlags-Anstalt, 2005), 35.

vulnerability to, popular opposition gave momentum to widespread terror, mass arrests, and gulags, conditions in Germany seemed benign by comparison – that is, by those whom the Gestapo and SD did not overtly threaten.

The Wehrmacht's attack on Poland in the early hours of the morning of September 1, 1939, illustrated Hitler's concern to keep popular anxieties within manageable boundaries. Conducting a charade of negotiations with the British, which included a proposal for a plebiscite in Danzig, was little more than an attempt to assure Germans that Hitler had made every attempt to prevent a war, even as he undercut Mussolini, who proposed a reprise of the Munich conference. The immediate justification for Germany's declaration of war was a staged "assault" on a German radio station in Upper Silesia, in which 150 concentration camp prisoners, poisoned by lethal injection, were dressed up as invading Polish soldiers. A good many Germans greeted the portentous announcement with ill-disguised dread, having recalled the consequences of the last disastrous war with little difficulty. Or they responded with equanimity, believing that the British and French would behave as they had during the Czech crisis.[115] Yet the führer's talent for deceit, parlayed by a rigidly controlled media and delivered to a population that viewed Poles through eyes colored by racial stereotypes, successfully played the card of Germany's persecution at the hands of external enemies, the depredations against German minorities, and the promise of a quick victory.[116] "All in all," noted Klemperer in his diary on September 3rd, "reports and measures taken are serious, popular opinion absolutely certain of victory, ten thousand times more arrogant than in '14. The consequence will either be an overwhelming, almost unchallenged victory, and England and France are castrated minor states, or a catastrophe ten thousand times worse than '18."[117] The more positive perspective of the university student Lore Walb confirmed Klemperer's observation as to the popularity of Hitler's war. Having been riveted to the daily radio broadcasts, she blamed Poland for the conflict, revealing her concern as to precarious status of "stranded" *Volksdeutschen.* "As was the case in the past under the Czechs, Germans have recently suffered under the Polish terror. Over the past five months, attacks against Germans, mistreatment, atrocities, and murder have piled on top of each other and increased

[115] *Sopade*, August-October 1939, 980.
[116] Müller, "Nationalismus": 38.
[117] Klemperer, *I Will Bear Witness*, entry of September 3, 1938, 307.

more and more." That Hitler had willingly ignored the plight of Polish Germans by signing his nonaggression pact with Poland five years earlier, was long forgotten.[118] Klemperer's emphasis on the coming catastrophe was telling: far from being a war of self-defense, the Nazi regime would fight for an empire. It would not be content to control and exploit diverse peoples to the metropole's advantage; rather, it would subject entire peoples to elimination because the regime perceived them as a threat to the survival of the "racial community."

[118] Walb, *Ich die Alte*, 129. See Richard Blanke, *Orphans of Versailles: The Germans in Western Poland 1918–1939* (Lexington: University of Kentucky Press, 1993), 220.

5

The Nazi Place in the Sun

German-Occupied Europe during World War II

The German invasion of Poland exploded from five fronts that opened from the Polish corridor in the north to the Carpathian Mountains in the south. It pitted the best air force and most combat-ready army in Europe against an overmatched enemy. Using panzer divisions, light and motorized divisions, most of its infantry divisions, and aerial fighter and bomber assaults, the German armed forces aimed to encircle and destroy the Polish forces quickly in order to meet the expected French assault from the west. A counterattack did not materialize, partially the result of the defensive presuppositions of the French military. In addition to overestimating German troop strength along their borders, the French assumed that a future war would resemble the previous one. Yet French operational planning only partially explains the inaction. Despite their frantic efforts to force the Wehrmacht to pull back after the German attack, the British and French entertained the prospect of attacking Italy first to undermine Germany's weak link. When Italy did not enter the war, they shifted their attention to squeezing Germany's new ally, the Soviet Union. The Allied generals drafted plans to attack the Soviet Union through Scandinavia, support Finland's war against the Soviets, and bombard the Soviet oil fields in the Caucasus to interrupt shipments of a natural resource that Germany could not do without.[1]

The Nazi-Soviet Nonaggression Pact, the consequence of the western powers' anti-Bolshevism and the collapse of collective security, as much as German tactical brilliance, made a German victory in the east

---

[1] Jost Düffler, *Nazi Germany 1933–1945: Faith and Annihilation*, trans. Dean Scott McMurray (London: Arnold, 1996), 119.

inevitable.[2] By the second week of the war, the Germans occupied the important industrial city of Łódź and had marched to the outskirts of Warsaw. By September 27th, the Polish capital surrendered, with the Germans taking formal control of the city a week later, only five weeks after the war began. Despite the brevity of the German assault, the campaign provided a frightening omen of the carnage that would result from a second world war that Germany unleashed. German losses included nearly 16,000 killed and another 30,000 wounded. Seventy thousand Poles lost their lives, while over 130,000 were wounded and an additional 700,000 taken prisoner.[3] When the Soviet Union occupied eastern Poland on September 17th, another creation of the post–World War I settlement was brought to an end. In the German half, the way was now open to reshape the territory under the Reich's control.

From the outset, the German attack was an ideologically motivated total war aimed at the destruction of the Polish nation.[4] Five mobile SS attack units (*Einsaztgruppen*), composed of men from the Gestapo, Security Police, Criminal Police, and the Security Service, were assigned to each of the invading armies. Charged with ruthlessly combating "anti-German elements" in the rear, they served notice that the German occupation of Poland would depart from the more routine procedures of military administration. There were to be no court-martials for suspected insurgents, who would be summarily shot. Although Hitler briefly considered the establishment of a semi-autonomous Polish rump state, he soon abandoned that idea. His dream of living space farther to the east and his fury at the Poles for refusing to accept the reintegration of Danzig into the Reich in exchange for membership in the anti-Comintern Pact concluded with the Japanese empire determined the outcome. Summoning his generals to his Bavarian Alpine retreat, the Berghof, on August 22nd while Joachim Ribbentrop was in Moscow to sign the Nazi-Soviet Pact, Hitler made it clear that he sought the complete elimination of Poland. "Have no pity," he ordered his listeners.

---

[2] See Michael J. Carley, *1939: The Alliance That Never Was and the Coming of World War II* (Chicago: Ivan Dee, 1999), esp. 144–241.

[3] Ian Kershaw, *Hitler 1936–45: Nemesis* (New York and London: W. W. Norton, 2000), 236; Czesław Madajczyk, *Die Okkupationspolitik Nazideutschlands in Polen 1939–1945* (Berlin, 1987), 4

[4] Madajczyk, *Okkupationspolitik*, 165–215; Jörg Echternkamp, "Im Kampf an der inneren und äusseren Front. Grundzüge der deutschen Gesellschaft im Zweiten Weltkrieg," in *Die Deutsche Kriegsgesellschaft: Politisierung, Vernichtung, Überleben*, Erster Halbband (Munich: Deutsche Verlags-Anstalt, 2004), 83.

The campaign was to be carried out with "the greatest brutality and without mercy."[5]

In the days leading up to the invasion, the SS attack units were given the task, tellingly code-named Operation Tannenberg after the iconic World War I victory in East Prussia, to eliminate Poland's military, aristocratic, clerical, and political leadership. As the invasion unfolded, the mobile attack units and Waffen-SS units engaged in the sweeping arrest and executions of Polish civilians, especially Jews. Despite periodic protests from officers on the ground, the armed forces (Wehrmacht) generally dispensed with court-martials as pointless, time consuming, and injurious of its security. In contrast to World War I when the initial reactions of German soldiers ranged from wonder or bewilderment at the exoticism of their environment, to sympathy for the population because of their poor treatment under the tsars, expressions of contempt now moved to the center. Indicative of the impact of the Nazi regime's antisemitic propaganda, such sentiments were especially directed against "menacing,' "filthy," "lice-ridden," and "ragged" Polish Jews, whose unhygienic villages violated the exacting German standards of cleanliness.[6] At times, Wehrmacht commanders expressed unhappiness with the challenge that the SS units' violations of procedure posed to their authority. They remained ambivalent about thousands of atrocities perpetrated in clear violation of international law and their negative impact on military discipline. Nevertheless, the Wehrmacht quickly ceded its control over the administration of the German half of Poland, including the enforcement of regulations by which conquered "enemies" would be dealt with.[7]

The violence that accompanied invasion extended beyond that which the Wehrmacht and SS initiated on their own. Believing that ethnic Germans would compose a fifth column, enraged Poles in the western regions of the country rounded up thousands of them and marched them eastward in boxcars or on foot, exposing them en route to beatings and

---

[5] Alexander B. Rossino, *Hitler Strikes Poland: Blitzkrieg, Ideology, and Atrocity* (Lawrence, Kansas: University of Kansas Press, 2003), 9; Notes from the diary of Admiral Wilhelm Canaris quoted in Winfried Baumgart, "Zur Ansprache Hitlers vor den Führern der Wehrmacht am 22. August 1939," *Vierteljahrshefte für Zeitgeschichte* 19, no. 2 (July 1971): 303.

[6] Debórah Dwork and Robert Jan Van Pelt, *Auschwitz 1270 to the Present* (New York and London: W. W. Norton, 1996), 113-4.

[7] Rossino, *Hitler Strikes Poland*, 58-87. Jochen Böhler, "'Tragische Verstrickung' oder Auftakt zum Vernichtungskrieg: Die Wehrmacht in Polen 1939," in *Genesis des Genozids: Polen 1939-1941*, eds. Klaus-Michael Mallmann and Bogdan Musial (Darmstadt: Wissenschaftliches Buchgesellschaft, 2004), 43-7.

shootings at the hands of villagers.[8] In response, thousands of young to middle-aged male Germans, whose families remained in Polish territory after 1919, formed their own militia, the Ethic German Self-Protection Force (*Volksdeutscher Selbstschutz*). Rather than simply an example of spontaneous self-organization, Hitler had actually ordered the creation of the militia shortly after the invasion began, subordinating it to the SS. The commander of its West Prussian wing, Ludolf von Alvensleben, an adjutant of Himmler, ordered his militia to engage in a Social Darwinian, no-holds-barred "ethnic struggle" befitting a master race. By early 1940, the Protection Force's killing spree had become so extensive and uncontrolled that its conflicts with the army and civil authorities forced its disbanding.[9] Emblematic of numerous scions of distinguished Junker clans, whose prior service in the Free Corps and subsequent loss of their estates – in this case to Poland – Alvensleben's career in the SS provided opportunities that had been denied him under the Weimar Republic. In addition to giving him a military career and an outlet for his anti-Polish resentment, Himmler granted him the right to manage two estates that had belonged to his family before 1918. Although Alvensleben's reward came as recognition for his performance in the field and not his noble pedigree, Alvensleben's assigned duty as a role model for the ethnic Germans under his command signified the recovery of the privileges of his caste.[10]

The most notorious case of local violence began on September 3rd in the Poznanian city of Bydgoszcz (Bromberg). Located in the volatile Polish Corridor, ethnic Germans, many of them sympathetic to Nazism, clashed with Polish troops. The conflict resulted in the deaths of an estimated one thousand Germans, whom the Nazi regime labeled as *Volksdeutschen*, and another one hundred who were shot later during a forced march. Following the Polish army's withdrawal, resident Polish militias took up arms against the incoming German troops until forced to surrender. Operating in the rear, the SS mobile attack units took revenge against the "insurgents" by executing hundreds of Polish hostages, many of them from the city's political and educated elite, while the Wehrmacht continued to give short shrift to the niceties of military justice.[11] Far from

---

[8] Richard Blanke, *Orphans of Versailles: The Germans in Western Poland 1918–1939* (Lexington: University of Kentucky Press, 1993), 232–7.

[9] Kershaw, *Nemesis*, 242–3.

[10] Stephan Malinowski, *Vom König zum Führer: Deutscher Adel und Nationalsozialismus* (Frankfurt am Main: Fischer Taschenbuch, 2004), 561; Peter Longerich, *Heinrich Himmler: Biographie* (Munich: Siedler Verlag, 2008), 445–6.

[11] Rossino, *Hitler Strikes Poland*, 59–74.

being a reaction to the murder of ethnic Germans, however, the German reprisals, especially the destruction of the local elite, implemented ideologically infused decisions made at the top, which "read" Polish resistance from below through the lens of race. Like Alvensleben, the chiefs of the attack units and their subunits, the Kommandos, fit the profile of SS officers. They were young, most in their thirties, middle-class, and possessed university educations, particularly law degrees. A significant number embodied the festering hatreds of the postwar conflicts in the eastern borderlands. Either they were raised in border regions and served in German border patrols, or they later served in the Gestapo there. All had been attracted to Nazism as students and all relished the opportunity to undo the "shame" of Versailles. By December of 1939, the SS and ethnic German auxiliaries had murdered fifty thousand Poles, which included seven thousand Jews.[12]

The German occupation of Poland, and the Soviet Union after June of 1941, seemed to resemble practices that European conquerors applied to their conquests overseas for over four hundred years. They included economic extraction, the ruthless exploitation of labor in which inhuman conditions often decimated the victims, the expulsion of indigenous peoples, which by the nineteenth century Social Darwinian and racist assumptions routinely justified, and the suspension of European rules of "civilized" warfare as inappropriate to engaging armed but inherently "backward," "inferior," and "savage" "natives."[13] Indeed the führer explicitly compared the Nazi *Lebensraum* project to the European conquest of the Americas, and in Poland, the German conquerors followed the colonial practice of minimizing the distinction between combatants and civilians. If some army commanders in Poland objected to the unlawful "actions" against Poles and Jews, cooperation between the Wehrmacht and the mobile attack units proved to be the rule rather than the exception. Such cooperation was assured before the campaign began, owing to the expectation of resistance from Polish paramilitaries and civilians.[14] Senior Wehrmacht officers differed little from SS leaders in their contempt toward the Poles, and believed that Poles, like "savages" or *frank tireurs* would not fight fairly. Both drew in equal measure from

[12] Ibid., 29–57.

[13] See Enzo Traverso, *The Origins of Nazi Violence*, trans. Janet Lloyd (New York and London: New Press, 2003), 47–75.

[14] Rossino, *Hitler Strikes Poland*, 1–28; Jochen Böhler, *Auftakt zur Vernichtungskrieg: Die Wehrmacht in Polen 1939* (Frankfurt am Main: Fischer Taschenbuch Verlag, 2006), 25–74, 201–39.

the historically ingrained hostility toward Poles that emerged well before 1871, festered under the Second Empire, and intensified after World War I as the redrawn borders heightened German perceptions of ethnic crisis. When procedural concerns were raised, they arose less from moral conviction than from the fear that other "civilized" nations might well consider the behavior of the Wehrmacht criminal, or they arose from concerns as to the potential ill effects of mass reprisals on military discipline. For the majority of officers, however, the Polish campaign amounted to an "ethnic struggle" (*Volkstumskampf*) that functionally equated the present European enemies with Africans. Still, if Nazi conceptions of *Lebensraum* would recall the long history of European imperialism and colonialism, the Third Reich's "drive to the east" (*Drang nach Osten*) differed from previous European and Imperial German practice in the consistency of its long-term goal of racial purification sanctioned at the top, and in the case of the Soviet Union, its fusion of civil and racial war. Even without including the Holocaust, the violence that the Third Reich unleashed would merit the term "catastrophe." The Nazi regime would triumph over Germany's tragic past by cleansing "superfluous" populations and mobilizing the resources of its living space to become a global power.

Despite debates among Nazi leaders as to whether to pursue more conciliatory policies toward conquered peoples, the dominant view assumed the legitimacy of ethnic cleansing and mass murder to a degree that most colonial administrations and imperial metropoles neither achieved nor ought to attain. Rather, the mass expulsion or killing of native populations often followed frontier conflicts on the ground between European settlers and indigenous peoples over land and resources. Neither senior colonial authorities nor metropolitan governments could be disentangled from, or exonerated of, the murderous outcomes of settler violence. European settler colonialism structurally linked empires to their frontier encampments of land-hungry immigrants through the logic of the international market and European legal norms regarding the ownership and disposition of property.[15] Yet at times, colonial officials tried to dampen conflicts between natives and settlers in order to keep the peace and maintain a

---

[15] Patrick Wolfe, "Settler colonialism and the elimination of the native," *Journal of Genocide Research* 8, no. 2 (2006): 390–5. See also A. Dirk Moses, "Conceptual blockages and definitional dilemmas in the 'racial century': genocides of indigenous peoples and the Holocaust," in A. Dirk Moses and Dan Stone, eds., *Colonialism and Genocide* (London and New York: Routledge, 2007), 148–80.

functioning colonial economy. Indeed, the British metropole's effort to restrain colonial settlement in North America after 1763 emerged as one of the principal settler grievances leading up to the American Revolution.[16] The most thoroughgoing case of genocide, the total eradication of the aboriginal peoples of Tasmania in the late 1820s and early 1830s, offers an instructive example. Although prepared to crush a formidable aboriginal insurgency, Arthur George, the British governor general of Tasmania, then known as Van Dieman's land, was caught between the restraint demanded by London and the rapacity of the convict settlers whom he was supposed to protect. "Only" the structural imperatives of colonialism, the protection of colonists and their property, forced his reluctant consent to settler actions. However minimal such tactical disagreements seem in light of the devastation that indigenous peoples suffered, the Nazi enterprise lacked even this modest level of restraint, particularly in the east where its empire would be anchored.

The logistical problems of expelling and resettling millions, which included the severe labor shortages that resulted as too few Germans replaced too many expellees, caused delays in the implementation of long-term goals and provoked rivalries among Nazi Party satraps. Turf wars erupted among the Wehrmacht, the SS, Göring's economic empire, and the civil administrations. Nevertheless, the outcome of the German *Lebensraum* project, a massively destructive program of settlement, exploitation, and murder was never in question. Moreover, unlike the migrations to North America or, to a more modest extent, German Southwest Africa, where settlers exercised considerable autonomy and initiative even when backed by metropolitan governments, the Nazi regime sought to procure settlers through bilateral diplomacy with its allies and satellites. Whereas Mussolini initiated the transfer of South Tyrolean Germans, Hitler initiated the resettlement of ethnic Germans from eastern Poland and the Baltic states with Stalin in the course of finalizing the Nazi-Soviet division of Poland during the second half of September.[17] Over the long term, the Nazi leadership expected that settlement in the east would be attractive

---

[16] Fred Anderson and Andrew Cayton, *The Dominion of War: Empire and Liberty in North America, 1500–2000* (New York: Viking, 2005), 104–206.

[17] For accounts of the Reich's negotiations over ethnic German settlers, see Vladis Lumans, *Himmler's Auxiliaries: The Volksdeutsche Mittelstelle and the German National Minorities of Europe, 1933–1945* (Chapel Hill and London: University of North Carolina Press, 1993), 158–75; Markus Leniger, *Nationalsozialistische "Volkstumsarbeit," und Umsiedlungspolitik 1933–1945* (Berlin: Frank and Timme, 2006), 58–60, and for the Soviet case, Philip T. Rutherford, *Prelude to Genocide: The Nazi Program of Deporting Ethnic Poles, 1939–1941* (Lawrence, KN: University of Kansas Press, 2007), 48–9.

enough to encourage Germans from the Old Reich and the Americas to migrate, yet few accepted the offer. For that reason alone, an unusual degree of mobilizing settlers from on high characterized the Nazi "drive to the east."

In addition, the Third Reich dispensed with the Christian imperatives of conversion, which important imperialist constituencies promoted during previous conquests and settlements. This was not just because the populations in question were Christian, or at least nominally so, including the Soviet Union where rural people tenaciously retained their allegiances despite the Bolsheviks' suppression of the Orthodox Churches. Rather, the pitiless Social Darwinian state-and-party-directed colonialism of the Third Reich provided little room for missionaries.[18] On the ground, varied and inconsistently applied criteria for ranking subject peoples did allow for the assimilation of those whom occupation officials believed capable of Germanization. Yet their approach differed from assimilationists elsewhere, notably on the American frontier. There the desire to eradicate native cultures derived from the Enlightenment's faith in education and self-improvement. Nazism's route to homogeneity, on the other hand, was grounded in the expectation, deeply held in the SS, that German blood could be extracted from the human residue that remained from the medieval German migrations and the conquests of the Hanseatic traders and Teutonic Knights.[19] The conquest of the east, finally, bore little resemblance to discussions of an overseas empire that occurred during the Weimar Republic and even the Third Reich, in which paternalism played a more prominent role. Such discussions imagined the cultural uplift of "natives" and large-scale structural improvements, including schools, which would partially benefit them, as well as the increase of the labor supply through education and proper medical care. While no doubt condescending, fundamentally exploitative, and self-serving, such goals were positively benign compared to German ambitions in the east.

To carry out its racist agenda, the Nazi regime created a new type of institution in the SS organized around the singular mission to eliminate

---

[18] Henry Reynolds, "Genocide in Tasmania,?" in *Genocide and Settler Society: Frontier Violence and Stolen Indigenous Children in Australian History*, ed, A. Dirk Moses (New York and Oxford: Berghahn Books, 2004), 127–49. See also in the same volume, Jürgen Zimmerer, "Colonialism and the Holocaust: Towards an Archeology of Genocide:" 63.

[19] See for example the different approaches to Indians in the American West, in Michael Hochgeschwender, "The Last Stand: Die Indianerkriege im Westen der USA (1840–1890)," in *Kolonialkriege: Militärische Gewalt im Zeichen des Imperialismus*, eds. Thoralf Klein and Frank Schumacher (Hamburg: Hamburger Edition HIS Verlag, 2006), 44–79.

"enemies" and bring about racial purification, an agency that stood in a class by itself in its calculating viciousness. As a self-styled racial elite, the admission to which required an acceptable genetic make-up and physical appearance, educational attainment, and military prowess, the SS expanded beyond its military and police functions to manage dispossession, ethnic transfer, and genocide. Having grown steadily more powerful because of its ultramontane fealty to the führer and its implementation of racial purification at home, the SS was well positioned at the outbreak of war to carry out its utopian ambitions. The channels of policy making in the east thus departed significantly from those of the first German genocide, the war in Southwest Africa. There, the military, having triumphed over the colonial office and the colonial governor, opted for genocide following conflicts between German settlers and the Herero. To be sure, few could best the German commander, Lothar von Trotta, in waging a ruthless war of annihilation. The colonial army's "pacification" in the name of "security" at the very least carried genocidal potential.[20] And German military culture as it had developed since the Franco-Prussian and Herero Wars likely had long-term consequences that influenced the armed forces of the Third Reich.[21] Nevertheless, Nazism's ideological project, the racial remaking of its *Lebensraum* largely unchecked by dissent at home, created its own unique agent.

The SS was neither the only agent of racial transformation, nor did its power go unchallenged. Its freedom of action was less contested in the east than in northern and western Europe where the Wehrmacht, civil administrations, and German business interests encouraged more pragmatic approaches to occupation. The civil administration in the occupied territories often played as significant a role in carrying out ethnic cleansing and genocide. The sheer scale of the Nazi enterprise institutionally interlocked the SS, the military, civilian bureaucrats, private industry, and Göring's own economic empire, which expanded with his management of the Four-Year Plan. Despite their initially close relationship, Himmler and Darré battled over their diverging conceptions of rebuilding the *Volk*. Although favoring expansion, Darré gave priority to the creation of racially healthy peasant elite, whereas Himmler's expansionism conceived

[20] On the genocidal implications of the "security syndrome," see A. Dirk Moses, "Empire, Colony, Genocide: Keywords and the Philosophy of History," in *Empire, Colony, Genocide: Conquest, Occupation and Subaltern Resistance in World History*, ed. A. Dirk Moses (New York and Oxford: Berg, 2008), 28–9.

[21] Isabel V. Hull, *Absolute Destruction: Military Culture and the Practices of War in Imperial Germany* (Ithaca and London: Cornell University Press, 2005), 7–130.

the Germanization of the east as the means of ordering space and creating an entirely new society of independent farmers. Himmler could more easily circumvent Alfred Rosenberg, the Reich Minister for the Occupied Eastern Territories, who advocated a slower place of settlement, than he could district leaders in regions of the Old Reich where settlers were to be recruited. They placed roadblocks in Himmler's way, unwilling to lose labor that they wanted to mobilize for economic development.[22] Similarly, the removal of Poles and Jews from territories annexed to Germany raised objections from civil administrators, who suddenly found themselves without farmers or skilled laborers. Nevertheless, as the beneficiary of Hitler's charismatic authority and the magnet for numerous, highly educated, well-trained, and ideologically committed young men, the SS set the bar sufficiently high to place the more commonplace practices of imperial rule on the defensive.

Finally, because it was imposed on Europe itself, Nazi colonialism fused politics and race in different and unprecedented ways. During the nineteenth century, the transformation of politics from the practice of elites to the mobilization of mass constituencies increasingly pressured European political classes to justify imperialism in light of the cultural, national, and material benefits they provided. Thus, they sought colonies because they provided labor and commodities that directly and indirectly raised popular living standards at home. In addition, they assumed that the acquisition of great power status, which the possession of empire defined, would encourage popular identification with the nation so as to mitigate class tensions. Although European middle classes frequently equated workers with colonized peoples of color, using words such as "uncivilized," "unclean," and "savage" to describe both,[23] metropoles fought colonial wars to exploit the labor and raw materials of indigenous societies, while using "divide and rule" policies to identify collaborators among indigenous social and political elites. Nazi imperialism, on the other hand, became a continental civil war and a racial war simultaneously. It became a perfect storm that combined contemptuous stereotypes of long standing, a loathing of the Bolshevik Revolution, and the wrenching impact of World War I and its aftermath, which exacerbated German perceptions of foreign domination and ethnic contamination. The Nazi

[22] Uwe Mai, *"Rasse und Raum": Agrarpolitik, Sozial-und Raumplanung im NS-Staat* (Paderborn: Ferdinand Schöningh, 2002), 154, 188, 305–8.
[23] Anne McClintock, *Imperial Leather: Race, Gender, and Sexuality in the Colonial Context* (New York and London: Routledge, 1995), 4–9, 104–20.

assault against Bolshevism as the vanguard of proletarian revolution and imperial disintegration joined with the expulsion and mass murder of Slavs and the total extermination of the Jews.

PRELUDE TO GENOCIDE: RESETTLEMENT, ETHNIC CLEANSING, AND THE NAZI ASSAULT IN THE WEST

Extending its boundaries beyond the German territories ceded to Poland after World War I to include land that once belonged to the Romanovs and Habsburgs, Germany incorporated Poland's western territories into the Reich. Following the elimination of the Polish Corridor, East Prussia was once again joined to the Reich, while Upper Silesia was reincorporated as a separate province. Two new provinces, named Danzig-West Prussia and the Wartheland, the latter more commonly referred to as the Warthegau, were created. Procedures that the regime had developed in the Protectorate to categorize and displace populations, as well as to transfer property to the racially suitable, would now apply farther east, laying the foundations for ethnic cleansing and genocide. "Old fighters," long-time Nazi Party members with experience in the Free Corps, headed the civil administrations of the annexed territories: Josef Wagner in Upper Silesia, Albert Forster in Danzig-West Prussia, and Arthur Greiser in the Warthegau. Alsatian by birth and a World War I veteran who transplanted himself to the Ruhr afterward, Wagner joined the Nazi Party in 1922 and became the Gauleiter of Westphalia South. After 1933, he was appointed the governor of Lower Silesia. Forster, born in 1902, joined the NSDAP and SA in 1924 in Fürth, the town of his birth, having been captivated by Hitler's defense of his role in the Munich Putsch. As a protégé of Hermann Göring and Julius Streicher, Forster became the Gauleiter of Danzig in 1930, where he made life miserable for the Poles and Jews who lived in the city and engaged in frequent confrontations with the League of Nations' High Commissioner, Carl Jakob Burkhardt. The Polish-speaking Greiser, who was raised in the Imperial German border province of Posen, joined the SA and Nazi Party in 1928 and the SS in 1931. After serving as an aviator in World War I and a fighter in the Baltic Free Corps afterward, the radical nationalist Greiser was elected to the Danzig senate in 1924, rising to become its president in 1935. Although bitter rivals while in Danzig, Forster and Greiser personified the anti-Polish revanchism and Pan Germanism that was especially pronounced in contested border regions, regions which produced a disproportionate share of the perpetrators of ethnic expulsions and mass murder.

MAP 5.1. Occupied Poland, 1939–1941. Source: Christopher R. Browning with Jürgen Matthäus, *The Origins of the Final Solution: The Evolution of Nazi Jewish Policy, September 1939–March 1942* (Lincoln: University of Nebraska Press, 2004), 38.

Although not a product of the German borderlands, Hans Frank, another "old fighter" with unimpeachable radical nationalist credentials, was appointed governor of the remainder of Poland, including its capital of Warsaw. Known as the General Government (*Generalgouvernement*), Frank's region was to become the temporary dumping ground for Poles, Sinti and Roma, and Jews displaced from the annexed territories, and subsequently a source for labor, food, and raw materials for the Reich. A native of Baden in the German southwest, Frank joined an infantry regiment in 1917 and served in the Free Corps under Franz Ritter von Epp in Bavaria when it suppressed the Munich soviet. In 1919, he joined the Nazi Party as one of its first members and later took part in the Munich putsch. Trained as a lawyer, he served as the party's legal counsel. When the Nazis took power, he won simultaneous appointment as minister without portfolio in the national cabinet and minister of justice in Bavaria. Despite Frank's lack of administrative experience on a scale that would be appropriate to his task, his appointment as governor general in 1939 amounted to the reward of a fiefdom to one of Hitler's most loyal vassals, a plum that Frank would exploit to the fullest during his tenure.[24]

In addition to installing the civil administrations, Hitler extended the authority of the SS still further by naming Heinrich Himmler as Commissar for the Consolidation of Germandom. In addition to this new embellishment to his personal power, Himmler could now make good on his sweeping plans to Germanize the annexed territories. Although the impracticality of the wholesale dispossession and expulsions of indigenous populations would soon make itself felt, millions of Poles and Jews were to be expelled to the General Government or deported to Germany as labor, while "superior" Nordic stock, namely ethnic Germans who lived outside the borders of the Old Reich, would be "repatriated" to replace them. Seemingly imitating the complicated relationship between the SS-led police and the judiciary, in which competition coexisted with ideologically grounded cooperation, the SS administration in the east engaged in frequent jurisdictional conflicts with the civil administration, even if those conflicts rarely produced fundamental ideological disagreements. In fact, the outright merger of the SD, the Gestapo, and the Kripo into Heydrich's Reich Security Main Office (RSHA) in September of 1939, anticipated the new responsibilities that the SS would assume in the conquered territories that would take precedence over those of the civil administration. The new office was to fight all internal and external "enemies of the Reich," giving "legal" cover to the SS mobile attack units currently operating in Poland.

---

[24] Christoph Klessmann, "Hans Frank: Party Jurist and Governor-General in Poland," in *The Nazi Elite*, eds. Ronald Smelser and Rainer Zitelmann (New York: New York University Press, 1993), 39–47; Dieter Schenk, *Hans Frank: Hitlers Kronjurist und Generalgouveneur* (Frankfurt am Main: Fischer, 2006)), 143–54.

Himmler wasted little time in importing ethnic Germans into the annexed territories, while moving out Polish Christians and Jews. After the arrest, confinement, or execution of Polish elites, all remaining Poles in the annexed territories were to be deprived of their property and deported, either to the General Government or to the Old Reich as forced labor. Those who were "resettled" would receive little provisioning and the minimum of medical care necessary to prevent epidemics that could put Germans at risk. Only a few Poles deemed suitable for Germanization, or those considered essential for menial labor, would be allowed to remain as long as they were politically unobjectionable and agreed to give up their "racially valuable" children to German families or orphanages.[25] According to the first long-range program for settlement, the "General Plan East" of January, 1940, a projected one hundred thousand "child-rich" families drawn from the German peasantry, over eight hundred thousand Germans in all, were to be resettled along the southern and western borders of the annexed territories. They would constitute a "wall" of Germandom to insulate the Reich from the Poles.[26]

That "fundamental cleansing" (*Flurbereinigung*) adhered to the führer's conception of Germanization as he expressed to the military immediately after the Nazi takeover in 1933 and his specific instructions of mid-October of 1939. There would be no Germanization of subject peoples as Bismarck and his successors had once attempted and failed to achieve, only the Germanization of the soil. On the day before Himmler was appointed Commissar for the Strengthening of Germandom, Hitler addressed the Reichstag to lay out his radical conception of a postwar continent. He rejected traditional power politics among nation states as irrelevant in an era in which the struggle among peoples had contributed to and profited from the postwar collapse of the multiethnic empires. Much less was he interested in restoring Germany's pre–World War I borders. Rather, in an echo of the latter phases of the Supreme Command's eastern policy during World War I, a "peaceful" new Europe would arise from a new, purified ethnographic order that would ensure the security and economic prosperity of the German *Volk*. The salvation of one's own kind was all that mattered.[27]

[25] Madajcyzk, *Okkupationspolitik*, 389–431; Götz Aly, *"Final Solution": Nazi Population Policy and the Murder of the European Jews*, trans. Belinda Cooper and Allison Brown (London: Arnold, 1999), 33–58; Longerich, *Himmler*, 457–66.

[26] Mai, "*Rasse und Raum*" 293–4.

[27] Michael Wildt, "'Eine neue Ordnung der ethnographischen Verhältnisse:' Hitlers Rede vom 6. Oktober 1939," *Zeithistorische Forschungen/ Studies in Contemporary History* 3

The expropriation of the property of Germany's victims, undertaken usually by Race and Resettlement and Central Emigration Offices of the SS, took place with maximum dispatch and a minimum of compassion. Tossed out onto the street, shoved into collection camps, or unceremoniously deported, the dispossessed were given few resources from their overlords, who focused their concerns on caring for their own kind, the ethnic Germans scattered elsewhere who would now come "home to the Reich." "Evacuations" normally occurred in the wee hours of the morning so that stunned owners would not have had time to flee with their possessions or leave their animals without food. Volunteers from the Nazi Women's League and the League of German Girls (BDM) waited in the wings while SS units evicted Poles from expropriated homes and farms. Once the Poles departed, they attacked the premises with mops, brooms, cleansers, starched white curtains, and hanging flower baskets in preparation for their new owners, engaging in the ritualistic as well as actual cleansing of space.[28] Occasionally, evicted Poles returned to their homesteads either to look for lost relatives or simply to see their farms once more, only to be intercepted by the police. Thus after his unsuccessful return and arrest, Anton W., who was evicted in June of 1940 from his small farm in the Warthegau, made his way to the General Government where he was forced to settle for work as the employee of another farmer. Others in his shoes, if they survived at all, became forced laborers for Germans.[29] Because the annexed territories constituted the most highly developed industrial and agricultural regions in interwar Poland, the occupation's expropriation and integration of their assets was nearly total, sparing but a few Polish artisanal and service enterprises.[30]

The polish physician, Zygmunt Klukowski, whose diary provides invaluable descriptions of the nerve-shattering horror of the occupation, witnessed the trauma of expellees from the annexed territories from his hospital in the Zamość region south of Lublin in the General

(2006), http//www.zeithistorische-forschungen.de/16126041-Wildt-1-2006. Accessed May 6, 2010.

[28] Nancy Reagin, *Sweeping the German Nation:Domesticity and National Identity in Germany, 1870–1945* (Cambridge: Cambridge University Press, 2007), 79, 201–2.

[29] Isabel Heinemann, *"Rasse, Siedlung, deutsches Blut": Das Rasse-und Siedlungshauptamt der SS und die rassenpolitische Neuordnung Europas* (Göttingen, Wallstein, 2003), 217–27.

[30] Bogdan Musial, "Das Schlachtfeldzweier totalitärer Systeme: Polen unter deutscher und sowjetischer Herrschaft 1939–1941," in Klaus-Michael Mallmann und Bogdan Musial eds., *Genesis des Genozids: Polen 1939–1941* (Darmstadt: Wissenschaftliche Buchgesellschaft, 2004), 18–19.

FIGURE 5.1. The evacuation of Poles from the annexed territories. 1939–1940.
Source: USHMM, photograph #81221.

Government. Given at most an hour to pack what few possessions the
Germans allowed them to take with them, deportees ended up briefly
in Łódź where the Germans confiscated their money. "They had been
forced to leave their homes where their families had lived for hundreds
of years," herded like cattle, pushed, and beaten. "These people are all
to be relocated in different villages in the Zamość region," continued
Klukowski. "What will they do, how will they live? Hundreds of them
who were farmers became beggars in one hour. The worst of it is that our
own farmers do not have enough even to feed themselves and many times
have refused to help."[31]

To take the place of the evacuees, Himmler began to resettle ethnic
Germans from the Soviet-occupied zone of Poland, the Baltic states,
and South Tyrol. Ultimately, Germans would come from southeastern
Europe, the poor agricultural regions of southwestern Germany, and the
Americas. Additional areas for settlement in the General Government and
further east would be specified later. The imagined German "wall" would
be more than the bricks and mortar of farms. In order to ensure that

---

[31] Zygmunt Klukowski, *Diary from the Years of Occupation 1939–1944*, trans.
George Klukowski, eds. Andrew Klukowski and Helen Klukowski May (Urbana and
Chicago: University of Illinois Press, 1993), 104.

"Polonism" had no chance of contaminating Germans, ethnic German immigrants themselves were ranked in terms of their suitability according to the German Ethnic Registry (*Deutsche Volksliste*, or DVL). The DVL, a series of four classifications, which originated with Greiser in the Warthegau and which the SS subsequently refined, joined a confusing and often arbitrarily applied array of linguistic, anthropological, eugenic, and political criteria, whereby hereditary health, political activism on behalf of German causes, fluency in the German language, and other cultural markers, such as efficient housekeeping, punctilious cleanliness, and the adherence to German customs, resulted in the highest ranking. Those immediately eligible for German citizenship would take over the farms, homes, shops, and furnishings confiscated from Poles and Jews. Such would be their compensation for the property that they had left behind. Ethnic Germans who ranked lower, starting with category three, which designated subjects "capable of being Germanized," received probationary citizenship and transfer to the Old Reich for further Germanization. If they sloughed off whatever Slavic characteristics they possessed, they would then receive their due reward, Reich citizenship and property. Those in the last category who were hopelessly polonized through generations of intermarriage or cultural laziness were relegated to SS-run labor and detention camps.[32]

Because the DVL embraced a fiction, the notion that a "pure" Germandom could be extracted from the traces of past Germanic colonization once cleansed of the accretions of "undesirable mixing," the borderline categories of three and four posed the greatest problems of identification. The irony was inescapable: If the purpose of ethnic cleansing and settlement was to secure Germany's future, the complex histories of potential settlers led to, at best, the intrusive and demeaning examinations for the regime's putative "*Volk* comrades," and at worst, deportation to Germany where the failure to achieve the appropriate standard of Germanness could have devastating consequences. The pressing

---

[32] On the application of the DVL, see Leniger, *Nationalsozialistische "Volkstumsarbeit,"*, 161–90; Bruno Wasser, *Himmlers Raumplanung im Osten: Der Generalplan Ost in Polen* (Basel, Berlin, and Boston: Birkhäuser Verlag, 1993), 21–46; Götz Aly and Susanne Heim, *Vordenker der Vernichtung: Auschwitz und die deutsche Pläne für eine neue europäische Ordnung* (Frankfurt am Main; Fischer Tachenbuch, 1993), 125–55; Heinemann, "*Rasse, Siedlung, deutsches Blut*," 250–82; Hans-Christian Harten, *De-Kulturation und Germanisierung. Die nationalsozialistische Rassen-und Erziehungspolitik in Polen, 1939–1945* (Frankfurt: Campus, 1996); Robert Koehl, *RKFDV: German Resettlement and Population Policy, 1939–1945* (Cambridge, MA: Harvard University Press, 1957), 89–160; and Reagin, *Sweeping the German Nation*, 181–217.

need for labor, which settlers alone could not satisfy, became the solution to ambiguity, as exemplified by Albert Forster, the self-confident district leader of Danzig-West Prussia. Responsible to Hitler alone, Forster considered his district his own to administer without interference from the SS, whose leader he once dismissed with the comment, "If I looked like Himmler, I would not talk about race!"[33] In Forster's hands, the DVL became a way to transform Poles into probationary Germans.

The Warthegau was another matter. Arthur Greiser, whose utopian ambitions were more in accord with Himmler's, held firm to his exacting standards. His extreme racism, which rejected any possibility of assimilating Poles, personified the ruthless potential of the expulsion and resettlement project. Assiduous to a fault in carrying out his desire to make his district a model, Greiser instituted a rigid policy of racial segregation, in which those Poles who were neither expelled to the General Government nor classified as capable of Germanization became little more than slaves. In addition to relating the fear that Greiser inspired among his subject people, the recollections of Greiser's housekeeper, Danuta Pawelczak-Grocholska, revealed the close relationship between "German" standards of housekeeping, the German imperialist mission, and the assiduous maintenance of consumer goods as a badge of racial superiority.

You were not supposed to see a speck of dust. Carpet fringes had to be combed in straight lines. God help us if there was one out of place! It was all done to perfection, with exaggerated opulence. On the coldest day of the winter, her ladyship would order the cleaning of the windows for New Year's Eve. Our hands would freeze to the window panes. We blew on our fingers but we had to carry on with the cleaning…The orangery, the fishponds, the gamekeeper…The whole economic base of the place was geared exclusively for the use of these two people. It was luxury, in every respect pure luxury.[34]

Typical of the planning mania that accompanied the Nazi imagination of space, Greiser engaged architects and urban planners to modernize and transform his domain. They were to reshape the land so that it would no longer reflect years of Polish backwardness and squalor. Posen and Lódź, the latter renamed Litzmannstadt in honor of the general who led the German forces in the area during World War I, were to become vast urban renewal projects, while forests, parks, and state-of-the-art highways would crisscross the province in a seamless blend of nature and

---

[33] Rutherford, *Prelude*, 66–7.
[34] Laurence Rees, *The Nazis: A Warning from History* (New York: New Press, 1997), 144–5.

technology. In addition to establishing viable farms for German settlers, which German planners considered essential to relieve the land hunger and low productivity of peasant holdings at home, Greiser envisioned new factories, as well urban and suburban homes with up-to-date appliances and comfortable furnishings. Together they would achieve the high standard of living that the Third Reich promised for racially acceptable Germans. Greiser's cultural mission was to provide the finishing touches on his project to eradicate Polonism. In addition to founding a new university in Posen, Greiser pursued the construction of cultural institutions, concert halls, theaters, and museums, which would promote German high culture and eliminate all vestiges of Polish low culture. Renamed cities, villages, and streets would erase all memory of the Slavic desecration of Germanness. In the process of rebuilding the towns that the war against Poland destroyed, Greiser would resurrect the glory of medieval times in buildings with high roofs and pointed gables that would signify the arrival of the Teutonic Knights of the twentieth century.[35]

Despite such visions of radical transformation, the demands of a war economy, especially as preparations for the invasion of the Soviet Union came to fruition in the spring of 1941, took precedence over evacuations of "undesirables." In addition to the overcrowding of the General Government with Poles and Jews, which prompted Frank's endless complaints, expulsions deprived the Reich of essential labor, as Forster recognized. While Jews could be done without, Poles were now indispensible. Even if they did not merit a favorable ranking according to the DVL and were deprived of their property, they could at least be housed with family or friends as long as their skills were useful. Even the Warthegau did not realize the hopes of its district leader. As late as 1944, Poles outnumbered by over three to one Reich Germans, resettled *Volksdeutschen*, and DVL-designated Germans taken together. The ratio of Germans to Poles looked "better" in Upper Silesia, Danzig-West Prussia, and the annexed territories of East Prussia, but only because of the more generous application of the German Ethnic Registry. Yet the impact of evacuation and resettlement should not be underestimated. By January of 1944, over

---

[35] Much if this is drawn from chapter 6 Catherine Epstein's *Model Nazi: Arthur Greiser and the Occupation of Western Poland* (New York and Oxford: Oxford University Press, 2010). I am grateful to Professor Epstein for her willingness to share this material. See also Niles Gustchow, "Stadtplanung im Warthegau 1939–1944, in *Der 'Generalplan Ost': Hauptlinien der nationalsozialistische Planungs-und Vernichtungspolitik*, eds. Mechtild Rössler and Sabine Schleiermacher (Berlin: Akademie Verlag, 1993),: 232–70; Leniger, *Nationalsozialistische "Volkstumspolitik,"* 20.

340,000 ethnic Germans had been resettled in the annexed territories, or according to some estimates, close to 400,000. Close to one million Jews and Christian Poles had been expelled. The 300,000 who were allowed to remain were deprived of their property.[36] Compared to the meager results that the Prussian Settlement Commission produced, the number of settlers imported by the SS was as impressive as it was ruinous for Himmler's victims.[37]

The outbreak of war and the ruthlessness of the occupation of Poland carried over to the home front with the full implementation of euthanasia. Having begun by eliminating deformed children as war approached, the threat of resistance from the churches deterred Hitler from the further implementation of the program until the outbreak of war diverted public attention. Nevertheless, enabling measures had been introduced previously, including the transfer of mental patients from private to state institutions. In 1938, following on the heels of the plaintive letter of a father asking for the mercy killing of his disabled child, Hitler ordered the head of the führer chancellery, Philipp Bouhler, and his personal physician, Dr. Karl Brandt, to head an advisory committee to implement the killing of mentally ill children. A subsequent decree from the interior ministry ordered physicians and midwives to report cases of "deformed" children, a significant broadening of the target population. In the last weeks before the outbreak of war, plans for a nationwide adult euthanasia program began to emerge, only to be implemented once victory over Poland provided the opportunity. The so-called T-4 project, named after the villa on Berlin's Tiergartenstrasse that housed its staff, came into being in late July of 1939 with an expanded pool of medical and psychiatric experts.[38]

---

[36] Elizabeth Harvey, *Women and the Nazi East: Agents and Witnesses of Germanization* (New Haven and London: Yale University Press, 2003), 79; Koehl, *RKFDV*, 130–1; Harten, *De-Kulturation*, 75, 116. See especially Rutherford's summary in *Prelude*, 211–20, which argues that the "de-racialization"of racial policy as applied to the Poles began much earlier than the second half of 1941, which most historians date as the reluctant beginnings in the use of Slavic forced labor. The need for labor competed with Germanization plans elsewhere, notably in the Protectorate, according to Chad Bryant, *Prague in Black: Nazi Rule and Czech Nationalism* (Cambridge, MA and London, 2007), 114–38.

[37] Some SS personnel recognized this. See Mark Mazower, *Hitler's Empire: Nazi Rule in Occupied Europe* (London: Allen Lane, 2008), 88.

[38] On euthanasia, see the summaries in Christopher Browning, *Origins of the Final Solution: The Evolution of Nazi Jewish Policy, September 1939-March 1942* (Lincoln: University of Nebraska Press, 2005); 184–93 and Peter Longerich, *Politik der Vernichtung: Eine Gesamtdarstellung der nationalsozialistischen Judenverfolgung*

Between the fall of 1939 and late summer of 1941, the overdosing of children was carried out in twenty-two specially designated hospital wards, beginning with infants and then extending to older children, including those with learning disabilities. In some cases, the means of killing was even more barbaric, such as that witnessed by Christine Weihs, whose younger brother died of mysterious circumstances in an asylum in Essen. While visiting him before his death, Weihs heard a child's cry from the next room. "And then I pushed the door handle and there lay a child," she said, "a boy, in the bed. And his scalp had been opened and the brain was gushing out. Of a living body."[39] The more centralized T-4 project soon encompassed a large number of doctors, psychiatrists, nurses, and orderlies in Germany's public, private, and religious asylums who were willing either to refer "life unworthy of life" for "special handling," or participate in the killing themselves. As of September 21, 1939, the interior ministry required all hospitals, nursing and senior homes, and sanitariums to identify patients with conditions ranging from criminal insanity to "feeblemindedness." Jewish patients needed no handicap to warrant a death sentence. To process those deemed suitable for euthanasia, six killing centers were established in remote areas to prevent news from spreading, for such actions violated the criminal code, which the regime simply ignored. The utterly bereft patients referred to them were loaded into vans, driven to remote locations, and poisoned by carbon monoxide. Later, the victims were herded into on-site gas chambers. Between the fall of 1939 and the spring of 1940, SS units in Poland emptied the asylums of ten thousand mentally ill patients, Polish and German, from hospitals located near the ports of Danzig, Swindemünde, and Stettin. They either shot them or disposed of them in gas chambers or mobile gas vans. A short time later, patients from the Warthegau and Danzig-West Prussia were killed. The district leaders of the annexed territories involved themselves directly in the action, as did the ethnic

(Munich and Zurich: Piper, 1999), 234–42. They build on the specialized works of Ernst Klee, *"Euthanasie" in NS-Staat: die "Vernichtung lebensunwertigen Lebens"* (Frankfurt am Main: Fischer, 1983; and Christian Ganssmüller, *Die Erbsgesundheitpolitik des Dritten Reiches: Planung, Durchführung, und Durchsetzung* (Cologne: Böhlau, 1987), 150–75 especially; Michael Burleigh, *Death and Deliverance: 'Euthanasia' in Germany 1900–1945* (Cambridge: Cambridge University Press, 1994); and Henry Friedlander, *The Origins of Nazi Genocide: From Euthanasia to the Final Solution* (Chapel Hill and London: University on North Carolina Press, 1997).
[39] Allison Owings, *Frauen: German Women Recall the Third Reich* (New Brunswick, NJ: Rutgers University Press, 1995), 415–7, quotation on 416.

German "protection forces." By the fall of 1940, the euthanasia program expanded from a targeted 70,000 to 140,000 victims, again German, Polish, and Jewish. Local initiatives, especially of Nazi leaders eager to reduce the populations of their mental institutions, complemented the decisions of Himmler and the euthanasia personnel in Berlin, Philippe Bouhler and Leonardo Conti. The SS used some of the freed-up space in hospitals to house ethnic German settlers or SS military units temporarily, yet the decision to kill "lives unworthy of life" proceeded less from practical considerations and more from ideological ones.[40] Cleansing the *Volk* of "useless eaters" was essential to self-preservation.

Although the euthanasia project fell below its ambitious projections, it still claimed nearly seventy thousand victims in the Old Reich by August of 1941, and thousands more without. It represented the outcome of trends in scientific thinking that first emerged during the Second Empire, and grew exponentially between the Great War and the Depression as eugenicists became obsessed by the "sacrifice" of the racially "valuable" on the battlefield without the comparable "sacrifice" of the mentally handicapped, or by social programs that encouraged the reproduction of the "unfit."[41] And it introduced a novelty, the "killing center," the assembly line of death that would become emblematic of Nazi Germany's racially purified empire. As the actions of the father of the disabled child, whose appeal to Hitler was the catalyst, the euthanasia program exploited the often unbearable stress and meager resources of care-giving relatives to persuade them that a "merciful" death would be in the best interests of the patient and the patient's family. Even party members revealed their mixed feelings of approval and dismay, as testified in a letter from a Nuremberg woman who was notified of the death of her two sisters, which suspiciously enough, took place on consecutive days. "I could only find peace if I had the certainty that through a law of the Reich it were possible to release people from their incurable sufferings," she said. "This is a good deed for both the patient himself and also for the relatives, and a great

---

[40] Recently, scholars have questioned the connection that Götz Aly has drawn between euthanasia and resettlement. See Longerich, *Politik der Vernichtung*, 238 and Volker Riess, "Zentrale und dezentrale Radikalisierung: Die Tötungen "unwerten Lebens" in den annektierten west-und nordpolnischen Gebieten 1939–1941," in Mallmann and Musial, *Genesis des Genozids*: 127–44.

[41] Stefan Kühl, "The Relationship between Eugenics and the so-called 'Euthanasia Action' in Nazi Germany: A Eugenically Motivated Peace Policy and the Killing the Mentally Handicapped during the Second World War," in *Science in the Third Reich*, ed. Margit Szöllösi-Janze (Oxford and New York: Berg, 2001), 185–210.

FIGURE 5.2 The corpse of a woman in an open casket at the Hadamar Institute near Wiesbaden where she was "euthanized," April 5, 1945. Although public outrage forced Hitler to suspend gassings, patients in institutions continued to be killed by overdoses or starvation until the end of the war.
Source: USHMM, photograph #05416, courtesy of Rosanne Bass Fulton.

lessening of the burden on Reich and people." Neither she nor her relatives would object to such a law, because for years they had witnessed her sisters' misery. "But that this, my most sincere wish, should be fulfilled in two days, that I cannot believe."[42]

---

[42] Quoted in Ian Kershaw, *Popular Opinion and Political Dissent in the Third Reich: Bavaria 1933–1945* (Oxford: Clarendon Press, 1983), 337.

Contrary to Hitler's expectations, however, an enormous popular backlash did arise, especially among Catholics already infuriated by confiscations of church property and the closing of denominational schools. Public anger forced the postponement of the euthanasia program. In a widely circulated sermon that even reached German troops in Norway, the profoundly conservative Bishop Clements August Graf von Galen of Münster, who otherwise objected little to Nazi anti-Bolshevism and antisemitism, denounced euthanasia for its assault upon the intrinsic value of human beings, warning that the logic behind the destruction of putatively "unproductive" lives could soon extend to wounded German soldiers.[43] Fearing popular demoralization as a result of the British bombing of German cities and the temporary stagnation on the eastern front, the führer stopped the killings.[44] Nevertheless, the regime encouraged more subtle and less traceable means of doing in "useless eaters," such as starvation and lethal injection, which allowed the program to continue to the end of the Third Reich. Although provoking crises of conscience, horror, and rage among those most directly affected, the next of kin of the victims, the euthanasia action faced no subsequent collective protest. Moreover, Hitler authorized the extension of "mercy killing" to the concentration camps. The experience and training that the euthanasia program provided, which in addition to involving more health care professionals took on the characteristics of assembly-line killing, proved indispensable once the Nazi regime's "solution" to the Jewish "question" became genocide.[45]

As the foundation of German *Lebensraum*, the Nazi war in Poland was well on the way to achieving the catastrophe that would define its "drive to the east." Nevertheless, the interlocking imperatives of race and empire informed the German campaigns in Scandinavia, western and southeastern Europe, and contributed to the accelerated murderousness in the east after June of 1941. Much like the campaign in Poland, the invasion of France especially would become the proving ground for strategies pursued later in the Balkans and the Soviet Union. Following the defeat of Poland, which occurred without the intervention of Britain and France that Hitler's generals feared, the führer believed for a time that

[43] Beth A. Griech-Ploelle, *Bishop von Galen: German Catholicism and National Socialism* (New Haven and London: Yale University Press, 2002), especially 59–135, provides a long overdue critique of the "lion of Münster."
[44] Aly, *'Final Solution,'* 205.
[45] Longerich, *Politik der Vernichtung*, 242.

the western powers would agree to peace terms that allowed Germany a free hand in the East and the return of the former German colonies in Africa.

The widening focus of German ambitions, however, arose not merely from the desire to reclaim prewar overseas possessions, although the Reich government repeatedly staked its claim to former German colonies in its diplomatic pronouncements and negotiations throughout the 1930s. Having progressed in achieving its first priority, acquiring *Lebensraum* in the east, plans for an overseas empire began to take on a more expansive cast immediately after the defeat of France and the Low Countries. Until the end of 1940 when it became evident that the Germans had failed to knock Britain out of the war, and that Britain put together a coalition to ensure that outcome, vocal elements within the Nazi Party and Reich government, the Reich Colonial Association, the Colonial Political Office headed by Hitler's one-time mentor Franz Ritter von Epp, the German Labor Front's Institute for the Science of Labor (*Arbeitswissenschaftliches Institut*), commercial and industrial interests, and the navy and the foreign ministry, resurrected the ambition to a central African empire. That idea once embedded in Bethmann's September Program, laid the foundation for a global confrontation with the United States. In preparation, von Epp's office, with financial support from the government, established a school in the town of Oranienburg outside of Berlin to train colonial administrators, nurses, and policemen.[46]

Faced with mounting labor and raw materials shortages at home and the growing hostility of the United States, which after the German attack on Poland abandoned its neutrality to sell weapons to the British and French, Hitler announced his plan for a strike in the west for November of 1939 against the advice of his generals. To ensure an adequate food supply, the regime conscripted Poles from the General Government to bring in the harvest, the first of millions of foreign workers who would toil in factories and on farms.[47] Unlike the German attack in 1914, this invasion of the west would violate the neutrality of both Belgium and the Netherlands, which in Hitler's view would render a British blockade impossible. Only bad weather forced a postponement until the spring. A

---

[46] Karsten Linne, "*Weisse Arbeitsführer*" im "*Kolonialen Ergänzungsraum*": *Afrika als Ziel sozial-und wirtschaftspolitischer Planungen in der NS-Staat* (Münster: Monsenstein & Vannerdat, 2002), 28–37. On the German acquisition of French territories, see Chantel Metzger, *L'Empire Colonial Français dans la Stratégie Du Troisième Reich (1936–1945)*, vol. 1 (Brussels: P.I.E. Peter Lang, 2002), 13–239.

[47] Tooze, *Wages of Destruction*, 326–67.

FIGURE 5.3. "Here also is our *Lebensraum*," ca. 1933–1938. Aspirations to recover and expand the African empire of the Imperial Germany, which persisted in the 1920s and 1930s, received an additional, if temporary, boost with Germany's victories in the west in the spring of 1940.
Source: Bundesarchiv Koblenz, Plak 003–008–024. Designer: Hanns Reindl.

failed assassination attempt against the führer, which met with widespread popular condemnation, undercut plans for a military coup provoked by Hitler's recklessness. Nevertheless, the führer turned his attention to invading Denmark and Norway to protect Germany's imports of Swedish iron ore from a British blockade of the North Sea. In an attack that took the British government by surprise, the Germans took over their two northern neighbors by mid-April of 1940, which required the stationing of three hundred thousand German troops for the duration of the war. The occupation of Denmark, however, proved to be unusually gentle. The Reich Plenipotentiary and former deputy to Reinhard Heydrich, Werner Best, who in 1942 succeeded a diplomat appointed by the Foreign Office, aimed to construct a "model" protectorate.[48] Despite severe constraints on its foreign policy and the size of its military, Denmark retained its monarchy, government, and constitution with a German plenipotentiary serving as an intermediary between Berlin and Copenhagen. Rapidly increasing Danish dairy and cement exports to Germany and the lack of Danish resistance to the invasion contributed, to be sure, but so did the belief that as Nordic peoples, racial similarities would ensure the Danes' cooperation. The Third Reich envisioned a similar arrangement for Norway, a prospect that the Norwegian fascist Vidkun Quisling eagerly promoted to capitalize on the Reich's hold on Norway's seacoast to establish his own government under German protection. Norwegian resistance to the Germans and especially to Quisling's, clumsy attempts to nazify Norwegian society, necessitated the imposition of the provincial governor of the Rhineland Josef Terboven as Reich commissioner, and backed up by assorted SS functionaries.[49]

The German invasion of the west in May and June of 1940, concluding with the so-called "sickle cut," a high-risk maneuver that sent the strongest German force through the Ardennes forest where French defenses were at their weakest, was a six-week affair that resulted in the annexation of Luxembourg, the conquest of Belgium and Holland, and the ignominious defeat of France. Although the military expected that Belgium and Holland would be allowed to remain independent, the party and SS advanced other ideas, which Hitler did not discourage. The putative racial affinity of the Dutch prompted dreams of the restoration

[48] Ulrich Herbert, *Best: Biographische Studien über Radikalismus, Weltanschauung und Vernunft 1903–1989* (Bonn: Verlag J.H.W. Dietz Nachf., 2001), 323–42.

[49] Michael Burleigh, *The Third Reich: A New History* (New York: Hill and Wang, 2000), 457–63; Mazower, *Hitler's Empire*, 103–5.

of the western wing of the Holy Roman Empire, which would ultimately include Switzerland. Belgium remained under the administration of the Wehrmacht. Similar to Norway, the Nazi Party and SS officials, including the new Reich Commissioner, the Austrian Nazi Arthur Seyss-Inquart, ruled the Netherlands, albeit with a relatively gentle touch to prevent the Germans from losing control of the colonies that belonged to the Dutch. As for France, the Germans continued to rule the northern and western seacoasts directly to protect themselves against a British invasion, while the poorer central and southern parts of the country were merged into a puppet state with its seat in the spa town of Vichy, headed by the elderly conservative war hero Marshal Philippe Pétain. The occupational authority in Belgium governed the industrial Nord and the Pas de Calais, with another zone reserved for German settlement. The provinces of Alsace and Lorraine, which went back to France in 1919, were once again the property of the Third Reich. The existence of the Vichy government testified to the necessity of relying on collaborators to ease the pressure on Germany's overextended military manpower,[50] yet the Nazi regime's exploitative policies in occupied Europe and its genocidal campaign against the Jews would strain German resources to the breaking point.

The führer's lighting victory in the west seemed miraculous in light of the experience of World War I, with nothing to show for four and one-half years of brutal trench warfare except Germany's humiliation at the peace table. Trapped in the coastal town of Dunkirk, the British Expeditionary Force required a Herculean, but ignominious, amphibious rescue to prevent its total destruction. The irony was not lost on Hitler, who ordered that the surrender take place in the forest of Compiègne in the exact site and in the same railway car where in November of 1918, the German and French delegations signed the armistice agreement. The comparative novelty of the German victory lay not merely in the demoralizing speed with which it unfolded, nor in the ruthless bombing of the Dutch port of Rotterdam, which cost the lives of one thousand civilians. Rather, it resided in the overt racism that informed the treatment that Wehrmacht and Waffen SS accorded to prisoners of war, which expressed Germany's answer to the French use of colonial troops to occupy the Rhineland. German forces committed numerous massacres of black soldiers from French West Africa, whom the French had pressed into service to supplement their manpower in light of the

---

[50] Mazower, *Hitler's Empire*, 107–8.

nation's population decline. Unlike white civilians and soldiers, whom the Wehrmacht now treated according to the standards of international law to prevent a repetition of the Entente's atrocity propaganda of the Great War, African POWs were segregated from white prisoners and then massacred. Although at minimum 1,500 African POWs were killed, the treatment of African prisoners varied by unit and by context. Summary executions occurred disproportionately among the most nazified units, notably the SS *Totenkopf* division, or regular infantry regiments such as the *Grossdeutschland*, whose commanders had been deeply influenced by Nazi ideology. Atrocities also became the practice of units that faced strong resistance from African troops, especially on the final push toward Paris. Nevertheless, the killings evidenced the deep racism stemming from Germany's colonial and postcolonial experience and the official encouragement that it received from Berlin.[51]

Unlike the invasion of the Soviet Union launched one year later, the führer issued no "Commissar Order" for the western campaign, which authorized the murder of designated categories of POWs. Yet Propaganda Minister Goebbels, most certainly with Hitler's approval, issued directives to the mass media that stated the regime's expectations in no uncertain terms. African troops were "jungle beasts" who deserved no quarter. Resurrecting military fears of "illegitimate" guerrilla fighters (*franc-tireurs*), which first emerged during the Franco-Prussian War and then gained renewed currency as a result of French attacks on German units from the rear, the German press challenged the Entente's justification for depriving Germany of its overseas colonies. Claiming that the French violated the laws of "civilized" nations by using colonial troops against Germany, the press depicted cruel mutilations of German soldiers that black "savage" soldiers allegedly committed, even as France purported to defend "civilization" against the invasion of the "Huns." Goebbels did not hesitate to draw upon the spectre of miscegenation and its horrific consequences. Luridly describing the white women whom the French government allegedly hired to service the "needs" of African soldiers, Goebbels asserted that such racial mixing had contributed to the decline of the "Germanic Franks." Those and similar tropes, which focused on the putatively inexhaustible sexual appetites of Africans motivated as much by the desire to destroy as to satisfy, belonged to the reparatory of the German right's media campaign against the "black horror"

---

[51] Raffael Scheck, *Hitler's African Victims: The German Army Massacres of Black French Soldiers in 1940* (Cambridge: Cambridge University Press, 2006), especially 17–74.

twenty years earlier. In *Mein Kampf*, Hitler himself had weighed in on French occupation as the product of a "Jewish conspiracy," which had transformed France into an "African state on European soil." Likewise, the German propaganda war of May and June, 1940, could not resist drawing a similar connection while targeting the French Minister of the Interior, Georges Mandel, who was also Jewish. Formerly minister of the colonies, Mandel, according to the Goebbels machine, recruited Africans as French "cannon fodder." Although antisemitism was not the dominant theme of the propaganda war, the presumption that Jews had contributed to the degeneration of the French by engineering France's reliance on colonial troops, revealed enough to show that for Germany, the Jew was the greater threat.[52]

Because many units did not massacre Africans, however, the Nazi leadership determined that its next campaign would require more thorough ideological preparation and a direct order from the führer so as to remove all ambiguity. Yet the campaign against the Soviet Union would build on the even deeper colonialist ambitions of the Third Reich, the extension of *Lebensraum* at the expense of Slavs. Already present by the end of the Great War, the hatred of "Jewish Bolshevism" would soon propel an even more murderous endeavor. Ironically in the French case, the resurrection of world policy, given a boost by Germany's success in the west, necessitated by the late summer of 1940 the improved treatment of West African POWs in accordance with the Geneva Convention. The desire for an African empire, which was to include French colonial territory and thus the need to discourage West Africans from defecting to the Free French forces of Charles de Gaulle, rendered the racialized murder of black troops counterproductive. The hope, however fanciful, that some of the Africans in POW camps would collaborate with a future German colonial administration reinforced this change of heart.[53]

The victory in the west resulted in significant territorial and economic gains. It harnessed the resources of France, Belgium, Luxembourg, and the Netherlands to the Third Reich. The industrial assets of the new conquests, combined with those of Germany, Austria, the Protectorate of Bohemia and Moravia, Polish Silesia, and northern Italy, had the potential of producing a GDP greater than that of the United States or the British Empire. If the empires of the conquered nations and Italy are included, the Third Reich could potentially have produced thirty percent

[52] Ibid., 108–9.
[53] Ibid, 48–9.

of the global GDP.[54] Despite his successful campaign, Hitler remained on edge because Britain did not respond as he expected. Instead of agreeing to peace negotiations brokered by Mussolini, the new British Prime Minister Winston Churchill, who replaced Neville Chamberlain after the German invasion of Scandinavia, refused to come to the bargaining table. Mindful of the threat that Germany posed to the British Empire, Churchill was also disturbed by reports that Hitler would install a pro-German puppet government in London.[55] Faced with the likelihood of the intervention of the United States, with its seemingly unlimited manpower and resources mobilized against him, the führer briefly considered a Wehrmacht proposal for a cross-channel invasion of the British Isles. Nevertheless, Hitler's nagging fear that an amphibious assault would fail led him to order an aerial attack against British coastal defenses and cities to force Churchill to come to terms. More importantly, he decided to attack the Soviet Union no later than the spring of the following year. Confident of a victory that would deprive Britain of a potential continental ally, the conquest of the Soviet Union would give him resource-rich territory that would support a future German conflict with the United States.[56] Defeating the Soviet Union, he hoped, would also force an agreement between Britain and Germany that would give Germany continental dominion and an African empire enlarged at the expense of Belgium and France, ambitions that moved significantly beyond Hitler's more modest, earlier claims to the recovery of Germany's former colonies in Africa.[57] The failure of the Battle of Britain the following September, despite an unrelenting aerial assault against British cities, reinforced the need to attack the Soviet Union even though Hitler knew that he would be fighting a two-front war.

The British refusal to countenance German expansion exposed a dilemma that would have been familiar to the general staff and civilian leadership of Wilhelmine Germany, the unwillingness of other European empires to accommodate German ambitions. To compensate for British intransigence, other voices from within the Reich government sought allies who would participate in a global division of spheres of influence in return for supporting Germany against Britain. Joachim von Ribbentrop,

---

[54] Tooze, *Wages of Destruction*, 383.

[55] Ian Kershaw, *Fateful Choices: Ten Decisions that Changed the World 1940–1941* (New York: Penguin, 2007), 11–53.

[56] Ibid., 75–6; Tooze, *Wages of Destruction*, 396–425.

[57] Wolfe W. Schmokel, *Dream of Empire: German Colonialism, 1919–1945* (Westport, CT: Greenwood Press, 1964), 133–4.

the foreign minister, proposed an anti-British blockade that would include Italy, Japan, the Soviet Union, Spain, and Vichy France, as well as Germany. The inducements to join such an entente included access to, depending on the signatory, Southeast Asia, the Middle East, and the Mediterranean once the British Empire collapsed. Similar to Tirpitz, the commander of the German navy Admiral Raeder proposed the rapid construction of a huge surface fleet, modified to meet new strategic realities. An enlarged navy would defeat the British at sea and enable an overseas German empire of sufficient size to rival the United States for global domination. In Raeder's view, the possession of the Mediterranean under a German-dominated alliance would prevent an American foothold in northwest Africa. It would ensure German influence in Palestine and Syria, and would prevent Turkey from siding with the Soviet Union. Moreover, contiguous possessions in central Africa between Senegal and the Congo, and stretching east as far as German east Africa, would keep the German navy from being bottled up in the North and Baltic Seas, and link the African empire to naval bases in the Indian and Atlantic Oceans.[58] The Tripartite Pact of September 27, 1940, which committed Germany, Italy, and Japan, and later Hungary, Romania, Slovakia, and Bulgaria, came closest to accomplishing the Reich's goals. In addition to stipulating mutual assistance in the event of an American attack on the pact's participants, the treaty allowed the major signatories their desired spheres of influence, and the satellite powers their opportunities to revise the postwar peace settlements to their advantage. Nevertheless, the pact was a far cry from the global schemes of Ribbentrop and Raeder.

Germany's hunt for allies foundered on the incompatible goals of its potential partners and the führer's limited tolerance for accommodation, starting with those with interests in the Mediterranean and northwest Africa. Aside from Italy, an understanding with Spain seemed most promising because the Axis supported the Nationalist forces of Francisco Franco during the Spanish Civil War. For opportunistic reasons, Franco considered joining the Axis after the fall of France. Yet if Spain ultimately contributed troops to the German invasion of the Soviet Union, Franco's and Hitler's separate wish lists undermined their proposed anti-British entente. In addition to economic assistance and military aid, Franco demanded much of the French north African empire, including Morocco and Oran, as well as the British-held island of Gibraltar off the Spanish

---

[58] Kershaw, *Fateful Choices*, 72; Schmokel, *Dreams of Empire*, 131; Linne, "Weisse Arbeitsführer," 33; Mazower, *Hitler's Empire*, 113–8.

coast. Although the führer was prepared to concede Gibraltar to Franco, and did not consider Spanish imperial demands as necessarily incompatible with a German central African empire, the French wild card came into play. Because Hitler needed a reliable Vichy defense against de Gaulle's Free French armies, a case that the Vichy regime strengthened by having staved off de Gaulle's attack on the Senegalese port city of Dakar, Germany could not cede French colonial territory to Spain. Moreover, Hitler's demand for German military bases in the Canary Islands and in Africa alienated both Spain and Vichy France, who expected a partnership with Germany, not subordination. Hitler's assumption that the French and Spanish would allow Germany to construct air bases on their territories was dismissed out of hand.[59]

Quite apart from the unlikelihood of Hitler accepting a long-range arrangement with the Soviet Union on ideological grounds, mounting tensions between Germany and the Soviet Union precluded the latter's participation in an anti-British alliance. The Soviet Union refused to sacrifice hegemony over its neighbors, especially on its western borders. The Soviet Foreign Minister Vyacheslav Molotov would not accept the role that Germany defined for it following Britain's defeat, a sphere of influence in India, the Persian Gulf, and the Middle East. In fact, the Soviet annexation of Bukovina and Bessarabia from Romania was its answer to Germany's takeover of Romanian oil fields. So were Soviet demands for a German withdrawal from Finland, the incorporation of Bulgaria in the Soviet sphere of influence, the session from Japan of the Sakhalin islands, and the placement of Soviet bases in Turkey. Even worse than those indications of deep fissures in the German-Soviet alliance of convenience was Germany's dependence on Stalin for the delivery of food and raw materials, which the weakened state of the economies of German-occupied Europe rendered even more acute.[60] Confronted by the Soviet barrier to German continental hegemony, Hitler's anti-Bolshevism combined with the force of circumstance confirmed his inclination to attack.

Because Hitler and his generals underestimated Soviet military strength, they believed that an attack on Russia was a risk worth taking. An invasion would check Britain and forestall American intervention until such time when Germany could challenge both from a position of strength. Basing their assessments on the Soviet Union's poor performance in the Winter War against Finland and Stalin's purge of his top commanders,

[59] Kershaw, *Nemesis*, 327–31.
[60] Tooze, *Wages of Destruction*, 422–5.

not to mention their deep-seated anti-Slavic racism, the führer and his commanders believed that the Soviet Union could be destroyed before the winter weather and before the Soviets could mobilize their full military and industrial potential. Yet despite their apparent confidence, pessimism hovered just beneath the surface. A quick and decisive victory simply had to be achieved because time was not on Germany's side. Echoing the foreboding that Hitler had enunciated in his announcement of the Four-Year Plan over four years earlier as to the consequences of Soviet industrialization, an army study from January, 1941, warned that the Soviet armaments industry was capable of mass-producing up-to-date weaponry. The report further noted that since the 1920s, much Soviet industry had been moved beyond the Urals to protect it from a future attack. Lastly, despite the purges, the Red Army remained formidable in its size.[61] In an eerie replay of the Second Empire's general staff's gamble in 1914, Hitler and the Wehrmacht chose preventive war. The Nazi-Soviet Nonaggression Pact had outlived its usefulness economically and strategically, and giving the Soviet colossus more breathing space would be suicidal.

The acquisition of living space at the expense of the Soviet Union promised to advance the regime's primary objective, the racial and biological remaking of eastern Europe. Already dependent on Soviet deliveries of grain and oil, which arose from subsidiary agreements to the Nazi-Soviet Pact, and anxious about the Soviet threat to the Romanian oil fields at Ploesti, German planners imagined the realization of economic autarky and German economic hegemony once "Jewish Bolshevism" met its demise. The appropriation of Soviet raw materials would enable a longer conflict with Great Britain and sooner or later the United States. Furthermore, the economic absorption of Russia would be the foundation of prosperity and security for the racially purified German "master race" (*Herrenvolk*), beginning with food supplies to compensate for the shortages in the Old Reich, which even imports from southeastern Europe could not satisfy. By January of 1941, one month after Hitler's decision to press ahead with the invasion, the Wehrmacht high command, Himmler, Heydrich, Goering, and State Secretary Herbert Backe, who had out maneuvered his superior Darré by claiming a seat on the General Council for the Four-Year Plan, counted on the "reduction" of some thirty

---

[61] Burleigh, *Third Reich*, 491; Ludolf Herbst, *Die Nationalsozialistische Deutschland 1933–1945: die Entfesselung der Gewalt-Rassismus und Krieg* (Frankfurt am Main; Suhrkamp, 1996), 348–9.

million Slavs. So that Ukrainian grain would feed German soldiers and civilians, the native population would have to starve. Contrary to prewar Russia, when an overwhelmingly rural population produced substantial grain surpluses, the Soviet Union's rapid industrialization and urbanization, and the population shifts that accompanied them, meant that food reserves were now more modest. According to the brutal logic of National Socialism Soviet civilians would thus suffer the consequences. By May of 1941, a "Hunger Plan" initiated by Herbert Backe and adopted by the Wehrmacht called for the shift of agricultural surplus from the Soviet Union's bread-basket regions, that is the food that normally provisioned Russia's cities and northern regions, to the Wehrmacht and the German home front.[62]

The Hunger Plan was not the only evidence of the horror to come. The führer's "Commissar Order" directed to the armed forces high command shortly before the invasion made it clear just what sort of treatment Soviet political leaders could expect to receive in the "struggle against Bolshevism." Because this was to be a war for Germany's very existence, the military was relieved of even the pretense of adhering to international law.[63] As was the case in Poland, shooting political and guerrilla leaders post-haste was permissible, as were reprisals against entire villages. Similar to the Herero War in Southwest Africa, the military's objective was "total annihilation" of the enemy. Because of its much vaster scale, however, Barbarossa's fusion of anti-Marxism, anti-Slavism, and anti-semitism, which combined mass starvation with the systematic elimination of the Soviet ruling strata and other "anti-German elements," would rival the decimation of native peoples that accompanied the colonization of the Americas and it would make the first German genocide pale by comparison. Yet in the Americas, murderous intent, although evident in numerous conflicts between Europeans and indigenous peoples, was not systematically applied from the top. In earlier overseas conquests, the deaths of millions of indigenous peoples because they lacked immunity to the diseases that Europeans brought with them, testified to the devastating consequences of European intervention. The Third Reich

[62] Christian Gerlach, *Krieg, Ernährung, Völkermord: Deutsche Vernichtungspolitik im Zweiten Weltkrieg* (Zürich and Munich: Pendo, 1998), 11–29; Alex J. Kay, *Exploitation, Resettlement, Mass Murder: Political and Economic Planning for German Occupation Policy in the Soviet Union, 1940–1941* (New York and Oxford: Berg, 2006), 61–2.

[63] Christian Streit, *Keine Kamaraden: deutsche Wehrmacht und die sowjetische Kriegsgefangenen 1941–1945* (Stuttgart: Deutsche Verlags-Anstalt, 1978), 28–61, 77–127.

stood out in its deliberate decision to destroy human lives, a policy that the commanding heights of the Nazi state orchestrated.

The contrast between the planning for Barbarossa and that for Africa could not have been more glaring. Advocates of overseas empire, spearheaded by the German Labor Front's Institute of Work Science, envisioned the imposition of apartheid between German colonial administrators and the "natives" to prevent miscegenation. Nevertheless, the proposals for Africa corresponded to the developmental paradigms of other European empires during the interwar period. By improving colonial infrastructures and the living standards of indigenous peoples, colonial rule would be sustained through negotiation instead of raw force. Instead of crass exploitation, functioning economies and reliable labor forces would produce for export. To ensure an adequate supply of labor, the Institute imagined the creation of nonproletarianized wage laborers, who would reside in communities supervised by German "white labor guardians." In turn, the guardians would oversee the education, well-being, and productivity of African workers. In addition to increasing the labor force by providing medical care for African women, the application of labor science would carefully regulate the supply and distribution of workers. Aside from a relatively few number of colonial administrators, missionaries, teachers, and health care professionals, Africa was seen less as a venue for German settlement, which would have opened the door to racial mixing, and more as the source of raw materials and food, which only a healthy native labor force could extract or produce.[64]

If the east was not Africa, neither was it simply the "atavistic relapse" to an earlier period of European colonization, as some historians have recently termed it.[65] Rather, *Lebensraum* was intended to solve contemporary obsessions, the perceived overpopulation of Slavs who jeopardized the German food supply, the chronic weaknesses of agriculture in the "Old Reich," the renovation of Germany's historically determined right to rule through settlement, and the final decisive triumph over the threat of annihilation by Germany's enemies, both internal and external. By capitalizing on the conquest of Nordic peoples or by unearthing the German blood

---

[64] Karsten Linne, "*Weisse Arbeitsführer*", 38–183. See also Robert Gerwarth and Stephan Malinowski, "Der Holocaust als "kolonialer Genozid"? Europäische Kolonialgewalt und nationalsozialistischer Vernichtungskrieg," *Geschichte und Gesellschaft* 33 (2007): 439–66.

[65] See Dirk van Laak's critique in, *Über alles in der Welt: Deutscher Imperialismus im 19. Und 20. Jahrhundert* (Munich: C.H. Beck, 2005), 149.

that could be extracted from the available Slavic mélange, the regime's plans proceeded beyond the murder and resettlement of "natives" to the biological recovery and expansion of Germandom. In addition to registering adults to determine their capacity for Germanization, the Race and Resettlement Office of the SS extended its mission to kidnapping "racially valuable" children for rearing by German families – some fifty thousand of them in southeastern Europe, Poland, and the Soviet Union alone. Be they the offspring of relationships between German soldiers and racially "suitable" Dutch, Danish, or Norwegian women, or Polish, Slovenian, Czech, Ukrainian, or White Russian children with the appropriate physical appearance and aptitude, or finally the children orphaned by German assaults against partisans, adoption by Germans would have been unimaginable in Southwest Africa where the possibility of extracting German blood did not exist.[66]

The impending invasion of the Soviet Union opened the floodgates of planning from the staff of the SS office for the Strengthening of Germandom (RKF), excited by the possibility of permanently resolving Germany's economic and population problems: the bottlenecks arising from transfer and resettlement in the annexed territories, overcrowding in the General Government, the inadequate resources to provision the conquests of 1940, and the Reich's own precarious shortages of raw materials and food. By the middle of July, 1941, three weeks after the invasion of the Soviet Union began, the rural development expert in the RKF, Konrad Meyer, submitted the first of three expanded versions of the General Plan East that would grow progressively more ambitious and radical over the next two years. The various iterations of the plan drew extensively from the ideas of the interdisciplinary specialists involved in the "eastern research" of the Weimar era.[67] Taken together, they proposed the expulsion of the vast majority of Slavs from Poland and the Soviet Union up to the Urals, for a total of some 31 million people, not including Jews. In some versions, up to 51 million people were to have been driven out. Following population transfers and the deliberate confiscation of food that would likely entail the physical annihilation of most of the population of eastern Europe, roughly five million ethnic German settlers would begin to replace the victims over a

[66] Isabel Heinemann, "'Until the Last Drop of Good Blood': The Kidnapping of 'Racially Valuable" Childen and Nazi Racial Policy in Occupied Eastern Europe," in Moses ed., *Genocide and Settler Society*: 244–66; and Heinemann, *Rasse, Siedlung*, 508–30.

[67] Wolfgang Wippermann, *Die Deutschen und der Osten: Feinbild und Traumland* (Darmstadt: Primus Verlag, 2007), 73–6.

generation, pushing Germany's ethnic boundary one thousand kilometers to the east.[68] Combining land drainage, reclamation, and modernization, SS planners initially envisioned self-sustaining German farms that would provide a decent livelihood for hard-pressed peasants and an abundant source of food for the Reich, and would remedy agrarian problems at home – rural landlessness, overcrowding, and peasant holdings too small to manage. Yet in keeping with the increasingly inflated expectations that would accompany an expanding empire after June of 1941, SS settlement plans evolved well beyond the historical aims of restoring the peasantry, preventing flight from the land, or erecting barriers between Germans and Slavs. Rather, they envisioned a biologically new society combined of Reich and ethnic Germans. In addition to populating living space, the revitalized *Volk* would be strong enough to resist future threats of degeneration.[69] As well as attracting Germans from overcrowded regions in the Old Reich and ethnic Germans scattered throughout the east and the globe, Dutch peasants, whom the SS presumed to be Germanic, would join them.[70]

During the 1930s, Nazi agricultural policy emphasized the revitalization of the German peasantry, whose position industrialization and urbanization had presumably weakened. The emergence of Herbert Backe and the additional accretions to Himmler's power resulted in a widened focus, balanced economies of agriculture, industry, crafts, commerce, and state service. The RKF drew deeply from a geographical imagination that was stimulated for decades by visions of the American frontier with its unlimited possibilities, and the historical migrations of Germans eastward, long-embedded in the collective memory of the German right.[71] Propelled by the desire to reenergize a model from the past, living space would heal a wounded and demoralized Germandom. Even in 1943, as Germany's military status grew weaker, Himmler and SS population experts continued to plan for German settlements that would extend from Burgundy and the Vosges mountains in Alsace to a line in the east that extended from

[68] On the General Plan East, see the documentation in Czesław Madajczyk ed., *Vom Generalplan Ost zum Generalsiedlungsplan* (Munich: K.G. Saur, 1994); Wasser, *Himmlers Raumplanung*; Rössler and Schleiermacher, 'Generalplan Ost;' Tooze, *Wages of Destruction*, 463–76; Aly and Heim, *Vordenker der Vernichtung*, 156–68; Heinemann, "Rasse, Siedlung, deutsches Blut," 359–76; and Mai, "Rasse und Raum," 302–19.

[69] Mai, "Rasse und Raum," 361–70.

[70] Koos Bosma, "Verbindungen zwischen Ost-und Westkolonisation," in Rössler and Schleiermacher, *Generalplan Ost*, 198–214.

[71] David Blackbourn, *The Conquest of Nature: Water, Landscape, and the Making of Modern Germany* (New York and London: W.W. Norton, 2006), 293–309.

MAP 5.2. The General Plan East (*Generalplan Ost*). Connected by a series of bases, the plan specified the Baltic regions, and the Crimea as prime areas for German settlement.

Source: Mark Mazower, *Hitler's Empire: How the Nazis Rule Europe* (London: Allen Lane, 2008), xxii.

the Waldaj plateau northwest of Moscow to the Sea of Azov. Although in the end the SS could not realize its institutional ambitions, the very attempt at their implementation uprooted and immiserated millions.

EUPHORIA AND DREAD: BARBAROSSA AND THE TENSIONS OF EMPIRE

A military coup against the pro-Axis government in Belgrade and Italy's military misadventure in Greece, which Mussolini launched in a fury against Hitler for having moved into the Romanian oil fields, necessitated the unwelcome diversion of Wehrmacht units to the Balkans. Nevertheless, the German war against Yugoslavia and Greece, which the führer launched in April of 1940, provided an ominous prelude to the Barbarossa campaign. Hitler's anger at Serbian officers, whose bitterness at Croatian influence in the Yugoslav government precipitated the coup just as it was on the verge of joining the Tripartite Pact, resulted in a punitive Blitzkrieg that exceeded the brutalities of the German campaign in the west. Luftwaffe attacks left Belgrade in ruins, while the Wehrmacht at Himmler's "suggestion" ferreted out "partisans," "saboteurs," "terrorists," Jews, and Communists for summary elimination. Such categories, interpreted capaciously, resulted in thousands of collective reprisals against civilians. Although the attack on Serbia was not initially planned as a racial war, the high proportion of Austrians among officers and enlisted men in the German occupation force, as well as among the civilian managers of the Serbian economy, predisposed the invaders to draconian measures as revenge for Serbia's role in the onset of the Great War. That, in turn, served as the foundation for even more extreme measures against Jews. If critical to the German war effort, the extraction of resources and securing the southeastern flank in preparation for the war against the Soviet Union, the war in the Balkans did not take long to expose the Nazi regime's ideological predilections.[72]

Like Czechoslovakia and Poland, Yugoslavia ceased to exist as a nation-state. The occupiers subdivided its regions as spoils for its Axis partners, especially Hungary and Bulgaria. Croatia, which became a German puppet state governed by the murderous fascist party, the Ustasha, was the exception. Fully 1.7 million Yugoslavs, two-thirds of them civilians

---

[72] Walter Manoschek, "Die Vernichtung der Juden in Serbien," in *Nationalsozialistische Vernichtungspolitik 1939–1945: Neue Forschungen und Kontroversen*, ed. Ulrich Herbert (Frankfurt am Main: Fischer Taschenbuch, 1998), 210–11.

including 65,000 Jews, died during the war. To be sure, Greece did not meet the same fate as Yugoslavia for its territory remained intact after a puppet government signed the armistice. Regardless, German plunder during the months that followed resulted in the deaths by famine of some 300,000 Greeks by the end of the war, which included a shortfall in the number of births because of hunger.[73] In addition to following the charge from above that they provision themselves at the expense of the local population, German soldiers pilfered food and furnishings, secure in the knowledge that their plunder would go unpunished. German corporations, which operated through the economics staff of the Wehrmacht, acquired the entire output of Greek mines, and assumed control of virtually the entire Greek industrial plant.

Despite the postponement arising from the diversion of troops to the Balkans and a late spring in Russia, the regime proceeded with its plan to attack the Soviet Union. In so doing, it adopted the nickname of the red-bearded, twelfth-century Holy Roman Emperor Frederick I Hohenstaufen, "Frederick Barbarossa," whose reign combined the solidification of royal power and the empire's consolidation with a crusading zeal that cost him his life in the Holy Land. Appropriately, Operation Barbarossa would follow its namesake by destroying the "infidel" and completing the German nation. A fixture of radical nationalist myth since the late nineteenth century, "Barbarossa" fused anti-Bolshevism with the yearning for ethnic salvation.[74] Launched at dawn on June 22, 1941, the anniversary of Napoleon's invasion of 129 years earlier, three army groups totaling three million soldiers advanced across the largely unattended Soviet border. The führer saw no need to bother with a formal declaration of war. With the weight of the past upon it, the Wehrmacht's Army Group North followed the route of the Teutonic Knights and the Hanseatic traders along the Baltic coast, on its way to its premier destination, Leningrad.[75]

Here and there, noted an SD internal situation report four days after the invasion began, some Germans wondered aloud whether their leader had bitten off more than he could chew. How would it be possible to avoid the fate of Napoleon? How could Germany administer such a vast

---

[73] Mark Mazower, *Inside Hitler's Greece: The Experience of Occupation, 1941–44* (New Haven and London: Yale University Press, 1993), 23–41.

[74] See Ian Kershaw, *The 'Hitler Myth': Image and Reality in the Third Reich* (Oxford: Clarendon Press, 1987), 15–47.

[75] John Keegan, *The Second World War* (New York: Viking, 1989), 181–2.

space with such diverse populations?[76] Nazi visions of settlement in the vast expanses of Russia held less appeal for many Germans, who feared Bolshevism more than they dreamed of repeating Medieval conquests.[77] Nevertheless, reported Victor Klemperer, the Germans he observed greeted the news with "general cheerfulness." If not as obsessed with *Lebensraum* as the Nazi leadership, the thrill of victory could not help but conjure up visions of empire. "Mood: 'Triumphant we shall conquer France, Russia and the whole wide world'....A new entertainment, a prospect of new sensations, the Russian war is a source of pride for people, their grumbling of yesterday is forgotten...." Consistent with his unhappy fascination with the hyperbolic, partially Americanized language of the Third Reich, Klemperer contrasted the understated and Spartan reports of the army during World War I to the bombast of the Nazis, "Military bulletin on the seventeenth from the East: 'Nine million are facing one another in a battle whose scale surpasses all historical imagination.' Bialystok was recently 'the greatest battle of attrition and annihilation in world history.' Curse the superlative, Barnum-cf. the style of army reports in 1914."[78] If accurately conveying the size of the Barbarossa undertaking, the regime's pronouncements revealed its boundless utopian expectations, as Klemperer later put it in more formal prose, "The bulletins of the Third Reich," he wrote, "start off in a superlative mode from the very outset...until everything becomes literally measureless, twisting the fundamental quality of military language, its discipline exactitude, into its very opposite, into fantasy and fairy-tale."[79]

During the first weeks of the campaign, the German armies progressed with astonishing speed, seemingly supporting the expectations of the führer and the Wehrmacht high command. Because it was rotten to the core "Jewish Bolshevism" would collapse like a house of cards and spare the German armies of Napoleon's miserable fate during the winter of 1812–1813. By the end of the first week, Army Group North had taken Latvia and Lithuania. Army Group Center, wherein the preponderance of

[76] *Meldungen aus dem Reich: Die geheimen Lageberichte des Sicherheitsdienst der SS 1938–1945*, ed. Heinz Boberach (Herrsching: Pawlak, 1984), vol. 7, no. 197, 26 June 1941.

[77] Wippermann, *Die Deutschen und der Osten*, 70.

[78] Victor Klemperer, *I Will Bear Witness: A Diary of the Nazi Years, 1933–1941*, trans. Martin Chalmers (New York: Viking, 1998), entries of June 22 and July 18, 1941, 390–1, 421.

[79] Victor Klemperer, *The Language of the Third Reich: LTI-Lingua Tertii Imperii: A Philologist's Notebook*, trans. Martin Brady (London and New York: Continuum, 2000), 217.

German troops were concentrated, and Army Group South had advanced well into Belorussia and Ukraine, respectively. That Stalin was ill-prepared for the German Blitzkrieg resulted from his belief that Hitler would not risk a two-front war immediately, even though he certainly knew that the Germans were amassing troops on the western border. Yet neither Stalin nor Soviet intelligence understood that the German build-up represented the majority of German divisions, and neither appreciated the Wehrmacht's capabilities. Soviet errors enabled the German rout, as did massive desertions from the Red Army and the impact of Stalin's purges on the military leadership.[80] By the end of July, the high command of the Wehrmacht confidently asserted that eighty-nine of the Soviet Union's 164 divisions had been either partially or totally destroyed, along with thousands of aircraft, tanks, and heavy artillery. Cities, such as the Belorussian capital of Minsk, were almost totally destroyed. In addition to suffering staggeringly high numbers of killed and wounded, the Soviet armies lost thousands upon thousands of POWs, who would suffer a miserable fate. The German high command had already decided that its treatment of Soviet captives, redefined as "commissars," would not adhere to the Geneva Convention. Out of some 5,700,000 Red Army soldiers whom the Germans captured between 1941 and 1945, some 3,300,000 million, or 57.5 percent, died in captivity.[81] Most succumbed as the direct result of the Hunger Plan, for like feeding Soviet civilians, feeding Soviet prisoners would unnecessarily deprive Germans of food.

To follow Barbarossa's progress, Hitler decamped to his new field headquarters, named the "Wolf's Lair," in East Prussia, shortly after the invasion began. Included in his entourage were scribes assigned to record the führer's late-night reflections, most of which centered on the place of the Nazi regime in the history of world empires. Hitler's dictations were to become the archive for a subsequent history of the "Thousand Year Reich." Beginning with the first entry from July 5, 1941, Hitler articulated his deep contempt for the Russians, who did not "incline toward a higher form of society." Although Russia had established a state to mimic

[80] Evan Mawdsley, *Thunder in the East: The Nazi-Soviet War 1941–1945* (London; Hodder Arnold, 2005), 32–7; Karel C. Berkhoff, *Harvest of Despair: Life and Death in Ukraine under Nazi Rule* (Cambridge, MA and London: Belknap Press of Harvard University Press, 2004), 12.

[81] Streit, *Keine Kamaraden*, 128–90; and "Die Behandlung und Erforderung sowjetischen Kriegsgefangenen," in *Gegen das Vergessen: Der Vernichtungskrieg gegen die Sowjetunion 1941–1945*, eds. Klaus Meyer and Wolfgang Wippermann (Frankfurt am Main: Haag Herschen 1992); Kay, *Exploitation, Resettlement, Mass Murder*, 159.

western forms of political organization, "it is not in fact," he continued, "a system which is either congenial or natural to her." Because the Russians were incapable of sustained organization, they were at the mercy of "an instinctive force that invariably leads [them] back to the state of nature." Using two remarkable analogies, Hitler likened the Russians as follows:

People sometimes quote the case of the horses that escaped from a ranch in America, and by some ten years later had formed huge herds of wild horses. It is so easy for an animal to go back to its origins! For the Russian, the return to the state of nature is a return to primitive forms of life. The family exists, the female looks after her children, like the female of the hare, with all the feelings of the mother. But the Russian doesn't want anything more. His reaction against the constraint of the organized State (which is always a constraint, since it limits the liberty of the individual) is brutal and savage like all feminine reactions. When he collapses and should yield, the Russian bursts into lamentations. This will to return to the state of nature is exhibited in his revolutions. For the Russian, the typical form of revolution is nihilism.[82]

What would be the benefits for Germans? Casting his eyes over the empires of history, Hitler envisioned a future of unbounded security and prosperity befitting the master race. If Russia were to become the German equivalent of India for the British, the centerpiece of an empire, a German-dominated Europe would replace America as "the country of boundless possibilities," which despite huge productivity no longer had a future. "Everything about the behaviour of American society reveals that it's half Judaised, and the other half negrified." Yet there was no greater measure of lasting achievement for Hitler than Imperial Rome. The granite-based classical monumentalism, which Albert Speer was simultaneously drawing on to transform Berlin into the imperial capital of "Germania," would leave one with "the feeling that one is visiting the master of the world. One will arrive there along wide avenues containing the Triumphal Arch, the Pantheon of the Army, the Square of the People – things to take your breath away! It's only thus that we shall succeed in eclipsing our only rival in the world, Rome." Moreover, in Hitler's view, Rome had promoted racial awareness "in the days of her glory," guarding against "any racial adulteration," and its warrior culture enabled its place in history until it delegated much of its defense to non-Roman tribes, who turned the tables on it. Above all, Rome unified its empire by constructing roads and reclaiming marshlands, which allowed it to colonize vast

---

[82] *Hitler's Table Talk 1941–1944: His Private Conversations*, ed. H.R. Trevor-Roper, trans. Norman Cameron and R.H. Stevens (New York: Enigma Books, 2000), 3–4.

spaces. Now Germany would do the same. Its super-highways would link countless villages of settlement, allowing not only expanded possibilities for tourism, especially to Croatia and the Crimea, but also permit a high standard of living for the master race, "material amenities" through the benefits of mass production and the labor of colonized peoples:

The mistress of the house must be set free from all the minor chores that waste her time. Not only must the children's play-gardens be near the houses, but the mother must not even be compelled to take her children there herself. All she should have to do is to press a button for the woman in charge to appear immediately. No more refuse to take downstairs, no more fuel to carry up. In the morning, the works of the alarm-clock must even switch on the mechanism that boils the water. All these little inventions that lighten the burden of life must be set to work.[83]

Subsequently, Hitler drew the practical consequences of his placement of Russians among the lesser races that were incapable of creative labor, higher forms of organization, and commitment to the whole rather than to the self. While Nordic peoples would populate and Europeanize the Russian steppe, where modern roads would connect German settlements and transform it into "one of the loveliest gardens in the world," the "Jew, that destroyer," would be driven out and Russian villages would be allowed to "fall to pieces without intervening. And above all, no remorse on this subject! We're not going to play at children's nurses; we're absolutely without obligations as far as these people are concerned." Regarding public health, "there is no need whatsoever to extend to the subject races the benefits of our own knowledge. This would result only in an enormous increase in local populations, and I absolutely forbid the organization of any sort of hygiene or cleanliness crusades in these territories." According to Hitler, the conquerors had only one obligation, "to Germanize this country by the immigration of Germans, and to look upon the natives as Redskins." Alluding to the probable fate of the conquered, the führer dismissed them with a shrug, "I don't see why a German who eats a piece of bread should torment himself with the idea that the soil that produces this bread has been won by the sword. When we eat wheat from Canada, we don't think about the despoiled Indians."[84]

The initial euphoria of the Soviet campaign, however, gave way to dread by the end of August in the high command's recognition that it

[83] Ibid., 53, 188, 81, 563, 435, 537–8, 5, 347–8.
[84] Ibid., 68–9, 425.

FIGURE 5.4. Albert Speer's model of the proposed reconstruction of Berlin, renamed "Germania," as befitting a world capital. This photo shows the north-south axis beginning with the south railway station at the bottom, proceeding through a new victory arch that would dwarf the Arch de Triomphe in Paris, and ending at the top of the photo with the Great Hall and its disproportionately sized dome. *Source*: Bundesarchiv Koblenz, Bild 146III-373.

had seriously underestimated the enemy. The Red Army's surprising resistance at Smolensk on the Dnieper River roughly 250 miles west of Moscow proved that the Soviet Union could produce enough reserves to replace its losses. The Wehrmacht had neither defeated the Red Army on its western frontier, nor had it accurately estimated its size. It had not appreciated the willingness of Soviet soldiers to fight on, despite the desertions, having been raised in a culture that had been on a war footing since well before the Bolshevik Revolution.[85] No doubt Soviet losses had been catastrophic. Stalin lost over 175 divisions by the end of 1941, most of them between June and the end of September. Yet German losses from June 22 through the end of August, 1941, exceeded those that of the period between September, 1939, and the end of May, 1941 – 185,000, as opposed to the 102,000 in the earlier campaigns.[86] By the end of 1941, fully one-quarter of the personnel of the German army was recorded as having been killed, wounded, or missing in action. The Germans were able to press deeper into Soviet territory, taking the Ukrainian capital of Kiev on September 19th, capturing some 665,000 Soviet soldiers in the process. That victory came after wrangling between the führer and his generals, in which Hitler insisted upon taking the industrial and economic resources of the western Soviet Union before concentrating on Moscow.[87] The capture of Kiev seemingly opened the door to prized possessions, the Donets industrial basin near Kharkov with its rich coal seams, and beyond that the oil reserves of the Caucasus. Leningrad, the target of Army Group North, was already under a horrendous siege, one that would remain in force for two and one-half years at the cost of 600,000 lives. Yet even leaving aside the difficulty of reconciling economic and political objectives, the high command confronted major problems, not the least of which were the Soviet partisan units who bedeviled German troops from the rear. Shortages in manpower had a negative impact, as did German supply lines that were stretched to the limit. Unexpectedly heavy fall rains, which turned primitive Soviet roads into impenetrable muck, made matters worse. Finally able to push onto Moscow in October, the German offensive by Christmas was stalled in conditions so frigid that frostbite put many German soldiers out of commission. Thus, what had begun as a Blitzkrieg had now been transformed into a war of attrition, much like the western front of the Great War, which

[85] Mark Edele and Michael Geyer, "States of Exception: The Nazi-Soviet War as a System of Violence, 1939–1945," in *Beyond Totalitarianism: Stalinism and Nazism Compared*, eds. Michael Geyer and Sheila Fitzpatrick (Cambridge: Cambridge University Press, 2009), 361–7.

[86] Mawdsley, *Thunder in the East*, 85–6; Kershaw, *Nemesis*, 407–19; Gerd R. Überschar, "The Military Campaign," in *Hitler's War in the East: A Critical Assessment*, eds. Rolf-Dieter Müller and Gerd R. Überschar (New York and Oxford: Berg, 2002), 73–205.

[87] Tooze, *Wages of Destruction*, 457.

was itself the product of unrealistic timetables and inflated expectations. Yet, rather than temper the predisposition to ethnic cleansing and mass murder by machine gun or starvation, the German invaders became even more brutal as they proved unable to defeat an enemy whose staggering losses belied its determination to fight to the death.[88]

Similar to the campaign in Poland, Barbarossa combined the murderous talents of the Wehrmacht and the SS, especially the mobile assault units assigned to each army group, whose task was to liquidate all those whom the Commissar Order identified as carriers of "Asiatic-Jewish-Bolshevism." Unlike the campaigns in Poland or France, however, where officers intermittently objected to atrocities, few scruples arose this time around. If the campaigns in the west and the Balkans gave evidence of mounting brutalization, Hitler's explicit orders for Barbarossa guaranteed that no quarter would be taken. Wehrmacht units usually did not hesitate to collaborate with the mobile killing squads and assorted police battalions in rounding up and murdering "commissars," whose numbers included those who simply failed to follow a German order or did little more than distribute leaflets. Reprisals against entire villages, as punishment for "sheltering" suspected enemy guerrillas, took place with increasing regularity. Consistent with the preventive war that was Barbarossa, to attack the Soviet Union before the Soviet military and industry could defeat Germany, German troops on the ground killed Soviets because of what the "Asiatic-Jewish" Soviets might do to the Germans if they remained alive. The unprecedented violence unleashed against POWs and civilians in the rear went beyond actions against "unruly natives,"[89] for this was no ordinary war. Barbarossa was, according to the Nazi leadership, the SS, and the majority of Wehrmacht field commanders, an apocalyptic struggle for existence between the German and the Slav, and between the Germans and "Jewish Bolshevism." Echoing the historical evolution of German nationalism, the prospect of annihilation coexisted with the euphoria of triumph.

The Barbarossa campaign aimed at total victory and the subjugation of local populations. Yet contrary to Hitler's professed admiration for the British rule of India, which he claimed would be his model in the east, this particular undertaking eschewed indirect rule. Aside from

---

[88] See Omer Bartov, *Hitler's Army* (New York and Oxford, 1991), and the critique of Bartov's thesis in Edele and Geyer, "States of Exception," 357.

[89] Wendy Lower, *Nazi Empire-Building and the Holocaust in the Ukraine* (Chapel Hill and London: University of North Carolina Press, 2005), 67–8.

FIGURE 5.5. The bodies of five civilians executed by German forces hang from the balcony of a building in an unidentified Soviet city, ca. November 1941. Unable to defeat the Soviet Union quickly, German assaults against suspected Soviet "partisans" testified to the increasing desperation of the Barbarossa campaign.
Source: USHMM, photograph #66702, courtesy of David Mendels.

seeking out ethnic Germans with sufficient qualifications for subaltern positions, the occupation failed to exploit the hostility of ethnic groups toward the Soviet Union, which would have served as the basis for collaboration between subject peoples and their new overlords. In line with its reluctant and haphazard efforts to recruit locals for administrative positions, the regime made no effort to educate indigenous elites, as was the practice of other European imperialist powers, for doing so would invite resistance.[90] To be sure, as it quickly became clear in the annexed territories, civil administrations could not do without Polish labor even as they became "German" by virtue of generous DVL rankings. Nor could Hans Frank, despite violating his own regulations, do without the thousands of Poles in the General Government, who collected taxes, supervised the harvest, distributed food, managed the forests, and maintained highways and railroads.[91] Yet assigning positions to Slavs with the potential to challenge German authority was more problematic. Thus, organizations such as the Organization of Ukrainian Nationalists (OUN), which had high hopes that Germany would support their drive for independence, received a rude awakening when the occupiers privileged ethnic Germans for subaltern positions such as mayors, elders, collective farm leaders, shopkeepers, and militia chiefs. Only because so few ethnic Germans in Ukraine possessed the skills necessary for such positions, did the occupation begrudgingly loosen its rules.[92]

In accordance with the Hunger Plan, the occupation proceeded with the elimination of "useless eaters," beginning with Red Army POWs. POWs whom the Germans determined were literate were immediately shot on the theory that they were most likely Bolsheviks. Otherwise, the racist contempt toward "Asiatic Russians" propelled the genocidal massacre of officers and enlisted men. The victims were transported to the rear either on foot in "death marches" or in railway cars poorly protected from the elements. They were subsequently and unceremoniously

---

[90] Gerwarth and Malinowski, "Holocaust als" kolonialer Genozid?, 458.

[91] Mazower, *Hitler's Empire*, 448–9.

[92] Lower, *Nazi Empire Building*, 38–43, 50–2; Martin Dean, *Collaboration in the Holocaust: Crimes of the Local Police in Belorussia and the Ukraine, 1941–44* (New York: St. Martin's Press, 2000), esp. 105–18; Bernhard Chiari, "Grenzen deutscher Herrschaft: Voraussetzungen und Folgen der Besatzung in der Sowietunion," in *Die Deutsche Reich under der Zweiten Weltkrieg*, vol. 9, *Zweiter Halbband: Ausbeutung, Deutungen, Ausgrenzung*, ed. Militärgeschichtlicher Forschungsamt (Munich: Deutsche Verlags-Anstalt, 2005), 949.

FIGURE 5.6. A mass grave for the bodies of Soviet POWs, after June 22, 1941. Owing to the Third Reich's ruthless occupation plans, starvation and disease claimed the lives of over 2 million Soviet POWs by early 1942.
Source: USHMM, photograph #50178.

deposited in transit or permanent camps with little to no provisioning. Not surprisingly, death rates spiraled. The Wehrmacht and SD brutally repelled the repeated attempts by sympathetic Ukrainian civilians to smuggle food to prisoners from the abundant harvest of 1941.[93] Observed the physician Zygmunt Klukowski, a transport of fifteen thousand Soviet POWs that crept through his home city of Sczbrzeszyn in the Zamość region of Poland was a picture of horror. "They all looked like skeletons, just shadows of human beings, barely moving...They looked like starved animals, not like people." Fighting for scraps of food thrown to them by sympathetic Polish Christians and Jews, according to Klukowski, the prisoners ignored the blows rained upon them by their German overseers, as did the bystanders who fed the victims. "Some crossed themselves and knelt, begging for food...This unbelievable handling of human beings is only possible under German ethics."[94]

[93] Christian Gerlach, *Kalkulierte Mord: Die deutsche Wirtschafts-und Vernichtungspolitik in Weissrussland 1941 bis 1944* (Hamburg: Hamburger Edition, 1999) 774–859; Berkhoff, *Harvest of Despair*, , 89–113.
[94] Klukowski, *Diary*, 173.

In light of the regime's priority, which was to encourage its armies to live off the land at the expense of the conquered, maltreatment was not only condoned, it was also actively encouraged. By February of 1942, a staggering 2 million out of the 3.3 million Soviet POWs had already died in transit or permanent POW camps.[95] Others were deported to Germany or Austria where they ended up in concentration camps, such as Buchenwald, Dachau, Mauthausen, and Sachsenhausen. There they faced execution by shooting or gassing after having received the sort of devious promises of work that temporarily assuaged the fears of Jews deported to death camps. In September of 1941, six hundred Soviet prisoners, who had been deported to Auschwitz, were among the first victims of a new and more effective method of gassing, Zyklon B. Only when it became clear by the fall of 1941 that the Soviet Union would not be defeated quickly did the Reich leadership deploy the surviving POWs as forced laborers. Even that begrudged decision promised sufficient misery as to minimize the odds for survival.

The conquerors treated civilians nearly as lethally, restricting their livelihoods and depriving them of basic necessities. In keeping with the predilections of the Reich's senior leadership, Soviet cities received harsh treatment. Like Kiev, which in September of 1941 was sealed off from the surrounding countryside to prevent peasants from delivering food, provisioning urban dwellers was considered an unaffordable luxury. Turning the iconic historical moment of German humiliation against the enemy of the present, Göring serenely remarked that, "this war will witness the greatest starvation since the Thirty Years War."[96] In contrast to most other European empires, where even in cases with astronomically high death rates, the securing of labor assumed top priority, increasing the supply and training of native labor was secondary to the deliberate attrition of subject populations until sheer exigency dictated otherwise. In cases such as Belorussia, which were not designated as areas for German settlement, the demands of total war sanctioned the ruthless plunder of food and raw materials and the transfer of forced labor to Germany. To provision themselves, soldiers, either individually or in groups, stole with abandon from peasants, seizing livestock, draft animals, food, wagons, and clothing. Even the victims' modest property was fair game. Yet the unorganized theft of soldiers would not by itself have provisioned the

[95] Götz Aly, *Hitler's Beneficiaries: Plunder, Racial War, and the Nazi Welfare State*, trans. Jefferson Chase (New York: Metropolitan Books, 2006), 175.
[96] Berkhoff, *Harvest of Despair*, 168.

occupation without the layers of the civilian administration, which took over Soviet collective farms to requisition food supplies. The Germans responded to popular resistance to their actions with all the weapons at their disposal, and the results were devastating. Between the beginning of Barbarossa in mid-1941 and the end of 1943, German seizures of agricultural commodities totaled over 106 million grain units in nutritional value, negatively affecting over 21 million Soviet citizens.[97]

In their letters home, many German soldiers betrayed their contempt for the conquered, seemingly unaware of the inconsistency between the consequences of their collective looting and their disdain for the poverty that they witnessed. On the one hand, the seemingly endless expanses of Soviet territory became a cornucopia for exploitation, in which the regime's rules of engagement laid claim to everything of value. On the other hand, soldiers frequently derided the "Soviet Paradise" for having failed to live up to communist promises of plenty for its citizens, expressing disgust at the impoverishment, filth, and primitiveness that they claimed to have witnessed, conditions to which Germans themselves contributed. The racism of their observations was explicit. In addition to characterizing Russia as "Asiatic," the frightening detritus of the Mongol invasions, the "destructive poison" of "Jewish Bolshevism" had incited those Slavic "subhumans" by promising a "workers' paradise." Nor did soldiers confine their impressions to writing. Snapshots, photo albums, and films abundantly documented their barbarous activities, showing that they had little to fear from their superiors as they murdered and pillaged.[98] Many soldiers, finally, welcomed the Nazi colonial project, envisioning settlements of armed German farmers, who would exploit the labor of Slavic helots. Some even imagined themselves as the landowner-settlers of the future.[99] Such cockiness did not endure as the euphoria of early victories faded and the reality of an impending and disastrous defeat became clearer.[100] The justifications for German violence, however,

---

[97] Aly, *Hitler's Beneficiaries*, 177–8. For food requisitioning in White Russia, see Gerlach, *Kalkulierte Mord*, 253–65.

[98] Despite the controversy over the misattributions of some of the photographs in it, *The German Army and Genocide: Crimes Against War Prisoners, Jews, and Other Civilians, 1939–1944*, ed. Hamburg Institute for Social Research (New York: The New Press, 1999), effectively depicts the German military *Alltag*.

[99] Sven Oliver Müller, "Nationalismus in der deutschen Kriegsgesellschaft 1939–1945," in *Die Deutsche Kriegsgesellschaft 1939 bis 1945*, Zweiter Halbband, *Ausbeutung, Deutungen, Ausgrenzung*, ed. Jörg Echternkamp (Munich: Deutsche Verlags-Anstalt, 2005), 79–80.

[100] Katrin A. Kilian, "Kriegsstimmungen. Emotionen einfacher Soldaten in Feldpostbriefen," in *Deutsche Kriegsgesellschaft*, Zweitern Halbband, 251–88.

did not evaporate. Only the grounds changed from contempt to dread as the perception of a life-or-death struggle meant the extreme escalation of violence.[101]

Following the Red Army's liberation of the Ukraine in 1944, the Soviet war correspondent Vasily Grossman, relaying reports received from eyewitnesses, described the racist hubris of the Germans who once occupied his home city of Berdichev, a racism that resulted in behavior that aped the stereotypes they held of Slavs:

In these villages, the Germans used to relieve themselves in the halls and on the doorsteps, in the front gardens, in the front of the windows of houses. They were not ashamed of girls and old women. While eating, they disturbed the peace, laughing loudly. They put their hands into dishes they were sharing with their comrades, and tore boiled meat with their fingers. They walked naked around the houses, unashamed in front of the peasants, and they quarreled and fought about petty things. Their gluttony, their ability to eat twenty eggs in one go, or a kilo of honey, a huge bowl of smetana, provoked contempt in the peasants... Germans who had been withdrawn to the rear villages were searching for food from morning till night. They ate, drank alcohol and played cards. According to what prisoners said and [what was written in] letters on dead German soldiers, the Germans considered themselves the representatives of a higher race forced to live in savage villages. They thought that in the wild eastern steppes one could throw culture aside. 'Oh, that's real culture,' I heard dozens of people say. 'And they used to say that Germans were cultivated people.'[102]

The introspective Wehrmacht private, Willy Peter Reese, who despite the initial German victories expressed his fear that Russia was an "everlasting Good Friday" to the soldiers in his unit as they marched slowly to Golgotha, dismissed the ordinary canons of morality as no longer useful in a mysterious and frightening land. Stealing from muzhiks was justified. "We were the victors. War excused our thefts, encouraged cruelty, and the need to survive didn't go around getting permission from conscience."[103]

There were voices among the occupiers who saw the pitfalls of an occupation policy geared solely to economic exploitation and the disregard for the lives harmed by it, even if pragmatic considerations rather

[101] Edele and Geyer, "States of Exception": 358–9.

[102] Vasily Grossman, *A Writer at War: Vasily Grossman with the Red Army, 1941–1945*, ed. And trans., Antony Beevor and Luba Vinogradova (New York: Pantheon Books, 2005), 249.

[103] Willy Peter Reese, *A Stranger to Myself: The Inhumanity of War: Russia, 1941–1944*, trans. Michael Hofman, ed. Stefan Schmitz (New York: Farrar, Strauss and Giroux, 2005), 67, 35.

than morality informed their concerns. Those voices that grew louder as the progress of Barbarossa slowed. Unlike Backe and Göring, they recognized the multiethnic complexity of the Soviet Union and the widespread resentment against Bolshevism among the Soviet Union's subject peoples. They proposed a less grotesque version of imperialism that believed Germany should exploit the Soviet regime's unpopularity and the deep religious and ethnic divisions of the Soviet empire to its own advantage, an imperialism that resembled the tactics that the Germans used during World War I. Could not Germany claim, as it had with good effect at the beginning of Barbarossa, that its objective was liberation and not subjugation? Hitler's virulently anti-Bolshevik appointee as Reich Minister for the Occupied Eastern Territories, the Baltic German "old fighter" Alfred Rosenberg, whom Hitler first met in Munich, personified this line of thinking. He wanted to combine the Baltic states and White Russia in a protectorate, establish the Ukraine as an enlarged, semi-autonomous state, and create a federation of the Caucasus and much reduced "Muscovy" that would serve as the dumping ground for "undesirables." Given the mass starvation in the Ukraine, which resulted from the Stalinist collectivization of agriculture and the NKVD death squads that executed thousands of Latvians, Lithuanians, and Estonians during the Soviet takeover of 1940–1941, not to mention the virulent antisemitism that was common on the Soviet Union's western borders, Rosenberg was not wrong to think that the Germans might be greeted as liberators. Seeking the voluntary cooperation of the peripheral nationalities of the Soviet Union, Rosenberg reasoned, would significantly aid the German colonization of the east.[104]

Similar arguments arose from the foreign and interior ministries, from public intellectuals, and even the SS, which suggested that the German leadership of Europe would be more effective if it permitted a degree of national autonomy, or if the German "New Order" was more effectively recast as a partnership. The need for greater latitude grew more urgent as Germany's enemies offered a brighter future for Europe's peoples than that conveyed by the practices of the Third Reich. Mussolini pleaded with his ally to offer an alternative to Roosevelt's and Churchill's Atlantic Charter of August, 1941, which promised national self-determination,

---

[104] Michael Kellogg, *The Russian Roots of Nazism: White Émigrés and the Making of National Socialism, 1917–1945* (Cambridge: Cambridge University Press, 2005), 263. See especially, Kay, *Exploitation*, who provides a thorough treatment of the division between the economic and political side of the occupation.

freedom from want and fear, equal access to the world's raw materials, free trade, economic cooperation and the advancement of social welfare, national borders determined by the wishes of the affected peoples, and, of course, the destruction of Nazism. Thereafter, military reverses in the Soviet Union, especially after early 1943 when the Red Army pushed the Wehrmacht westward, prompted even Goebbels to proclaim Germany as the savior of western civilization from "Asiatic Bolshevism."[105]

Nevertheless, such relatively conventional proposals could not compete with the führer's imperial vision wherein German survival was to be placed *über alles*. If those interests gobbled up the property and ended the lives of the subjugated, so be it. They could not compete with the utopian agenda of Himmler, whose control over ethnic cleansing enhanced his power. They could not retard the aggressive expansion of Göring's Reichswerke, which absorbed captive heavy industries, thus laying the groundwork for a huge industrial basin that would stretch from central Germany to the Donets Basin, the heavy industrial and mining region of the Ukraine. German corporate interests assumed control of Soviet firms that Göring had not grabbed for himself, particularly in coal, iron and steel, and engineering. The Business Administration Main Office of the SS developed its own enterprises powered by concentration camp and civilian forced labor, enterprises that included the design and construction of settlements for the "child-rich" German families.[106] Millions of German settlers would move into this vast territory to take the place of the even larger number of indigenous peoples, who would be deported, starved, or at best conscripted to toil on German farms or in German industries.

Even in regions that spawned the most fanciful dream worlds, such as the Crimea, the dreams evaporated in the face of Soviet resistance. Renamed the Gotengau, or "Goth District," because Aryan ancestors once inhabited it, the Crimea to Nazi leaders would become the site of new Rivieras and Monte Carlos, a German Hollywood, and a paradise for retired German soldier-settlers. Yet because the peninsula was never

---

[105] Mazower, *Hitler's Empire*, 245–54, 144–57, 320–1, and 553–5; and Birgit Kletzin, *Europa aus Rasse und Raum* (Münster, Hamburg, and London: LIT, 2002), 110–217. For the Charter, see the Avalon project at Yale Law School, http://avalon.law.yale.edu/subject_menus/wwii.asp. Accessed May 6, 2010.

[106] Richard Overy, "German Multi-Nationals and the Nazi State in Occupied Europe," in R.J. Overy, *War and Economy in the Third Reich* (Oxford: Clarendon Press, 1994), 315–42; Michael Thad Allen, *The Business of Genocide: The SS, Slave Labor, and the Concentration Camps* (Chapel Hill and London: University of North Carolina Press, 2002), 97–112,

safe from Soviet counterattack, the military did not turn it over to a civilian administration, and it called a halt to deportations.[107] Regardless, the Third Reich inflicted catastrophic damage. In Belorussia alone where the implementation of the Hunger Plan fell especially hard, well over two million died out of a population of 9.2 million. An additional one to one and one-half million fled the German invasion in 1941, while another two million were forcibly resettled. Three million were left homeless and around five thousand Belorussian villages and towns were wasted and depopulated. In addition to bearing the brunt of the Wehrmacht's initial assault on the Soviet Union, Belorussia suffered from an occupation policy that placed a priority on the murder and starvation of its urban population and the thorough requisition of its agriculture produced by a subjugated and dependent peasantry.[108] The loss of life in another primary battleground, the Ukraine, was nearly as high, especially from mass starvation.[109]

Instead of semi-autonomy or independence, which anti-Soviet Ukrainians especially expected and Rosenberg advocated, Ukraine was dismembered in line with the needs of German colonial administration. Eastern Galicia became a province of the General Government in Poland, while parts of its southern rim were transferred to Romania and renamed "Transnistria." The congenitally vicious Erich Koch, a veteran of the eastern front during World War I and the Upper Silesian Free Corps afterward, became Reich commissar over the remainder. Dismissive of Ukrainians as "niggers" (*Negervolk*), whom he exploited and repressed, Koch outmaneuvered Rosenberg to run his fiefdom on his own terms.[110] With equal dispatch, the Germans crushed aspirations to independence of the Baltic states, even though the SS considered Latvians and Estonians racially acceptable enough to serve in its units, especially those that massacred Jews. The Baltic states and Belorussia became the Reich Commissariat of the Eastern Lands (*Reichskommissariat Ostland*) under the leadership of yet another party apparatchik, Hinrich Lohse. Moreover, to a

---

[107] Norbert Kunz, *Die Krim unter deutscher Herrschaft 1941–1944: Germanisierungsutopie und Besätzungsrealität* (Darmstadt: Wissenschaftliche Buchgesellschaft, 2005), 15–53, 234–5.

[108] Christian Gerlach, "Deutsche Wirtschaftsinteressen, Besatzungspolitik und der Mord an den Juden in Weissrussland 1941–1943," in Herbert, *Nationalsozialistische Vernichtungspolitik*: 283; and Gerlach, *Kalkulierte Mord*, 1159.

[109] Berkhoff, *Harvest of Despair*, 164–86.

[110] Ralf Meindl, *Ostpressens Gauleiter. Erich Koch – eine politische Biographie* (Osnabruck: Fibre Verlag, 2007), 323–80

degree that the führer would likely have appreciated, the eastern-occupied territories become a frontier of unlimited possibilities for hundreds of party functionaries, who found positions in civil administrations that allowed them to prosper beyond their wildest dreams. A "master race" mentality that caused many to abuse and humiliate "subhumans" fused easily with the material comforts and increased status that came with empire. Military turning points, which began with the failure to reach Moscow in December of 1941, certainly necessitated modifications. They included the deployment of indigenous ethnic groups in Wehrmacht and Waffen SS divisions, or the increased use of "auxiliary volunteers" as supply troops and staffing for anti-Jewish "actions." The most notorious example of collaboration with the Germans was the creation of a Russian National Army under the leadership of General Andrei Vlasov, which Vlasov saw as the foundations of a "new Russia" without communism. Nevertheless, the only task that Hitler could conceive of assigning Vlasov was the encouragement of desertions from the Red Army. It took until September of 1944 when a German rout on the Soviet front became clear to Himmler, who as defeat approached sought a separate peace with London and Washington, to give Vlasov command of two divisions. In that capacity, he could be used in a future war between Germany, the British, and the Americans against the Soviet Union.

In the west and Scandinavia, the German occupation was comparatively milder. With the obvious exception of the Jews and political opponents, their peoples were ranked higher on the Nazi racial scale. Neither western nor northern Europe would, except for Alsace and Lorraine, become sites of German settlement. Unlike Czechoslovakia or Poland, which the Germans considered unworthy of statehood, the territorial nation-state remained in force while under occupation.[111] To be sure, before moving onto Denmark, Werner Best occupied his time in Paris as the RSHA's representative to the military occupation by devising ambitious plans to restructure western Europe according to races rather than nation states. Best proposed the incorporation of the Netherlands, Flanders, and French territory north of the Loire River into the Reich, the transformation of Wallonia and Brittany into protectorates, the merger of Northern Ireland with the Irish Republic, the creation of a decentralized British federation, and independence for the Basques, Catalonians, and Galicians of Spain. Yet, in addition to running up against the RSHA's priority of colonizing

---

[111] Mazower, *Hitler's Empire*, 586–7.

MAP 5.3. Europe at the end of 1941.
Source: David Blackbourn, *The Conquest of Nature: Water, Landscape and the Making of Modern Germany* (New York and London: W. W. Norton, 2006), 276.

and settling the east, Best's plans foundered in the face of resistance from the foreign office and the military, which continued to envision a western Europe of national states, albeit one that was suitably dominated by Germany.[112]

[112] Herbert, *Best*, 295–8.

Nevertheless, the Reich's aim of creating a "greater economic region" (*Grossraumwirtschaft*) to meet its own need for resources and labor power weakened the position of collaborators over time, despite widespread support for fascism and the discrediting of liberal democracy in the interwar period. As the prospects for a quick military victory in the Soviet Union receded, the pressure mounted on the Nazi regime to extract what could be extracted, even at the cost of losing whatever sympathy existed. Resistance movements sprang up in response to Germany's crass imperialism. Defeated nations such as Vichy France, where fascist sympathizers had fervently sought a partnership between equals with the Third Reich, were sorely disappointed by policies that refused even the pretense of equality among states. Hitler would hear of no other solution but subordination, even for the Nordic Norwegians and the Germanic Dutch. Even Denmark, which enjoyed an unusual degree of political latitude, was subjected to a permanent state of emergency in the summer of 1943 after Denmark's integration and subordination within the German currency bloc increased domestic unrest.

Whether directly or by proxy, the Nazi regime imposed the ruthless economics of colonialism. Although the east bore the brunt of the Reich's insatiable need for resources, Nazi Germany's acute shortage of manpower, which its impressive record in forcing women into the labor force could not assuage, meant that no part of occupied Europe would be spared its exactions.[113] The huge influx of foreign workers – some 13.5 million between 1939 and 1945, 11 to 12 million of them forced –[114] led to obsessions about liaisons between such laborers and Germans, which could threaten the purity of the race. Those fears gave as good a demonstration as any of the contradiction between Nazism's primary goal, the biological salvation of Germans, and the means to achieve it, the war to acquire permanent living space.[115] In addition to receiving wages well below those earned by Germans despite legal commitments to the contrary, and suffering higher deductions for taxes and social benefits, the

[113] See Tooze, *Wages of Destruction*, 514–5. Tooze overturns the long-held view among historians that the Third Reich, as compared to Britain and the United States, was reluctant to press German women into service because of the bad morale that could result.

[114] Mark Spoerer, "Die soziale Differenzierung der ausländischen Zivilarbeiter, Kriegsgefangenen und Häftlinge im Deutschen Reich," in *Die Deutsche Kriegsgesellschaft 1919 bis 1945, Zweiter Halbband: Ausbeutung, Deutungen, Ausgrenzung*, ed. Jörg Echternkamp (Munich: Deutsche Verlags-Anstalt, 2005), 575.

[115] Mazower, *Hitler's Empire*, 294–318.

nations that yielded foreign laborers in the first place were saddled with the burden of compensating their families for lost labor.[116] Moreover, the quality of treatment accorded to foreign workers depended on racial status. Russians, Poles, and Ukrainians especially became little more than conscripted slaves for German industry or for the Economics and Administrative Office of the SS. Their deaths from malnutrition and disease, although mitigated by better working conditions late in the war when labor was at an absolute premium, mattered little in light of the seemingly millions available to replace them.[117] If accused of "racial defilement," sexual relations with a German woman, their execution was a near certainty, especially if the worker was from the east. Yet even workers from nations allied with Nazi Germany, such as Italy, France, and Spain were hardly treated with kid gloves. The labor draft in France in 1942 significantly contributed to broadening the resistance beyond its Communist instigators. Volunteers who signed up for duty in the Reich as compensation for unemployment at home; the Italians, Greeks, and Spaniards who toiled on Germany's farms and in its factories, saw promises in their contracts of good wages, benefits, and annual trips home repeatedly violated.[118]

On top of dragooning labor, the Third Reich imposed huge reparations in the form of "occupation costs" and "accommodation services." In addition to exceeding the prewar budgets of occupied nations, those exactions went well beyond what was required to maintain German troops. The Nazi regime relied on a wartime debt-clearing system that by sleight of hand allowed German to retain foreign credits while Germany's suppliers received payment in local currency. Revenue obtained through occupation costs and accommodation services went to the purchase of everything from locomotives to motor vehicles to gold from Belgian colonies. The absorption of state-owned and Jewish-owned enterprises proceeded apace. Reich Credit Bank certificates allowed German soldiers to purchase foreign consumer goods at highly beneficial exchange rates, emptying shelves so rapidly that little remained for local people

[116] Aly, *Hitler's Beneficiaries*, 156–8.

[117] Mark Spoerer, "soziale Differenzierung," in Echternkamp, *Deutsche kriegsgesellschaft*, 500–1, 521, 527, 571,

[118] Wayne H. Bowen, *Spaniards in Nazi Germany: Collaboration in the New Order* (Columbia and London: University of Missouri Press, 2000), 103–56; Hans Mommsen and Manfred Grieger, *Das Volkswagenwerk und seine Arbeiter im Dritten Reich* (Düsseldorf: Econ Verlag, 1997), 711–99; Mazower, *Inside Hitler's Greece*, 73–9.

to purchase. The certificates proved especially useful in acquiring goods from countries such as France, where living standards were comparable or even higher than Germany's.[119] Despite visions of huge acquisitions, Germany was less successful in western Europe in using corporate capital to assume control over foreign industries, for privately owned companies simply transferred ownership to their offshore offices. Moreover, collaboration between French and German capitalists provided a measure of equality. In industries such as insurance, cars, textiles, and chemicals, joint ventures between French and Germans proved profitable and effective in keeping the Hermann-Göring Werke and the Nazi Party at bay.[120] Nevertheless, even Albert Speer's effort as armaments minister, following the sudden death of his predecessor of Fritz Todt, to promote economic cooperation persuaded few Belgians, Dutchmen, and Frenchmen that the leopard had really changed its spots, especially when the agents of the Nazi labor czar, Fritz Sauckel, relentlessly hunted down thousands to work for the Reich.

With the exception of the violence and pestilence that accompanied the settlement of the Americas, Barbarossa exceeded the worst atrocities inflicted by Europeans against subject peoples. And if one could argue that the diseases that killed millions of indigenous peoples across the Atlantic were the unintended by-product of colonialism, there is no doubt that the Third Reich intentionally created the conditions for massive loss of life in the east. The Nazi goal of racial engineering combined with the means to achieve it, war with Germany's rivals, escalated the violence. Even in the west where the conditions of occupation were less extreme, German conduct did nothing to strengthen the case of Nazis who proposed "partnerships" between the Third Reich and its subject peoples. Yet by the end of 1941, Germany had defeated neither Britain nor the Soviet Union, who were now joined by the United States. Despite the vast territory under the control of the Third Reich, the worried German civilians whom the SD monitored a few days after Barbarossa began were not wrong to fear the possibility of defeat. The tension among Germans would only grow

---

[119] Harold James, *The Deutsche Bank and the Nazi Economic War Against the Jews: The Expropriation of Jewish-Owned Property* (Cambridge: Cambridge University Press, 2001), 172–3; Aly, *Hitler's Beneficiaries*, 84–93, 136–7.

[120] R.J. Overy, "The Reichswerke 'Hermann Göring': A Study in German Economic Imperialism," in Overy, *War and Economy* 44–74; Tooze, *Wages of Destruction*, 380–93; Aly, *Hitler's Beneficiaries*, 136; Mazower, *Hitler's Empire*, 268–9. On the east, see Madajczyk, *Okkupationspolitik*, 551.

in proportion to the tenacity of the Soviet resistance.[121] What was the Nazi regime's answer? During the late summer and fall of 1941, actions in the field and decisions at the top signaled that the time had come to "settle accounts" with the "real" enemy, the Jew who used rival empires to destroy Germany.

[121] See in particular the astonishment at Soviet resistance in Leningrad, in *Meldungen*, vol. 8, no. 231, 23 October 1941, 2902.

6

The "Final Solution"

Global War and Genocide, 1941–1945

As the Nazi regime's anti-Jewish attacks before September of 1939 made clear, Nazi antisemitism was exclusionary and violent, all the more so for having fused popular hatreds and the sanction of a state that defined the expulsion of "Juda" as its first priority. Antisemitism only became more vicious with the growing threat of war. On January 30, 1939, the sixth anniversary of the Nazi assumption to power and nearly three months after the Crystal Night pogrom, Hitler delivered a two-hour speech to the Greater German Reichstag, which now included deputies from Austria and the Sudetenland. After the führer began by recalling the blood that generations had shed to achieve a greater Germany, Hitler cast himself in the role of "prophet." Infuriated by the international condemnation of the Reich's persecution of the Jews, he issued a warning: "Should the international Jewry of finance (*Finanzjudentum*) succeed, both within and beyond Europe, in plunging mankind into yet another world war, the result will not be a Bolshevization of the earth and the victory of Jewry, but the annihilation (*Vernichtung*) of the Jewish race (*Rasse*) in Europe." Having accused the "Jewish world enemy" of plotting to exterminate the German *Volk*, the führer articulated the Nazi leadership's conviction that the Jews dictated government policy in the nations that most directly threatened Germany, the Soviet Union, Great Britain, and the United States.[1] Unlike the Imperial German war of annihilation in Southwest

---

[1] Max Domarus, ed., *The Complete Hitler: A Digital Desktop Reference to His Speeches and Proclamations 1932–1945, Reden und Proklamationen 1932–1945*, vol. 3 (Wauconda, IL: Bolchazy-Carducci Publishers, 2007), 1047–71, quotation on p. 1449. See also Jeffrey Herf, *The Jewish Enemy: Nazi Propaganda during World War II and the Holocaust*

Africa against Herero and Nama "savages," the target in Hitler's address was the "Jew," the personification of Bolshevism and international capitalism, the global enemies who threatened Germany with extinction.

Despite Hitler's rhetoric, the Nazi regime's attempt at the total extermination of European Jews was not yet in play. The outbreak of war certainly increased the potential for genocide for German conquests brought millions more Jews into the orbit of the Third Reich, 1.7 million Jews in German-occupied Poland alone. Yet during the first two years of the conflict when its military victories seemed assured, the regime sought to "solve" its Jewish "problem" by deporting Jews to inhospitable places beyond the territories that Germans were to settle. Between September of 1939 and the fall of 1941, the various schemes that Nazi leaders proposed for resettling ethnic Germans and evacuating Jews and Slavs unfit for Germanization, took for granted that most of their victims would perish in unforgiving surroundings. Nevertheless, that cynical expectation did not yet achieve what would become the "final" solution, the physical elimination of every Jewish man, woman, and child as far as the Third Reich could reach. That would result from a confluence of roadblocks arising from the regime's colonialism: the logjams of settlers and expellees, the need to extract resources, and the mounting difficulties with its war, which by threatening Germany with the disaster that empire was supposed to prevent, "demanded" a more direct and systematic retaliation against the Jews. Barbarossa transformed the regime's "solution" to the Jewish "problem" into an orgy of killing that exceeded even the bloodletting visited upon the Slavs. The determination to kill Jews permeated every level of decision making and involved nearly every agency of the regime. If some questioned the wisdom of the regime's brutal occupation policies on pragmatic grounds, and advocated more conventional strategies of collaborating with subaltern peoples, the fate of the Jews prompted no such disagreement.

RESETTLEMENT AND RESERVATIONS: TERRITORIAL SOLUTIONS TO THE "JEWISH QUESTION," 1939–1941

After the defeat of Poland, the regime's ambitious plans for annexation, expulsion, and resettlement, spearheaded by Heinrich Himmler as the

(Cambridge, MA and London: Belknap Press of Harvard University Press, 2006), 50–91; and Adam Tooze, *The Wages of Destruction: The Making and Breaking of the Nazi Economy* (London: Allen Lane, 2006), 462.

newly named Reich Commissar for the Strengthening of Germandom, tried to realize long-standing dreams of reestablishing a German dominion in the east. Nevertheless, the scale of such a project, moving millions of Poles, Jews, and ethnic Germans within the exacting timetable that the Reichsführer SS stipulated, created enormous bottlenecks that repeatedly forced Himmler to postpone a final determination in the status of Jews. Even the order of September 21, 1939 by Himmler's deputy Heydrich, which mandated the concentration of Jews in urban ghettos within three to four weeks' time, a temporary palliative that would enable their deployment as forced labor and facilitate their deportation once a "permanent" solution was found, proved impossible to achieve. Heydrich's plan ran afoul of the Wehrmacht's chief of staff, Walther von Brauchitsch, who insisted for security and logistical reasons that the military should have a say in population transfers. In the meantime, Polish and Jewish property would be confiscated at will to enable the resettlement of ethnic Germans. Also in the interim, discussions continued as to the long-term disposition of the Jewish "question," during which several proposals arose to "rid" German territory of Jews by dumping them elsewhere. Although momentarily attractive, they would only be shelved as more pressing military, economic, and demographic concerns intervened.[2]

The first such project involved the planned resettlement of Jews from the old Reich, Austria, and the annexed territories to a transit camp near the town of Nisko on the River San near the eastern Galician border in the Lublin district of the General Government. The transit camp was to become the staging ground for resettlement in that region. Initiated by Hitler's direct order, the task of evacuation fell to the former vacuum salesman- turned-official in Heydrich's SD, the thirty-two-year-old Adolf Eichmann, who, like so many young men, saw National Socialism as an opportunity for adventure, advancement, and ideological fulfillment.

---

[2] Although they differ in their identification of turning points, the following recent works are indispensible to tracing the unfolding of the Final Solution: Götz Aly, *"Final Solution": Nazi Population Policy and the Murder of the European Jews*, trans. Belinda Cooper and Allison Brown (London: Arnold, 1999), 1–184; Christopher R. Browning with Jürgen Matthäus, *The Origins of the Final Solution: The Evolution of Nazi Jewish Policy, September 1939–March 1942* (Lincoln: University of Nebraska Press, 2004), 36–110; Saul Friedländer, *Nazi Germany and the Jews 1939–1945: The Years of Extermination* (New York: HarperCollins, 2007), 3–194; and Peter Longerich, *Politik der Vernichtung: Eine Gesamtdarstellung der nationalsozialistischen Judenverfolgung* (Munich and Zürich: Piper, 1998), esp. 419–586. For a superb analysis of recent scholarship on the Holocaust, see Peter Fritzsche, "The Holocaust and the Knowledge of Murder," *Journal of Modern History*, 80, no. 3 (2008): 594–613.

Having established a successful career in Vienna by exploiting the wave of antisemitic terror following the Anschluss to promote Jewish emigration, in which he had "encouraged" 150,000 Jews to emigrate in a single year, Eichmann's prospects might have dimmed without the new opportunities presented by the east.[3] As a result, he capitalized on the plan that Hitler and Heydrich authorized to concentrate the expelled Jews at the furthest reaches of German-controlled territory. In their view, the Nisko project would provide a more workable "solution" than previously unsuccessful attempts to deport them to the Soviet zone, whereupon the Soviets forcibly returned those whom they did not send to the NKVD's labor camps.

Beginning in October of 1939 with some nine hundred Jews from the town of the Protectorate, and 1,800 Jews from Vienna and Upper Silesia, Eichmann expanded his initiative to include Jews, Sinti, and Roma from the Reich, especially from Berlin. Although depositing their victims in a swampy field where they were forced to build barracks, and cynically exchanging their Reichsmarks for Polish złoty at well below the official exchange rate, Eichmann and other engineers of the Nisko program pitched their enterprise as an opportunity for their victims to begin new lives without the legal restrictions that inhibited them at home. Resettling Jews to the Lublin "reservation" took for granted that their victims would suffer severe attrition in the marshy land in the dead of winter, deprived of the essentials for human existence. Nevertheless, Himmler, preoccupied with resettling the ethnic Germans who had disembarked in Danzig, all but terminated the Eichmann's scheme by ordering that trainloads of Jews be halted in transit and temporarily repatriated. Eichmann's subsequent efforts to evacuate Jews from the eastern Prussian provinces and the annexed territories, and to resettle them in the General Government foundered on the existing problem created by too many incoming ethnic Germans and too few Poles or Jews with enough property to accommodate the new arrivals. By January of 1940, Himmler was forced to scale back the resettlement of ethnic Germans and indefinitely postpone Jewish deportations. The protests of Hans Frank, who preferred to make the General Government "Jew free" rather than manage thousands of deportees, contributed to the delay. So did the objections of Hermann Göring, who wanted to avoid paralyzing the Polish economy by losing

[3] Yaakov Lozowick, *Hitler's Bureaucrats: The Nazi Security Police and the Banality of Evil* (London and New York: Continuum, 2002), 35–42; Hans Safrian, *Eichmann's Men*, trans. Ute Stargardt (Cambridge: Cambridge University Press, 2010), 14–45.

the cheap Polish labor necessary to run it. Yet Hitler's own intervention was likely decisive, inasmuch as a reservation for Jews interfered with his conviction that the General Government should serve as a military staging area for future operations farther east.[4]

The German victories in the west briefly raised the possibility of an overseas alternative that would resettle Jews on Madagascar, an island that was to become a German mandate following the conclusion of a peace treaty with France. As such, it held greater potential than prewar Nazi attempts to resettle German Jews in formerly German East Africa, which foundered on fears that the deportees would infect Africans with communist propaganda or discourage the British from returning the colony to Germany.[5] A French colony since 1895, located in the Indian Ocean off the southeast coast of Africa, the putatively underpopulated Madagascar had long figured in the imaginations of antisemites as a conveniently distant place to dispose of European Jews. The idea originated among geographers, anthropologists, and missionaries who determined that the Jews were ancestors of the Malagasy.[6] Beginning in the 1880s with the German racist writer Paul Lagarde,[7] visionaries of Madagascar's potential as a site for the segregation of Jews came to include the right-wing and deeply antisemitic Polish government, which in 1937 entered into negotiations with France over the resettlement of as many as seven thousand Jewish families there. In 1938, as the regime increased the pressure on German Jews to emigrate, the French foreign minister and arch appeaser, Edouard Daladier, suggested to the German foreign minister, Joachim von Ribbentrop, that the island could accommodate ten thousand German Jewish refugees. Despite that, the French government's proposal came to naught because of the resistance of Leon Cayla, the xenophobic and ultranationalist colonial governor of Madagascar.[8]

After the fall of France, the initiative for implementing the Madagascar scheme fell to Franz Rademacher, head of the Jewish Desk of the German foreign ministry and his superior, Martin Luther, who defined the task

---

[4] Aly, *"Final Solution,"* 33–58; Browning, *Origins of the Final Solution*, 36–43; Safrian, 46–58.

[5] Sandra Mass, *Weisse Helden, schwarzer Krieger: Zur Geschichte der kolonialer Männlichkeit in Deutschland 1918–1964* (Cologne, Weimar, and Vienna: Böhlau, 2006), 272–7.

[6] Eric Jennings, "Writing Madagascar Back into the Madagascar Plan," *Holocaust and Genocide Studies* 21, no. 2 (2007): 187–217.

[7] Ian Kershaw, *Fateful Choices: Ten Decisions that Changed the World, 1940–1941* (London: Penguin, 2007), 446–7.

[8] Jennings, "Writing Madagascar": 202–9.

before them as a now European-wide "problem" in light of the breadth of the Third Reich's military conquests. For the first time, a "solution" to the "Jewish Question," one projected to affect some four million deportees, was to include the Jews in western Europe.[9] In addition to ridding German-occupied Europe of the Jewish "bacillus," the plan contained another putative advantage. On the theory that Jewish wire-pullers controlled the Roosevelt administration, the regime could use its Jews as hostages to keep the United States out of the war.[10] The intervention of the German foreign office illustrated a broader trend that would come to distinguish the Holocaust. However internally competitive, most agencies of government in the Third Reich, military, party, or state, would become directly involved in a task to which they all became fundamentally committed.[11]

Determined to protect its jurisdiction in racial matters, however, Himmler and Heydrich quickly moved to assume control over the Madagascar "solution." Madagascar's virtues seemed obvious. Whereas the confused process of expulsion and resettlement to and from the annexed territories had created insurmountable bottlenecks and frequent conflict among Nazi epigones as to what to do with literally millions of uprooted Jews and Poles, the huge island off the African coast now presented itself as the solution to the "Jewish problem." Madagascar's strategic benefits, which derived from a clause in the proposed peace treaty between Germany and France, included the placement of German air and naval bases there. Hans Frank, who unceasingly complained about the Jews summarily dumped in the General Government, could hardly contain his relief at this new "solution," which promised to render his jurisdiction "Jew free." The expectations that the Madagascar Plan generated took no account of the island's existing population – over three and one-half million Malagasy, over ten thousand Africans and Asians, and the twenty thousand French colonists, whose own racism and antisemitism, including that of the island's governor, ill-disposed them to accept millions of Jewish expellees. Yet the dream of a Jewish reservation on Madagascar was not limited to the foreign ministry, the SS, and the General Government. Because Jews would only be allowed to take two

[9] Kershaw, *Fateful Choices*, 447.

[10] Peter Longerich, *The Unwritten Order: Hitler's Role in the Final Solution* (The Mill, Brimscombe Port, Stroud, Gloucestershire: Tempus, 2001), 93.

[11] Christopher Browning, *The Final Solution and the German Foreign Office* (New York: Holmes & Meier, 1978), 35–43; Aly, *"Final Solution,"* 88–104; Lozowick, *Hitler's Bureaucrats*, 67–8, 70–3.

hundred kilograms of property with them, the administrators of Göring's Four-Year Plan saw the island as a way to replace Jewish with German economic influence in Europe. Confiscated Jewish assets were to be liquidated through an intra-European bank for the utilization of Jewish property to cover the costs of the resettlement. By the middle of August of 1940, Eichmann and his staffers had composed a plan to deport four million Jews each year over a four-year period. To be directed by the SD, the Jews would be confined to a huge reservation managed by the SS on the driest, hottest, and most inhospitable part of the island. The Nazi regime's planners did not envision the reservation as a place for its victims to prosper.

The Madagascar project, however, fell by the wayside, an artifact of Germany's long-standing inability to maintain a permanent maritime foothold due to the superior position of its rivals. Because the British controlled the sea lanes and refused to sue for peace after the fall of France, the Madagascar plan was impossible to implement, even if the idea continued to resurface over the following year.[12] Moreover, Germany's annexation of Alsace and Lorraine that had been lost to France after World War I, and which was now joined with Baden and the Saar Palatinate, only increased the number of Jews under German administration, the disposal of whom local Nazi leaderships eagerly sought. Thus with Hitler's explicit authorization, the callous attempt of Robert Wagner and Josef Bürckel, the Gauleiters of Baden and the Saar Palatinate respectively, to deport "their" Jews to France ran into the immediate opposition of the Vichy government. Although unable to effect a complete cessation of the deportations, the Vichy protests presented yet another complication to the German plans for racial engineering. To add to that, tentative agreements over the following months to resume the transfer of Jews to the General Government in order to resettle Volhynian Germans met with resistance from Hans Frank and the military.

Still, the relentless pressure of district leaders and Reich governors, determined as always to "free" their districts of Jews, including those of Baden and the Saar Palatinate whom the French had rebuffed, motivated Hitler to once again permit limited deportations in the fall of 1940. His decision was immediately complicated by Germany's promise in September to Hungary to take tens of thousands of ethnic Germans

---

[12] Phillippe Burrin, *Hitler and the Jews: The Genesis of the Holocaust*, trans. Patsy Southgate (London: Edward Arnold, 1994), 78–9.

from Transylvania, and its further agreement with the Soviet Union and Germany to repatriate over 137,000 Germans from Bessarabia and Bukovina. The resulting impasse between too many people being shoved hither and yon and too few homesteads upon which to settle those with the requisite DVL classifications, forced Himmler into open-ended promises in December of 1940 of a Jewish resettlement "to a territory yet to be determined." Himmler's vagueness was most certainly designed to conceal the probable new "solution," the deportation of Jews into the interior of the Soviet Union. Going public with the new objective would have compromised the secrecy of the planning for Operation Barbarossa, the attack on the citadel of "Jewish Bolshevism." As discussions unfolded throughout the spring of 1941, the Pripet Marshes, which straddled the interwar border between the Soviet Union and Poland, emerged as the new area of Jewish "resettlement." There, the victims would be put to work on massive drainage and reclamation projects with a twofold purpose: to create fertile agricultural lands for German settlers who would wipe away the effects of years of Polish "mismanagement," and to erect another barrier between Germans and Slavic "undesirables."[13] Yet, despite the temporary emergence of another, seemingly inviting, "solution," the regime's inability to solve its huge Jewish "problem," forced its deputies in the field into, in their view, undesirable holding actions. In addition to creating more impatience and thus the greater potential for more radical strategies when the occasion arose, the present stalemate allowed the concentration and dispossession of Jews, which would facilitate their destruction later.

In the Old Reich, Austria, and the Protectorate, the impact of the Nuremberg Laws, which broadened the denaturalization of Jews, the property expropriations, the punitive taxes, and bank-account blocking that accelerated after Crystal Night, converged with a host of municipal ordinances that barred Jews from public spaces, theaters and restaurants, swimming pools, and tourist destinations. By the same time, Jews had also been excluded from public welfare services as welfare offices,

---

[13] Dieter Pohl, "Die Ermordung der Juden im Generalgouvernement," in *Nationalsozialistische Vernichtungspolitik 1939–1945: Neue Forschungen und Kontroversen*, ed. Ulrich Herbert (Frankfurt am Main; Fischer Taschenbuch Verlag, 1998), 102; Thomas Sandkühler in the same volume, "Judenpolitik und Judenmord im Distrikt Galizien, 1941–1942," 126; David Blackbourn, *The Conquest of Nature: Water, Landscape and the Making of Modern Germany* (New York: W. W. Norton, 2006), 251–61, 268–79.

without bidding from the Reich government, abandoned the principle of care for the individual for the care of the *Volk*.[14] With the introduction of segregated forced labor teams of Jews who could not afford to emigrate, and who mediated by labor exchanges would work for starvation wages for municipalities, the military, and private corporations, the removal of Jews from the day-to-day lives of "Aryan" society made their conditions even more claustrophobic.[15] In April of 1939, a new law that restricted the right of Jews to rent housing from Aryans while compelling other Jews to take in Jewish renters, created "Jew houses," or ghettoes in miniature that allowed the Gestapo to keep close tabs on its victims. Although the number of German Jews who had emigrated by the outbreak of war reached over three hundred thousand, the well over three hundred thousand who remained, many of them poor and elderly, struggled with deeper impoverishment and new humiliations. The increased confinement and fear took their toll on Victor Klemperer and his wife Eva, who had been forced to rent their home to an Aryan and relocate to a crowded "Jew house" in the summer of 1940. "The worst thing is Eva's declining powers of resistance," he said. Succumbing to melancholy, she played solitaire. "Not a note is played, hardly a book and no newspaper opened," he continued. "The bad weather, the early darkness stop us from going for walks, the shivering in the unheated apartment, the terribly meager food add the finishing touches. She looks pale, has lost weight. I am deeply depressed."[16]

In light of Hitler's menacing post-Crystal Night "prophecy," which threatened the "annihilation" of the "Jewish race," the increasingly draconian impositions, when added to those already in place, contemplated

---

[14] On the confiscation of Jewish assets, see Martin Dean, *Robbing the Jews: The Confiscation of Jewish Property in the Holocaust, 1933–1945* (Cambridge: Cambridge University Press, 2008), 132–44. On welfare, see Wolf Grüner, "Public Welfare and the German Jews under National Socialism: On Anti-Jewish Policies of the Municipal Administrations, the 'German Council of Municipalities' and the Reich Ministry of the Interior (1933–1941)," in *Probing the Depths of Antisemitism: German Society and the Persecution of the Jews 1933–1941*, ed. David Bankier (New York: Berg, Jerusalem: Yad Vashem and the Leo Baeck Institute, 2000), 102.

[15] Wolf Gruner, *Jewish Forced Labor Under the Nazis: Economic Needs and Racial Aims, 1938–1944*, trans. Kathleen M. Dell'Orto (Cambridge: Cambridge University Press, 2006), 3–8.

[16] Victor Klemperer, *I Will Bear Witness: A Diary of the Nazi Years 1933–1941*, trans. Martin Chalmers (New York: Random House, 1998), entry for December 10, 1940, 363.

a fate for its victims far worse than what could have been determined during the Nazi regime's first years in power. Even the civic and sexual segregation encoded in the Nuremberg Laws stipulated apartheid, not mass murder. Following the successful invasion of Poland and then the Soviet Union, even more restrictions were imposed on Jews, which included curfews, further cutbacks in rations, the denial of wage supplements, imprisonment in concentration camps for even the slightest infraction, and even the denial of the radios, telephones, and house pets, which determined one's membership in German middle-class culture. By the middle of 1941, the confinement of Jews in camps, "Jew houses," forced labor gangs, and ghettos were accomplished in Austria and the Protectorate, completing the transfer of anti-Jewish measures from the Old Reich.

In the haphazardly organized urban ghettos of Poland, the largest of which were Łódź and Warsaw, German administrators and ghetto managers struggled to master the chaos and congestion that Himmler's resettlement schemes created. To spare the German occupation from assuming the responsibility for internal governance and deflect the hostility of imprisoned Jews onto their own leaders, Heydrich ordered the formation of Jewish councils for each ghetto, while subsuming them under the control of German city administrations, particularly the food and economic offices. Deprived of sovereignty, the councils nonetheless had to assume the thankless tasks of distributing living quarters, allocating labor, collecting taxes, enforcing arbitrary German laws, as well as operating schools and public utilities under conditions that the term "straitened" does not even begin to describe. Beyond the designation of councils, however, German authorities had initially few long-term ideas as to what to do with their "charges" beyond warehousing them, or, as was increasingly the case, forcing able-bodied Jews into labor gangs to work in war-related industries and road construction.

As a consequence, two interim solutions evolved, emblematic of what would emerge as a periodic and largely microeconomic debate between exploiting Jewish labor or extermination that would decisively swing to the latter during the second half of 1941. The first advocated the "attrition" of Jews through disease and starvation. The "virtue" of this approach, according to those who presented this case, was that the Reich would not have to provision the ghettos with scarce resources that rightly belonged to the *Volk*. The second argued that until such time as the deportation of Jews could resume, the economic potential of ghetto inmates through forced labor needed to be utilized. The benefit to the Reich's economy would more than offset the cost of providing the ghettos with minimal food and other necessities. With a political leadership that remained focused on resettlement, Germans on the ground opted for the utilitarian course, in which only the pace of implementation varied. That such pragmatism triumphed for a time hardly meant sympathy for the captives. Rather, the "productivists" sought only to exploit ghettoized Jews with enough provisioning to keep them alive until further military advances allowed for the complete implementation of the territorial solution. In fact, the miserable conditions of the ghettos became a self-fulfilling prophecy for their German overlords. The combination of overcrowding and impoverishment yielded the predictable consequences of filth, hunger, and disease, which only reinforced German stereotypes of Jews as carriers of decomposition.[17]

As the first ghetto to be established in the face of delayed deportations, Łódź became the model for others that followed, even emerging as a tourist destination and a chilling example of "dark tourism," the travel to sites made infamous by their association with death and suffering.[18] Created in December of 1939 as a transit station in the northern part of Łódź, now located in the Warthegau and renamed Litzmannstadt in honor of the German general who captured it during World War I, the ghetto became a suffocating prison for Jewish captives, whom German authorities systematically extorted before and during their confinement. Jews who remained alive after the occupiers eliminated the city's Jewish elite would pay for their upkeep while awaiting further determination of their fate. By May of 1940 when the Germans sealed off the ghetto, the population stood at 163,000 Jews. As a temporary transfer point for Jews from the Warthegau, Old Reich, and the Protectorate, the population would rise and fall according to the pace of new arrivals and deportations from the ghetto to killing centers.[19]

Because the Jews did not have the money to pay for food, the increased likelihood of starvation and the declining possibility of deportation further east, brought together the converging interests of Łódź's pragmatic

[17] On the two camps, see Browning in *Origins of the Final Solution*, 151–69.

[18] As befitting a tourist attraction, the ghetto became the subject of postcards. See the entrance to the ghetto in 1940–1941 provided by the United States Holocaust Memorial Museum, www.ushmm.org under the encyclopedia listing for Łódź. On the formation and management of the ghetto, see Browning, *Origins of the Final Solution*, 115–20.

[19] Saul Friedlander, *The Years of Extermination: Nazi Germany and the Jews, 1939–1945* (New York: HarperCollins, 2007), 104–5.

German mayor, Karl Marder, the head of the Jewish Council, Mordechai Chaim Rumkowski, and Hans Biebow, a Bremen businessman, who had been appointed ghetto manager. All aimed to make the ghetto productive, albeit for different reasons. Having received a loan from funds confiscated from Jews, Marder and Biebow ultimately created a self-sustaining ghetto economy that consisted of 117 factories, warehouses, and sorting houses that employed 85 percent of the ghetto's population. In addition to the Jews who worked internally, the ghetto served as a reservoir of forced labor rented to private companies for construction or other military-related projects in the Warthegau and the Old Reich. Altogether, ghetto enterprises proved sufficiently profitable to entice the interest of German insurers, most prominently Allianz, who in calculating fashion held the ghettoized Jews responsible for keeping equipment in good condition.[20] Rumkowski was widely condemned during and after the war for maintaining a harsh, forced-labor regime, collaborating in the deportation of those too weak to work to the death camps, and distributing the ghetto's scarce resources to the privileged Jews on the council. "The Germans couldn't find a better man than Rumkowski," complained the precocious young Communist Dawid Sierakowiak, who would later die in the ghetto.[21] Yet Rumkowski's efforts, although suffused with corruption and callousness, and fueled by nepotism were not without effect, even if they only postponed the inevitable. The existence of labor projects helps to explain why so many Jews, whom the Germans "resettled," continued to hope for their survival.[22] The ghetto was not closed until mid-1944 when its remaining inmates were transported to Chełmno and Auschwitz, well after the others had been dissolved and its prisoners disgorged to the death camps. That the ghetto was located in the district of Arthur Greiser, whose militance in making the Warthegau "Jew

[20] Gruner, *Jewish Forced Labor*, 177–95; Gerald Feldman, *Allianz and the German Insurance Business, 1933–1945* (Cambridge: Cambridge University Press, 2001), 402–3.

[21] *The Diary of Dawid Sierakowiak: Five Notebooks from the Łódź Ghetto*, ed. Alan Adelson, trans. Kamil Turowski (New York and Oxford: Oxford University Press, 1996), 118. See also the introduction in *The Chronicle of the Łódź Ghetto 1941–1944*, ed. Lucjan Dobroszycki, trans. Richard Lourie and Joachim Neugroschel (New Haven and London: Yale University Press, 1984), xlv–xlviii.

[22] Andrea Löw, *Juden im Getto Litzmannstadt. Lebensbedingungen, Selbstwahrnehmung, Verhalten.* (Göttingen: Wallstein Verlag 2006), 263–333; Monika Kingreen, "'Wir warden darüber hinweg kommen': Letzte Lebenszeichen deportierte hessischer Juden: Eine dokumetarisiche Annäherung," in *Die Deportation der Juden aus Deutschland: Pläne-Praxis-Reaktionen 1938–1941*, eds. Beate Meyer and Birthe Kundrus (Göttingen: Wallstein Verlag, 2004), 86–111.

FIGURE 6.1. Jewish workers manufacture wooden shoes in a workshop in the Łódź ghetto, sometime between 1940 and 1944. Although Łódź was the last ghetto to be liquidated because of its value as a manufacturing center, the warehousing of Jews in ghettos overdetermined deportation and ultimately extermination rather than the use of Jews as labor.
Source: USHMM, photograph #65816, courtesy of Robert Abrams.

free" (*Judenrein*) could not be equaled and only deepened the irony.[23] Despite its relatively long life, the Łódź ghetto typified the Third Reich's begrudged and improvised approaches to Jewish labor: Only when the "better" alternative of evacuation was foreclosed did the desire to create self-sustaining ghetto economies emerge. Even then, hunger, overcrowding, disease, poverty, and isolation claimed thousands of lives, as debates among their captors wavered between pragmatic, if limited, provisioning and attrition.

Where no alternative to German sovereignty existed, most obviously in the Old Reich, Austria, the Protectorate, and German-occupied Poland, the increasing impoverishment, persecution, and deportation of Jews were ominous enough, even if the "territorial solutions" under discussion did not yet approach the horror to come. Legal discrimination,

---

[23] The delay in liquidating the ghetto resulted from the inability of the communal, regional, and ghetto administrations to agree on which "solution" to implement. See Peter Klein, *Die "Gettoverwaltung Litzmannstadt" 1940–1944: Eine Dienststelle im Spannungsfeld von Kommunalbürokratie und staaticher Verfolgungspolitik* (Hamburg: Hamburer Edition, 2009).

concentration, impressed labor, and enforced impoverishment not only limited Jews' room to maneuver, they also made it easier to mobilize Jewish populations once the regime decided to exterminate en masse. This was especially true in Poland where the debilitating economic and social impact of antisemitic legislation in the 1930s had already isolated Polish Jews from Polish Christians.[24] Nevertheless, even when alternatives to Germany's direct rule remained, the combination of local antisemitism embedded in centuries of Christian anti-Judaism, and the pursuit of self-interest that the status of German satellite engendered, resulted in a similar outcome by the middle of 1941 as the invasion of the Soviet Union commenced, the increased marginalization and endangerment of Jews.

In the west with its mostly assimilated Jews, more universalist political traditions, and the willingness of the German occupiers to depend on local administrations to conduct business, curtailing the Jewish "influence" nonetheless proved tempting to conservative puppet regimes. Although the Pétain government of Vichy France objected to the use of its territory as a dumping ground for Jews from Baden, the Saar Palatinate, Alsace, and Lorraine, it showed little reluctance to introduce anti-Jewish measures without much prompting from Germany, not only in metropolitan France but French colonies, notably Algeria and Madagascar.[25] The inherent authoritarianism, xenophobia, and anti-British disdain of the Vichy regime no doubt contributed, as did the expectation of its leaders that it could preserve its autonomy from Third Reich and allow France to retain its colonial empire.[26] In July of 1940, the Vichy regime denaturalized Jews in the unoccupied zone who had become citizens after the passage of the

---

[24] William Hagen, "Before the 'Final Solution': Toward a Comparative Analysis of Political Antisemitism in Interwar Germany and Poland." *Journal of Modern History* (July, 1996): 1–31; Bogdan Musial, *Deutsche Zivilverwaltung und Judenverfolgung im Generalgouvernement* (Wiesbaden: Harrassowitz Verlag, 1999), 101–5.

[25] Eric Jennings, *Vichy in the Tropics: Pétain's National Revolution in Madagascar, Guadeloupe, and Indochina, 1940–1944* (Stanford: Stanford University Press, 2001), 46–7.

[26] Gerhard L. Weinberg, *A World at Arms: A Global History of World War II* (Cambridge: Cambridge University Press, 1994), 138–40. On the relevance of the French empire, see Charles-Robert Ageron, L'Idée d'Euroafrique et le débat colonial franco-allemand de l'Entre-deux-Guerres," *Revue d'histoire moderne et contemporaine* 22, no. 2 (1975): 446–75; and Bernard Bruneteau, "L'Europe nouvelle" de Hitler: Une Illusion des intellectuals de la France de Vichy (Monaco: Rocher, 2003). On Vichy Jewish Policy, see Michael R. Marrus and Robert O. Paxton, *Vichy France and the Jews* (New York: Basic Books, 1981), esp. 73–176; and Susan Zuccotti, *The Holocaust, the French, and the Jews* (New York: Basic Books, 1993), 31–80.

liberal citizenship law of 1927, which covered thousands of Jews who immigrated after the turn of the century and Germany after 1933. The law also affected Jews who fled the country, which allowed for the confiscation of their property.[27] By the following October, the Vichy regime's Jewish Laws (*Statut des Juifs*) had defined Jews racially, and barred them from a wide range of occupations following a similar measure imposed in the occupied zone.[28] In June of 1941, the Vichy government ordered a Jewish census that required declarations of property. Overseen by the German military but executed by the French finance ministry, the declarations ultimately enabled aryanization.[29] Because the Vichy government retained sovereignty in the occupied zone as long as its measures did not conflict with the dictates of the occupiers, Vichy measures spawned a mutually reinforcing radicalization between it and the German military government, which also affected Jews in the occupied zone.[30] Eager to assert its sovereignty in order to claim at least some of the Jewish-owned property for itself, the Vichy regime acted according to the imperatives of an antisemitism that intensified during the Depression. It chose not to pursue what might have been an obvious means of protecting its own citizens, exploiting the German dependence on French labor. Vichy measures enabled the intervention of the Reich Security Main Office (RSHA) through its agent in France, Theodor Dannecker, Eichmann's associate and head of the Paris RSHA office. Dannecker could easily register Jews in and around Paris with the help of the data compiled by the Paris police. Dannecker won the agreement of the French government to establish a Commissariat on Jewish Questions in March of 1941 under French authority, which extended its jurisdiction over both unoccupied and occupied zones. The Commissariat centralized the registration and surveillance of Jews, as well as the aryanization of Jewish property.[31]

In the Netherlands, the German military presence was less significant than in the occupied zone of France. As was the case in Norway, the occupation consisted of an administration dominated by the Nazi

---

[27] On the financial consequences of Vichy's anti-Jewish measures, see Dean, *Robbing the Jews*, 300–10.

[28] Friedlander, *Years of Extermination*, 111. One was designated a Jew if one had three Jewish grandparents or two Jewish grandparents and a Jewish spouse.

[29] Götz Aly, *Hitler's Beneficiaries: Plunder, Racial War, and the Nazi Welfare State*, trans. Jefferson Chase (New York: Metropolitan Books, 2006), 210–23.

[30] Browning, *Origins of the Final Solution*, 197–201.

[31] Pim Griffioen and Ron Zeller, "Anti-Jewish Policy and the Organization of Deportations in France and the Netherlands, 1940–1944: A Comparative Study," *Holocaust and Genocide Studies* 20, no. 3 (2006): 441–2; Friedlander, *Years of Extermination*, 171–2.

Party and SS, which meant that German administrators could enact anti-Jewish measures, including property confiscations and aryanization, with greater speed and efficiency than in France or Belgium where the military occasionally sought to limit the influence of party officials.[32] Although to a lesser extent than in Denmark, Dutch elites encouraged sympathy for their Jewish citizens, which was not true of the Vichy regime. Nevertheless, Dutch civil servants who remained at their posts after Queen Wilhelmina and her government fled into exile, efficiently implemented Nazi racial policy after some initial resistance, defining Jews according to the criteria of the Nuremberg Laws, registering Jews and their property, and promulgating exclusionary legislation.[33] The Amsterdam stock exchange, which the Dutch still administered, sold the shares of Jewish-owned companies in compliance with the effort of German firms to acquire a controlling interest in Jewish-owned businesses[34] By February of 1941, the Dutch police had become fully compliant in persecuting Jews. Led by their pro-German constable, Sybren Tulp, a retired colonel in the Royal Dutch East Indian Army and avowed National Socialist, who cut his teeth by enforcing racial discrimination in Indonesia where the Dutch colonial administration had steadily hardened racial boundaries,[35] the Amsterdam police effectively carried out German orders. Similarly, the chief constables in Utrecht and The Hague appointed by the Reich Commissar, Arthur von Seyss-Inquart, had also learned their trade as colonial administrators.[36] If the German occupation was less draconian in the west than in Poland, Belorussia, or Serbia, the collaboration that the Germans received would make French, Dutch, and Belgian Jews nearly as vulnerable once deportations to the labor and death camps began.

The nations of southeastern Europe remained nominally independent, except for the Protectorate of Bohemia and Moravia. Nevertheless, in this

---

[32] Dean, *Robbing the Jews*, 264–70, 284–6.

[33] Griffioen and Zeller, Anti-Jewish Policy: 445; Friedlander, *Years of Extermination*, 121–5 and 178–82; Bob Moore, *Victims and Survivors: The Nazi Persecution of the Jews in the Netherlands 1940–1945* (London: Arnold, 1997), 42–90, 190–211.

[34] Aly, *Hitler's Beneficiaries*, 207–10.

[35] See Ann Laura Stoler, *Carnal Knowledge and Imperial Power: Race and the Intimate in Colonial Rule* (Berkeley, Los Angeles, and London: University of California Press, 2002), esp. 41–139.

[36] Guus Meershoek, "The Amsterdam Police and the Persecution of the Jews," *The Holocaust and History: The Known, the Unknown, the Disputed, and the Reexamined,* eds. Michael Berenbaum and Abraham J. Peck (Bloomington and Indianapolis: Indiana University Press, 1998), 284–300.

region, part of the European "shatter zone" of empires, the Third Reich exploited economic dependency and a deep-seated local antisemitism, an equally entrenched hostility toward the Soviet Union, and in one notable case post–World War I revisionism, to force an alignment of domestic policies with the interests of the Third Reich. That combination rendered Hungary particularly susceptible. Having lost over two-thirds of its pre-war territory, over 60 percent of its population, and its military sovereignty as a result of the Treaty of Trianon, Hungary found Germany's influence hard to resist, especially after the annexation of Austria created a common border and weakened Hungary's previous understanding with Italy that had supported and preserved an independent Austria. Having been terrified by the Bolshevik Revolution and Béla Kun's proletarian dictatorship, Hungarian fascists and conservatives, including Catholic clergymen, deemed "Jewish Bolshevism" responsible for Hungary's losses. By the late 1930s, the Arrow Cross, Hungary's own home-grown fascist movement, which had originated in the "white terror" against the Kun government, increased the pressure for anti-Jewish legislation.[37]

Beginning in 1938, new antisemitic measures redefined Jews as a race, which by permitting aryanization, squeezed them out of the economy. Jews of military age were drafted as forced labor. Although Hungary's regent, Admiral Miklós Horthy distrusted the Arrow Cross and opposed antisemitic legislation because the predominantly middle- and upper-middle-class composition of Hungarian Jews all but guaranteed a negative economic impact if legal restrictions were imposed, Hungary's closeness to Germany yielded substantial rewards. As a result of the Munich agreement, Hungary received the southern part of Slovakia. In March of 1939 it took over the Carpatho-Ukraine following the German dissolution of Czechoslovakia. After the Soviet Union occupied its half of Poland later that year, which pushed Horthy further into the German orbit, Hungary received the northern half of Transylvania at Romania's expense in return for signing the Tripartite Pact. Annexations and antisemitism reinforced each other. Having expanded its Jewish population by 275,000 by November of 1940, Hungary ensured that more Jews would be trapped in the widening web of legal persecution and ultimately deportation once

[37] Christian Gerlach and Götz Aly, *Das letzte Kapitel: Der Mord an den ungarischen Juden 1944–1945* (Frankfurt am Main: Fischer Taschenbuch, 2004), 30–1. On Hungarian Catholicism, see Paul Hanebrink, "Transnational Culture War: Christianity, Nation and the Judeo-Bolshevik Myth in Hungary, 1890–1920," *Journal of Modern History* 80, no. 1 (2008): 55–80.

Hungary committed troops to the Reich's crusade against the Soviet Union. Hungary's increasingly suffocating economic dependence on the Third Reich, which redirected its agriculture and subordinated its oil fields to German needs, further tightened the noose around the necks of Hungarian Jews.[38]

If Slovakia's native antisemitism did not suffice by itself, the inevitable dependence of that small and impoverished nation on Germany for having won its "independence" after Czechoslovakia' dismemberment, guaranteed that Slovakia's conservative clerical dictatorship of Monsignor Josef Tiso would consent to the registration of and legal discrimination against its Jewish population as long as it retained control of its anti-Jewish policy. In 1939, the government decreed the removal of Jews from public offices, limited their access to academically trained professions and aryanized Jewish-owned agricultural and forested property to aid its economically hard-pressed peasantry. The aryanization of Jewish commercial and business enterprises followed in the spring of 1940.[39] Although Tiso insisted on the right to exempt baptized Jews from the anti-Jewish legislation, the agitation of yet another home-grown clerical fascist movement, the Hlinka Guard, allowed Eichmann's deputies in the SD to influence the appointment of government officials who sympathized with more radical antisemitic measures.[40]

Romania's Ploesti oil fields might have provided leverage, but the inability of the British and French to stop German expansion, and the growth of the fascist and antisemitic Iron Guard with its commitment to "purifying" Romania of its ethnic minorities, soon weakened the neutrality of the Romanian government. As early as the end of 1937, it deprived most Jews of full citizenship and banned mixed marriages.[41]

---

[38] Gerlach and Aly, *Das letzte Kapital*, 32–3; Randolph L. Braham, *The Politics of Genocide: The Holocaust in Hungary*, rev. ed., vol. 1 (New York: Columbia University Press, 1994), 1–76; 121–97; István Deák, "A Fatal Compromise? The Debate over Collaboration and Resistance in Hungary," in *The Politics of Retribution in Europe" World War II and Its Aftermath*, eds. István Deák, Jan T. Gross, and Tony Judt (Princeton and London: Princeton University Press, 2000), 48–53; Péter Hanák and Joseph Hled, "Hungary on a Fixed Course: An Outline of Hungarian History," in *The Columbia History of Eastern Europe in the Twentieth Century*, 1918–1945, ed. Joseph Held (New York: Columbia University Press, 1992), 164–204.

[39] Aly, *Hitler's Beneficiaries*, 224–29.

[40] Dean, *Robbing the Jews*, 317–22; Debórah Dwork and Robert Jan Van Pelt, *The Holocaust: A History* (New York and London: W. W. Norton, 2002), 168–9.

[41] Longerich, *Politik der Vernichtung*, 521.

Under pressure from domestic fascists and reeling from the terms of the Nazi-Soviet Pact, which allowed the Soviet Union to absorb Bessarabia and Bukovina, the Romanian government gave Germany carte blanche to manage its oil fields. Then followed a raft of antisemitic legislation that, in addition to feeding the desires of home-grown antisemites, satisfied the Reich's demands.[42] Between early 1938 and the conquest of Poland, roughly the same period in which Romania signed over its agricultural production and the management of its oil fields to Germany, over 225,000 Jews lost their citizenship. The antisemitic laws ensured poverty and social death of the remainder. With the cession of Northern Transylvania to Hungary, a cruel blow to a state that had sought less draconian population exchanges with and territorial cessions to its neighbors, Romania's compliant royal dictatorship under King Carol collapsed in September of 1940 in favor of the unambiguously pro-German and antisemitic "legionary" regime of Ion Antonescu and Huria Sima. In addition to the emergence of Antonescu, an avowed ethnic cleanser with close ties to the Iron Guard, the defeat of France, once Romania's ally, took away what little leverage the Romanians possessed.[43]

"AGAINST HUMAN DIVERSITY AS SUCH": BARBAROSSA AND GENOCIDE

By the middle of 1941, the status of Jews in German-occupied Europe and in the German satellites had been dangerously undermined. The looming prospect of expulsion threatened thousands of Jews with physical destruction, as well as the ruination of Jewish cultures. Nevertheless, during the first two years of World War II in Europe, the Nazi regime's persecution of the Jews appeared to combine historical precedents, beginning with the medieval and early modern markers of marginalization and segregation, the requirement that Jews don a yellow armband with the Star of David and be confined to ghettos. "We are returning to the Middle Ages," observed the Łódź ghetto prisoner Dawid Sierakowiak in November of 1939 as "the yellow patch once again becomes a part of Jewish dress."[44]

---

[42] Aly, *Hitler's Beneficiaries*, 233–5.
[43] On the rise of Antonescu, see Dennis Deletant, *Hitler's Forgotten Ally: Ion Antonescu and His Regime, Romania 1940–1944* (New York: Palgrave Macmillan, 2006), 8–51. See also Dwórk and Van Pelt, *Holocaust*, 177–90; and Vladimir Solonari, "An Important New Document on the Romanian Policy of Ethnic Cleansing during World War II," *Holocaust and Genocide Studies* 21, no. 2 (2007): 268–73.
[44] Sierakowiak, *Diary*, 63.

Moreover, the camps, expulsions, and massacres visited upon Jews and non-Jews was derived from the European and German experience of overseas colonialism of the nineteenth century. If pushing westward in North America at the expense of indigenous peoples had been necessary for European settlers, according to Hitler, it was therefore equally logical and necessary for Germans to make space for themselves at the expense of Slavs and Jews in order to construct their own "Garden of Eden." And although during that period, Jews received the worst treatment among the Third Reich's victims, which included fewer rations, registration, and spider webs of discriminatory legislation with potentially genocidal impact if activated in the right circumstances, the lethality of German colonial rule did not yet reach the level that it would achieve in the months that followed the German invasion of the Soviet Union.

The attack on the Soviet Union unleashed a cataclysm that would engulf Jews in a way not shared by the Reich's other colonial subjects, including Slavs. By the summer of 1942 when the death camps were operating at full tilt, the "final solution" would, in addition to exemplifying the explosiveness of homogenizing nationalism, bring about the Third Reich's own horrific contribution to the history of European imperialism. The distinctiveness of the Nazi Judeocide arose first of all from its context, which combined global war with "total" war in its assault against civilians. Second, the apocalyptic danger that the victims putatively embodied as the threat to Germany's imperialist goals that would in turn ensure the survival of the *Volk*, led to a comprehensiveness unmatched by previous genocides, which embraced the Nazi leadership and its agents in the field in a murderous dialectic.[45] Finally, the weakness of organized opposition to imperialism or genocide from within the Reich allowed the Nazi regime extraordinary latitude to pursue its goals.

Although Nazi epigones liked to compare their "civilizing mission" of dispossession and decimation in the east to the Indian wars of North America, Jews, unlike Africans or Native Americans, assumed an altogether different status. In the past, colonizers and settlers spoke of "natives" or "savages" as either "declining," "dying," or "disappearing" in order to make way for the superior races – an inevitability that neatly elided the agency of Europeans whose actions assured that outcome. Yet the perpetrators of Nazi genocide proved less reticent to express their own responsibility for mass murder

---

[45] As Ben Kiernan points out in his comparative study, *Blood and Soil: A World History of Genocide and Extermination from Sparta to Darfur* (New Haven and London: Yale University Press, 2007), 454.

as the "solution" to the Jewish threat, even as they sometimes resorted to the obfuscating language of the past.[46] On the contrary, as propaganda minister Goebbels asserted, the war allowed the gloves to come off. "In these circumstances, one can't allow sentimentality to prevail. The Jews would destroy us if we didn't fend them off ourselves. This is a struggle of life and death between the Aryan race and the Jewish bacillus." "Thank God" that the war provided "an entire range of possibilities" that would have been impossible to implement during peacetime. "This," Goebbels concluded, "we must exploit."[47] In the Nazi scheme of things, Jews collectively emerged as the prime mover behind the industrialized imperialist rivals that threatened Germany's very existence and as the source of "racial mixing," which weakened the *Volk* from within. In the words of Victor Klemperer, the adjective "Jewish" had "the bracketing effect of binding together all adversaries into a single enemy." Thus, "from 1933 every single hostility, regardless of its origin, can be traced back to one and the same enemy, Hitler's hidden maggot, the Jew, who in moments of high drama is referred as 'Judah' or with even greater pathos, '*Alljuda* (Universal Judah).'"[48]

Hints of the coming catastrophe were already embedded in the regime's planning for the invasion in the spring of 1941. Although a high degree of ideological agreement and tactical coordination had existed between the army and the SS mobile attack units during the Polish campaign, the military's scruples over the treatment of civilians and the turf conflicts between it and the SS, reduced the units' participation in the Scandinavian and western campaigns the following spring. The army's treatment of captured French colonial troops had been murderous but inconsistent. Yet, because of the ideological stakes this time around, the führer ensured that there would be no such ambiguity. SS mobile attack units and order police were assigned to each army and charged with pacification in the rear. There was no disagreement as to who would be designated as anti-German partisans. Be it the SS, the army, the Nazi leadership, or the civil administration that was to be put into place once the Soviet Union met its demise, all shared in the anti-Slavism, anti-Bolshevism, and especially antisemitism that infused the operational and occupation planning of Barbarossa.

---

[46] Enzo Traverso, *The Origins of Nazi Violence* (New York: The New Press, 2003), 54–63.

[47] *Die Tagebücher von Joseph Goebbels: sämtliche Fragmente*, ed. Else Fröhlich (Munich and New York: KG. Saur, 1987–96), Part II, vol. 3, entry for March 27, 1942, 561.

[48] Victor Klemperer, *The Language of the Third Reich: LTI-Lingua Tertii Imperii*, trans. Martin Brady (London and New York: Continuum, 2000), 176–7.

On the eve of Barbarossa, the regime once more claimed Germany's victimization by an international Jewish conspiracy bent on exterminating the *Volk* – a conspiracy plainly evident in the common plan of British and American plutocrats allied with Bolshevism to destroy the Reich.[49] Embedded in the initial confidence that the Wehrmacht could destroy the Soviet Union quickly was the fear that the "real" enemy lurking behind the visible one would require more than just an army to annihilate. Thus, even before the invasion began, Jewish men of military age, because of their presumed association with communism, were to be singled out for immediate elimination. Soviet Jews were already at risk because they were concentrated in the former Pale of Settlement, established by the Empress Catherine the Great in the late eighteenth century on Russia's western borders. Although formally abolished by the Russian Provisional government in early 1917, hundreds of thousands of Jews remained. To add to that, the transfer of German practices in Poland, in which Jews held the least claim to food supplies, determined that Jews would an even a worse fate in the Soviet Union. And if German economic planning took for granted the starvation and forced labor of millions of Russians, and the deportation of the rest to the frozen wastelands of Siberia, few Jews would have any prospect of surviving acute hunger, random executions, or the "natural wastage" that would result from the backbreaking effort to drain the Pripet Marshes in Belorussia and Ukrain border. By the middle of July it became clear that the marshes would not be used to press Jewish work gangs into service but to liquidate them. The Reichsführer SS commanded that Jewish men should be shot en masse. Their women were to be driven into the swamps to drown.[50] At the time of Himmler's order, Germany's war in the Soviet Union was being radicalized to a degree that guaranteed that the fate of Jews would depart markedly from that meted out to Russian "redskins." To this point, segregated labor gangs, especially in the Old Reich, Austria, and the Protectorate had pressed some one million Jews into service. Yet once genocide commenced, the use of Jews as laborers would decline precipitously.[51]

The conduct of the mobile attack forces and order police suggested something new on the horizon. During the first days of the Barbarossa

---

[49] Herf, *Jewish Enemy*, 97–100.
[50] Christian Gerlach, "Deutsche Wirtschaftsinteressen, Besatzungspolitik und der Mord an den Juden in Weissrussland 1941–1943," in Herbert ed., *Nationalsozialistische Vernichtungspolitik*, 278. See also, Longerich, *Politik der Vernichtung*, 352–401.
[51] Grüner, *Jewish Forced Labor*, 261.

campaign, the ruthless pacification inflicted by SS units in the rear, was "limited" to the execution of Jews in Communist Party and state positions, as well as assorted "Gypsies," "saboteurs," "agitators," "snipers," and "propagandists." Yet even from the beginning of the campaign, the SS and the Wehrmacht exceeded their written orders to follow the cold-blooded directions of attack force leaders on the ground. Thus, it did not take long for the SS, with the army's cooperation, to extend its "actions" to women and children as well, either on their own initiative or by encouraging pogroms initiated by local antisemites.[52] On June 27th, only six days after Barbarossa began, a German police battalion murdered two thousand Jews in Białystok in eastern Poland, one-quarter of them women and children crammed into a synagogue that the troops set ablaze.[53] Nor did the "pacification" efforts of the police battalions end there. Responding to Heydrich's request for authorization as the mobile attack units murdered with abandon, Göring gave the order to the former on July 31st to prepare a "total solution" to the Jewish "question."

Although the precise meaning of Göring's order remains debated, the apocalyptic nature of the Barbarossa campaign, especially at that particular juncture when the mass shootings had escalated, most likely indicated that the term "solution" had taken on a new and more radical meaning. In fact, the SS Cavalry Brigade led by Erich von dem Bach-Zelewski, murdered some 25,000 Jews in the Pripet Marshes between late July and late August, extending his campaign to "de-Jewify" large swaths of Belorussian territory by early October.[54] The progress of the German armies, which by the middle of September had broken through the Soviet lines outside of Kiev and encircled Leningrad, further elevated the desire for a complete reckoning with the apocalyptic enemy. Having decided in August of 1941, when the German advance temporarily stalled, that the Jews would be deported farther east at the end of the Soviet campaign, the führer suddenly accelerated his plan. On the 18th of September, Hitler ordered the earliest possible deportation of Jews from Germany, Austria, and the Protectorate to the east, primarily to the ghettoes of Łódź, Riga, Kaunas, and Minsk to await further deportation in

---

[52] Geoffrey Megargee, *War of Annihilation: Combat and Genocide on the Eastern Front, 1941* (Lanham, MD: Rowman and Littlefield, 2006), 67–8.

[53] Longerich, *Politik der Vernichtung*, 345–8.

[54] Longerich, *Unwritten Order*, 117, and *Politik der Vernichtung*, 367–9; Christian Gerlach, *Kalkulierte Mord, Die deutsche Wirtschafts-und Vernichtungspolitik in Weissrussland 1941 bis 1944* (Hamburg: Hamburg Edition, 1999), 555–74.

the spring.[55] By the end of 1941, the order police numbered over 33,000, more than eleven times the combined numbers of the mobile attack units that crossed the Soviet border in June, an indication of the scale of the extermination already underway.[56]

One of the most horrifying massacres occurred at the end of September in the Ukrainian town Babi Yar. With many Jewish males of working age absent, most of them skilled workers whom the Soviet government transported behind the lines to work in the armaments industries, the victims were composed overwhelmingly of women, children, and the elderly. From the moment of their arrival in Babi Yar, the Germans engaged in hundreds of gratuitously brutal acts in response to their heavy losses from Soviet mines. Then came the three day "death procession" of Jews from Kiev to the ravines outside of town where, after giving up their clothing and valuables, Jews were machine-gunned at point-blank range, falling into the burial pits on top of one another. During the entire episode, they killed children before their mothers' eyes, callously murdered the disabled and elderly, and crowded Jews into a theater in order to set it on fire. The looting of Jewish property by the Germans and their Ukrainian accomplices occurred simultaneously with the mass shootings, signifying the infernal marriage of ideological hatreds and material gain.[57] Eyewitness accounts of Jewish survivors testified to their abandonment by neighbors who had been friends for years. The now-former friends included Communist Party members, eager to take advantage of genocide.[58]

Nor was the Babi Yar massacre exceptional despite the special notoriety it has since acquired. Twelve thousand of the thirty thousand Jews in the Ukrainian city of Berdichev were mowed down on a single September day in a field near the airport, the vast majority of them women, children, and the elderly. The preceding death march of Jews forced from their homes in the early morning hours presented a scene of indescribable horror: "The executioners murdered many of those who could not walk,

[55] Browning, *Origins of the Final Solution*, 323–30.

[56] Kershaw, *Fateful Choices*, 456.

[57] Ilya Ehrenburg and Vasily Grossman, *The Complete Black Book of Russian Jewry*, ed. and trans. David Patterson (New Brunswick, NJ and London: Transaction Publishers, 2002), 3–8. See also, Karel C. Berkhoff, *Harvest of Despair: Life and Death in Ukraine under Nazi Rule* (Cambridge, MA and London; Belknap Press of Harvard University Press, 2004), 65–9.

[58] *The Unknown Black Book: The Holocaust in the German-Occupied Soviet Territories*, eds. Joshua Rubenstein and Ilya Altman (Bloomington and Indianapolis: Indiana University Press, 2008), 74–5.

frail old people and cripples, right in their homes. The terrible wailing of the women and the crying of the children woke up the whole city. Residents living on the most distant streets awoke and listened in fear to the groans of thousands of people merging into a single soul-shaking cry."[59] At the mass execution of the Jews of Chudnov in the Zhitomir region of Ukraine, the freshly dug burial grounds awaited the victims of the shooting squads. A young woman waiting her turn at the death pit, according to an eyewitness, "went into labor before she even reached the pit. With his own dirty hands, a German butcher tore the baby out of the womb of its mother along with her innards, and then took the newborn by its little leg and smashed its head against the trunk of an old pine tree – that was how he awakened its life – and then tossed the infant to its bullet-riddled mother in the common grave."[60]

By the fall of 1941, the radicalization at the commanding heights of the Reich government converged with personal ambition and initiative in the field, as more and more Nazi functionaries in the field spoke openly of "extermination."[61] The thousands of Jews, who crowded into their jurisdictions increased the anxiety of Reich governors and security police in the affected districts, who pressed the Reich Security Main Office of the SS and Rosenberg's Ministry for the Occupied Eastern Territories for relief. Faced with the influx of more Jews to the General Government, Hans Frank once again protested against the use of his jurisdiction as the dumping ground for "undesirables." The weight of Hitler's decision to deport Jews from the Old Reich, Austria, and the Protectorate thus made it more likely that a "solution" to the "Jewish question" would mean death rather than resettlement. The implementation of the General Plan East in Soviet territory ruled out the relocation of Jews there.[62] The emerging food crisis provided an added, and arguably decisive, impetus, an indication of how Nazi colonialism would determine not just who would be deported or who would be subject to forced labor, but also who would be eliminated outright. Poor harvests in 1940 and 1941, coupled with the influx of huge numbers of foreign forced laborers whose labor was essential and whom the regime had no choice but to feed if it hoped to win the war, resulted in the application of the Hunger Plan to Poland.

---

[59] Ibid., 12–16.
[60] *Unknown Black Book*, 162–3.
[61] Peter Longerich, *Heinrich Himmler: Biographie* (Munich: Siedler Verlag, 2008), 568–9.
[62] See Christian Gerlach, *Krieg, Ernährung, Völkermord: Deutsche Vernichtungspolitik im Zweiten Weltkrieg* (Zürich and Munich: Pendo, 1998), 53–78 on the impact of the crisis in provisioning Jews; and Musial,, *Deutsche Zivilverwaltung*, 203.

To make up for the shortfall, the Reich government demanded that Frank's district now deliver food rather than receive it. The diversion of food would result in near starvation rations for Poles and absolute starvation levels for Jews. The extension of the Hunger Plan to the General Government provided additional context to discussions devoted to finding more efficient means of eliminating Jews.[63] Moreover, the recognition by September of 1941 that the Soviet Union would not be defeated by the end of the year had a pernicious impact on Jews, even in Soviet regions, such as Belorussia, that were not slated for colonization. The delay of victory necessitated a new food procurement plan for 1942 to ensure adequate supplies for the Wehrmacht and the civilian labor force. According to the zero-sum logic of National Socialism, Jews would die so that Germans could live.[64] By the Japanese attack on Pearl Harbor in December of 1941 when Hitler declared war against the United States, the regime had likely committed itself to the European-wide extermination of the Jews. Well before then, Philipp Bouhler's and Viktor Brack's team of euthanasia experts had found a new task to which to apply their skills, the construction of secret killing centers in Poland.[65]

The perpetrators of genocide were a diverse lot. They were district leaders and governors throughout German-occupied Europe who seized the opportunity to solve once "their" Jewish "problem" once and for all. They were higher SS and police leaders, such as the vitriolically antisemitic commander for Southern Russia, Friedrich Jeckeln, whose enthusiastic supervision of the elimination of thousands of Jews in Ukraine justified his meteoric rise in the SS police. They also included Wehrmacht generals with distinguished Prussian backgrounds, such as Erich von Manstein, who informed soldiers under his command in the Crimea that they were to ensure that Jews never again threatened the German living space. Regardless of their roles, charisma from the top simultaneously encouraged and legitimized the murderous activism from below.[66] In addition

[63] Tooze, *Wages of Destruction*, 538–49.

[64] Gerlach, *Kalkulierte Mord*, 503–774.

[65] See Christian Gerlach, "The Wannsee Conference, the Fate of the German Jews, and Hitler's Decision in Principle to Exterminate All European Jews," *Journal of Modern History* 70 (1998): 759–812; and Browning's answer in *Origins of the Final Solution*, 309–73, 540 no. 112. Browning, p. 373, also answers Peter Longerich, who questions whether European Jews were to be executed immediately. Cf. Longerich, *Politik der Vernichtung*, 466–72.

[66] Wendy Lower, *Nazi Empire-Building and the Holocaust in the Ukraine* (Chapel Hill and London: University of North Carolina Press, 2005), 75–8; Norbert Kunz, *Die Krim*

to Himmler's frequent presence at mass executions, the Reichsführer SS ordered significant increases in manpower, especially for the uniformed German police battalions, the heavily indoctrinated units that were charged with "pacifying" the rear. The SS counted on the collaboration of the Wehrmacht, which shared a commitment to military camaraderie and Nazi ideology. Special units drawn from local populations in the Baltic States and the western Ukraine, who were eager to act out their hostility toward the Soviet Union and the perceived connection between Jews and "Bolsheviks," were also mobilized.[67] The scale of the massacres in those regions sufficed to limit the extent of ghettoization that had occurred in Poland. Writing in the fall of 1943, the Soviet Jewish war correspondent Vasily Grossman underscored the special treatment that the Jews received compared to that which the Ukrainians experienced: "There are no Jews in the Ukraine," Grossman noted. "Nowhere – Poltava, Kharkov, Kremenchug, Borispol, Yagotin – in none of the cities, hundreds of towns, or thousands of villages will you see the black tear-filled eyes of little girls; you will not hear the pained voice of an old woman; you will not see the dark face of a hungry baby. All is silence. Everything is still. A whole people has been brutally murdered."[68]

The widening assault against Jews in the second half of 1941 extended to Eastern Galicia, a mixed Ukrainian, Jewish, and Polish region that had belonged to the Austro-Hungarian Empire before 1918. Ceded to Poland after the war, and then to the Soviet Union following the Nazi-Soviet Pact, the Germans merged the province with the Lublin district of the General Government. The mobile attack units, in combination with the Order Police and Ukrainian militia, murdered nearly thirty thousand Jews in the fall of 1941, making no distinction in gender or age. Ukrainians seeking revenge for the putative Jewish complicity in NKVD roundups of suspect locals during the Soviet occupation, unleashed ferocious pogroms that the Germans made no secret of tolerating. Unlike the rest of the General

---

unter deutscher Herrschaft 1941–1944: Germanisierungsutopie und Besatzungsrealität (Darmstadt: Wissenschaftliche Buchgesellschaft, 2005), 179.

[67] Lower, *Nazi Empire Building*, 78–83. On the order police, see Edward B. Westermann, *Hitler's Police Batallions: Enforcing Racial War in the East* (Lawrence, KN: University of Kansas Press, 2005), 163–99; and Christopher R. Browning, *Ordinary Men: Reserve Police Batallation 101 and the Final Solution in Poland* (New York: Harper Perennial, 1993), esp. 38–142. Of the two, Westermann places greater emphasis on ideology in the training and motivation of the order police.

[68] Vasily Grossman, *A Writer at War: Vasily Grossman with the Red Army 1941–1945*, ed. and trans., Antony Beevor and Luba Vinogradova (New York: Pantheon Books, 2005), 251.

Government, the haphazard ghettoization of Jews in the province's cities immediately provoked mass executions of Jews deemed unfit for work. The German authorities, claiming insurmountable housing shortages that that could barely accommodate the non-Jews under their charge, sought to reduce the Jewish population to a manageable size until the Jews could be deported farther east. The significance of developments in Eastern Galicia became clear. In Warsaw, the confinement of Jews straddled months of debate over the pace of resettling ethnic Germans and various "solutions" to the Jewish "problem." In Eastern Galicia's largest cities, Lviv, Tarnopol, and Stanislawow, however, the expectations arising from Barbarossa shortened the time frame between confinement and mass murder.[69]

Vicious attacks on Jews occurred not merely in German-occupied territories, but also in German satellites that stood to benefit from Barbarossa. Thus, in Romania, pogroms unleashed against Jews soon mushroomed into episodes of mass annihilation, in which rampant looting accompanied murder. In January 1941 Ion Antonescu assaulted his erstwhile allies who tried to overthrow him, the fascist Legionnaires of the Archangel Michael and its paramilitary, the Iron Guard. Nevertheless, Antonescu's military and police did nothing to stem the Iron Guard's pogroms against Romanian Jews, whom they alleged had delivered Bukovina and Bessarabia to the Soviet Union. The attacks included dozens of Jews killed in a forest near Bucharest or in the capital itself, where the victims were murdered in a slaughterhouse and suspended on meat hooks to mimic kosher butchering practices.[70] "The stunning thing about the Bucharest bloodbath is the quite bestial ferocity of it," remarked Mihail Sebastian, the Romanian-Jewish playwright and novelist, in his journal. It was "apparent even in the dry official statement that ninety-three persons ("person" being the latest euphemism for Jew) were killed on the night of Tuesday the 21st in Jilava forest."[71]

---

[69] See Dieter Pohl, *Nationalsozialistische Judenverfolgung in Ostgalizien 1941–1944: Die Organisierung und Durchführung eines staatlichen Verbrechens* (Munich: Oldenbourg, 1996), esp. 139–210; and Thomas Sandkühler, *"Endlösung" in Galizien: Der Judenmord in Ostpolen und die Rettungsinitiativen von Berthold Beitz, 1941–1944* (Bonn: Dietz, 1996), 110–66.

[70] For an assessment of Antonescu's role, see Deletant, *Hitler's Forgotten* Ally, 127–204. On the populist and religious origins of the fascist pogroms, see Armin Heinen, *Rumänien, der Holocaust und die Logik der Gewalt* (Munich; Oldenbourg, 2007), 99–108. On the integral relationship between murder and plunder, see Dean, *Robbing the Jews*, 330–3.

[71] Mihail Sebastian, *Journal 1935–1944: The Fascist Years*, trans. Patrick Camiller (Chicago: Ivan R. Dee, 2000), entry for February 4, 1941, 316.

Anticipating the return of Bukovina and Bessarabia once the Germans invaded the Soviet Union, Antonescu ordered his generals to prepare for "cleansing the ground" of Jews there by liquidation or deportation, the first step in a long-term plan to "purify" the returned territories of "foreign" elements, including Slavs.[72] Within days after the invasion of the Soviet Union began, thousands of Jews, including women and children, were mercilessly slaughtered in Iasi, the regional capital of Moldavia. Once Romania re-acquired Bukovina and Bessarabia as Germany's reward for the Romanian troops who joined the Barbarossa campaign, nearly half of the 375,000 Jews in those regions were murdered outright. Many thousands of others were dumped in camps in Transnistria, a small slice of Ukrainian territory between the Dniester and Bug Rivers that the Germans had awarded Romania. Reported Sebastian:

> The roads in Bessarabia and Bukovina are filled with corpses of Jews driven from their homes toward Ukraine. Old and sick people, children, women – all quite indiscriminately pushed onto the roads and driven toward Mogilev…It is an anti-Semitic delirium that nothing can stop…It would be something if there were an anti-Semitic pogrom; you'd know the limits to which it might go. But this is sheer uncontrolled bestiality, without shame or conscience, without goal or purpose.[73]

Moreover, Romanian army units, infuriated by their losses in the battle for Odessa, which included partisan attacks that killed dozens of Romanian troops, machine-gunned, hanged, or burned alive over 20,000 Jewish women, children, and the elderly. Eyewitnesses described nightmarish scenes of "gallows everywhere you turned your eyes" and the disappearance of any semblance of humanity: "The Romanians and Germans tested the strength of their bayonets on tiny children. A mother was feeding her baby, when a Romanian soldier tore it from her breast with his bayonet and flung it into the pit of the dead."[74] Along with Jews from Bukovina and Bessarabia, the remaining Jews of Odessa were crammed into concentration camps in Transnistria, only to be murdered in cold blood several months later. It was a crime that exceeded the bloodbath of Babi Yar in its scale.[75] Acutely sensitive to the novelty of the antisemitic violence that he witnessed, Sebastian recorded the following observation: "It is a European event. Organized anti-Semitism is going

---

[72] Solonari, "Important New Document:" 273–6.

[73] Sebastian, *Journal*, entry for October 20, 1941, 430–1.

[74] Ehrenburg and Grossman, *Complete Black Book*, 56–7; see also Heinen, *Rumänien*, 109–62.

[75] Jean Ancel, "Antonescu and the Jews," in *The Holocaust and History*, eds. Berenbaum and Peck, 462–79.; Friedlander, *Years of Extermination*, 166–7, 225–6.

FIGURE 6.2. The bodies of Jews removed from the last transports from the Romanian city of Iasi, June 30, 1941. These survivors of the Iasi pogrom succumbed to heat exhaustion, dehydration, and suffocation on the trains that the Romanian military and the SS used to deport them to Transnistria. The antisemitic bloodshed in Romania, as well as in the Soviet Union, gave indication that the anti-Jewish genocide would spread across Europe.
Source: USHMM, photograph #27473, courtesy of Serviciul Roman De Informat.

through one of its darkest phases. Everything is too calculated for effect, too obviously stage-managed, not to have a political significance. What will follow? Our straightforward extermination?"[76]

The wholesale slaughter of Jews that unfolded in the Soviet Union, Eastern Galicia, and Romania represented a turning point for Germany and its allies. What began as an assault against Jewish males of military age suspected of being "commissars," ended with the attempt to eliminate all Soviet Jews in the path of the Wehrmacht, one which opened the door to the slaughter of Jews elsewhere in occupied Europe. From the outbreak of the European war in 1939, the führer accused the Jews without respite of having launched the conflict to assure their own global dominion. Hitler repeated his threat of annihilation as the German armies pressed toward Moscow, and especially after he declared war against the United States on December 11th in what was now, in Hitler's words, a

[76] Sebastian, *Journal*, entry for October 29, 1941, 436.

"world war." In private meetings with his Gau leaders and a subsequent one with Rosenberg, Hitler made clear that extermination would open the route to victory. Barbarossa and the American entry brought the convergence of two global forces that the Jews allegedly embodied. Not recognized as human, Jews metamorphosized into a world-destroying evil that combined bloodthirsty Bolshevision from the borderlands of Asia and the predatory international finance and stock exchange capitalism now centered in America. Given theoretical vitality in *The Protocols of the Elders of Zion*, to which Hitler was introduced as a young veteran in Munich after World War I and the destruction of the Munich Soviet, the present shape of the Jewish menace demanded the translation of theory into action. Despite the similarities between the Armenian genocide and the Holocaust, among them the context of total war, their initiation at the highest levels of state, and the perpetrators' perceptions of being under siege by enemies from all sides, the imaginings of the CUP and the Nazi regime differed in at least one fundamental way. Christian minorities in the Ottoman Empire, including the Armenians, had indeed attracted the protection and intervention of the great powers, in which the proclamation of Tsar Nicholas II at the beginning of the Great War that the Armenians' "hour of liberty" had arrived was then the most recent example.[77] For the Nazis, the power of "Juda" ascended into the realm of myth. The Jew was not merely the satanic evil doer of Christian legend and not merely the beneficiary of foreign patrons whose loyalty could not be ensured. The "Jew" was the visible and invisible manipulator of Germany's enemies who would exterminate it.

With its promise of world revolution, Bolshevism used the wedge of international proletarian solidarity to destroy the biological health of the ethnic nation. It violated the laws of nature by presuming that class, rather than racial, struggle shaped history. Instead of accepting the necessity of racial hierarchies, including the elimination of the "unfit," Bolshevism sought to achieve the impossible, social egalitarianism. As the "culture destroying" race par excellence, the Jew with "his" Bolshevik face fostered reproduction of other racial "inferiors." Even the bloody massacres of French African prisoners in the spring of 1940, saturated by

---

[77] See Mark Mazower, "The G-Word," *London Review of Books*, 8 February 2001; Taner Akçam, *A Shameful Act: The Armenian Genocide and the Question of Turkish Responsibility*, trans. Paul Bessemer (New York: Metropolitan, 2006), 25–35. Suffice it to say, neither sees foreign intervention on behalf of the Armenians as a justification for genocide.

racist images of primitive, sex-crazed savages, arose from the assumption that the African presence in Europe itself resulted from the machinations of Jews, who strove for the dilution of French and German blood through miscegenation. On the other hand, the Jew in "his" capitalist guise elevated multinational exchange over "national" industry and weakened national economies. "He" enriched Jewish banking, stock exchange, and department store-owning plutocrats, while depriving peasants and workers of the fruits of their honest labor. The incorporation of highly developed western and northern European economies within the Nazi empire, did little to relieve German from the ever-present menace in light of the British and American alliance with the Soviet Union. The belief that the Jew was the wire puller behind the Roosevelt administration, American banks, multinational corporations, and the New York Stock Exchange, was simply a given among Nazi leaders; a terrifying image that Goebbel's propaganda network regularly transmitted.[78] In the context of a global war "caused" by the Jew, Hitler's charismatic leadership motivated thousands of ambitious Germans, who to a greater or lesser extent, shared the führer's belief that unlike the Russian or the Pole, the Jew should be made to "disappear" forever.

"...THE SOLE RESPONSIBILITY FOR THE MASSACRE MUST BE BORNE BY THE TRUE CULPRITS: THE JEWS"[79]

The inclination to exterminate became European-wide and explicit in early 1942, as the stalled offensive on Moscow and America's entry in the war converged in the perceived need to "settle accounts" with the Jews once and for all. To coordinate the deportations of Jews and address the concerns of the regime's governors in the field, Himmler's deputy, Reinhard Heydrich, called a meeting of high Nazi-party functionaries, state secretaries, representatives from the SS Reich Security Main Office, and delegates of the Reich governors on December 9th, only to postpone it because of the Japanese strike on Pearl Harbor and the führer's declaration of war against the United States. Reconvened on January 20th in a villa in the upscale Berlin section of Wannsee, Heydrich made it clear that the SS would coordinate the "final solution" from above, reaffirming Himmler's authority. He defined tasks that would be assigned to

---

[78] Herf, *Jewish Enemy*, 92–137.
[79] Hitler's political testament of 1945, *Hitler's Letters and Notes*, ed. Werner Maser, trans. Arnold Pomerans (New York: Harper & Row, 1973), 350.

the appropriate ministries, and stipulated the "evacuation" to the east of eleven million Jews from across Europe, including England, Ireland, Sweden, Switzerland, Portugal, and Turkey.[80]

Because of the inability of the German armies to defeat the Soviet Union quickly, the Wannsee meeting confirmed its consequences. Jews were to be destroyed outright, and not indirectly as the by-product of expulsions elsewhere. Jews capable of work would temporarily be assigned to labor gangs to build roads, "in the course of which action doubtless a large portion [would] be eliminated by natural causes." Those who somehow managed to survive would be liquidated soon enough. After all, as Heydrich blandly noted, survivors would become the germ cell of a revived Jewry. Heydrich did concede a temporary exemption for Jews working in armaments industries to satisfy Erich Neumann, the representative of Göring's Four-Year Plan agency. Military and corporate demands for Jewish labor could forestall deportations and liquidations on a case-by-case basis. Indicative of the RSHA's desire to eliminate the most problematic element of the Nuremberg Laws, the hybrid classification of "mixed-race" people, Heydrich ordered that first and some second degree *Mischlinge* and Jews in mixed marriages were to be evacuated immediately. At best, his victims could expect transport to the combined ghetto and transit camp of Theresianstadt in the Protectorate. For most, Heydrich imagined immediate execution. The führer, however, was unwilling to allow the SS to proceed with Heydrich's order. Because of the continuing social ties of "mixed-race" Germans and Jews in mixed marriages, Hitler wanted to avoid traumatic episodes that could damage morale on the home front.[81]

Upsetting the intimate lives of German civilians was not the only issue. The slowing advance against the Soviet Union made three problems more urgent, the declining prospect of deportation beyond the territories planned for conquest, the overpopulation of Jews in occupied Poland, and especially the messy, distressing violence of mass shootings, which

---

[80] See Browning, *Origins of the Final Solution*, 410–4, and especially Mark Roseman, *The Wannsee Conference and the Final Solution: A Reconsideration* (New York: Picador, 2002), 79–156. Roseman includes the Protocol of the meeting on 157–72.

[81] Roseman, *Wannsee Conference*, 118, 146–8, and Thomas Pegelow, "Determining 'People of German Blood', 'Jews' and '*Mischlinge*': The Reich Kinship Office and the Competing Discourses and Powers of Nazism, 1941–1943," *Central European History* 15, no. 1 (2006): 61. On the status of "mixed-race" people according to the Nuremberg Laws, see Cornelia Essner, *Die "Nürnberger Gesetze" oder Die Verwaltung des Rassenwahns 1933–1945* (Paderborn: Schöningh, 2002), 327–83.

led Nazi leaders to fear that there forces were "going native" by adopting "Bolshevik" methods. The carnage in the Soviet Union, in which the perpetrators directly faced their victims in day-long shooting sprees, required a less disturbing means of ending Jewish lives. To be sure, there were perpetrators such as the sergeant-major in an SS mobile attack force assigned to Eastern Galicia, Felix Landau, who groused about his wife and pined for his mistress while matter-of-factly recounting the day's round up and murder of Jews.[82] Yet as the German experience in the Soviet Union revealed, the mass killings of the mobile attack units, especially when broadened to include women, children, and the elderly, placed sharp shooters and machine gunners under stress. The desperate fear of Germany's destruction by its enemies did not eradicate pangs of conscience.

Frequently drinking became the indispensable lubricant for troubled perpetrators. According to an SS sergeant-major assigned to the mobile attack unit A in the Baltic regions, "it emerged that the men, particularly the officers, could not cope with the demands made on them. Many abandoned themselves to alcohol, suffered nervous breakdowns and psychological illnesses; for example we had suicides and there were some cases where some men cracked up and shot wildly around them and completely lost control." A flyer circulated by the leftist German underground movement, the Red Orchestra, documented the "furies" that raged in a military hospital filled with soldiers from the Russian Front. Among the profoundly disturbed patients was an order policeman who could not get past the memory of a dirty rag doll, the toy of a two-year-old girl he had executed together with her mother and brother. The rivers of blood that he regularly witnessed in the course of his work unsettled him less than the tragic remnant of a little girl's life.[83]

Having himself witnessed the shootings in the summer of 1941, Himmler expressed enough concern about the "psychological burden" placed on the killers that, according to the recollection of the sergeant-major, the Reichsführer SS established a convalescent home for such cases near Berlin.[84] The higher SS police commander in Belorussia, Erich von

---

[82] *"The Good Old Days." The Holocaust as Seen by Its Perpetrators and Bystanders*, eds. Ernst Klee, Willi Dressen, and Volker Riess, trans. Deborah Burnstone (Old Saybrook, CT: Konecky and Konecky, 1991), 87–106.

[83] *"Good Old Days,"* 81–2; Anne Nelson, *Red Orchestra: The Story of the Berlin Underground and the Circle of Friends Who Resisted Hitler* (New York: Random House, 2009), 246–9.

[84] *"Good Old Days,"* 82.

dem Bach-Zelewski, feared that his commandos would be turned into "savages" or "neurotics" if Germans continued to participate directly in the mass shootings.[85] Like Himmler, who sought a putatively "humane" and "non-Bolshevik" approach to address concerns that Germany would be compared to "uncivilized" or "uncultured" peoples, Bach-Zelewski's background hardly allowed him to oppose extermination, only the means by which it was carried out. Yet another scion of the Junker aristocracy who joined the NSDAP, embittered by Weimar democracy and the lack of suitable occupations for young nobles, Bach-Zelewski enlisted in the army during World War I at fifteen, rising to the rank of lieutenant by the war's end. Thereafter he fought with the Upper Silesian Free Corps, affiliated with several right-wing organizations, and dabbled in several careers until joining the SS and rising rapidly through its ranks.[86] For his part, Hans Frank demonstrated that the obsession with carrying out a "civilized" extermination was not confined to the SS. In an interview with an Italian journalist, who had witnessed the massacre of Jews in Iasi, Frank disparaged the "uncivilized" crudeness of the Romanians. In keeping with Germany's "higher culture," he claimed the Third Reich would devise a better solution. "We Germans are guided by reason and method and not by bestial instincts; we always act scientifically."[87]

"Civilized" means of killing extended to assigning the dirty work to non-Germans to ease the burden on Germans as the knowledge of atrocities and discomfort spread. Soldiers' letters and snapshots from the front, as well as their furtive comments to acquaintances while on leave, frequently recalled incidents of cold-blooded mass murder that they had either witnessed, participated in, or heard about.[88] Within the borders of the Soviet Union, the Germans relied increasingly on local police units composed of subject peoples to ease the burden, capitalizing on the fusion of anticommunism and antisemitism that fueled local collaboration since the beginning of Barbarossa. Or the regime returned to its previous mechanism of racial purification to build the foundation for the new "solution" to the "Jewish question," the concentration camps and

---

[85] *Unknown Black Book*, 8–9.

[86] Stephan Malinowski, *Vom König zum Führer: Deutscher Adel und Nationalsozialismus* (Frankfurt am Main: Fischer Taschenbuch, 2004), 561–2.

[87] Quoted in Dwórk and van Pelt, *Holocaust*, 285.

[88] David Bankier, *The Germans and the Final Solution: Public Opinion under Nazism* (Oxford: Blackwell, 1992), 104–7; Bernward Dörner, *Die Deutschen und der Holocaust: Was niemand wissen wollte, aber jeder wissen konnte* (Berlin: Propyläen Verlag, 2007), 417–51.

gassing technology derived from its dragnet against its internal enemies and the genetically "inferior." At the very moment at which the charge of the SS mobile killing squads were being broadened, that is, mid to late summer 1941, talk about using the bottled gas and gas vans employed in the euthanasia project became rife among SS agents in the field. Yet even the use of gas vans, which were supposed to make killing easier, failed to produce the desired effect because the condition of the victims upon unloading and the expressions of horror on their faces unnerved the executions.[89] Thus, stationary camps supplemented the use of subject peoples to carry out the dirty work. Placed in concealed locations on the Reich's new frontiers where everyday rules and mores no longer applied – sites where fewer agents were needed – would keep the killing under the radar and cause less psychological stress. By September and October, the supervisory personnel of the Upper Silesian camp Auschwitz were conducting lethal experiments on Soviet prisoners of war. Trapped in airtight cells and asphyxiated by Zyklon B gas, they were among the first victims of the extension of euthanasia to the SS camp system.

Ironically, Hitler's order to suspend the euthanasia program because of popular and clerical outrage at home, a seeming capitulation to the moral sensibilities of Reich Germans that threatened to undermine the morale of the home front, resulted in the diversion of the euthanasia project's top-ranking personnel, Philipp Bouhler and Viktor Brack and their subordinates, to the General Government. Their new task was to apply their expertise in the construction of the secret killing centers directed by civil administrators and SS personnel. In addition to the camps in the Warthegau and Upper Silesia, one near Chełmno (Kulmhof), where by December of 1941 Jews from the Łódź ghetto were being gassed in vans, and a second camp at Auschwitz-Birkenau where stationary gas chambers and a crematorium were being put into place, construction was underway on three additional killing centers and a large labor camp in the Lublin district. Under the direction of the former district leader of Vienna and now SS and Police Leader, Odilo Globocnik, whose new position put him at forefront of SS plans to Germanize the region,[90] the camps at Bełżec, Sobibór, and Treblinka became operational in the late spring and summer of 1942. They liquidated Jews from Germany and Austria, the Protectorate, and the General Government, as well as the Ukraine and Belorussia. Although also used as a killing center, the fourth camp

[89] Kunz, *Krim unter deutscher Herrschaft*, 185.
[90] On Globocnik, see Musial, *Deutsche Zivilverwaltung*, 201–8

at Maidanek was to provide forced labor for SS construction projects. Deportations of Jews from occupied western Europe, France, Belgium, and the Netherlands, the majority of them sent to Auschwitz-Birkenau and Sobibór, began in July. By the end of 1942, an estimated four million of the roughly six million Jews who lost their lives during the Holocaust, had already been killed, a figure that included those murdered by the mobile attack units in Poland and the Soviet Union.[91]

Germany's modern, industrial, technological, and scientific sophistication obviously enabled its preferred means of genocide, gas chambers and crematoria, which disposed of their victims on conveyor belts of death. Although mass shootings continued where it proved impractical to transport Jews to death camps – indeed death by means other than asphyxiation by gas claimed a large proportion of the victims within the camps and without[92] – the gas chambers absorbed the majority of the captured Jews after the spring of 1942. Few better captured the chillingly Fordist efficiency of the killing centers than the Soviet war correspondent Vasily Grossman, who on the basis of eyewitness accounts, tried to reconstruct the final moments of the victims in his article on Treblinka, a camp that in a mere thirteen months between 1942 and 1943 gassed 750,000 victims. As the condemned approached the gas chamber, Grossman noted:

They stepped into a straight alley, with flowers and fir trees planted along it. It was 120 metres long and two metres wide and led to the place of execution. There was wire on both sides of this alley, and guards in black uniforms and SS men in grey ones were standing there shoulder to shoulder. The road was sprinkled with white sand, and those who were walking in front with their hands up could see the fresh prints of bare feet in this loose sand: small women's feet, very small children's ones, those left by old people's feet. These ephemeral footprints in the sand were all that was left of thousands of people who had walked here recently, just like the four thousand that were walking now, like the other thousands who would walk here two hours later, who were now waiting for their turn at the railway branch in the forest. People who'd left their footprints had walked here just like those who walked here yesterday, and ten days ago, and a hundred days ago, like they would walk tomorrow, and fifty days later, like people did throughout the thirteen hellish months of Treblinka's existence.[93]

The death camps seemed to epitomize the soullessness of technology, or the rational, calculated, and dehumanizing side of modernity.

[91] Browning, *Origins of the Final Solution*, 374–423.

[92] Ulrich Herbert, "Vernichtungspolitik: Neue Antworten und Frage zur Geschichte des Holocausts," in Herbert, ed., *Nationalsozialistische Vernichtungspolitik*, 57.

[93] Grossman, *Writer at War*, 293–4.

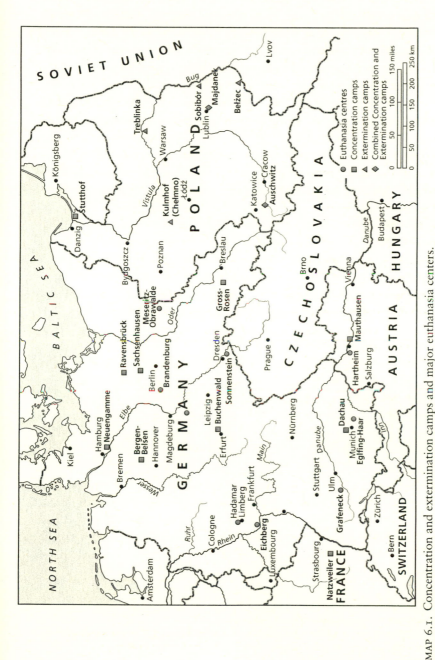

MAP 6.1. Concentration and extermination camps and major euthanasia centers.
Source: Nazism 1919–1945, vol. 3, Foreign Policy, War and Racial Extermination: A Documentary Reader, eds. J. Noakes and G. Pridham (Exeter: University of Exeter Press, 1995), 1223.

Their slaughter house–like "efficiency" had much to recommend them because they required fewer executioners and putatively fewer burdened consciences, especially when "worker Jews" or other subject peoples unloaded the gas chambers and either buried or cremated the victims. The lack of ceremony and the relative anonymity of gassing, which consisted of dropping a pellet of Zyklon B through a grate, distanced executioners from their victims, whose individuality and ability to resist had been stripped from them. In the words of Grossman, who imagined the paralyzing fear of the Jews about to be gassed at Treblinka as best as he could reconstruct it: "When stripped, a person immediately loses the strength of the instinct to live and accept[s] one's destiny like a fate. A person who used to have an intransigent thirst for life becomes passive and indifferent."[94] Yet because the Germans depended increasingly on the labor of collaborators and even skeleton crews of Jews to ensure the smooth running of genocide, the Final Solution derived from something more basic to the Nazi enterprise, the desire to destroy the apocalyptic enemy "humanely" without succumbing to pogrom-like "barbarism." The executioners' "higher duty" to the survival of the *Volk* required, in Himmler's words, hardness and detachment combined with the decency that Germans extended to animals. Only savages engaged in killing out of sadism or the unmodified desire for personal enrichment. Such determination to distinguish civilized from barbarous killing would have sounded familiar to post-colonial writers, notably the francophone Martiniquan intellectual Aimé Césaire, who excoriated Europeans for concealing their savagery toward colonized peoples under the pretense of "civilizing" them. Nazism, continued Cesairé, had simply turned European barbarism on Europeans themselves. Yet the German obsession differed from the "pseudo-humanism" that Cesairé ascribed to European colonialism. Having subjected the Jews to the mass-produced death of the gas chambers or the assembly lines of machine guns, the Nazi regime's goal of racial purity to prevent ethnic annihilation arose from the self-conscious rejection of "humanitarianism" and its redesigned moral imperative: The only bonds that counted were not those of a common humanity, but of one's own kind.[95]

---

[94] Ibid., 293.

[95] Aimé Césaire, *Discourse on Colonialism*, in *Postcolonial Criticism*, eds. Bart Moore-Gilbert, Gareth Stanton, and Willy Maley (London and New York: Longman, 1997), 74–7. Although focusing on the thirties, Claudia Koonz's *The Nazi Conscience* (Cambridge, MA and London: Belknap/Harvard, 2003), effectively lays out the Nazi "transvaluation of values."

In Auschwitz and Maidanek, which combined genocide and forced labor, some survived selections to win a temporary reprieve from elimination. Even for non-Jewish prisoners, the conditions under which they toiled inverted the value that the regime ascribed to the work of Germans, barely mitigating the regime's profligate waste of human beings. Whereas "German work" represented the expression of creativity, in which the worker's artisanal vitality infused his product and proclaimed his humanity, the work of slaves stripped them of their identity and ultimately killed them. In the fall of 1941, the SS established its Business Administration Main Office (*Wirtschaftsverwaltungsamt*, or WVHA) under the leadership of Oswald Pohl to exploit the labor power of concentration camp prisoners, Soviet POWs and Jews temporarily ghettoized in occupied Soviet territory. Assigned to the backbreaking unskilled tasks, the road and tunnel building and other construction projects supervised by German civil engineers or the dirtiest and most dangerous jobs in the armaments industry, prisoners succumbed to the effects of their miserable provisioning as well as to on-the-job accidents – only to be replaced by others whose lives had equally minimal value other than as a temporary source of weak muscle power. The cooperation between the WVHA and armaments industrialists resulted in the fusion of technocracy and routinized horror for their victims.[96]

Charlotte Delbo, a non-Jewish member of the French resistance who in 1942 was arrested and deported to Auschwitz, vividly described the anonymity and torment of her battalion of women prisoners as it marched to its daily round of back-breaking work of breaking rocks and hauling bricks. Like Vasily Grossman, her attention to the movement of feet conveyed the slow evaporation of people slated for death. "To walk in rank formation creates a sort of obsession. You tend to look at feet moving in front of you. You have these feet going forward, heavily, walking before you, those feet you are avoiding and you'll never catch up with, feet preceding yours, always, even at night in a nightmare of trampling, these feet so fascinating that you would see them even if you were in the front rank, feet that drag or stumble yet keep on going."[97] Few Jewish women survived long enough to work themselves

---

[96] Longerich, *Politik der Vernichtung*, 476–82; Michael Thad Allen, *The Business of Genocide: The SS, Slave Labor, and the Concentration Camps* (Chapel Hill and London: University of North Carolina Press, 2002), 128–201.

[97] Charlotte Delbo, *Auschwitz and After*, trans. Rosette C. Lamont (New Haven and London: Yale University Press, 1995), 44.

to death, for that privilege was generally confined to Jewish men with immediately applicable skills. Having the "good fortune" to be selected because of his training to work in the labs of the IG-Farben Buna plant on the camp grounds, the Italian-Jewish chemist Primo Levi, deported to Auschwitz following his capture in December of 1943, described the gulf between the German civilian employees and him, a chasm created by their refusal to recognize him as human. If the memoirs of Holocaust survivors are by definition exceptional because the majority was killed, this was especially true of Levi for the assignment of skilled work to camp labor was rarer still.[98]

The genocide would not be limited to Jews in Europe. As indicated by the explicit mention of France's North African colonies in the Wannsee protocol, the regime would pursue Jews trapped by the expansion of its conflict with its enemies. If the Barbarossa campaign and food shortages provided the impetus for the escalation from mass murder to genocide, the Afrika Korps of General Erwin Rommel, which in February of 1941 landed in Libya to support the Italian army against the British, was to become the instrument of the destruction of the Jews in the Middle East. By July of 1942, Rommel's Panzers had pushed as far as El Alamein in Egypt, which would have become the jumping off point through the Suez Canal to engage the British in Palestine. Following in Rommel's wake was to follow an SS mobile killing squad under the command of Walter Rauff, among those responsible for introducing gas wagons in the east. His unit was to eradicate the Zionist community of Palestine. In the regime's view, one SS squad would suffice. The Germans would exploit Arab anti-semitism and hostility to British imperialism that derived from the bitter postwar conflicts between Arabs and Jewish settlers in Palestine. After the American landings in North Africa in November of 1942, the Grand Mufti of Jerusalem, the Nazi-sympathizing Amin Al-Husseini, that urged Arabs over the radio to "join the Axis powers and their allies in common struggle against the common enemy." If England and her allies were to win the war, he continued, "Israel would rule the whole world, the Arabian fatherland would suffer an unholy blow, and the Arab countries would be torn apart and turned into Jewish colonies." Because Jews were agents

---

[98] Primo Levi, *Survival in Auschwitz: the Nazi Assault on Humanity*, trans. Stuart Woolf (New York: Collier, 1961), 128–9; See Wolfgang Sofsky, "An der Grenze des Sozialen: Perspektiven der KZ-Forschung," in *Die nationalsozialistischen Konzentrationslager – Entwicklung und Struktur*, vol. 2, eds. Ulrich Herbert, Karin Orth, and Christoph Dieckmann (Göttingen: Wallstein Verlag, 1998), 1148.

of British, American and Soviet imperialism, an Axis victory would eliminate "the Jewish danger."[99] Unlike the setbacks of Barbarossa, the defeat of Rommel's forces at the Egyptian town of El Alamein prevented the extension of genocide, even if the regime remained committed to building alliances with Arabs and engaged in the bloody persecution of Jews in Tunisia.[100] The German failure in the Middle East to cut the British off from their empire spared the Jews of Palestine the fate of Jews trapped in Europe.

The Nazi crusade against the Jews combined ideological zeal and personal ambition in the blending of bureaucratic murder from on high and what Primo Levi, who well understood the mixture of hubris and desperation that fueled the Holocaust, described as the "millennial anger" from below.[101] The extent to which the extermination of the Jews united the Third Reich from top to bottom complicates the long-standing description of the Nazi regime as having been fueled by Social Darwinian competition, in which nearly constant turf wars undermined the normal processes of government while promoting the inefficiencies characteristic of competing feudalities.[102] Yet if that picture remains accurate as far as it goes, Hitler's charismatic authority, a product of the perceived crisis of German ethnicity after World War I, put a premium on personal loyalty, ideological commitment, and the ambition to prove it. The expression "working toward the führer," coined in 1934 by Werner Willikens, State Secretary in the Prussian Agriculture Ministry, testified to the shared assumptions behind the decisions of bureaucrats, military officers, and Nazi Party men in positions of power, who acted according to their perception of Hitler's wishes, perceptions that Hitler's radical rhetoric justified in turn. A key element in Prusso-German military practice, encouraging subordinates to exercise initiative without detailed orders from superiors, found its postwar application in the Nazi

---

[99] Quoted in Herf, *Jewish Enemy*, 172–3. On the appeal of National Socialism to young Arabs and its relationship to the Palestine question, see Matthias Künzel, *Jihad and Jew-Hatred: Islamism, Nazism and the Roots of 9/11*, trans. Colin Meade (New York: Telos, 2006), 6–48

[100] On the German extension of the Holocaust to Palestine and North Africa, see Klaus-Michael Mallmann and Martin Cüppers, *Halbmond und Hakenkreuz: Das 'Dritte Reich', die Araber und Palästina* (Darmstadt: Wissenschaftliche Buchgesellschaft, 2006), esp. 137–97.

[101] Levi, *Survival in Auschwitz*, 15.

[102] For an analysis of this and similar arguments, see Ian Kershaw, *The Nazi Dictatorship: Problems and Perspectives of Interpretation*, 4th ed. (London: Arnold, 2000), esp. 69–92,

leadership principle.[103] In most cases, a multiplicity of motivations, along with competition and infighting, paradoxically ensured that the führer's wishes would be carried out. Thus, the debates that took place within the various levels of Nazi administration as to what to do with the millions of Jews under German suzeraignty ultimately settled on the common goal of extermination in the radicalizing context of total war. Whatever the infighting among Nazi paladins, the comprehensiveness of the extermination campaign exposed an underlying shared commitment in all its lethality.

Countless minor bureaucrats, noncommissioned officers in the army or SS, and police battalions participated in the roundups, shootings, transfers, and supervision of the death camps, becoming inured over time to their bloody tasks. A recent sociological survey of over fifteen hundred perpetrators who stood trial for war crimes, ranging from camp and SD officers to proportionately fewer district leaders, senior attack unit officers, and higher SS and police officers reveals the ease with which imperial imaginings flowed ineluctably into full-scale genocide. Overwhelmingly male and drawn from all social classes, one-third of the perpetrators had become hardened through their participation in organized violence before 1939. The male comradeship and *esprit de corps* conferred by membership in Free Corps, as well as the SA, SS, and the military, deadened sensibilities against lethal solutions to political problems. Many sought careers in professions most threatened by economic hardship, the postwar peace settlement, and the uncertainty of career opportunities, including education, medicine, law, the police, and the military – professions in which status encouraged the relatively early gravitation to National Socialism. Not surprisingly, those were professions which had already absorbed the ideology of racial hygiene and the justifications for legal exclusion. In addition to the presence of a number of Sudeten Germans, the religious affiliations and regional heritages of the perpetrators proved most striking. Catholics from borderlands, particularly those lost after World War I, comprised the most over-represented group. Refugees from Alsace and Lorraine, Schleswig-Holstein, the Baltic, and Poland, disgruntled evacuees from regions simultaneously well disposed to revanchism, Greater

---

[103] See Ian Kershaw, *Hitler 1889–1936: Hubris* (New York and London: W. W. Norton, 1998), 527. On relationship of the leadership principle to German military practice, see MacGregor Knox, *To the Threshold of Power 1922/33: Origins and Dynamics of the Fascist and National Socialist Dictatorships*, vol. 1 (Cambridge: Cambridge University Press, 2007), 339.

German imperialism, and antisemitism, translated hatreds into action. Although less in evidence than refugees, Austrians as well contributed more than citizens of the Old Reich to the enterprise of mass death.[104]

Another important cohort, the five hundred or so race and resettlement experts of the RSHA, who before the war cut their teeth on processing the applications of prospective SS men for their racial pedigree and that of their spouses, presented in many respects a similar profile that began with experience in the Free Corps for those in the older age brackets. Academic training and career opportunities that declined particularly during the Depression motivated many to join the NSDAP as the solution to their professional needs and ideological inclinations. In this group, however, academic backgrounds in agronomy and anthropology predominated, indicative of the politicization and racialization of agriculture, which took hold during the 1920s as the "drive to the east" was increasingly seen as the remedy for two major problems: a weak domestic primary sector and ethnic decline in Germany's border regions.[105] Like the numerous planners, lawyers, geographers, statisticians, and population experts in on the design of German schemes for settlement and economic development in the east, or the young professionals, many of them historians, in the SD who were charged with political and racial "security" policy, academic training and personal ambition converged with ideological commitment.[106] The same was true for the several thousand young women, whom the regime mobilized from the Old Reich to deliver education and welfare services in the annexed territories of western Poland, the General Government, and the occupied territories of the Soviet Union. Although pressure from Nazi Party organizations most certainly contributed to their decision to head eastward, many young women availed themselves of the opportunity to demonstrate their competence, their sense of responsibility, self-reliance, and ideological commitment.[107]

---

[104] Michael Mann, *The Dark Side of Democracy: Explaining Ethnic Cleansing* (Cambridge: Cambridge University Press, 2005), 225–78.

[105] Isabel Heinemann, '*Rasse, Siedlung, deutsches Blut*': *Das Rasse-und Siedlungshauptamt der SS und die rassenpolitsche Neuordnung Europas* (Göttingen: Wallstein Verlag, 2003), 561–65.

[106] Götz Aly and Susanne Heim, *Vordenker der Vernichtung: Auschwitz und die deutschen Pläne für eine neue europäische Ordnung* (Frankfurt am Main: Fischer, 1991), 69–124; Gerd Simon, "Germanistik und Sicherheitsdienst," in Michael Wildt, ed., *Nachrichtendienst, politische Elite und Mordeinheit: Der Sicherheitsdienst des Reichsführers SS* (Hamburg: Hamburger Edition, 2003), 190–203.

[107] Elizabeth Harvey, *Women and the Nazi East: Agents and Witnesses of Germanization* (New Haven and London: Yale University Press, 2003), 79–118.

For civil servants in the east, district commissioners and town prefects, most of them Germans disproportionately from the frontiers of the Old Reich, commitment to the party's mission and the desire for adventure dovetailed with the promise of personal advancement and a higher standard of living.[108]

Although ideological motivations behind those decisions were obviously prevalent, the desire for personal enrichment and advancement emerged as the outward signs of belonging to the racial elect. Assigned to the American embassy in Prague from the Munich conference to 1940, the diplomat George Kennan observed as much in the privileges of thousands of German white-collar employees, who assumed positions in Czech government offices, Reich organizations, and aryanized local firms, and who either replaced Czechs or supervised them. "They are," remarked Kennan, "in the most literal sense of the term, the carpetbaggers of the occupation."[109] The tangible benefits of plundering one's victims lubricated genocide, which by extending Nazism's prewar promises of a future of abundance, displayed one's status as a member of the master race in material terms. Occupied Europe became the setting for countless individuals, women as well as men, to realize dreams of upward mobility and a standard of living that would have been impossible to achieve at home. Even the poorer east opened the door to the attainment of plenty, even as it allowed the regime's agents to express their "idealism" in the service of the Nazi empire. If personal gain no doubt helped to overcome sympathy for one's victims, the participants in plunder saw no contradiction between the pursuit of ideological ends and self-enrichment.[110] The civil administration of the General Government or "gangster gau," widely known as the field of dreams for aspiring officers, civil servants, and entrepreneurs whose careers had otherwise stagnated, became notorious for its corruption. Eastern Galicia, which had been annexed to the General Government, took on the elegant pun, *Skandalizien*.[111] With stylish homes in Munich and Berlin and four residences in the General

[108] See David Furber, "Going East: Colonialism and German Life in Nazi-Occupied Poland," (PhD Diss: State University of New York at Buffalo, 2003), 148–272.

[109] George F. Kennan, *From Prague after Munich: Diplomatic Papers 1938–1940* (Princeton: Princeton University Press, 1968), 232.

[110] See Adam Tooze's critique of Götz Aly's materialism in "Economics, Ideology and Cohesion in the Third Reich: A critique of Götz Aly's *Hitlers Volkstaat*, English version of essay for *Dapim Lecheker HaShoah*, http://www.scribd.com/doc/4099126/toozealy. Accessed May 7, 2010.

[111] Musial, *Deutsche Zivilverwaltung*, 79–96.

Government, including the royal castle in Cracow and the Belvedere Palace in Warsaw, the governor general Hans Frank set high standards for ostentation that matched the lifestyles to which the Nazi elite had become accustomed. Following the affinity to high fashion that enraptured the wives and female companions of the Reich leadership, who shopped at elegant couturiers, purchased Gucci accessories and Ferragamo shoes, and decorated their homes lavishly,[112] Frank's wife indulged in compiling a huge collection of furs. Among the purveyors of luxury goods that Frank regularly extorted on his and his relatives' behalf was the Jewish council of the Warsaw ghetto.[113] Not surprisingly, Frank's conduct sanctioned similar behavior from those under him. SS operatives engaged in their share of the plunder, but that did not prevent the Higher SS Police Leader for the General Government from attributing the pervasive graft among civil administrators to their inability to resist the "materialistic-Polish-Jewish lifestyle."[114] The common dread of colonialism, that is, that the colonizers would "go native" and thus lose what made them superior, applied here as well.

Despite its paradigmatic status, the General Government was hardly exceptional, for German occupation, extraction, and colonization removed the constraints of delayed gratification, the regime's official position toward consumption before the war. Generals, field marshals, and admirals received generous monthly supplements to their pay or deeds to land in the occupied territories.[115] It was far from unusual for satraps in the SS or civil administrations to have shipped at the Reich's expense furnishings, culinary delicacies, and works of art purchased from elsewhere, be it Italian travertine marble, motor boats or horses from the Netherlands, or even the furniture of a hotel in Cannes – paid for by slush funds derived from "enemy property."[116] Although corruption undeniably cut into the economic proceeds of empire for the Reich as a whole, the acquisition and display of goods wrested from the regime's victims became a badge of racial superiority for the appropriators of such wealth, as well as the sign of personal achievement. Living next to the machinery

---

[112] Irene Guenther, *Nazi Chic: Fashioning Women in the Third Reich* (Oxford and New York: Berg, 2004), esp. 131–41,

[113] Frank Bajohr, *Parvenüs und Profiteure: Korruption in der NS-Zeit* (Frankfurt am Main: Fischer, 2001), 77–8.

[114] Ibid., 81.

[115] Fabrice d'Almeida, *Hakenkreuz und Kaviar*: Die Mondäne Leben im Nationalsozialismus trans. Harald Ehrhardt (Patmos, 2007), 293–4.

[116] Ibid., 82–3.

of mass extermination neither lessened the sense of entitlement nor the enjoyment of living high on the hog. The wives of SS men stationed at the camp described their lives in the occupiers' compound as positively "idyllic." Luxurious homes and furnishings, a seemingly endless supply of goods at their disposal, purloined of course from the daily transports of Jewish victims, and the ready availability of slave labor to clean their homes and make their clothing, made life bearable.[117] For Rudolf Höss, the commandant of Auschwitz, the material and familial well-being that prevailed in his home off the camp grounds, assuaged the emotional consequences of his daily oversight of "heartbreaking scenes" of horror, such as the moment when a desperate mother about to be gassed frantically begged the guards to spare the life of her child. "Yes, my family had it good in Auschwitz, every wish that my wife or my children had was fulfilled. The children could live free and easy. My wife had her flower paradise."[118] If the accommodations were less posh for other Auschwitz personnel, the perquisites of power sufficed to relieve the daily experience of horror. Trips to the SS retreat at Solahütte a few miles from the camp provided fun and respite for select SS guards and other staff for their exemplary performance on the job.

The higher the position in the Nazi hierarchy, the more flagrant the acquisition of booty. Nevertheless, the German rank-and-file, which included enlisted men in the Wehrmacht, also recognized that battlefield triumphs yielded the material rewards of Germany's resurgence as a global power. Benefiting from exchange rates that reflected the leverage of the occupation, German soldiers swept prized goods from the shelves of shops at a fraction of their cost to locals who, even if the inventory remained available, could no longer afford them. In any case, even the more mundane commodities, which German troops gobbled up as gifts for families and girlfriends at home, could not be procured. Not surprisingly enlisted men, whose wages would otherwise have denied them all but the basic necessities, look upon Paris or Riga as "Eldorados" of material plenty. Without a trace of irony, soldiers referred to the army that provided them their bonanza as the "Kaufhaus der Wehrmacht," a take-off on the name of the famed Berlin department store, Kaufhaus des Westens, once owned by Jews.[119] In the Soviet Union, rampant theft

[117] Gudrun Schwarz, *Eine Frau an seiner Seite: Ehefrauen in der "SS-Sippengemeinschaft"* (Berlin: Aufbau Taschenbuch Verlag, 2001), 115–69.

[118] Rudolf Höss, *Death Dealer: The Memoirs of the SS Kommandant at Auschwitz, Rudolf Höss*, ed. Steven Paskuly (New York: Da Capo Press, 1996), 159, 164.

[119] Aly, *Hitler's Beneficiaries*, 94–117.

FIGURE 6.3. Nazi officers and female auxiliaries pose on a wooden bridge at the SS retreat in Solahütte, near Auschwitz, July, 1944. This photo is found in the album of the then-adjutant to the commandant of Auschwitz, Karl Hoecker.
Source: USHMM, photograph #34585, courtesy of Anonymous Donor.

accompanied rampant brutality, especially against Jews. In Minsk, "as soon as the ghetto was fenced in," according to reports, "the plundering and violence began. At all hours, day and night, Germans would drive up in cars or come on foot and go into Jewish apartments where they took themselves to be the absolute masters. They plundered and confiscated anything in the apartment that pleased them. With the robbery came beatings, humiliations, and often murder."[120] Elsewhere in Belorussia, according to others, "for days on end the Germans hauled off truckloads of stolen clothing, shoes, linens, and dishes, as well as sewing machines, machines for making stockings and hats, milling machines, and all sorts of household goods."[121]

In occupied western Europe, local authorities helped themselves to the spoils of deportation. Even in the Netherlands, where the population often did not support German anti-Jewish policy, the Dutch police took what they could take when arresting Jews.[122] In eastern Europe, the Judeocide capitalized on the antisemitic resentments and virulent

[120] Ehrenburg and Grossman, *Complete Black Book*, 115.
[121] Ibid., 163.
[122] Dean, *Robbing the Jews*, 283.

anticommunism of the former subjects of the Austro-Hungarian, Russian, and Soviet empires, as well as the desire for material benefit. Without the collaboration of local populations, the occupiers could not have accomplished what they did, the near total decimation of Jewish communities.[123] Similar to Arabs who looked upon the Jews in Palestine as the instruments of British imperialism that denied their own nationalist aspirations, eastern Europeans read the Jews as the personification of the oppression of Bolshevism as the Soviet Union sought to anchor its influence after 1918. In Poland, where German rule was harshest, relatively few Poles took part in mass killings, at least as compared to their neighbors. Poles were allowed few weapons and little authority to murder with abandon. Nevertheless, few Poles expressed regret at the dispossession and murder of their Jewish neighbors, many of whom favored the Soviets over the Germans because they correctly feared that the agents of the Third Reich would treat them worse. And if given the opportunity, many Poles unleashed their hatreds, to which the horrific mass murder of Jews in the village of Jedbawne testified. Recently liberated from Soviet control, Polish Christian villagers, many of whom had collaborated with the Soviet occupiers, attacked their Jewish neighbors to deflect attention from their prior complicity.[124] The grinding poverty of the Polish countryside intervened too. Accustomed to interpreting their circumstances as the product of Jewish treachery and exploitation, the Jews having gained their "wealth" at their expense, countless Poles justified their acquisition of the property of Jewish victims as legitimate restitution for Jewish wrongs.[125]

In Lithuania, Latvia, and Estonia, the harshness of Soviet rule in 1940–1941, which included massive expropriation and the deportation of thousands to Siberia, and the support that Jews gave to the Soviets as the "lesser evil" to the Germans, provoked thousands of "liberated" Balts, notably those on the far right, to launch lethal pogroms against their Jewish neighbors. In addition to believing that their contributions would encourage the Germans to support their independence, Baltic collaborators saw anti-Jewish "actions" as an opportunity for plunder. "For the Germans 300 Jews are 300 enemies of humanity," according to the

---

[123] Theodore Hamerow, *Remembering a Vanished World: A Jewish Childhood in Interwar Poland* (New York and Oxford: Berghahn Books, 2001), 119.

[124] Jan Gross, *Neighbors: The Destruction of the Jewish Community in Jedbawne, Poland* (Princeton and London: Princeton University Press, 2001), 40–53, 111–21, 152–67.

[125] Hamerow, *Remembering a Vanished World*, 119.

Polish journalist Kazimierz Sakowicz who regularly observed the mass shootings of Jews from his cottage in the forests of Ponary, a suburb of Vilna, "for the Lithuanians they are 300 pairs of shoes, trousers, and the like."[126] Over 100,000 Balts joined the Wehrmacht, Waffen SS, or order police units. On the surface, Belorussia resembled Poland in its relatively small number of active collaborators, most of them anti-Soviet nationalists and career policemen, who fled to Germany after Polish-controlled Belorussia fell under Soviet control and then returned with the Wehrmacht. As was true for nationalists in the Ukraine, who after welcoming the Germans grew disillusioned when they learned that they would be subjugated once again, Belorussians who sympathized with the German occupiers were soon disappointed. In addition to those whom the Germans reluctantly recruited to fill lower-echelon positions in the colonial administration, thousands of Belorussians and Ukrainians enlisted in local police forces that in 1942 launched the "second phase" of anti-Jewish actions. Those assaults eliminated Jews whom the occupation no longer considered essential as workers or those who hid from the mass shootings of 1941. Although the material rewards of collaboration motivated many, the combination of anti-Bolshevism and antisemitism was indispensible to enlisting the support of local people until German military reverses strengthened local opposition to the Third Reich.[127]

Ethnic Germans contributed their share to dispossession, expulsion, and mass killing. Following the annexation of the Sudetenland, ethnic Germans predominated in local administrations even though to the dismay of local Germans, the shortage of trained personnel required an influx from the Reich. Aryanization could not have been accomplished without local collaboration, and many Sudenten Germans profited handsomely.[128] In addition to the bands of Germans organized in the Protection

---

[126] Kazimierz Sakowicz, *Ponary Diary 1941–1943: A Bystander's Account of a Mass Murder*, ed. Yitzak Arad (New Haven and London: Yale University Press, 2005), 16. For Latvia especially, see Andrej Angrick and Peter Klein, *The "Final Solution" in Riga: Exploitation and Annihilation, 1941–1944*, trans. Gary Brandon (New York and Oxford: Berghahn, 2009), passim.

[127] Martin Dean, *Collaboration in the Holocaust: Crimes of the Local Police in Belorussia and the Ukraine, 1941–44* (New York: St. Martin's Press, 2000), esp. 60–77; Lower, *Nazi Empire-Building*, 205; Olga Baranova, "Nationalism, anti-Bolshevism or the Will to Survive? Collaboration in Belarus under the Nazi Occupation of 1941–1944," *European Review of History* 15, no. 2 (2008): 113–28.

[128] Jörg Osterloh, *Nationalsozialistische Judenverfolgung im Reichsgau Sudetenland* (Munich: R. Oldenbourg, 2006), 563–4; Chad Bryant, *Prague in Black: Nazi Rule and Czech Nationalism* (Cambridge, MA and London: Harvard University Press, 2007) 83–4.

Forces, who brutally murdered thousands of Poles and Jews during the German invasion of Poland, the SS recruited hundreds for the Waffen SS and for service as death and labor camp guards, and distributed the goods of murdered Jews to ethnic Germans in the Soviet Union. Even if ethnic Germans had once seen themselves as Ukrainians or Hungarians, the bestowal of privileged status by their benefactors from the Old Reich rekindled long-forgotten identities or created new ones. The prospect of acquiring property, possessions, and a place at the top of the ladder mixed with virulent antisemitism. To be sure, many Germans whom Himmler's racial experts had sent to resettle the annexed territories faced broken promises and indeterminate stays in transit camps. Yet others who remained in the occupied east took advantage of the opportunities given to them until the withdrawal of their protectors exposed them to the rage of their neighbors.[129]

Among racially akin occupied nations and the nominally independent client states of the Third Reich, German pressure to carry out the final solution became no less intense, not least because local antisemitism and anti-Bolshevism reinforced it. Yet, when the tide turned against Germany in late 1942 and early 1943 with the devastating military reverses at El Alamein and Tunis in North Africa, and Stalingrad in the Soviet Union, resistance mounted against deportations, especially of assimilated Jews. Thus, when the Germans sought to deport Danish Jews to the death camps in September of 1943, the Danish government arranged for their asylum in Sweden while ordinary Danes, emboldened by the prospects of an Allied victory, aided in the escape. Organizing fleets of fishing boats that carried Jews to refuge in Sweden, all but five hundred of Denmark's 7,500 assimilated Jews survived the war. In contrast to other occupied lands of western Europe, no legal confiscation of Jewish property was implemented.[130] Although until the spring of 1943, Bulgaria willingly deported Jews to Treblinka from its newly acquired territories of Thracia and Macedonia (its reward for having joined the Tripartite Pact) and confiscated Jewish assets, public protest, backed by the Bulgarian parliament and the Orthodox Church, erupted against the imminent deportation of

[129] Doris Bergin, "The 'Volksdeutschen' of Eastern Europe, World War II, and the Holocaust: Constructed Ethnicity, Real Genocide," in *Germany and Eastern Europe: Cultural Identities and Cultural Differences*; *Yearbook of European Studies*, vol. 13, eds. Keith Bullivant, Geoffrey Giles, and Walter Paper (Amsterdam and Atlanta: Rodopi B.V., 1999),70–93.

[130] Friedlander, *Years of Extermination*, 545–6; Dean, *Robbing the Jews*, 290–1.

Bulgarian Jews from the "old kingdom," undermining King Boris' promise to cooperate with the Germans.[131]

Romania's vicious pogroms, many of which went after Jews in the territories that it acquired after World War I, managed to disgust even the Germans. In the summer and fall of 1942, however, as the German advance on Stalingrad slowed, the destruction of the Romanian army near Stalingrad and Allied gains in North Africa persuaded the Antonescu regime to change course. Under pressure from the Allies to change sides and eager to save his own skin, Antonescu spared the remaining Romanian Jews, the vast majority of them "civilized" Jews, who resided in the Regat, Romania's core territory. To be sure, Antonescu was unwilling to give up his vision of an ethnically homogeneous nation, in which Romanian colonists would replace expelled "foreigners" in the border regions, and he anticipated a tidy profit from Jews upon their emigration to Palestine after the war. For the moment, however, Antonescu substituted tactical discretion for ideology.[132] The Romanians also turned the tables on the Germans by revealing their appreciation of irony. Its vice prime minister Mahai Antonescu, a distant relative of the dictator, complained to Himmler's delegate in Bucharest that the German behavior toward the Jews was "barbaric."[133] Even Slovakia, which in the spring of 1942 earned the dubious distinction of being the first to deliver its Jews to the forced labor and death camps after the Reich and the Protectorate, demurred in the spring of the following year as its clergy circulated pastoral letters in support of baptized Slovakian Jews who had thus far escaped the German dragnet.[134]

In Hungary, the strength of the Arrow Cross and the pervasive and malignant antisemitism in the army worked to the Germans' advantage when Regent Horthy sought negotiations with the Allies to withdraw his country from the Axis. In March of 1944, the Wehrmacht directly intervened to force Regent Horthy to deport Hungarian Jews to the death camps after months of Hungarian foot-dragging in the belief that Hungarian Jews could be used as bargaining chips to achieve favorable

---

[131] Friedlander, *Years of Extermination*, 484–5. King Boris promised to deport Jewish communists and place an additional 25,000 Jews in labor camps as a sop to the Germans. See also Dean, *Robbing the Jews*, 335–42.

[132] Salonari, "Important New Document:" 282–87; Deletant, *Hitler's Forgotten Ally*, 205–29; Dean, *Robbing the Jews*, 330.

[133] Solonari,"Important New Document," 449–51.

[134] Friedlander, *Years of Extermination*, 372–4, 485–7: Longerich, *Politik der Vernichtung*, 491–3.

terms from the Allies. Well before October of that year, when the Germans finally removed Horthy's prime minister and replaced him with the Arrow Cross leader Ferenc Szalasi, the infiltration of fascists in key ministries enabled the round up and deportation of some 435,000 Jews in just seven weeks' time, the largest such operation during the Holocaust. The remaining sixty thousand Jews, most of them in Budapest, met their deaths in forced marches and in mass shootings at the hands of the Arrow Cross. Horthy's congenital anti-Bolshevism prevented him from turning against the Axis with the speed of an Antonescu, despite the loss of Hungarian forces in the Soviet Union. Yet, in addition to his temporizing, Horthy's dependence on the military, police, and state administration proved fatal to Jews as Hungarian administrators eagerly cooperated with Eichmann and the German plenipotentiary, Edmund Veesenmayer Jews. Although spared the fate of Polish and Soviet Jews in 1941 and 1942 as the Third Reich reached its lethal apogee, Hungarian Jews were killed after it was clear that Germany was losing the war.[135]

Like Vichy France, and the Netherlands, prior colonial experience contributed to the willingness of the Mussolini's Fascists to impose racial antisemitism at home. Between the wars, Italy sought to atone for its disastrous defeat at in Ethiopia in 1896 and the psychic wounds that had resulted from it by striving to obtain its own "place in the sun" in north and east Africa. Italy's pacification of the former and its invasion of the latter, both motivated by the desire to create Italian settlements that would ensure the nation's biological reproduction, proved exceptionally violent. The Italian invaders killed nearly one-quarter of the population of the Libyan city, Cyrenia, and an estimated 250,000 Ethiopians. The use of weapons that international law proscribed as unlawful and "uncivilized," such as mustard gas, were entirely appropriate when applied to Africans. Because Fascist colonial policy legally mandated segregation between Italians and "natives," colonialism increased the propensity for legalizing exclusion at home, especially after the Anschluss when Mussolini grew closer to the Third Reich. Without bidding, the Fascist regime imposed anti-Jewish legislation on its relatively small community of assimilated Jews, in part as revenge for the putative support of Jews for the League of Nations

---

[135] Lozowick, *Hitler's Bureaucrats*, 238–67; Aly and Gerlach, *Das letzte Kapitel*, 249–343: Longerich, *Politik der Vernichtung*, 565–70; Dean, *Robbing the Jews*, 342–52; and Safrian, *Eichmann's Men*, 196–207. For the full details, see Braham, *Politics of Genocide*, vol. 1, 510–710, and vol. 2, entire, for the region by region breakdown of the deportations.

FIGURE 6.4. Jewish women and children from Subcarparthian Rus (Carpatho-Ukraine, then part of Hungary), await selection on the ramp at Auschwitz-Birkenau, May, 1944. Like the image that follows, this photo is found in the "Auschwitz Album," compiled by SS Hauptscharführer Bernhardt Walter, the head of the camp's photographic laboratory, to document the selections for the commandant.
Source: USHMM, photograph #77254, courtesy of Yad Vashem (Public Domain).

sanctions against Italy during the Ethiopian war. Antisemitic laws introduced in 1938 trapped even those who belonged to the Fascist party.[136] Nevertheless, the relative unpopularity of racial segregation and antisemitism in the metropole and colonies, except among ardent Fascists, meant that Italian Jews were not threatened with genocide until 1943 when Mussolini was overthrown. Thereafter, persecution and deportation was limited to the Italian Social Republic in the north, where Mussolini survived under German protection until his murder by partisans. Italian army units in Croatia and southern France resisted German pressure to turn over Jews in their districts, resentful of German domination and the

---

[136] Michele Sarfatti, *The Jews in Mussolini's Italy: From Equality to Persecution*, trans. John Tedeschi and Anne C. Tedeschi (Madison: University of Wisconsin Press, 2006), 42–177; Longerich, *Politik der Vernichtung*, 553–4, 560–1.

FIGURE 6.5. Jewish men from Subcarpathian Rus having undergone selection are about to be gassed at Auschwitz-Birkenau, May, 1944. The "Auschwitz Album," from which this photo is drawn, documents the deportation and extermination of over 400,000 Hungarian Jews in the spring of 1944.
Source: USHMM, photograph #77304, courtesy of Yad Vashem (Public Domain).

poor military performance of the Fascist regime. Even before the rupture of the Italian-German alliance in the fall of 1943, Italian officials engaged in bureaucratic sleights-of-hand to circumvent German orders to deport Jews.[137]

Italy's internal autonomy until relatively late in the war, its small, assimilated Jewish community and few Jews who could be designated as "foreign," and the ineffectiveness of the Fascist regime's apartheid in its brief experience with colonialism, meant a better outcome for its Jews than in France, where one-quarter of its Jewish population was killed. Nearly 80 percent of Italian Jews survived. Having already rendered defenseless those Jews who had recently settled in France with its antisemitic legislation,

[137] Susan Zuccotti, *The Italians and the Holocaust:Persecution, Rescue, and Survival* Lincoln: University of Nebraska Press, 1987), esp. 52–228; Daniel Carpi, *Between Mussolini and Hitler: The Jews and the Italian Authorities in France and Tunisia* (Hanover: Brandeis University Press, 1994), 39–66, 103–63, 228–49; Jonathan Steinberg, *All or Nothing: The Axis and the Holocaust 1941–43* (London and New York: Routledge, 1990), 168–242.

the Vichy government beginning in mid-1942 provided the police necessary to round them up for deportation. As long as the Germans observed international law by funneling Jewish assets into supposedly legitimate "occupation costs," French authorities did not object.[138] The lethal cooperation of the Higher SS Police Chief, Carl Oberg, now reassigned from Poland, and the rabidly pro-Nazi and viciously antisemitic Vichy Commissioner for Jewish Affairs, Louis Darquier de Pellepois, ensured the proper coordination of the raids on terrified Jews.[139] Nevertheless, the occupation's continuing need to assure the Vichy regime's cooperation against a probable Allied invasion produced a different result than in the neighboring Netherlands where fully 75 percent of Dutch Jews lost their lives. Darquier's own laziness, which contributed to the failure to meet Eichmann's requirements by spring 1943, illustrated the relevance of individual decisions, or the lack of them. Yet Darquier's inefficiency was but one explanation for the declining willingness to cooperate among the French. German labor drafts, the unpopularity of measures taken against assimilated Jews, especially in highly publicized roundups, the rise of an underground resistance, and the growing reluctance of the Catholic hierarchy to sanction deportations created a different climate than in the Netherlands, where the occupation assumed the sole authority for deportations and could proceed with few impediments.[140]

Despite the collaboration of Axis sympathizers, which increased the scale and depth of the Judeocide, the vision, design, and implementation belonged to Germany alone. The racist-inspired viciousness of colonial wars is a matter of record. So are the catastrophic demographic declines that resulted from disease, wars, forced labor, and even the environmental disasters made worse by the distortions of the British-dominated liberal imperialist international economy of the nineteenth century. Yet if one should not exaggerate the political impact of anti-imperialism or the opposition to the cruelty of colonialism, conflicts over the means and ends of empire exposed divisions in the European metropoles.[141] What was particularly striking about the Third Reich, however, was the lack

---

[138] Dean, *Robbing the Jews*, 310–1.
[139] Carmen Callil, *Bad Faith: A Forgotten History of Family, Fatherland, and Vichy* France (New York: Knopf, 2006), esp. 240–99.
[140] Griffioen, "Anti-Jewish Policy", 459–60; Longerich, *Politik der Vernichtung*, 501.
[141] Such as the examples of opposition to the worst consequences of British rule in India in Mike Davis, *Late Victorian Holocausts: El Niño Famines and the Making of the Third World* (London: Verso, 2001), 50–9, 164–5, and 336–8.

of a sustained, collective dissent either against Nazi expansionism generally or to the extermination of the Jews specifically. To be sure, SD and
Gestapo reports, diaries, and letters to family and friends from soldiers
recorded frequent, furtive expressions of dismay and even outrage over
the deportations of German Jews to the east. Widespread reports of mass
shootings in Poland and the Soviet Union troubled the consciences of
many, as did the equally widespread dissemination of rumors of camps
in the east into which thousands disappeared into gas chambers never
to be seen again. Although most Germans either did not perceive, or did
not want to grasp, the systematic nature of the Holocaust, the growing
uncertainty of a German victory caused many to dread the revenge that
Jews would take against them if they returned. With the onset of large-
scale Allied strategic bombing of German cities and the Ruhr conurba-
tion in mid-1942, and especially after the catastrophic German defeat at
Stalingrad in early 1943, many civilians concluded that their punishment
was revenge for killing the Jews. Church-going Germans interpreted the
reversal of Germany's military fortunes to divine judgment.[142] Ironically,
the connection that Germans drew between the regime's treatment of
the Jews and the hand of God at work in the ever-increasing likelihood of defeat suggests that the regime had made the case that a greater
enemy lurked behind the Allied enemy. After all, many asked, hadn't the
Jewish determination to exterminate Germany started the war in the first
place?[143] Yet such expressions of dismay coexisted with the deeply held
desire to know as little as possible in order to avoid assuming responsibility for the regime's crimes, or to believe that the Reich, now mortally
threatened from without, could have done such things. Despite their letters from the front that conveyed their suffering and their fading hopes
that the führer would pull them through, German soldiers fought on to
the bitter end, dreading what they feared would be the alternative, Allied
revenge and total subjugation.[144]

[142] Frank Bajohr, "Über die Entwicklung eines schlechten Gewissens: Die deutsche Be-
völkerung und die Deportationen 1941–1945, in *Die Deportationen der Juden aus
Deutschland: Pläne-Praxis-Reaktionen 1938–1945*, ed. Christoph Dieckmann (Göttin-
gen: Wallstein Verlag, 2004), 180–95. For further development of Bajohr's argument, see
Frank Bajohr and Dieter Pohl, *Der Holocaust als Offenes Geheimnis: Die Deutsche, die
NS-Führung und die Alliierten* (Munich: C. H. Beck, 2006), 65–79.

[143] See Herf, *Jewish Enemy*, 183–230: Longerich, '*Davon haben wir nichts gewusst!*,'
201–310; and Dörner, *Deutschen und der Holocaust*, 483–92.

[144] As conveyed in riveting detail in Jens Ebert, ed., *Feldpostbriefen aus Stalingrad:
November 1942 bis Januar 1943* (Göttingen: Wallstein, 2003). See also Katrina

There were loosely connected clandestine resistance groups, such as the Munich university students who called themselves the White Rose, whose leaflets documented German atrocities in the hope of mobilizing opposition to a criminal regime. In addition to circulating their own leaflets with damning evidence of German war crimes and aiding Jewish victims, the Red Orchestra, some of whose members worked from within the Reich government, transmitted information to the Allies, including their desperate messages of warning to the Soviet embassy about the imminence of Barbarossa. The bureaucratic and military resistance, whose attempt on July 20, 1944, to assassinate Hitler and overthrow the regime failed, acted out of a loathing of Nazism not only for its criminality but also for having upended conservative values and institutions. Yet in all cases, few of the conspirators believed that they had, or would receive, much support from the German population. They were right. After the collapse of the plot, many Germans denounced the conspirators even as the would-be assassins suffered through show trials and gruesome executions. The Red Orchestra received minimal recognition in postwar East and West Germany, having appeared as too independently leftist for the rulers of the German Democratic Republic, the Socialist Unity Party. In the Federal Republic, especially in the conservative 1950s, the Red Orchestra was condemned for having collaborated with the Soviet Union.[145]

Instances of collective dissent were few and far between. Even when one considers the accelerated repression that the regime imposed after the calamity at Stalingrad to bludgeon the *Volk* into holding its ground, and even when the regime's courts severely punished those who passed rumors of death camps and gas chambers, terror alone does not suffice as an explanation. If the SA, Gestapo, and the SD took care of the regime's political enemies, which included those most disposed to antifascism, neither the Gestapo nor the concentration camps could fully prevent Germans from mobilizing on behalf of issues that mattered to them. The publicly expressed fury against euthanasia in the summer of 1941 provides one example. The well-organized protests of Bavarians

Kilian, "Kriegsstimmungen: Emotionen einfacher soldaten in Feldpostbriefen," in Jörg Echternkamp, ed. *Die Deutsche Kriegsgesellschaft: Politisierung, Vernichtung, Überleben*, Erster Halbband (Munich: Deutsche Verlags-Anstalt, 2004), 251–88.

[145] See Gerd R. Überschar, *Für ein anderes Deutschland: Der deutsche Widerstand gegen den NS – Staat 1933–1945* (Frankfurt am Main, 2006); Peter Hoffmann, *The History of the German Resistance 1933–1945* (Montreal: McGill University Press, 1969), 397–534; and Nelson, *Red Orchestra*, 287–329.

at roughly the same time against the attempt of local party leaders to remove crucifixes from schools, provides another.[146] At the height of the Nazi regime's power and at a time when the Wehrmacht's advance in the Soviet Union seemed unstoppable, the Nazi Party was forced to relent in both cases to avoid damaging popular morale. Indeed, friendships, marriage, and conscience saved some Jews from deportation to the east. The most striking episode occurred in Berlin in early 1943 when the spouses of 1,700 Jews who were rounded up for deportation by the Gestapo congregated at the collection center in defiance of a shoot-to-kill order by the SS.[147] As a result, Goebbels agreed to release the detained Jews. For the majority, however, the relentless bombing raids, the struggle to survive among ruins, mounting anxiety over the approaching Allied armies, and the threat of denunciation by neighbors if one complained too loudly, ensured that Nazism would only be defeated from outside. Despite widespread disillusion with the Reich leadership, to which the situation reports of the SD steadily testified, civilians withdrew into themselves as they struggled to survive.[148]

Sensitive to the manner in which Nazi vocabulary had permeated the language and conceptualization of ordinary Germans, Victor Klemperer underscored another aspect of the German predicament, the "religious intensification of the already extremely religious term 'Reich,' which dragged the listener into the realm of faith." In fact, Goebbels' propaganda regularly resorted to Christian themes of death and resurrection, especially when the propaganda minister recognized that he could no longer conceal military disasters from the public. Thus, after the surrender of the Sixth Army at Stalingrad, Germans were informed that their soldiers "died so that Germany could live."[149] Religious preoccupations carried over to faith in Hitler himself, who despite the gradual erosion of confidence in him over the last two years of the war, remained a given

---

[146] Ian Kershaw, *Popular Opinion and Political Dissent in the Third Reich: Bavaria 1933–1945* (Oxford: Clarendon Press, 1983), 331–57.

[147] Nathan Stolzfus, *Resistance of the Heart: Intermarriage and the Rosenstrasse Protest in Nazi Germany* (New Brunswick, NJ and London: Rutgers University Press, 2001), esp. 209–57.

[148] Echternkamp, "Im Kampf an der inneren und äusseren Front," in *Deutsche Kriegsgesellschaft*, Erster Halbband, 49–50, 66–7. Not surprisingly, popular disaffection was clearest during the last six months of the war. See Heinz Boberach, ed., *Meldungen aus dem Reich: Die geheimen Lageberichte des Sicherheitsdienst der SS 1938–1945* (Herrsching: Pawlak, 1984) vols. 16 and 17 especially.

[149] Richard J. Evans, *The Third Reich at War* (New York: Penguin, 2009), 421.

among many.[150] Indeed less than two months before Germany finally surrendered, the Danish war correspondent Jacob Kronika recorded in staccato sentences the persistence of the "Hitler myth" in a woman gone made with grief. "A shocking scene on the Vossstrasse. A woman comes running from the ruins of the Wertheim warehouse. She screams and gesticulates with her arms. She has the appearance of being drunk. The truth is that she has lost all sanity. She approaches the entrance of the Reich Chancellery. A policeman runs after her. 'My child is dead! My child is dead! I have to speak with the führer,' cries the unfortunate one."[151]

While preparing to take his own life as the Soviet armies approached Berlin, the führer derived his own meaning from the collapse of the Nazi empire. Yet his was an interpretation that echoed the mythologized triumphs and tragedies in nationalist renderings of the German past. Despite all the setbacks, he asserted, the war would "go down in history as the most glorious and heroic manifestation of the struggle for the existence of a Volk." Having decided to share the fate of so many Berliners and remain in the capital, he would nonetheless refuse to "fall into the hands of the enemy who requires a new spectacle, presented by the Jews, for the diversion of the hysterical masses." Moreover, he expelled his closest associates beginning with Hermann Göring, who upon learning that Hitler intended to commit suicide, peremptorily designated himself as the führer's successor. Hitler removed Himmler for violating his "all or nothing" creed of total victory or a fight to the death by seeking a negotiated peace with the western Allies. In attempting to save his own skin and continue the fight against Bolshevism, Himmler dangled Jewish prisoners as bait. "Apart together [sic] from their disloyalty to me," Hitler wrote, "Göring and Himmler have brought irreparable shame on the whole nation by secretly negotiating with the enemy without my knowledge and against my will, and also by attempting illegally to seize control of the State." A new government headed by Grand Admiral Karl Dönitz would continue the war "with all the means at their disposal." In the future, the seed of resistance sewn in the present will "grow to usher in the glorious rebirth of the National Socialist movement in a truly united nation."[152] During

---

[150] Victor Klemperer, *The Language of the Third Reich: LTI-Lingua Tertii Imperii: A Philologist's* Notebook, trans. Martin Brady (London and New York: Continuum, 2002), 117–9. See especially, Peter Fritzsche, *Life and Death in the Third Reich* (Cambridge, MA and London: Belknap Press of Harvard University Press, 2008), 225–307.

[151] *Reisen ins Reich 1933 bis 1945: Ausländische Autoren berichten aus Deutschland*, ed. Oliver Lubrich (Frankfurt am Main: Eichborn Verlag, 2004), 375.

[152] "My Political Testament," *Hitler's Letters and Notes*, 346–9, 354, 358–61.

the last three months of the war alone, 1.4 million Wehrmacht soldiers lost their lives, while the number of civilian deaths in Allied air-raids averaged over one thousand per day.[153] In light of such destruction, it was to be expected that the führer would remind his listeners of the possibility of resurrection. The dialectic of annihilation and resurrection, of having an empire, losing it, and striving for it once more defined German national identity.

By giving priority to *Lebensraum* in the east, Hitler made good on his critique of the Second Empire. An alliance with the Austria-Hungarian "corpse" and a commercially motivated world policy led to Imperial Germany's demise. Then followed a republic weakened by internal divisions and ruled from outside by the victors of World War I. By contrast, the Nazi regime briefly achieved continental hegemony and a vast land empire that extended from the Atlantic coast to the Caucasus. When competition among the European great powers frustrated Imperial Germany's attempt to acquire its "place in the sun," the Third Reich exploited the transformations and weaknesses in the European state system after 1918 to secure an empire of its own, an empire that unlike its predecessor would resettle and revitalize German communities scattered throughout the globe. In the name of biological necessity, it made no accommodations to legality and certainly none to humanity, for its ethical priority was the redemption of the *Volk*. Nevertheless, the Third Reich succumbed to the encirclement and strangulation of its more powerful enemies, enduring an even more devastating defeat than that inflicted in 1918. In its desperate effort to secure homogeneity and invulnerability, the Nazi regime created the catastrophe that it sought to prevent.

---

[153] Michael Geyer, "Endkampf 1918 and 1945: German Nationalism, Annihilation, and Self Destruction," in eds. Alf Lüdtke and Bernd Weisbrod, *No Man's Land of Violence: Extreme Wars in the 20th Century* (Göttingen: Wallstein Verlag, 2006), 35–67; Fritzsche, *Life and Death*, 291.

Index